The Mammoth Book of
Celebrity Murder

The Mammoth Book of
Celebrity
Murder

Chris Ellis and Julie Ellis

CARROLL & GRAF PUBLISHERS
New York

Carroll & Graf Publishers
An imprint of Avalon Publishing Group, Inc.
245 W. 17th Street
New York
NY 10011-5300
www.carrollandgraf.com

AVALON
publishing group incorporated

First published in the UK by Robinson,
an imprint of Constable & Robinson Ltd 2005

First Carroll & Graf edition 2005

ISBN 0-7867-1568-5

Printed and bound in the EU

Contents

Introduction

The world of the celebrity would appear to be a complex one. Never short on material wealth or the trappings of success, the celebrity leads a busy, often nomadic lifestyle, travelling, socializing and of course making the money that allows them to maintain their star status. Celebrity is a tag shared by an ever-increasing range of people. The stars of film, television and sport are now joined by those men and women famous for being the offspring of those in the first category. There are those who are famous for being rich, whose entrepreneurial skills have made them household names. And there is a more recent addition to this exclusive club, the "it" girl, famous for being seen in all the right places, with all the right people but without any other generally required qualification. Yet once we, the watching and reading public, get to know someone, we want to continue our media-driven relationship with them.

They are generally familiar to the public, either through newspaper commentary, the television or the gossip magazines. So if they commit a crime or are the victim of one, we tend to feel it as though it was a member of our own family. The shock value comes from the perception that they have so much more to lose, therefore their lives and lifestyles are more worthy of protection. When O. J. Simpson was arrested for the murder of his ex-wife, Nicole Brown-Simpson, the world held its breath while this famous football player had his day in court, watched by millions of television viewers around the world. At times the evidence seemed overwhelming, yet Simpson was exonerated and many people wondered at the way justice had been dispensed in the cosmic glow of his celebrity, enriched further by the glare of unprecedented publicity.

Within these pages you will find many tales of celebrities who have been accused of murder, but who have walked free, and tales of famous people who have been murdered, often resulting in the perpetrator becoming more famous than the victim. Typical of this scenario is the murder of Sharon Tate and her house guests by members of the Charles Manson gang. Since his imprisonment more than thirty years ago Charles Manson has become a cult figure, more infamous than most Hollywood A-listers are famous. He still receives more mail than any other convict in the US penal system.

Mark Chapman sought to find his own place in the history books when he gunned down John Lennon outside the Dakota Building in New York City. Hated by millions for an act that deprived the world of a musical genius, Chapman's name is synonymous with premeditated celebrity murder, geared to ensuring one's own notoriety.

Yet there are other anomalies associated with celebrity crime, beyond the celebrities' ability to buy the best justice. When a celebrity is murdered the Establishment appear to make additional efforts to catch the criminal, thus proving their additional worth in society. When popular television presenter Jill Dando was shot outside her London home, the police authority attached fifty officers to the investigation and a reward of £250,000 was offered for information leading to an arrest.

The media play a significant part in maintaining the public's interest in the lives of the rich and famous, often running stories day after day, affording the case in question significant advance trial publicity. The advance publicity can be good or bad depending on the spin the media wishes to give it. In many cases the presiding judge has had to enforce a media-gagging order to help ensure the trial is carried out without the pressure of media prejudices.

The media can be a force for good one minute and fickle the next. Following the conviction of Barry George for the slaying of Jill Dando, the press, having doubts about the legality of the conviction, sought to present new information in a bid to reopen the case. George remains in prison still hoping for a retrial. However, when gangster rapper Tupac Shakur was gunned down in a drive-by shooting in Las Vegas, the headlines told a different story. No longer prepared to use the power of the press to secure a conviction, they sought instead to simply draw the public's attention to the drug-cultured gang warfare that existed on the mean streets of America's many cities.

The system of law which prevails in most democratic countries exists in order to provide a fair means of establishing guilt or innocence and a method by which punishment can be consistently and fairly dispensed. Yet there are many cases here which would suggest there is one rule for the celebrity and another for faceless millions. The inconsistencies are there to be seen – some say they are coincidental, others that they prove a two-tier system is in operation.

Wherever you find the opposing worlds of celebrity and murder meshed together, you will find the breeding ground of the conspiracy theory. The death of JFK sparked rumours that it was the Mafia, the Cuban dictator, Fidel Castro, Lyndon Johnson, the Vice President, or even all of them. To many John Lennon was killed by the CIA, to silence him and prevent him from bad-mouthing the government in respect of its various foreign policies.

Whatever the truth about celebrities, their murderers and their crimes, we the public are drawn to them more than we are to any other type of crime. At the time of writing, Michael Jackson, the most famous of the Jackson Five, is entrenched in a California court case, over allegations of his relationship with various minors. The world's attention is focused heavily on this story; both the press and the television media provide a day-by-day, sometimes hour-by-hour comment on the progress of this trial. Too late for this volume, Phil Spector, the musical maestro who helped create the sound of the Beatles, is being held pending his trial for the murder of Lana Clarkson. Robert Blake, the actor who played the 1970s detective Baretta, is presently on trial for the murder of his wife. It is the type of mass coverage that these people would normally dream of, yet delivered within the context of what must seem like the nightmare scenario.

We are yet to see if the celebrity status these people hold will be of benefit to them in a court of law; many believe it will. The press will continue to provide detailed coverage and the public will continue to absorb as much detail as they can. It is difficult to conclude anything other than that the combined effect of celebrity and the reports filed by the media have a significant impact upon the outcome of some if not all such trials.

Annie Get Your Gun

Ann Eden

The year of 1874 was to prove life changing for the Woodward family and all of its many descendants. Mr James T. Woodward took the decision to join the board of directors at the Hanover National Bank, which, after numerous aquisitions and mergers is now famously known as JP Morgan Chase. After two years of diligent work James was elected president, a position in which he excelled, keeping him busy for the next 34 years. His nephew, William Woodward, ascended to the grand role after his long-serving uncle finally stood down.

William Woodward proved to be an equally successful president, who also maintained a strong interest in the other family business, the Belair Stud in Maryland, which during the 1930s to 1950s sired many excellent thoroughbred horses. Some of its more noteworthy horses went on to win the Triple Crown duo, once with a famous father-son combination called Gallant Fox and Omaha. The Belair Stud was regarded as one of the best in the world. One horse, Nashua, was regarded as the most valuable horse on the planet, earned more than $1 million in prize money, and only ever lost one race throughout its professional racing life.

The Woodward family lived an elite lifestyle in their Belair mansion, close to their valuable stud farm. William's son Billy was set to follow in his father's footsteps and join the banking profession, as well as learning the family business at the stud. Prior to taking up his position at the bank Billy served for a time in the United States Navy, during which he was awarded the prestigious Purple Heart after surviving a torpedo attack which sank the ship on which he served. When he returned to New York he had matured into an eligible bachelor, and was indeed quite a catch, coming from one of the wealthiest families in America, all of whom moved in the upper echelons of New York high society. And as if lady luck had not bestowed enough good fortune on him already, he was handsome, a fine sportsman and quite witty, so not surprisingly he was very popular with all the debu-tantes.

Billy's father, William, was also very popular with the ladies, being successful, powerful and charismatic. He was, for a short time, involved in an extramarital affair with a young radio actress known as Ann Eden, though this was not her born name. She had elected to change it from Angeline Crowell when she had made the move from Kansas to New York City, seeking fame and fortune. She was brought up by her mother who worked in a taxi cab office, earning a meagre wage so that the young Angeline was without material comfort, though much loved. Ann was described as brainy, talented, beautiful and too good for Kansas. She moved to New York City and took various radio station jobs, becoming well regarded in her field. Her beauty did not go unnoticed either for she was voted the "Most Beautiful Woman on Radio", a strange accolade and not one awarded in humour.

By 1942 William Woodward Sr, apparently unfulfilled by his relationship with Ann, decided to introduce her to his son Billy, by now 22 years old, some five years younger than Ann. The plan worked and Ann was soon besotted with the younger, more attractive man. Luckily for her Billy was similarly impressed and the two struck up a relationship, soon becoming lovers. After a whirlwind romance, hot with the passions of youth, the pair announced their intentions to be married.

The marriage was well received by family and friends, with the apparent sole exclusion of Elsie Woodward, Ann's new mother-in-law. Elsie Woodward did not consider Ann to be good enough for her wonderful son, her poor upbring-ing and the obvious class differences between the pair suggesting only one thing. She concluded that Ann was only marrying Billy to get her hands on a share of his $10 million inheritance, and deduced that she was some kind of conniving gold-digger. Elsie was not satisfied with her son's choice of wife, believing her daughter-in-law to be too voluptuous and pretty to be a good person, and advised people to be very careful of her.

Because of this family rejection, Ann found it difficult to be accepted in her husband's social circle – Elsie was very highly regarded among her peers and when she rebuffed Ann, others dutifully followed suit. Even Billy's sisters began to cool towards their brother's choice of wife, their initial acceptance gradually turning into resentment. In fact the only person in the highest social circles whom Ann could call a respected friend was the Duchess of Windsor, better known as Wallis Simpson, the wife of Edward, the former king of England. Simpson had experienced for herself the hardship of marrying above her station, consequently the two women formed a friendship based on their mutual difficulties.

As Ann was not tolerated within Billy's social group, the couple spent more time alone together, really getting to know one another. They became more than just a happily married couple, they became each other's best friend. In time though, cracks did begin to show and the couple were observed arguing, others speculating that they were each involved in illicit affairs. Typically, as often occurs within the bounds of a top-class respectable family, any activities of this type were swept under the carpet, never admitted to, never mentioned, glossed over and hidden beneath a thick veneer of wealth.

Rumours circulated which inferred that Billy not only enjoyed the company of other young women, but also spent time with men. Word of his bisexuality spread, eventually reaching the ears of his wife, who, having already lost a great deal of self-esteem, took Billy to task. A public argument was witnessed and Ann was overheard shouting, "Why don't you just bring a man into our bed if it's what you want." Despite their differences, the couple had two sons, the first, William III, was born in 1944, with James arriving some three years later. It was obvious that Ann and Billy had no intention of splitting up their marriage – even Billy's diverse sexual tastes seemed unable to break the weakening bonds of their marriage.

The couple enjoyed evenings out with mutual friends, always appearing to be the epitome of a happily married couple. One such party was held on 29 October 1955, hosted by the Duke and Duchess of Windsor. Some of the guests later noted that the couple seemed to be overly concerned with a spate of burglaries which had occurred close to their home in Oyster Bay, Long Island. A sneak thief had had the audacity to break into homes while the residents were in their beds, a terrifying thought for the Woodwards. They had told friends that they were taking no chances and were prepared for any such eventuality. They were under the impression that a break-in at their home was imminent, as strange footprints had been found within the grounds of their mansion, and on several occasions Ann's dog had disturbed her during the night, something he was not normally prone to doing.

By the time that Ann and Billy arrived home it was already the early hours of the morning around 1.00 a.m. Their sons, now aged eleven and seven were both fast asleep in their bedrooms, as were the servants, who occupied rooms at the opposite end of the house. Ann and Billy did not share the same bedroom, so after wishing each other good night, they retired to their respective rooms for the night. Each of them had a firearm in their bedrooms – Billy was armed with a revolver, while Ann, strangely, had a 12-bore double-barrelled shotgun. While neither of them ever expected to use the weapons, they felt safer and slept more soundly knowing that they had them should the need ever arise.

At approximately three in the morning, Ann's dog, Sloppy, broke the silence and started barking, waking Ann from her deep slumber. With her heart pounding, a fresh burst of adrenalin raced into her blood stream and Ann instinctively reached for the shotgun. Then, as she later described to the police, she walked slowly and silently to her bedroom door, pausing momentarily. She slowly opened the door and peered out along the hallway, where, in the darkness of the night, she saw a shadowy figure standing outside her husband's closed bedroom door. Without pausing for thought, or indeed to warn the intruder, she pulled the trigger, spraying birdshot over the wall next to her husband's bedroom door; taking better aim she fired again, this time the pellets hitting their target, blasting the would-be robber to the floor. Once the man had hit the floor and danger began to recede, Ann moved closer to look at the now still figure laying on his back in her upstairs hallway, her fear turning to horror when she looked down at the man and realized that she had just shot her husband. She did not know if he was dead, though it was obvious that he needed help, so dragging herself to her feet she raced to the phone and rang the police and the ambulance service. Then, rather suspiciously, she also phoned for her attorney.

Sadly before any help could be offered to Billy, he died outside his bedroom door on the hallway floor. He had been shot in the head, examination later showing that his brain contained tiny fragments of pellets. When the police arrived they spent time consoling Ann, who readily admitted that she had shot her husband, believing him to be a burglar. She offered her explanation to police as soon as they arrived on the scene: "I did it. I thought he was the man who has been around here." Shortly after her admission of guilt she became inconsolable and had to be given a drug to sedate her.

Her powerful and very much respected attorney, Sol Rosenblatt, arrived at the mansion and soon demanded that owing to Ann's obvious stress, she be transferred to a Manhattan hospital to be monitored by professionals. This proved to be an ingenious ploy, for while Ann was in the hospital recovering from her shock, detectives investigating the death of her husband were unable to question her until two days after the shooting.

The status of Billy Woodward, as a man of wealth and position elevated the investigation above the lowly police officers of the local police force, and immediately involved the Nassau County prosecutor and the Oyster Bay chief of police, who began gathering the details of the night's misadventure. Like others in Nassau, and even those living in the greater area of the Bahamas, the chief of police and the prosecutor were well aware of the gossip surrounding Billy and Ann Woodward and of the public humiliation she had experienced because of her husband's various philanderings.

As the sun rose on the morning of 30 October 1955, tongues were already wagging, news having quickly spread of the death of Billy Woodward. Speculation was rife and suspicion was falling on Ann, people believing that she had not innocently shot a "shadowy figure", as she had claimed. The consensus of opinion was that she had tired of her family problems and the embarrassment that Billy had caused her, and had decided that it was time to do away with him, claiming her part of the Woodward fortune in the process. There was, however, one small fact that the gossip mongers were not aware of, a fact, which to some extent, removes the motive. During a period of separation from his wife, Billy had taken steps to remove her from his will, leaving the majority of his wealth, in the form of trusts, to his two sons, William III and James.

The newspaper hounds were also gathering and were quick to assess the situation. In short, Ann had shot dead her husband in the belief that he was an intruder. That they lived in a vicinity popular with a local and very active burglar was why they had both elected to be armed. And then the under-current of doubt flooded through – the Woodwards had not enjoyed perfect marital relations, on the contrary, they had been stretched to breaking by Billy's extramarital activity. Scandal surrounded Billy's murder and his family formed their own views – as far as they were concerned this was a blatant attempt by Ann to secure her financial independence.

Billy Woodward's death, just like his life, would not be without its drama. The police investigation was advancing routinely when officers made an arrest in connection with the spate of burglaries occurring in the Oyster Bay area. The man they arrested was Mr Paul Wirth, a known villain and accomplished domestic burglar. Once under police guard and subject to police interrogation he quickly admitted that he was the man responsible for the break-ins, even giving specific details of his activities. Then, without need or enticement, he also added that on the night of the shooting of Billy Woodward, he had indeed been in the process of breaking into their property when he heard the gunshot.

The whole Woodward saga and family drama became the hottest news of the day and filled many newspaper column inches. A murder story is always popular, but the death of such a wealthy socialite, at the hands of his own wife, was inceasing readership by a massive margin. The media speculation and their perpetual theorizing was increasing the pressure on the police to either make an arrest or offer a suitable explanation. It would have been easy to simply ignore death and put the whole sorry set of events down to a tragic accident, but the public and the press wanted more. The police department wanted the case closed as swiftly as possible, yet needed to be seen to be making a thorough enquiry – they therefore chose to convene a grand jury to investigate every detail of the now world-famous shooting.

Just a short while after attending the funeral of her husband, Ann was summoned before the grand jury to give her account of the events leading to her husband's death. During the hearings the newspapers continued to serve up titillating facts and pieces of gossip to an ever-hungry readership. Their stories were badly timed as Ann did not want to attract any publicity let alone bad publicity. Her standing within the Woodward family could not have been lower and now she had lost most of her social circle, practically all of whom were known to her through her husband. At the mercy of the court and a scurrilous press, it was surprising therefore to find that Elsie Woodward, a woman who now loathed Ann, was prepared to defend her. The rich and powerful attach more value to their family names than mere mortals; to these elite upper classes, the honour of the family name is something to defend, a wrapper in which family members present themselves to other majestic families. Whatever the truth of that evening's events, justice could only be served if it preserved the Woodwards' prestigious heritage. And to do that, it would need to be dealt with quickly, before the press could could swamp them in more scandal.

Sadly for the Woodwards the press investigation appeared
to be swifter and more detailed than that carried out by the
police. One story which appeared more than once, to the
embarrassment of both Ann and the larger Woodward family, alleged that Ann had been married once before, and
worse, that she had not dissolved that marriage fully before
joining Billy at the altar. These stories painted a terrible
picture of Ann, who was even more made to look as if she had
married in haste, hoping not to miss the Woodward gravy
train.

The rumour mill continued to produce more stories, almost all of which found themselves printed in the daily press;
on one occasion her father was researched. In the Woodwards' marriage announcement her father was referred to as
the late Colonel Crowell, but this was seemingly untrue as he
was in fact alive and kicking. Ann had not kept in contact
with her father and owing to his daughter's name change he
had not been able to trace her, being under the impression
that she was actually the actress called Eve Arden, though he
never considered contacting her to find out if this was
correct.

It was to this background of press and media intrusion that
Ann was forced to describe the events leading up to her
husband's shooting. She described how she and Billy had
arrived home to a quiet house, retiring to their own separate
bedrooms soon after arriving home, tired and ready for bed
after a night of relaxation and fun with some friends. She
went on to describe how she was awoken by the sound of her
dog barking in the early hours of the morning. Careful to
emphasize the fear she experienced when she woke up, she
explained how the recent glut of house burglaries had got her
and Billy on edge and how, in the middle of that night, she
felt fearful that someone was in the house with them. She
explained to the jury the joint decision she and Billy had
made to arm themselves in case they were isolated, and how
she instinctively reached for the weapon upon waking, terrified of what might happen. With much emotion, some of
which was possibly dredged up from her acting days, Ann
described how she took the double-barrelled shotgun and

ventured out of the safety of her own bedroom and into the
corridor outside her room. Having built up the tension thus
far, her description of her entrance into the bedroom corridor was equally spellbinding. Having described the gloomy
darkness as being alleviated by only a small amount of
moonlight, Ann then described her first sight of the sil-
houetted figure stood by her husband's bedroom door. She
explained away her actions as a pure response to seeing what
she believed was an intruder about to enter her husband's
bedroom. Believing she was now defending her home, her
children, her husband and herself, without a second thought
she pulled the trigger. The room was silent as Ann, continuing her dramatic performance, described how the first
shot missed, the majority of the shot ending up in the wall
next to her husband's bedroom door – how she then fired a
second shot and how this time, it had blasted the target.
Turning to look at the jurors Ann mustered up more emotion
when she described her relief when the figure slumped to the
floor, but her horror and panic when she finally realized that
the man on the floor was none other than her husband Billy.
She had made a fatal error, one caused by the threat of attack,
but nonetheless one which had ended her husband's life. By
now she described herself as in a total state of panic, struggling to summon the strength to call for assistance, which she
eventually managed to do. Shortly after this she said she
could recall very little, having been prescribed a sedative to
calm her nerves, which had the effect of sending her to sleep.
Relieved at stitching off the nightmare she then told the jury
that when she regained consciousness she found herself in a
Manhattan hospital, where she stayed for a couple of days
until she was well enough to face the world.

The jurors, most of whom were aware of the negative press
surrounding the case, took a little over half an hour to come
to the conclusion that Ann had mistakenly shot her husband,
without premeditation and that it had not been an act of
malice. The jury were happy to believe that Ann and Billy
Woodward had both been disturbed by Paul Wirth, the
Oyster Bay burglar and were then both subject to an appalling act of terrible coincidence, both emerging into the

bedroom corridor at the same time, in order to investigate the noise of the dog barking. Strangely though, it appeared that Billy, having agreed to be armed in case of such an emergency, had apparently chosen to investigate the possible intrusion without his weapon, which was found stored in its usual place inside the bedroom.

Ann was able to breath a sigh of relief as she was declared free of any blame. She had lost her husband due to her own mistake, had suffered enough and was able to leave the hearing a free woman, though not necessarily with her head held high – she had after all shot one of the prestigious Woodward family dead and now her children were without a father.

Despite her success at the grand jury, her name was not cleared as far as her peers were concerned. It has been heavily suggested that Elsie Woodward paid Paul Wirth to state that he had been planning to rob the Woodwards as they slept, but that he had been disturbed when the dog had started to bark and had fled when he heard the shotgun being fired at around 3 a.m. on the morning in question. But why would Elsie Woodward offer Ann this unexpected rescue? Elsie was a particularly proud woman – almost royalty within her own social empire – and as such she was determined that any family scandal should be hushed up as quickly as possible. She simply could not face her prestigious family name being dragged through the mud throughout a protracted murder trial. Even though this meant giving Ann support at a time when she was absolutely beside herself with loathing for the woman, who she had, and would continue to treat as a lower-class citizen.

Ann was a free woman, but found that she was totally ostracized by any of her previous acquaintances and her life became almost unbearable. Her beloved sons were sent away to boarding schools in Switzerland, where they were to be schooled in the tradition of the Woodward family. Ann hardly had any face-to-face contact with them, even to explain what had happened to their father. Thankfully the boys had managed to sleep through the events on the night of their father's death, but were left to piece together the little information they had regarding it. James, the youngest child, coped less well at school than his older brother William, finding school life difficult to bear and thoroughly detesting the boarding school experience.

As her husband had not left her well catered for after his death, Ann found herself financially embarrassed and unable to make ends meet, the Woodwards continuing to give her the cold shoulder.

On the other hand Elsie found herself to be extremely popular after the terrible death of her son and found that her social status had soared to new heights. By now she was able to name the likes of Andy Warhol and Hollywood actor Frank Sinatra as her new friends. She clearly wanted to bring the criminal investigation to an end and was reported to have paid over $300,000 to achieve her ends. The never-ending news stories regarding her daughter-in-law's unsavoury past were a major strain on Elsie. With Ann seeking legal assistance to secure a portion of her dead husband's estate, she made her a very tempting offer.

In exchange for a generous annual income of around half a million dollars, Elsie insisted that Ann move out of America and set up home in Europe. The offer was accepted gratefully. By now Ann was just as keen to remove herself from her socially hostile environment and ready to flee the embarrassing position she found herself in with the media stories.

Ann moved to Europe and managed to enjoy the not insignificant income her deal with Elsie afforded. As the years went by she started to long to return to America, though when she did it was soon obvious that she was not fondly remembered and was coldly received.

One person who was glad of her return to New York was author Truman Capote, who considered that Ann's life story was worthy of recording in print. He set about collecting information on her and gradually started to produce a piece about her life. Ann was aware of the imminent publication date and became very nervous about it, not wanting her past retold to another generation of Americans.

On the night before the publication was due to appear in *Esquire* magazine, Ann met with her son James who had taken to referring to himself as Jimmy. The meeting did not go well and Ann left on a sour note. She must have felt that her world was about to fall in on her for the second time in her life. That night rather than washing and going to bed, she decided to reapply her makeup, and, looking perfect, she took a capsule of cyanide which ended her life.

What might have been considered to be true justice in the eyes of the Woodward family, and what should have been the start of a happier chapter, turned out not to be. Jimmy was now without his mother and father and sought solace in drugs, initially cocaine, but later moving on to heroine. His life was in ruins and he could see no way out – before the anniversary of his mother's death Jimmy took his own life by jumping out of a multi-storey building.

William Woodward, known as Woody to his friends, managed to survive his family problems and studied for an MBA in politics at Harvard University. He started in politics, serving under Hugh Carey, but this career was only fleeting, as he decided after much scrutiny to live outside the public eye. Married in 1985 he chose to live overseas, away from the red-hot glare of the US media. The marriage lasted for over ten years, but in 1996 the couple separated, his wife and daughter moving away. Woody, who was now suffering from a bipolar disorder, causing the sufferer to experience great mood swings, found the changes to his life too great to bear. At the age of 54 he ended his life in the same way as his brother by jumping out of a building to his death. He left all of his estate, over $30 million, to his only child and so ends this terrible family tragedy.

The Woodwards reacted to a family member's gruesome death in the only way they knew how – they closed ranks and sought to minimize the rapidly forming public relations disaster. Only in the realms of the rich and famous would the mother of a dead son pay a significant annual sum to the person who had blasted to death the child she reared in such a closeted, upper-class environment.

Ann of course was found not guilty and she was still the mother of Elsie Woodward's grandchildren, which perhaps explains her generosity towards her lower-class daughter-in-law. We will never know.

Drama at Ford's Theatre

President Abraham Lincoln

Most people would agree that the assassination of a president
has a great effect on the course of history – who knows what
the future would have been if JFK's term had been allowed
to continue past his ill-fated visit to Dallas, or if his brother
Robert had made it to the White House. The assassination of
Abraham Lincoln during the closing phases of the civil war
changed the future of America probably more than any other
event before or since.

By 1865, the civil war had raged for nearly four years and
Lincoln, the presiding President of the United States, was
preparing to demobilize nearly one million soldiers who were
serving under the expert guidance of General Ulysses Grant,
commander of the Union troops. The Confederates fighting
for the South were led by Robert E. Lee but were finding
themselves under more and more pressure. The North had
significantly more troops and were now making more progress in overcoming the tired and demoralized Confederates.

An air of desperation seemed to exist amongst those who
supported the South; to them Lincoln had amassed too much
power, a power he was wielding against them. Whereas the
South had grown rich on the back of the slaves who toiled in
their fields, Lincoln dreamed of a united America where all
Americans could live as equals, irrespective of creed or
colour. It was Lincoln's intention to abolish slavery and
give freedom to each and every black person who was
presently owned by a white family. Those who lived in
the South had a lot to lose, but there were also those in
the North who felt that Lincoln's meddling had gone too far

and some of them felt the time had come to contribute to the war effort.

Like many presidents Lincoln had endured a lot of hate mail, many containing threats to his life. As the man in charge of a country at civil war he was very much a potential target. Throughout the early years of the war Lincoln had always struggled with his desire to be close to his people and the need to protect himself from would-be attackers, but he was at least able to take some comfort from the track record of his predecessors – all of the fifteen presidents who had held the office before him had died of natural causes. Only Andrew Jackson had been the target of an assassin's bullet, but a misfire saved him. Lincoln's Secretary of State, William H. Seward noted with pride the orderly succession of power from one president to the next, saying, "assassination is not an American practice or habit". Strange words considering Lincoln had come close to losing his life in the summer of 1862, when an assassin's bullet punctured the President's hat as he was out riding; the assailant was never caught.

By 1864, with Lee's troops penned into the trenches around Petersburg, Virginia, sympathisers with the South were more willing than ever to take revenge on the President and as more and more bad news emerged regarding the downfall of Lee's army, the desire for revenge seemed to reach fever pitch. One southern gentleman placed an advertisement which suggested that if his fellow southerners could raise $1 million dollars he would see to it that Lincoln met with a violent end. Government detectives in Washington heard rumours of murder or abduction of the President, as did Lincoln's best friend and self-appointed head of the President's security, Ward Hill Lamon. Lamon persuaded the President to make alterations to the White House which would allow him to walk around without passing windows and which would keep him out of view of visitors. And to ensure he was always protected Lamon assigned four Washington police officers to keep an around-the-clock vigil.

In general though Lincoln took a fatalistic approach to the perils of his high office: "I cannot possibly guard myself against all dangers, unless I shut myself up in an iron box, in which condition I could hardly perform the duties of the President," concluding, "if anyone is willing to give his life for mine, there is nothing I can do about it."

Strangely it would appear that Lincoln had some sort of a premonition of his death in a dream just seven days before he was killed. While sat in the White House with Lamon, some other friends and his wife, the conversation turned to dreams. It was thought that it was through dreams that God was able to communicate on a personal level – the Bible had numerous references to this. Lincoln looked a little withdrawn as he mentioned to the crowd that he had dreamt only a few nights before and that he had been thinking of it ever since. His wife now keen to know what the dream had been about encouraged the President to tell them. He explained how having gone to bed he had quickly fallen into a deep sleep. He had dreamt that he had got out of his bed and walked through the White House where he had come upon a crowd of people gathered around an open casket. The crowd were clearly upset as many of them were crying. Approaching them he asked who had died and to his shock and horror was told, "The President, he was killed by an assassin."

Lincoln loved the theatre and knew many of the leading actors of the day. Ironically it was to be one of the thespian fraternity who was plotting the President's demise and with the Confederates losing ground by the day the need for drastic action, something which might stem the tide, was fast needed.

John Wilkes Booth was born of acting stock. His father Junius Brutus Booth – named after Caesar's assassin – was a British-born thespian renowned for his powerful renditions of Shakespearian characters. Leaving his wife and children he fled to America in 1821, finding a new love and setting up home in the Baltimore area. Junius fathered ten children and was an attentive if erratic father who never settled on just one religion and therefore selected pieces of wisdom from all of the prominent religions of the day. The one principle he did maintain and one that he passed on to his children was his belief in reincarnation – that every animal had once been a human being with an immortal soul – and for this reason they should never harm any of God's creatures. As a successful actor he was able to bring his children up well, during the summer living on a spacious farm and in the winter living in a town house in Baltimore.

John Wilkes Booth was the ninth child to be born, arriving in 1838; his siblings described a young boy full of fun and playfulness with a kind and sensitive nature. Booth's mother could not deny that he was the favourite of her ten children and in her opinion the best looking, with dark eyes, black hair and tawny coloured skin. Although their father tried to dissuade all his children from following his footsteps onto the stage, Booth was consumed with a desire to be famous as was his elder brother Edwin. Edwin later became one of the most accomplished actors of his day, demanding up to $1,000 dollars a week, a huge sum in those days.

Booth's desire for fame was not confined to the realms of acting – once in discussions with friends at school he pondered out loud the prospect of him knocking over the Colossus of Rhodes, one of the Seven Wonders of the World. He remarked that if he could achieve this task then he would live for a thousand years in print, each generation learning his name.

In 1855, at the age of seventeen, Booth made his theatrical debut in *Richard III* at Baltimore's St Charles Theatre. His first experience of the limelight was not good – suffering stage fright he forgot his words and was booed off the stage. His subsequent attempts drew better results and he was soon regarded as a splendid actor who brought great realism to his roles.

Booth travelled widely throughout the United States and was well received everywhere, especially in the South. Although illegitimate – his father still had a wife in England – Booth considered himself to be of fine stock, coming from one of Maryland's most respectable families. During the late 1850s, with regional tensions signalling the threat of civil war, Booth made his views clear, sympathizing with the South, probably because he had enjoyed so much success there. He was even on record as stating that slavery was morally correct and was beneficial to all parties. He also got into frequent heated debates with his siblings who mostly held Union views.

Booth found that his Confederate views became stronger over time, occasionally translating his thoughts into action. One day he was drawn to a group of men marching in uniform, members of a volunteer militia group called the Richmond Greys. The group were heading to Charlestown, Virginia, where the Confederates were holding a young man called John Brown, who had gone to the South to try and inspire a black uprising but had been caught and imprisoned. The Richmond Greys were en route to act as Brown's prison guards when Booth managed to borrow a uniform and join the group. Booth was one of the guards near the scaffold when Brown was hung, the sight of which affected him greatly, his southern sympathies now stronger than ever.

When the war did finally break out Booth managed to avoid any uniform, let alone that of the Confederate Army. Outspoken in his support of the South it played upon Booth's mind that he did not contribute to the war effort in a more direct way. It was said that he had promised his mother that he would never go to war – they were extra-ordinarily close – but others suggest that Booth had an almost pathological fear of being disfigured and of the effect this would have upon his acting career. He managed to assuage his guilt at not becoming a soldier by smuggling medical supplies to the South, but increasingly the guilt returned in direct proportion to the South's decline. More and more the focal point of his hatred was Abraham Lincoln, whom he thought wanted to destroy the South and its way of life. It was with these troubled thoughts that Booth once more began to think of his place in the history books.

During the final months of the war, Secretary of War Stanton and chief of the Union Army, General Grant, changed their policy of prisoner exchanges. Recognizing that they could now win a war of attrition they decided to hold on to their 50,000 Confederate prisoners. Booth was one of a number of people who hatched a plan to give the South a boost – he would kidnap Lincoln and transport him to Richmond, where they would then demand a range of concessions in exchange for the President's release.

Booth moved quickly to put his plans together and by September 1864 he had started to assemble his gang, those who would assist in his daring plot. Arriving at Barnum's Hotel in Baltimore he was met by a couple of old school friends, Samuel Arnold and 26-year-old Michael O'Laughlin, both men who had been Confederate soldiers at one point. Over food and wine and a lot of talk about the war Booth let the two in on his plan and asked if the pair would join him. Had it not been for Booth's invitation the pair would certainly have gone through their lives unnoticed, but now, flattered by their famous friend's attention, they readily agreed to assist. Through his links in Canada Booth was given the names of Confederate agents who were operating in the Maryland area, people who might be able to assist in his kidnapping plot. Meanwhile the South was losing ground fast, so any plan, no matter how outrageous, was worth a shot.

Booth now started to add detail to his plan, working out the best route for transporting Lincoln from Washington to Richmond. There were many back ways through Maryland, some of which were used by spies passing back and forth, and it was during his forays along the lanes of Maryland that Booth recruited David Herold, an out-of-work Washington drug store clerk. Booth, always accessible to his fans, had met Herold in 1863 when he invited him backstage after one of his performances. Running into him again Booth thought he might now be able to make use of the adoring Herold, who spent much of his time bird watching around Maryland, an area he obviously knew well, having spent hours in the swampy waterways of the Maryland peninsula. Herold, a southerner who had moved north before the war, was pleased to help, both for the sake of his Confederate colleagues and to assist the charismatic Booth.

Over the next few months Booth made many visits into the Maryland countryside, often acting as a potential real estate buyer, or claiming to be looking for horse stock. One day he attended a Catholic service in Bryan town, about thirty miles from Washington, and there was introduced to Dr Samuel A. Mudd, a Charles County physician. The thirty-year-old Mudd was the son of a wealthy planter who had employed up to one hundred slaves before the war broke out. On commencement of hostilities the slaves had dispersed and Mudd had been forced to give up his medical practice to help out on the farm. After their introduction Booth was invited to stay over at Mudd's residence, during which they grew to know more of each other, although Booth did not indulge Mudd in his scheme to kidnap the President.

With his new friendship with Mudd cemented, Booth returned to Washington, buying a new horse on the way back. Part of Booth's kidnap plan involved having a horse stabled near the theatre as part of the escape plan – he intended to keep the horse in a run-down stable at the rear of Ford's Theatre. Edman Spangler, the theatre's handyman and joiner, was a person Booth knew quite well, having been employed to work at Junius Booth's home where he carried out repairs and improvements. Now a middle-aged widower he was employed at the theatre, creating sets and generally helping out. Booth reacquainted himself with Spangler and soon they were seen out and about drinking together, Spangler enjoying the attention of his famous friend. Like many before him Spangler soon fell under Booth's spell and agreed to help the actor with his plan.

Through his links with Confederate agents Booth was now given the name of John Harrison Surratt, another sympathizer. When the two men met, Surratt was accompanied by a friend, Louis Weichmann, and the three men went out for food and drinks during which time Booth was able to size the two men up. Booth was of the opinion that Surratt was an intelligent man, more so than his other recruits, and he and Weichmann exhibited the same Confederate sympathies. Booth asked them so many questions that they began to suspect he was a Federal agent. When they refused to talk to him any further Booth was forced to reveal his plan to kidnap the President to Surratt, but not Weichmann. Later Weichmann would report that the two men had held a number of private conversations in his company, to which both men had claimed they were discussing a private property deal. Surratt listened to Booth's foolhardy plan sceptically, but Booth was nothing if not persuasive and he soon had him considering the enormity of what they could achieve. Surratt was well aware of the Union's dominance over the South and was keen to see if they could swing the South's fortunes in the other direction. A few days after learning of the daring plot Surratt agreed to join the clan, keen to assist his southern allies.

Surratt had gone with his mother to live in Washington after his father died, moving into a ten-room boarding house which Mrs Surratt now intended to run as a going concern. Mrs Surratt kept the boarding house scrupulously clean and its rooms were always in reasonable demand, although it would later be better known as the dwelling where the egg of conspiracy was hatched.

Surratt gave up his job to commit himself full time to the plot and made a contribution early on by managing to recruit another willing helper, a 29-year-old German immigrant named George A. Atzerodt. Surratt realized that any workable plan would involve them escaping across the Potomac River and decided to visit Port Tobacco, a small town on the edge of Pope's Creek in southern Maryland, six hours hard ride from Washington. It was here that Surratt met Atzerodt, a cabinet maker by day and an oarsman by night. The two men had previously met and Surratt knew that Atzerodt would be available for a price so was easily able to persuade him to visit Washington to discuss terms with Booth.

Booth gave the pathetic-looking Atzerodt the full treatment – fancy food and lots to drink. Atzerodt had a slightly sly look to him as well as being particularly scruffy and in need of a wash, yet Booth decided to invite him to join the group as a co-conspirator, not just an employed river man which had been the original intention.

By now Booth had decided that the abduction would happen at one of Washington's many theatres, as it gave Booth, the well-known actor, a legitimate reason for being there and no doubt appealed to his sense of drama. The plan was simple. Booth and an accomplice would accost the President in his box at gunpoint and then truss him up. They would then lower the President onto the stage by rope where the athletic Booth and his other helpers would whisk him out of the back of the theatre and away into the night, where, using their knowledge of the country lanes of Maryland, they would smuggle the President to Richmond via the Potomac River.

Even though Booth recognized the need for yet another helper, it was folly to believe that an entire audience would simply sit and watch while the President of the United States was manhandled out of the theatre by kidnappers. What he needed was someone with an intimate knowledge of the theatre who would be able to extinguish the gas lights, plunging the place into darkness. To this end Booth set off to New York where he tried to enlist the help of a boyhood friend who was working with his brother Edwin, but the man turned the offer down flat. Booth returned to Washington where he again tried to recruit another young man but he too declined the offer. He was of course running a grave risk that any one of those he tried to recruit, especially those who refused to help, might have turned him over to the authorities. None did, probably not because they held Confederate sympathies, but more likely because they didn't ever believe the plan would be put into action.

Daily press reports relayed news of the North's successes and most people, even the southerners, were convinced of the North's impending victory. Day by day General Grant's army was winning Confederate flags while Lee's armies were being trapped and demolished in all of the main fighting zones. The daily newspapers made depressing reading for Booth who now wanted to push ahead with his plans.

Booth had heard news that Lincoln was to attend Ford's Theatre on 18 January, where he would watch a production of *Jack Cade*, so he put the word out to his conspirators to meet him in Washington, although how many showed is not known. In any event the night in question was stormy and Lincoln decided to stop at home.

This turn of events made Booth reconsider his plan. He

wasn't convinced of the reasons that the President stayed home that evening and wondered whether news of his plan had reached official ears. He put the plan on hold and the conspirators went their separate ways for a while, Booth moving to New York and the others simply went back to where they had come from. Had it been left up to the others then it is most unlikely that the plan would have been enacted at all, for it is thought that with the exception of Surratt the others were sceptical that the plot would ever come to fruition.

By February, with yet more bad news gracing the front pages of America's newspapers, Booth tried to rekindle the interest amongst his band of merry plotters. During his efforts to rally the troops, a number of whom seemed to have lost their enthusiasm, Booth came across another potential helper and one who seemed significantly more competent than the others. Lewis Thornton Powell had been a private in the Confederate Army, who had had once seen Booth on the stage which was the basis of a chance conversation they had. Somehow the two reached an understanding, Powell was recruited and Booth rewarded him with new clothes and money to spend. Powell became Booth's most trusted associate and was considered to be an excellent recruit. Powerfully built and with a violent temper, he could be relied upon in times of trouble, yet was docile and obedient in Booth's company, referring to Booth as "Cap".

In February 1865, Powell arrived in Washington having in the meantime changed his name to Lewis Paine after turning himself over to the Federal authorities and swearing an oath of allegiance to the Union. He called at the boarding house of Mrs Surratt, where as others would later testify, Paine was warmly welcomed and offered supper and a room in the attic.

With Paine now in Washington Booth's assembled gang of conspirators were all ready and present, with Surratt travelling back and forth between Washington and Richmond, and Arnold and O'Laughlin on call in Baltimore. The others, David Herold, George Atzerodt and the theatre's handyman, Ned Spangler, were also awaiting instructions.

Throughout this period of extended planning Booth had

also managed to collect an impressive array of knives and guns. One of his associates would later recall how he had barged in on Booth one day and caught him with several guns spread out on a bedroom table – the day in question just happened to be Inauguration Day. Whether Booth had planned to shoot the President at this most special event is not known for sure – he certainly had a viable opportunity for he had been given a special ticket to the event and would have been perfectly placed to carry out the attack, although this approach lacked the benefit of a realistic escape plan.

Booth was amongst the crowd when Lincoln gave his famous, five-minute inaugural address, during which he uttered words of reconciliation. Looking much older than his 56 years, Lincoln spoke of his hopes for a land soon to be at peace. He spoke of freedom for all, the need to bind up the nation's wounds and the desire to look after the country's widows and orphans. The crowds who had gathered to listen absorbed the words and were keen to move to a more united future, all that is except for Booth – the speech hadn't moved him at all.

As Booth had anticipated, the security on Inauguration Day was tight, with marksmen positioned all around the great room. The entrances were manned by armed guards and only those with legitimate passes were allowed in. All coats and garments that could have concealed a weapon had to be removed at the door – thanks to Lincoln's friend Lamon, no chances had been taken.

By now Lincoln had begun to believe that the need for high security had been overstated. As the war was about to end he received an invitation from General Grant to witness the end of the Confederacy at first hand. The President was keen and on 23 March 1865, he made his way to Grant's headquarters on the James River, near Petersburg. Believing that the situation was safe Lincoln even brought along his wife, Mary Todd Lincoln, a decision which would in due course have an influence on future events. Mrs Lincoln did not get on well with General Grant's wife, Julia, and the two had a number of cross words, after which Julia Grant spent much of her time trying to avoid being in Mrs Lincoln's company.

During Lincoln's visit to the front line General Grant launched the full might of his army against the entrenched Confederates and was soon rewarded with their retreat. Lincoln quickly wired his War Secretary that Robert E. Lee's army had abandoned the Petersburg trenches; this was followed by another wire a short time later declaring that Richmond had fallen.

Lincoln now chose to visit the captured Confederate capital to see the situation for himself. Accompanied by only a dozen armed soldiers the President walked through Richmond's downtown area, moving from building to building. The white people who saw him looked glum but none appeared to bear him malice and none made any attempt to attack him. As a result of this Lincoln now believed that if he could walk safely through a one-time Confederate stronghold he must surely be safe in Washington; from then on he began to take less precautions for his personal safety.

Booth was in Washington when news of Richmond's fall was received and had to watch as the streets erupted into thunderous celebration, a bitter pill for a Confederate sympathizer to swallow. In the days that followed the papers reported the events, presenting victorious headlines and reflecting on the euphoria which now engulfed the capital city. Whether it was in reaction to the public celebrations that spurred Booth on is not known, but he strongly resented the outpouring of glee which was visible on all but a few of Washington's residents.

Shortly after the fall of Richmond, on 13 April, Grant and his wife returned to Washington where they became the centre of the public's attention, everyone wanting to see the hero who had defeated the Confederacy. A police escort had to be provided to ensure the unrestricted passage of Grant from his hotel to the War Office where he had some administrative duties to take care of. From there he was escorted to the White House where he met with the President, during which Lincoln invited General Grant and his wife to a theatre performance the following evening.

Grant was well aware of the frosty relations which existed between his wife Julia and Mary Lincoln and did not relish the thought of having to spend an evening in the tight squeeze of a theatre box with them. With the war now over he was also keen to visit his children who were elsewhere at boarding school. It would be this reason he would give for not being able to attend the theatre, but in reality it was Mrs Lincoln's brash manner which kept them away and which saved them from the possible danger they would have been in had they gone to the theatre that night.

On the morning of 14 April 1865, Lincoln called together his war cabinet for a brief meeting, during which Grant reviewed the surrender of Richmond with them. When the meeting was concluded Grant was able to make his excuses and went back to his hotel to collect his wife and belongings.

Booth too had heard of Grant's arrival in Washington and watched as the crowds continued their merry celebrations at the expense of people like himself. The overzealous nature of the town's elation left Booth with a strong desire to wipe the smiles off their faces and so he set about planning his revenge. The one observation which Booth had noted was the President's habit of visiting the theatre with any special guest who arrived in town. He concluded therefore that he would extend the same invitation to General Grant and began making enquiries as to where the President might go. Booth began visiting the multitude of show houses and enquired within if any were expecting the President. By checking the billboards Booth could see that Ford's Theatre was presenting a long-running show called *Our American Cousin*, whereas Grover's Theatre was staging a brand-new show called *Aladdin, or the Wonderful Lamp*, and concluded that Grover's was the better bet. Enquiring within he found the theatre manager in discussion with a colleague; interrupting he enquired if they were intending to invite the President along. The manager confirmed they were and then quickly turned to his assistant to remind him to send the invitation.

For Booth, the morning of 14 April commenced with him carefully dressing and then going for breakfast at the National Hotel. Wanting to look his best for what would be the most important day of his life, Booth then went for a haircut before returning to his rooms where he met with Michael O'Laughlin. O'Laughlin, despite his southern sympathies, could not resist joining in the merriment and arrived from Baltimore with the intention of joining the party. Booth attempted to re-engage him in the conspiracy but failed – O'Laughlin was too busy enjoying himself and had more partying planned for that very evening.

After O'Laughlin left the hotel Booth set about organizing his own plans. He visited Ford's Theatre which he used as a mailing address and was handed a bundle of letters by Henry Clay Ford, brother of the theatre owner. During their brief discussion Ford told him that the President and Mrs Lincoln would be accompanied by General Grant to their theatre that very night. Booth's guesswork had been wrong – they would not be at the Grover Theatre as he thought and now he would need to change his plans rapidly.

Leaving the theatre he headed over to the livery stable where he kept the horse he had bought while in Maryland and instructed the liveryman to deliver the large, heavy horse to Ned Spangler who would put it in the stables he had readied just behind Ford's Theatre. His plan now was to allow Lewis Paine to use the horse as his getaway and so he now needed a horse of his own. It was mid-afternoon when visited a stable on C Street, where he ordered the stable lad to make the horse available and ready to go by 4 p.m.

Booth next arrived at Mrs Surratt's boarding house where he found her preparing to leave for a brief visit out of town with Louis Weichmann, her long-time lodger. Booth now fully implicated Mrs Surratt by handing her a small package wrapped in coarse brown paper and tied with twine, which he requested she take with her and deliver to a man named John Lloyd at the Surrattsville Tavern. The package would play a major part in Surratt's life although she nearly set off without it and had to return to collect it, keeping Weichmann waiting in the carriage. Weichmann was soon to find out what whispers had passed between Booth and John Surratt the first time they met, that it was not a property deal they were engaged in, but rather a murderous conspiracy.

Booth next called on Lewis Paine whome he found lolling

on his bed. Booth quickly brought Paine up to date with the plan, telling him he intended to shoot the President that very evening and demanding that he take care of General Grant. Paine accepted the assignment with little emotion, shortly thereafter checking out of his hotel and heading out for something to eat.

Booth then unsuccessfully tried to track down George Atzerodt, leaving him a note, before heading back to Ford's Theatre where he was seen by a number of people. It is thought that Booth then reconnoitred the presidential theatre box. Making his way up to the mezzanine floor he would be able to see boxes six and seven, normally separated by a screen, but now enlarged to accommodate the President's party. As Booth made his way back out he came across a man who he had dealt with previously in respect of buying properties. When the man suggested they go for a drink in an adjoining bar, Booth readily accepted.

At around 4.00 p.m. Booth collected his horse from the stable and had the liveryman shorten the stirrups for him before heading off towards Grover's Theatre. Finding the manager's box empty Booth settled to write a letter to the *National Intelligencer*, a prominent Washington newspaper. In a surprising turn of events, as Booth was leaving the theatre he bumped into John Mathews, one of the men he had visited in New York and who had turned him down in his quest to kidnap the President. He greeted Mathews cordially and the two spoke for a short while before Booth asked if Mathews would kindly deliver his letter to the newspaper the following day, a task which on this occasion Mathews accepted. As Mathews was in the play at Ford's Theatre that night and would witness the events for himself at close quarters, no longer would he doubt the resolve of Booth to carry through his daring plan. Worse still, Mathews read the letter and in fear of implicating himself in the plot burned it, not forewarning those who could have prevented the murder. Mathews would remain tight lipped about the letter for two years following the assassination.

Booth took his own horse to the stable behind the theatre and then invited Spangler and two other theatre staff out for a drink, after which he bought them a bottle of whiskey which he asked them to enjoy on him. He meanwhile went back into the pretty much deserted theatre and continued to make his plans. Taking a block of wood he approached a white door that led to the corridor outside the presidential box. Practising a few times he was able to be sure that by jamming the wood between the door and the wall, the door would be secure from anyone trying to get in – the President would therefore be unable to get assistance immediately after the attack. Once he was sure the door could be secured he hid the block of wood in a dark corner where it would go unnoticed.

Happy that his plans were now in place Booth returned to the National Hotel where he enjoyed a light supper and a liqueur before returning to his room. Upstairs he changed his clothes and loaded his pistol, a .44-calibre, single-shot Derringer, which though small, fired a lead ball nearly half an inch in diameter.

Booth held the final meeting of his remaining accomplices at around 8 p.m. when Paine, Atzerodt and Herold were informed of a more ambitious plot. Booth had learned earlier that although Grant had been invited to the theatre he had since left town. Paine therefore would not be able to deal with him as previously thought. Booth now suggested that instead of Grant he intended that Paine should ride to the home of William Seward, the Secretary of State, and murder him. Herold would act as Paine's guide, leading him to Seward's address and then guiding him away afterwards. Atzerodt meanwhile would seek out the Vice President, Andrew Johnson, who was staying at a local hotel and shoot him. Booth looked at his cohorts and told them the time of the attacks should be 10.15 p.m. Afterwards they would meet at the Navy Yard Bridge before fleeing to Surrattville; where they would be able to pick up the package that Mrs Surratt had delivered – a package containing more weapons. From there they hoped to cross the Potomac River and find a safe haven in the South.

All but Atzerodt seemed happy – he was not so keen on the ever-changing plans and complained that he had only agreed to the plot when it involved the kidnapping of the President. Atzerodt would later testify that Booth had said they would all be hung anyhow so backing out was not an option. By the time the men left the meeting President Lincoln was already seated in his box at Ford's Theatre watching *Our American Cousin.*

Sometime between 9.30 p.m. and 10 p.m. Booth rode into the alleyway behind the theatre and called for Ned Spangler, who appeared on the third call. Booth asked him to hold the horse but Spangler said he would be missed if he weren't inside and that he would ask Joseph Burroughs, the junior handyman, to come and hold it instead. Ironically Spangler and Burroughs had argued earlier in the day while preparing the presidential box. Spangler had cursed Lincoln and Burroughs had taken exception, asking him why he was blaspheming against Lincoln. Now Burroughs was about to hold the getaway pony for the President's assassin.

Once inside the theatre Booth took a route beneath the stage and crossed to the other side into the lobby. It was now a little after 10 p.m. and Booth had already passed a number of people who knew him by sight. He walked briskly up the stairs to the dress circle and paused, looking around; more people in the audience recognized him as he turned and headed to the white door which gave entry to the corridor outside the presidential box. Army Captain Theodore McGowan, who was close by, testified later that Booth took a pack of visiting cards from his pocket. Booth then showed one of them to the President's footman and messenger, Charles Forbes, who was sitting near the white door, before going through the door, closing it behind him. He was now within touching distance of the President – the bodyguards who should have been guarding the door were clearly not in attendance. Years later one would admit that they had moved in order to get a better view of the stage, leaving Lincoln completely vulnerable.

Safely ensconced in the corridor Booth now took the wood block he had hidden earlier and positioned it to prevent the door from being opened. The play was now in full flow and laughter filled the theatre. With the sound more than covering his own movements Booth slipped stealthily into the presidential box and moved towards Lincoln's rocking chair. The presidential party were so engrossed in the play that Booth's arrival went unnoticed by them, although a restaurant owner sat opposite noticed the stranger's arrival. James P. Ferguson had come to the theatre that night in the hope of seeing his idol, General Grant, so when he saw the shadowy shape of someone moving in behind the President, he hoped and expected it to be Grant.

Lincoln was sat forward in his chair, his arms resting on the railings and looking down at someone in the orchestra pit. Ferguson saw what happened next. The President suddenly turned as if to look at the stranger and in that very instance he saw the blue flash of Booth's Derringer. The audience were still laughing when the shot splintered into Lincoln's skull. Almost immediately he slumped into his chair, while Mrs Lincoln leaned toward her husband to hold him up. Major Henry Rathbone, who was sharing the presidential box, looked through the smoke and could see Booth standing there. Rathbone lunged towards Booth knocking the pistol out of his hand but Booth had drawn a dagger and was slashing mercilessly at him. In the heat of the struggle Booth managed to break free, leapt onto the railings and then off towards the stage. Unfortunately for Booth one of his spurs got caught in one of the flags shrouding the presidential box, his normally perfect balance was disrupted and he landed heavily on just one foot, breaking two small bones in his left leg.

Amazingly the 1,000-strong audience did nothing; many presumed the madman jumping onto the stage was all part of the act. It had taken just thirty seconds from Booth entering the presidential box to leaping onto the stage and escaping, most people still unaware of the monumental tragedy which had unfolded in their presence, all that was left was a curl of smoke drifting through the air. A moment later and everyone knew something terrible had happened as Major Rathbone shouted instructions to stop the escaping man, his voice barely audible above the screams of Mrs Lincoln.

Two men who did react quickly were A.C. Richards,

superintendent of the Metropolitan Police, who was sitting in the dress circle, and Joseph B. Stewart, a Washington lawyer. When Richards saw the man limping away, he dashed down onto the stage and began searching the back-stage area, where he was joined by Stewart.

Booth meanwhile was heading towards the back door, his dagger still drawn and flashing dangerously in the dim light. As he hobbled down the passageway leading to the rear exit door he found his way blocked by William Withers Jr, the leader of the orchestra, who had gone backstage during a break. Booth was in no mood to make requests and slashed out at Withers twice, the first slicing through his clothing the second delivering a nasty wound to his neck. Once outside he screamed at Burroughs to bring the horse around; when Burroughs did not respond quickly enough Booth knocked him to the ground with the butt of his knife and kicked him. Climbing into the saddle he spurred the horse on and galloped away. Within seconds Richards and Stewart arrived at the open door in time to hear the frantic sound of a galloping horse heading away down the alley and into the night.

By now the theatre had erupted into panic and misery, people were stood around crying as news of the attack on the President spread. A doctor in the audience who had been attached to an army unit and was familiar with gunshot wounds made his way to the presidential box. When he arrived Rathbone was just removing the wooden door jam that Booth had used to secure the white door. As he entered the room he saw Mrs Lincoln cradling the President, whose head was bowed, his chin resting on his chest. The dis-traught First Lady asked if the doctor would be able to help the President, although at first glance he had assumed the President was dead. Laying him out on the floor he ran his hand through the President's blood-matted hair, his finger finding the half-inch hole at the back of his head. Having found no pulse the doctor pushed his finger into the bullet hole and removed a blood clot in the vain hope of reducing the pressure on the President's brain. Another doctor then arrived, 23-year-old Dr Charles Sabin, who had been helped

up over the railings and into the President's private box. The
two doctors began to applying artificial respiration, pushing
the President's diaphragm in and out; when this didn't work
Sabin tried mouth-to-mouth resuscitation. Eventually Lincoln's breathing returned feebly on its own. Having worked
hard to maintain the President's life Sabin now faced the
reality of the President's injury – he had suffered a mortal
gunshot wound to the brain and would ultimately die of his
injuries. However, no one wanted him to die in the theatre
box, the White House was too far and so he was carried
across the street to a boarding house where more doctors
arrived, eventually sixteen in total attending the dying President, who lingered on despite his severe injury. Throughout the night Lincoln's life ebbed slowly away; the gunshot
wound to the head had caused major damage. Had he been
shot today his wounds would have been difficult to treat and
his prognosis poor. At 6.40 a.m., Dr Albert King jotted in a
notebook that Lincoln's breaths were prolonged and groan-
ing. At 7 a.m. King noted that the President was still breathing but with long pauses. Then, at 7.22 a.m., some nine
hours after the attack, the President's chest rose, fell and did
not rise again. Lincoln was dead, the victim of a most
audacious assassination.

At the same time as Lincoln was being shot, Booth's
cohorts were involved in murderous activities themselves.
At 10.10 p.m., Lewis Paine arrived at Seward's three-storey
mansion on Lafayette Square, adjacent to the White House.
Paine was accompanied by David Herold who, after refusing
to be actively involved in the murder, was acting solely as the
guide. Paine's plan was to pretend to be delivering medicine
to the sick Seward and to insist on seeing the man so as to
provide strict dosage instructions. Knocking at the door
Paine was initially met by Seward's black servant William
Bell, to whom he gave his story. When Bell refused to allow
him entry Paine became more insistent and barged past the
servant into the hallway. The commotion drew the attention
of the other guests who were now wondering what all the
noise was about. As Bell climbed the stairs to see if Seward
could receive a visitor, Paine noisily followed on behind,

quite aware that his presence was unwanted. At the top of the stairs Bell and Paine ran into Seward's son Frederick, whereupon Paine once again explained his errand. Frederick was concerned at disturbing his father but decided to check on him to see if the visit was possible. Unfortunately Frederick had now unknowingly given Paine Seward's location. When Frederick refused Paine permission to enter his father's bedroom Paine turned as if to walk down back down the stairs, then suddenly spun round with a pistol in his hand, pointed the gun directly at Frederick and pulled the trigger, but to Paine's disappointment the gun did not go off. Faced with a situation he had not foreseen Paine lunged at Frederick and whipped him about the head with the butt of the gun, breaking it in the process. Frederick sustained two skull fractures in the attack yet managed to grapple with the much bigger Paine, right up to his father's bedroom door. Outside William Bell had run into the street to find some help, screaming, "Murder! Murder!"

Hearing the commotion outside, Private George F. Robinson, who had been sitting with Seward, opened the door to the bedroom and was met by Paine who had drawn his bowie knife. Robinson was struck immediately on the forehead and was forced to the ground with blood pouring from the open wound. Also in the room was Seward's daughter, Fanny, who was shoved out of the way as Paine jumped on to the sick man's bed. Striking ferociously with his knife, Paine inflicted several severe injuries, the first opening a wound so deep on Seward's cheek that his tongue could be seen through it. Other stabs hit the beleaguered Seward in his neck, narrowly missing major arteries.

Robinson had by now got to his feet and had struck Paine from behind, but he continued slashing away with his knife, injuring Robinson even more, twice cutting him through to the bone. Another house guest now joined the affray, Seward's other son, Major Augustus Seward, who had been asleep in the room next door. He and Robinson grappled with Paine and the three men gradually moved towards the bedroom door. Once at the top of the stairs Paine broke free and dashed down into the hallway where he ran into Seward's State Department messenger, who had his back to him, and stabbed the man before running for his horse. By now David Herold had already departed, afraid the screams of William Bell would draw in help before Paine could complete his work.

Inside the house, Seward had suddenly regained consciousness, declared that he was not dead and that a surgeon should be called along with the police. He subsequently survived the attack and would live to see justice dispensed.

Vice President Johnson, George Atzerodt's intended victim, would also survive. Atzerodt, who was not a killer by nature, had become less and less happy with his role as the evening had progressed. Typical of the man he handled his unease in the best way he knew how – he got drunk in the bar of Kirkwood House, the hotel where Vice President Johnson was staying. The timing of Atzerodt's attack was of great significance, as was his victim, for once Johnson became aware of Lincoln's condition, as the next in line to the presidency he would be forced to visit and potentially take control. Atzerodt allowed the 10.15 p.m. deadline to come and go, instead sinking further into a whiskey induced haze. With the task still preying on his mind, he decided to leave the hotel and instead find lodgings for the night, he had decided he would not be able to progress with Booth's plan. Out on the street he noticed a large contingent of cavalry troops ride past, and suspected he knew their business. As if to distance himself further from the evening's plans he threw his dagger away and staggered off to find a bed for the night.

News of the attack on the President spread fast – even in these early days of the fledgling newspaper industry reporters were prepared to sell their papers on the back of some startling headlines. Secretary of War Stanton had assumed the responsibilities of the President and had already set in motion plans to capture the perpetrators. All southbound trains from Washington had been halted, all boats on the Potomac were prevented from touching shore south of Alexandria and all other members of the cabinet were under the watchful eyes of armed guards.

Ford's Theatre had been closed down and hundreds of

statements taken from eyewitnesses, all of whom claimed to have recognized the man who jumped from the presidential box as John Wilkes Booth. The weight of evidence seemed beyond doubt. Stanton now turned the full focus of his attention to catching the killer.

After Lincoln had died his body was removed to the White House and preparations were made to swear in Vice President Johnson, thus releasing Stanton from his temporary presidential duties, to concentrate on Booth. He released a cable at 3 a.m., naming Booth as the assassin and effectively put all authorities on alert.

The opportunity to catch Booth within an hour of the attack had come and gone. Booth had ridden his horse hard towards the Navy Yard Bridge arriving at around 10.45 p.m. The bridge had normally operated a curfew which prevented anyone crossing after 9 p.m. but with the war over this rule had been relaxed. When Booth reached the bridge he slowed to a stop, allowing the sentries to question him. Amazingly Booth gave his correct name and even told the two sentries that he was heading towards south Maryland. Not knowing the events that had unfolded in Washington they allowed Booth to continue on his way. A short time afterward the sentries allowed David Herold to cross the bridge, having enquired of him only briefly.

Ten minutes after Herold crossed the Navy Yard Bridge he caught up with Booth whose lower leg was causing him severe pain. The pair swapped horses as Herold's had an easier gate and they rode on towards Surrattsville and the tavern owned by Mary Surratt. Here they collected the guns they had shipped out earlier with Mrs Surratt, drank some whiskey and set off again heading south-east. Before they departed they told John Lloyd, the operator of the tavern, that they were pretty sure they had killed the President and Secretary Seward.

With Booth's leg causing him severe pain the pair headed to Bryan town and the home of Dr Samuel Mudd, where Booth had previously spent a night. At 4 a.m. Mudd was awakened by the sound of approaching horses and opened his door to find two men standing there, later testifying that he did not recognize Booth from his previous encounter, although many years later he changed his story to say he did recognize Booth but was not aware that he was a fugitive.

Dr Mudd prepared a splint for Booth's leg, put him to bed for the evening and retired once more for the night himself. Mudd did not sleep well and rose early the following morning preparing breakfast for Booth and Herold, most of which Booth could not face because of the searing pain he was still experiencing in his lower leg. As soon as the pair were up they enquired with Mudd as to the fastest route to the Potomac River. Mudd pointed out an old cart track which led directly into the Zekiah Swamp, a forbidding wilderness of bog land and dense undergrowth, swarming with flies, lizards and bugs.

That afternoon the two men set off into the swamp and were soon miserably lost. At 9 p.m., tired and disorientated, they came across the log cabin of black tobacco farmer, Oswell Swann, to whom they offered $12 if he would guide them out of the swamp and to the home of Samuel Cox, a wealthy farmer and known Confederate sympathizer. Oswell accepted the offer and they set off through the wilderness, often ending up in thick undergrowth with no apparent way out, but finally they emerged and were thankfully just across the fields from Cox's farmhouse; it was late but they hoped for a warm welcome.

Booth identified himself as Lincoln's assassin and requested that Cox help him across the Potomac and away to the South. Cox, Confederate though he was, decided that he could not provide a comfortable bed for the night and instead had them sleep in a dense thicket about two miles from the farmhouse. The next day he despatched his adopted son to fetch a Confederate agent named Thomas A. Jones. A daring and resourceful man, Jones had helped couriers across the Potomac many times and knew the shoreline well.

When Jones arrived at the thicket he gave a small whistle and announced that he had been sent by Cox to help. By now federal agents were swarming all over the area and Jones knew it would be difficult to get the two men across the river. Booth had given away his route and now he was being pursued day by day, while the rest of his accomplices had already been rounded up and were spilling the beans on the brains behind the plot.

The press had announced to the world the murder of Lincoln, but unlike modern assassinations, the population were split on the news. So soon after the fall of the Confederacy many of those in the South still resented their loss and downfall after the civil war. In the North though, the citizens were baying for Booth's blood and also that of his band of murderous helpers. Washington prepared itself for revenge; the trial would be just a precursor to the main event. In the hours following the assassination the police had already gathered the names of those involved: John Surratt, George Atzerodt, David Herold and Ned Spangler. Atzerodt had been easily detected. When a detective named John Lee visited Kirkwood House where Vice President Johnson had been staying, dropping by the bar he was told of a suspicious person who had been drinking there that night having booked into one of the rooms the previous day. Lee broke down the door to Atzerodt's bedroom and soon found incriminating evidence of the crime. Amongst the guns, cartridges and a knife, Lee found a Montreal bank book made out in the name of J. Wilkes Booth. From here the connection from one suspect to the next unfolded easily. Booth's known relationship with John Surratt led a police squad to Mrs Surratt's boarding house where she and Louis Weichmann were hauled in for questioning. During questioning Weichmann revealed all he knew about the Surratt house, its visitors and the comings and goings of John Wilkes Booth. At the time of the assassination John Surratt had been in New York and was astounded when he became aware of a $25,000 dollar bounty on his head. He quickly headed north over the border into Canada where he remained hidden for the next two years. His absence would have a great impact on the fate of his mother, who was now considered to be heavily implicated in the plot.

In another twist to this saga and one bordering on the ridiculous, another chance arrest was made at Mrs Surratt's boarding house. During the police search a large man with

a pick axe over his shoulder called at the house and claimed
he had been employed by Mrs Surratt to dig some drains.
Mrs Surratt claimed she had never seen the man before let
alone hired him to do a job for her. As a precaution the
police arrested him and took him in for questioning. The
man later confessed to being Lewis Paine and was eventually identified as the man who had attempted to kill
Secretary Seward. He had been in hiding for three days
near the Navy Yard Bridge and had been forced out
through desperation and hunger.

Booth and Herold were still hiding in the thicket near the
home of Samuel Cox, Thomas Jones regularly supplying
them with food and brandy. After a long wait, news that the
search for Booth and Herold had moved further away arrived
and it seemed time to make a move. Jones had secured them a
small boat hidden on the shores of the Potomac and now
guided them through the final stretch of undergrowth, he
walking ahead and whistling to confirm that the way was
clear. The two men climbed in the boat and rowed away from
the shore, until Jones vanished out of sight. Herold kept
rowing all through the night until finally at daybreak the
reality of their bid for freedom became obvious. Not only
had the incoming tide carried them several miles back up the
river but they were also still on the Maryland side. Tired,
hungry and disappointed they brought the boat back into the
shore and headed once more into the foliage, this time
heading for the farm of Perigrinne Davis, another Confederate sympathiser. Hoping to gather provisions and then
move on again the two men were forced to lay low again as
they found themselves back in the heart of the search zone
with hundreds of officers scouring the land and surrounding
countryside.

Eventually the two men made another attempt to cross the
Potomac and were this time successful, landing at Gambo
Creek. Their hope however of finding refuge in the bosom of
their Confederate allies was not one they would realise.
Virginia had now been taken over by Federal troops and
there were few now brave enough or stupid enough to aid the
President's assassin. Fleeing from place to place they were

occasionally given food and drink but never refuge, no one wanting to be the harbourers of the two most wanted men in America. Anyone who did consider it had only to read the newspapers to catch the mood of those back in Washington and the fate of anyone caught assisting the villains.

Deciding that they needed to move on again the two men made their way to the Rappahannock River where they planned to cross into West Virginia and put even more distance between them and Washington. Arriving at the jetty they found that the ferry was on the other side and so were forced to wait. Herold manage to get into conversation with a number of Confederate soldiers who were returning home and asked for their assistance, admitting that he and his friend were the ones responsible for the President's death. It was a risky and foolhardy admission but one that paid off. The two men were asked to share the cavalrymen's horses and were escorted across the river to Port Royal, from where the two men made their way to the farm of Richard Garrett, another man who had total loyalty to the Confederacy. They were offered food and shelter under assumed names and for a while were able to relax, more comfortable than they had been since they had gone on the run.

Not long after the cavalrymen had departed they returned with awful news, Federal soldiers had crossed the Rappahannock River to Port Royal and were heading towards them. Wishing the two men luck the cavalrymen rode off again towards the town of Bowling Green.

Booth and Herold considered their next move but were soon forced to hide at the sound of approaching horses. Luckily the troop went straight past; they too were heading for Bowling Green. They decided that they would stay at Garrett's ranch another night and made themselves comfortable in the barn, planning to make their escape the following morning. Unfortunately for them both, the Federal troops were hot on the trail of the cavalrymen who had been identified by someone when they themselves had docked at Port Royal. When the cavalrymen were finally tracked down they immediately gave the game away. Tired but determined the troops turned around and headed back to Garrett's ranch, arriving there at 2 a.m. Their hope of arriving undetected were dashed when Garrett's dogs started barking, drawing Garrett from his slumber.

When Garret denied any knowledge of the two men the troops threatened to hang him there and then, a threat which encouraged Garrett's son to blurt out that the wanted men were asleep in the barn. The soldiers surrounded the building and ordered the two men to surrender themselves, at which they heard then arguing – Herold clearly wanted to surrender but Booth was not of the same opinion. After a while the troops shouted in again at which point the barn door opened and David Herold emerged empty handed, his hands above his head. Booth, having previously called Herold a coward and a traitor, now shouted, "There is a man here who wants to surrender awful bad; he is innocent of any crime whatever."

The gibbering Herold was tied to a tree as the soldiers turned their attention back to the barn. Booth now offered to face the entire troop in a shoot-off, an offer the troop declined. One of the officers now went to the rear of the barn and lit some hay, throwing it through one of the larger gaps in the wooden building. Soon the barn was ablaze and the troops could see Booth's silhouette against the dancing flames. Booth started to head towards the barn door where upon one of the troops fired a shot through another gap in the wood which floored Booth. He was pulled from the blazing structure and laid out on Garrett's porch. A gaping wound in his neck had caused severe damage and injured Booth's spine and he lay paralysed on the floor.

Panic now spread among the troops who had been instructed to capture Booth – Washington wanted a public trial but now it looked like that opportunity had passed. During the night Booth's condition, just like the President before him, worsened and he eventually died at 7 a.m. in the morning.

Disappointment spread as the press confirmed that the President's assassin was dead. They would be denied the trial and the satisfaction of passing the death penalty, so in

Booth's absence attention now turned to those who had collaborated with Booth.

Lincoln's death triggered an outpouring of public emotion beyond anything America had ever seen. Within hours of the news of his death being known Washington was shrouded in black. On 18 April 25,000 people filed through the White House where Lincoln's body lay in state. The next day the body was taken to the Capitol Rotunda under escort. Minute guns boomed as the procession travelled up Pennsylvania Avenue, past 40,000 mourners. On 21 April Lincoln and the remains of his disinterred son Willie, who had died in 1862 at the age of 12, began their journey back to Illinois. Each city the train passed through on the 1,700 mile journey held its own public salute. By 4 May, when Lincoln and his son were entombed near his Springfield home, more than seven million people had shared in the emotional goodbye.

All of those who had been arrested on suspicion of being involved in the conspiracy of murder were now being held in the most atrocious conditions aboard two prison ships. Kept in stifling holds the male prisoners were manacled with cuffs connected by a 14-inch long iron bar, intended to impede movement of the hands and arms. Their feet were chained and the chain anchored to 75-pound iron balls. For the purpose of preventing communication between the prisoners they had also been forced to wear a canvas hood with thick padding intended to block out noise. The hood had a small opening for the mouth, through which food could be eaten, but that was all – no eye holes and the whole thing tied at the neck. These tortuous hoods were worn day and night; removal even for the purpose of having a wash was not permitted. Mrs Surratt faced slightly less arduous conditions; spared the discomfort of the hood and wrist manacles she did however wear ankle chains.

With the conspirators now firmly under lock and key, Secretary Stanton now focused his attention on the trials. Like the modern-day media the papers of the day were highly demanding in terms of representing what they perceived to be the public's desire for justice and vengeance. The headlines screamed out for punishment and with Booth, the main perpetrator, now dead, it must be the others who should pay the price.

Stanton, himself once an able attorney, was intent upon pursuing a military trial for the prisoners. The military justice system was not so constrained by the burden of proof, so guilt was more easily established, and once established the penalties were often more severe. Stanton was convinced that the need for swift and strong punishment was vital if Booth's action were not to ignite an uprising in the South.

Andrew Johnson as the new President was, however, uneasy about the legality of the prisoners undergoing a military trial and sought the opinion of the Attorney General, James Speed. Speed believed that if the prisoners had committed a crime against the United States then they must face a military court. Also, because he believed they may have broken the laws of war, they would not be allowed to face a civil court. With this news the President asked that nine competent officers form a commission with a view to trying the defendants.

The commission was ostensibly made up of friends and colleagues of Stanton, many of whom would be criticized during the trial for showing favouritism to the prosecution. Not only was the commission deemed to be biased – all had Republican sympathies – but the commission itself was allowed to formulate its own rules and procedures. And unlike a normal court of law, the commission would be allowed to convict with a two-thirds majority, rather than the unanimous decision normally required to secure a conviction.

Stanton asked the acting Adjutant General, Edward D. Townsend, to select the officers for the tribunal, all of who were committed Republicans. Appointed to the role of President of the commission was 62-year-old Major General David Hunter, a personal friend of Lincoln's before his death. As Judge Advocate for the trial Stanton chose another old friend, Brigadier General Joseph Holt, who headed the War Department's Bureau of Military Justice. Holt had been given the role of Judge Advocate General of the Army by Lincoln and in this capacity had set up many military commissions to prosecute political prisoners accused of disloyal practices, a procedure that had been criticized widely as despotic and unconstitutional. Finally to assist Holt, Stanton selected another long-time friend, Ohio's John A. Bingham, a radical member of Congress who was a hellfire-and-brimstone lawyer; and Colonel Henry L. Burnett, an army prosecutor who had successfully won the death penalty in a number of Western military trials.

Against this backdrop the defendants arrived in court on 9 May 1865, shuffling in one after the other, under strict armed guard. One by one they took their positions on a foot high platform, behind a wooden rail at the front of the guardhouse. Each sat looking glum: Sam Arnold, Lewis Paine, David Herold, Edman Spangler, Michael O'Laughlin, George Atzerodt, Dr Samuel Mudd and Mary Surratt, their hoods specially removed for the court appearance. The first day in court was a short one and the trial was adjourned as the accused had not yet been allowed to seek a defence council. On the second day, still without representation, the commission read out the charges and noted the not guilty pleas given by each prisoner.

The spectators' gallery was full and the courthouse was surrounded by members of the public and the press; the interest in the trial was immense, and in the outcome, already believed to be a foregone conclusion, even stronger.

During the opening phases of the trial other conspirators were caught and found themselves in strange predicaments. Jefferson Davis was caught near Irwinville, Georgia and a day later, Clement Clay gave himself in to Federal authorities. Both were imprisoned in Fort Monroe, Virginia, during which time the court in Washington progressed as if they too had been charged and were there to present a defence.

The trial was soon adjourned again as friends and family members fought to find legal representation for those imprisoned, a task which proved daunting as no one seemed willing to defend a bunch so publicly despised. By 12 May, all of the defendants had retained a defence council, many of whom were of an unusually high calibre. They were however expected to perform their duties under the most onerous of conditions – they were not for instance allowed to talk to their clients in the privacy of their cells, and the only communication allowed was in the full glare of the courtroom.

As one of the lawyers later stated, "This was a contest in which a few lawyers were on one side and the whole of the United States was on the other, the verdict was known beforehand."

In another procedural restriction the prosecution were able to produce 198 prosecution witnesses, many of whom came and went without the opportunity of a cross examination. The defence on the other hand had to inform the Judge in advance of any witness who was to be called for the defence. The prosecution frequently called surprise witnesses who would add more fuel to the Confederate conspiracy theory and then disappear.

The prosecution lawyers fought with an intensity that would shock a modern practitioner of the law – from the moment the trial commenced not only were the accused under attack but also the defence lawyers.

The outcome for the most part seemed inevitable, certainly for three of them. Paine had been identified as the man who attacked Seward, Atzerodt had been identified as acting suspiciously in Vice President Johnson's hotel and David Herold had been caught on the run with Booth. The defences presented on behalf of these men were at best long shots. Paine's lawyers suggested he was insane, although an expert witness called by the defence suggested otherwise. Atzerodt's defence was based on the fact that he did not commit a crime and was therefore portrayed as someone who couldn't actually kill. Herold was described as being too simple minded to know what he was doing.

The case against Ned Spangler was weak and ultimately hung on the statement of Jacob Ritterspaugh, the Ford's Theatre stage hand who claimed he was struck by Spangler shortly after Booth made his escape. Ritterspaugh claimed Spangler had instructed him not to tell anyone the direction in which Booth had gone.

Sam Arnold and Michael O'Laughlin's cases were more complex – they had been involved with Booth on the original kidnap plot but had not been involved in the assassination. Under the rules, these two men were on trial for involvement in the assassination and so their previous involvement should not have counted against them. As they could prove they had not been involved in the assassination they should have been safe from conviction, however, the government lawyers were more inclined to prove that both men had served in the Confederate Army and therefore would want to harm members of the US government.

Samuel Mudd's case was the most time consuming as he was able to produce 79 defence witnesses against the prosecution's 23. He was however shown to have had links with Booth in the past, to have fixed his leg after the assassination and to have held views sympathetic to the Confederate South.

The trial was a showpiece of its day; as such tickets to the daily drama were much in demand and the courtroom looked on most days to be the meeting hall of the rich, famous and the well connected. Each attendee would examine each of the accused in turn, looking for signs of guilt or repentance.

All of the defendants looked like frightened rabbits, except for Lewis Paine who for the most part looked bored and disinterested, at one point admitting his attack on Seward and demanding they hang him quickly and get it over with.

At the end of the row of prisoners sat Mrs Surratt, a veil over her face and dressed entirely in black. To make their case against Surratt the government called nine witnesses, the main two being Surratt's lodger, Louis Weichmann and the Surrattsville tavern keeper, John Lloyd. Both men had been threatened by government interrogators and were talking to save their own skins. Weichmann had been summoned by Stanton who apologetically seemed to imply that he would have to put the terrified man under lock and key. John Lloyd had even more reason to be scared – he had hidden the weapons given to him by John Surratt, thus involving himself even more deeply than some of the defendants. And so each man, terrified of doing otherwise, took their places on the witness stand, in the courtroom of the old penitentiary.

The defence council put up a brave defence but the harm was already done – when John Bingham put forth his closing statements he effectively put the rope round Mrs Surratt's neck. He accused Surratt of being as guilty as her son, encouraging him to commit an act of treachery against his country.

On 29 June, with these words still ringing in their ears, the nine officers of the court retired to consider their verdicts against all of the accused. The verdicts were quickly reached, with all but one being found guilty of treasonable conspiracy. Ned Spangler was found guilty of the lesser crime of aiding and abetting Booth in his bid to escape.

After the verdicts the court then dispensed the sentences. Spangler was given six years hard labour. Dr Mudd, Arnold and O'Laughlin were given life sentences, though Mudd only avoided the death penalty by one vote. The rest received the death penalty, including Mrs Surratt, although in her case five members of the commission signed a recommendation to President Johnson suggesting her sentence be commuted to life imprisonment on the grounds of her age and sex; sadly this never came to pass. The President approved the death penalty in each case and the date of execution was set for 7 July, although two years later when John Surratt was captured Johnson would claim that he never saw the document asking for clemency for Mrs Surratt and recalled the great reluctance he felt at agreeing to her death. Although Holt continued to maintain that the President had discussed the clemency plea but had refused it, the mystery was never resolved.

The procedures dictated that the accused should not know their fate until the day before the sentences were due to be carried out. Thus on 6 July the prisoners were told of their impending executions on the scaffold. Hours later Mrs Surratt's shocked lawyers heard the news only when they heard a young newsboy shouting out the headlines. In another twist, an opportunity to save Mrs Surratt arrived when Anna Surratt visited the White House in the hope of securing her mother's release. Hoping to see the President she was referred instead to Joseph Holt who turned her away.

At 1.15 p.m. on 7 July, a small crowd gathered in the courtyard outside the Washington Arsenal; it was a blisteringly warm day. Through a small doorway the condemned foursome marched toward the scaffold, soldiers on either side of them, Mrs Surratt at times looking like she might faint. To add a sense of reality to the occasion the group walked past their own freshly dug graves, each with a pine coffin beside it before climbing onto the scaffold. In contrast to the harsh realities of the day's proceedings, chairs had been provided for the prisoners' comfort.

Even at this late stage, General Hancock, who was in overall charge of the proceedings, had expected a reprieve to be given for Mrs Surratt, and had made sure his cavalrymen were ready to pass the instruction through to him rapidly when it came. The hangman, Christian Rath, who would tie the customary seven knots in the women's noose, had tied only five, saving himself time when the fully expected reprieve came through.

But the reprieve never did come through and the instruction was given to proceed with the planned executions. Each person in turn had their hands tied behind their backs before a white hood was placed over their heads. David Herold trembled violently as more restraints were tied around his legs. George Atzerodt managed a few brave last words, "Goodbye gentlemen, I hope we meet on the other side." Paine, the bravest of them all, seemed prepared for his own death. Standing tall he said, "Mrs Surratt is innocent. She doesn't deserve to die with the rest of us." The hangman fully agreed, respecting Paine's last-ditch attempt to save her. Putting the noose around the big man's neck himself, he then muttered, "I want this man to die quick." Paine calmly responded, "You know best."

Just before 2 p.m., General Hancock clapped his hands three times, whereupon soldiers knocked away the supports for the platform on which the prisoners stood. As the platform swung down their bodies fell and were soon hanging in the bright afternoon sunshine. Justice, driven by anger and vengeance, had been done, and through the press was seen to be done, although much controversy raged over the validity of the trials and of Holt's claim that the President had wholeheartedly agreed to Mrs Surratt's sentence.

Two years later, after being on the run in Italy and Egypt, Surratt was caught and returned to the United States where he faced the same charges as those who had gone before him. This time, though, Surratt was tried in a civil court and when the jurors couldn't agree on a verdict the case was dismissed and Surratt walked away a free man.

Like many other controversial events which have taken place, the assassination of Lincoln generated its fair share of conspiracy theories. Just as the demise of JFK gave way to the rise of Lyndon B. Johnson, the demise of Lincoln allowed Andrew Johnson to ascend and this created the suspicion that Booth and Johnson had somehow conspired together. Booth had been at Johnson's hotel earlier in the evening, although most people believe he was there to check on Atzerodt. Others have put forward the notion that Lincoln was the subject of a Confederate plot, designed to destabilise the Union and inspire another uprising. This idea is not without merit and to some extent is what Booth was hoping to achieve, although there is no evidence to support an organized Confederate plan involving leaders from the South. Even Edwin Stanton, the man who appeared to organize the manhunt for Booth, has come under suspicion. It was thought that Stanton wanted Lincoln out so that he could pursue a more radical policy of reconstruction after the war. It is also suggested that it was Stanton who ordered General Grant not to visit the theatre on the night Lincoln was murdered. Grant's absence therefore left Lincoln vulnerable to attack as it is thought that Grant's guards would never have allowed Booth to enter the theatre box. Again though there is nothing concrete to support this hypothesis.

The whole saga of how the families of Booth and Lincoln became entwined is one rich in sadness, yet along with this there is yet one more tale of coincidence, though this time of how a Booth helped a Lincoln.

Long before the assassination of Lincoln by Booth, two other members of these families had met in quite different circumstances. The encounter took place on a crowded train station platform in New Jersey, as President Lincoln's eldest son, Robert, was waiting to buy a sleeper ticket to Washington. Suddenly the impatient crowd surged forward, pinning Robert against a railway carriage, just as it began to move out of the station. Robert was carried along before being dropped into a space between the carriage and the platform. An alert bystander rushed across and dragged Robert out by his coat collar. As Robert later recalled, "On turning to thank my rescuer I saw it was Edwin Booth, whose face was well known to me, and I expressed my gratitude to him, and in doing so called him by name."

The two men never met again, but in the years following his brother's assassination of Lincoln, Edwin Booth would often take comfort from the fact that he had saved the life of President Lincoln's son.

The Stunt that Went Wrong

John Landis

The world of the Hollywood actor could not be more far removed from that of your average person. Famous actors and actresses enjoy all the trappings of their high-profile lives, lavish homes hidden in the hill of Los Angeles, apartments in the most chic cities in the world, chauffeur-driven limos and stopovers at the world's best hotels. Even on the film set, those with audience-pulling power can demand the most opulent of surroundings, plush trailers with colour-coordinated decor, bowls of expensive fruit and their preferred drinks all cooling nicely in the refrigerator. Some stars are renowned for their very specific instructions – fresh flowers all of a certain colour, even sweets in a bowl, but only the red ones. Generally then the film set is just an extension of the pampered lives the stars lead off set. If on the other hand an actor is called upon to take part in an action scene then the film set can be a very dangerous place, especially if the director takes risks with safety – when this happens people lose their lives.

In 1981 when the acclaimed movie director Steven Spielberg, director of *Jaws*, *Close Encounters of the Third Kind* and *Raiders of the Lost Ark*, decided he wanted to make a film version of the popular 1950s sci-fi programme, *The Twilight Zone*, he chose his friend and fellow movie maker John Landis to share production billing with him. Although not in the same league as Spielberg, Landis had shown himself more than capable of coming up with the goods with hit films like *Kentucky Fried Movie*, *American Werewolf in London* and *The Blues Brothers*. The two men agreed that they would both co-produce the new film, which would be based around four stories of equal length, three of which were based on plots out of the original series, the fourth to be written by Landis.

Landis hit upon a great idea with a wonderful moral at the heart of the story that fitted nicely with the format of the original series. At the heart of this particular story was the character Bill Connor, a racist bigot who is initially seen in a bar shouting down the rights of blacks and Jews – as he leaves the bar he steps back in time and finds himself in war-torn, Nazi-occupied France. The Germans see him as a Jew and the character experiences for the first time what it is like to be on the receiving end of the illogical persecution. As he flees from the Germans Connor suddenly finds himself back in the southern states of America at the time when the Klu Klux Klan are at large. He now finds that those who see him perceive him to be black and once again he endures the hardship of being pursued by a gang who want to lynch him. By the time Connor ends up in his third and final encounter, he is launched into the jungles of Vietnam being shot at by the advancing Americans who see him as a Vietnamese soldier. The final scenes show Connor's rehabilitation. Pursued through a Vietnamese village he comes across two orphans; collecting them in his arms he races away from the village and crosses a river to safety. In the final scene, Connor, played by the actor Vic Morrow, tells the kids, "I'll keep you safe! I swear to God" – just as an American bomb destroys the village.

The script was approved by Warner Brothers and Landis began making plans to recruit the other actors and secure a shooting location. The first obstacle which Landis encountered was the strict child labour laws which forbade children to work past eight-thirty in the evening, a problem as the final scene showing Morrow with the two children crossing the river was to be shot as a night-time scene. Not only that but the children needed to have a teacher-welfare worker with them at all times, for their own protection and representation. If Hollywood is anything, it is fair – audiences and staff get exploited to the same degree. The requirement for the children to work late together with the nature of the scene meant that the production's normal casting company, Fenton-Feinberg Casting, declined to assist. Not only would they have had to have got a special waiver for the children to work late, but the scene involved a low-flying helicopter and high explosives for the village bombing scene. For the casting company at least, the whole arrangement seemed too dangerous, a comment they recalled making to Landis.

For reasons that would be a cause of major debate later, Landis decided he would not bother with the waiver, deciding instead to ignore the law and make alternative arrangements. In 1982 Landis asked his associate producer George Folsey to find him two Asian kids who would be able to play the two Vietnamese children, having already decided that he would pay them out of petty cash to avoid having to include their names on the payroll. Another member of the production team recalled Landis and some colleagues coming out of a production meeting and joking that they would all be thrown in jail over the illegal hiring of the child actors.

George Folsey began looking around for a family who might be prepared to indulge the production in some "cash-in-hand" work. Contacting his friend Dr Harold Schuman, he was eventually put in contact with Dr Peter Chen, whose brother and sister-in-law had a six-year-old daughter named Renee. They discussed the proposition and decided it would be an exciting opportunity for the child, something for her to remember when she was older, and agreed to the deal. In a bid to help secure the second child Renee's father asked his colleague Dr Daniel Le if his seven-year-old son, My-ca, would like to be the other child, joining his daughter for the fun and experience. The little boy loved the idea, adored having his photo taken and found the prospect of being on a film set exciting beyond belief. The children were introduced to Landis who felt that they would be ideal and readily agreed for them to have the parts.

Tension was the order of the day right from the start. First assistant director Dan Allingham and his colleague, Anderson House, the second assistant director, had spoken about their unease at working the children after the official hours and neither was comfortable with their proximity to the helicopter, which would have to fly low, and the special-effects explosives, which would be triggered to explode all around the scene to simulate an air attack. House expressed the most concern and pursued Allingham over a number of issues, first asking if Landis intended to shoot the shots in the day and then simulate night later. Allingham explained this was not Landis' plan. House also enquired if Landis would be prepared to use dummies for the river-crossing scene, or even dwarf stunt people, but again was told that Landis felt this would look phoney and ruin the scene. Landis had made up his mind and there seemed little point in trying to discuss it further.

The location team had found the perfect place to simulate the Vietnamese village scene – Indian Dunes Park, a private property which had the benefit of high cliffs covered in green foliage and a flat basin where a temporary village had been built out of bamboo poles. In the foreground the Santa Clara River snaked along slowly, with just the right amount of waist-deep water for Morrow to look like he needed to carry the kids.

Once everyone was on location the detailed planning for the scene began, but there were problems and the production experienced several delays in shooting. Morrow had been told to throw a piece of wood up at the passing helicopter but the pilot, Dorcey Wingo, was concerned at the unpredict-ability of something hitting the helicopter rotors, either causing damage to the helicopter or the rotors batting a block of wood through the set. They eventually decided that it might be possible to use a piece of balsa wood.

Having never been on a film set before the children were understandably nervous so Morrow kept them entertained by pulling funny faces at them. Their laughter, however, continued when the cameras started rolling and Landis had to stop shooting on several occasions while the children composed themselves. The first scene was captured at 3.30 a.m. and both sets of parents were handed envelopes with the agreed 500 dollar cash payment.

On 23 July 1982, the evening of the river-crossing scene,

Renee and her parents arrived late on set annoying Landis who needed one last scene capturing before the big action scene. In this scene Morrow collects Renee and My-ca from a small hut and carries them to the river bank. In a prophetic warning of what was to come, a water bomb exploded and the terrified Renee burst into tears, afterwards saying that dust had blown into her eyes from the explosion. The concerned parents asked George Folsey if the explosion had indeed been dangerous, to which he replied, "No, not dangerous, just a loud noise."

With the parents and children reassured they were all sent back to their trailers where they could relax before the night's big shoot. Their nerves were still tingling as they could still hear the sounds of gunfire and explosions in the background as Morrow filmed his other scenes.

The first scene was shot from inside the helicopter as it approached the village; Wingo was at the controls as Allingham shone a beam of light illuminating the scene below. The first sign of trouble emerged when Landis gave the instructions for the special effects to be set off. A water bomb exploded and sprayed water all over the helicopter's perspex windscreen, obscuring Wingo's view. He leaned out of the helicopter in order to see where he was headed and swore loudly as the heat seared his face.

The location fire safety officer had watched the scene and was concerned that the force of the explosions might hinder the flight of the helicopter, but having discussed the issue with his superior nobody brought it to the attention of the film crew.

Wingo however was not so reserved. Having landed the helicopter he shouted to Allingham that he should tell Landis that the explosions were too strong, that they were flaring up right into the path of the helicopter. There was equal concern from the camera crew – Roger Smith said he would not film the scene unless the explosions were toned down.

Allingham later told Smith that he had spoken with Landis who had assured him that the force of the explosions would be dealt with, although just what he meant by this only became clear later. When Wingo and another cameraman were discussing the explosions, Landis was said to have responded, "You ain't seen nothing yet."

A bit later George Folsey visited the trailer where the children and their parents were staying. The kids were asleep so Folsey woke them and asked if they would like a bite to eat before the commencement of the scene. As the time was fast approaching Folsey also warned them not to speak with the firemen who would be operating around the location – he did not want to let them know that the children were working late, and asked the parents to say that they were friends of his and that the children were just watching.

As the children emerged from their slumber they arrived on a very tense set, the atmosphere seemed full of expectation and the parents too felt a degree of trepidation. Folsey tried to reassure them once more, "It'll be scary – but don't worry."

With Morrow now knee-deep in water and with a child under each arm Landis ordered the cameras to start rolling – the time 2.20 a.m., 23 July 1982.

Landis was slightly elevated above the river; from his vantage point he could clearly see the action to be filmed in the water and the approaching helicopter. He wanted the helicopter even lower than it already was and screamed through his bullhorn, "Lower, lower, lower," an instruction aimed at an operative who was in ground-to-air contact with Wingo.

Landis then shouted the instruction "Fire, fire", indicating that the special effects should commence. The special effects technicians pressed the keys on the control panel and a spray of fake bullets exploded in the water around Morrow. Multiple cameramen filmed from various angles – the final scene would be edited together later.

James Camomile, the technician in charge of the explosive devices at the back of the village, ran his finger across the firing board and the whole scene exploded in a kaleidoscope of light and noise. The explosions were so strong that the two cameramen who intended to film the exploding village had to run up a slope to escape the searing heat that stung their skin.

My-ca's father, Daniel Le, was completely taken aback by the ferocity of the explosions – he had personally witnessed real scenes of attack while in Vietnam and thought the effects seemed far too realistic. When a second blast went off Le fell to the ground; afterwards he recalled thinking that everyone was in real danger and that the situation was well past make-believe.

Up in the air Wingo was already struggling with the helicopter which had been affected by the initial blasts. Allingham, who was sitting next to him, suggested he fly away from the action zone and not into the special effects explosions, but the request came too late – the helicopter was already heading in low through the smoke.

Landis and his colleagues were unaware of the problems Wingo was facing in the air and continued with the explosive sequences as planned. Two more massive blasts went off and the helicopter span out of control – somehow the explosion had caused something to go wrong with the controls.

Now concerned himself, Morrow dropped Renee Chen into the water as the helicopter descended from the sky onto the terrified actors. As Morrow made a grab for Renee he was beaten to it by the helicopter rotors which slammed into the small child killing her instantly. The rotors continued to rotate at great speed even after the initial impact with the water as Morrow quickly became the next victim and he was sadly joined by My-ca Le. The helicopter's main rotor blades swept through the air and decapitated Morrow; My-ca met with the same fate, losing his head and a part of his shoulder. The scene was one of pure devastation – in a matter of moments three people had lost their lives and all for the sake of entertainment. Dorcey Wingo and John Allingham walked away from the crash, bruised and shaken but otherwise unhurt.

Whether it can be described as a form of professionalism or a totally misplaced comment has been debated by many, but on surveying the scene in front of him Landis held the bullhorn one more time to his lips and shouted, "That's a wrap," signalling for all that the filming could stop – it already had of course.

As the production crew sat staring in awe at the crashed helicopter and the now blood-red river they became painfully aware of the screaming coming from behind them. The mother and father of Renee Chen and My-ca Le were screaming, unable to stop to draw breath, having seen with their own eyes their children killed in the most gruesome way. Both would now need treatment for shock. As they were ushered into cars ready take them to the hospital Landis issued his last pleading instruction, "Everyone go home. Please, go home."

Why Landis wanted his crew to leave is not known – they had all witnessed the three cruel deaths and were all in a state of shock, so they needed each other more than ever. Landis, though, wanted time to think – he had illegally hired the children and the action scene had presumably used too many explosives; the results were just too terrible to contemplate.

In the aftermath of the three deaths the media sprang into life wanting to know what had gone on. There were many who wanted to tell their side of the story – not in support of Warner Bros or Landis. Early on it became obvious that Landis had allowed two children to work beyond the strict time barrier, apparently doing so to avoid having to obtain a waiver, which in turn would have required an official representative for the children to be there, who may have objected to the scene. The reports did not look good for Landis or other members of his senior production crew and when pictures of the children were aired the nation felt more pain for the parents. This pain had a second airing when it was time for the funerals to take place.

The question as to whether Landis should have attended any of the funerals is a difficult one – being there might have made him the focus for the emotions of those grieving; not to go might have looked callous and uncaring, while delivering a eulogy may have seemed foolhardy; a respectful silence at the back of the auditorium might have been a more appropriate action to take. But Landis was a man who had recently experienced foolish action and had survived – one more step in the wrong direction would therefore not matter. And Landis was not alone in his desire to pay his final respects to Morrow for George Folsey also wanted to say a few words.

Both Landis and Folsey did read eulogies at the funeral service and both managed to deliver what appeared to many as being shallow, self-promoting, hollow words. For the press the words were a reflection of the hard-faced Hollywood promotions machinery everyone expected – the show must go on, apparently at any cost.

When Folsey stood to deliver his message he could not have judged things worse as he tried to look for the positive side to the otherwise tragic story. "If there is any consolation in this it is that the film was finished. Thank God. This performance must not be lost. It was Vic's last gift to us."

With Folsey's words ringing in the ears of the mourners like insults heaped upon their injury, Landis took his place at the lectern and followed suit. "Tragedy can strike in an instant, but film is immortal. Vic lives forever. Just before the last take, Vic took me aside to thank me for the opportunity to play this role."

Whether the latter conversation ever took place will never be known for sure; what is known is that Landis had to endure the accusing stares of others in attendance at the funerals and at one point the distraught director had to be supported by his wife.

Landis was certainly severely traumatized by the events and possibly even more so after the funerals when he realized that most of those around him felt that he and his colleagues were culpable. As the families of those who had lost loved ones talked to their lawyers, Landis turned to his doctor for help, requiring medication for weeks afterwards, wondering if he would ever be able to take command of a film set ever again.

When the furore over the funerals had calmed down the lawsuits started flying. The Chens filed a suit on 3 August 1982 asking for damages of $200 million and citing Landis, Spielberg, Folsey, Wingo, Warner Bros, Western Helicopters and the owners of the Indian Dunes Park amongst many others. My-ca Le's family filed a suit a year later.

Vic Morrow's daughters, Carrie Morrow and actress Jennifer Jason Leigh filed a suit against Warner Bros, Landis, Spielberg and a number of others in late 1982. They agreed an out-of-court settlement within a year and the details of their agreement have never been made public.

Warner Bros hired a firm of lawyers who clumsily, in public relations terms, responded to the remaining suits by suggesting that the risk had been assumed by the children who had died when they accepted their roles – a starting point for the defence but one which sat badly with members of the public, who could only see that the all-powerful studio was seeking to wriggle out of its responsibilities.

Beyond the civil suits the Los Angeles County district attorney's office needed to establish for themselves if there was a criminal liability for the accident. The district attorney appointed prosecutor Gary Kesselman to the case and he was assisted by Sergeant Thomas Budds of the Los Angeles County Sheriff's Department. Between them they needed to gather all of the facts and assess whether Landis or others should face a criminal court in addition to the civil proceedings already underway against them.

The wheels of justice certainly appeared to turn slowly and while they were grinding away Landis managed to find the heart to work again. It would take four years for the trial to be brought to court and in that time Landis found himself back in the director's chair – at least some people in Hollywood were prepared to give him another chance. During this period Landis worked on the now highly regarded "Thriller" video with Michael Jackson. He directed and starred in the movie *Into the Night*, in which he played a slightly comical murderer. His work proved once more that he could make money for the studios and this factor easily overrode any other consideration, including the safety of actors and crew. Many were happy to believe that Landis had learned his lesson and would henceforth be more careful. But even as he continued to prove his prowess as a top Hollywood director, in the background the long arm of the law was still reaching out to him.

Gary Kesselman applied himself to the task in hand with some vigour and soon established that there was much

conflicting information regarding the facts of this particular
case. For a start Dr Schuman, who helped to recruit the
children, denied that he knew that they would be in close
proximity to such violent explosions, let alone that they
should be directly underneath a low-flying helicopter. Quick
to blame Landis, others testified that Landis and Folsey
knew they were breaking the law when they hired the
children and that Folsey had joked they would be jailed
because of it.

Hollywood and the acting profession as a whole is a heavily
controlled cartel; if you speak out against the powers that be
you might never work in show business again. The prosecutor therefore had to use some leverage to get those on the
set that night to confirm from their own perspective what
actually happened, both before the disaster and afterwards.
Kesselman came up with a plan whereby he would grant
several members of the crew immunity from prosecution in
exchange for them providing the much-needed information.
These were second assistant director, Anderson House,
James Camomile, the man who had been responsible for
setting off the explosives and all of the special effects crew
who served under Paul Stewart, but excluding Paul Stewart
himself.

Anderson House painted a terrible picture when he explained that the children had been deliberately hidden from
Jack Tice, the fire safety officer. Tice also occasionally acted
as a teacher-welfare worker and would have almost certainly
reported the fact that the children were working after the
agreed hours. Casting further blame onto his colleagues
House also suggested that Allingham had been warned about
the risks to the children. The evidence of premeditated
malpractice seemed to grow and grow and this meant that
those involved could be culpable.

The allegations were so serious that Dorcey Wingo and
Paul Stewart both pleaded the Fifth Amendment, trying to
avoid incriminating themselves. Folsey, however, was prepared to testify and without admitting there had been any
wrongdoing, he now wished he had shot the helicopter
sequences separate to the actors in the water.

John Landis on the other hand not only did not accept any wrongdoing on his own part, he felt he knew who should be held responsible. And in his view those who had created the deadly situation were the technicians and experts who worked for him, together with those who allowed the explosive devices to be too big or badly placed, and Wingo for not controlling the helicopter and for allowing himself to come in so low that he got caught in the blasts. He assumed Paul Stewart and Wingo had worked out the co-ordination of the scene – it was they after all who were experts in special effects and piloting the helicopter. Kesselman would not accept that Landis, as the man in overall charge of the shoot, could disassociate himself from the details of the one piece of the film which was actually dangerous. From all accounts Landis had requested the biggest explosions and had shouted from his director's chair for the helicopter to come in low. Landis stuck with his argument: when you employ experts you let them get on with the job and if the director asks you to do something dangerous, you refuse.

The enquiry got heated. When Kesselman pressed Landis, "The final authority in terms of camera, actor positions, helicopter –" Landis jumped in. "Not mine," he interjected. "If I asked an actor to stick his hand in a waste disposal unit the actor would say no."

As the arguments went back and forth the media could not help but represent the Warner Bros crew as a group who were trying everything they knew to avoid taking responsibility – come what may, the children would not be dead if Landis had gone through the official channels to gain proper authorization to have the kids work after 8.30 p.m. No one ever suggested that the deaths were anything other than an accident rather than murder, but if you do not take precautions, break some basic rules and do not check and recheck the safety of your plan, then you are responsible for any resultant deaths – or in this case three deaths.

On 15 June 1983, the grand jury delivered its indictments. Landis, Folsey and Allingham were each charged with two counts of manslaughter in respect of the deaths of Renee Chen and My-ca Le. The decisions were based on the legal premise that if death occurs as a result of the commission of an "inherently dangerous" unlawful act, then that constitutes manslaughter. The hiring of the children was most certainly unlawful and as such the grand jury had found its unlawful act.

Landis added one more manslaughter charge to his record, bringing the manslaughter count to three, as did Stewart and Wingo. They were found guilty due to the nature of their actions, which were described as aggravated, reckless and grossly negligent, resulting in the deaths of Morrow and the two children.

In a shock move, noted by the media and commentators alike, Kesselman decided not to pursue Landis, Folsey and Allingham of the crimes they were most certainly guilty of – that of hiring the children and then requesting they work past the curfew. His logic was simple – there was a reasonable chance that the jury might see the deaths as being purely accidental, nobody's fault; if they did then they might decide to hand down a guilty verdict based on the lesser charges and let the trio off the more serious charges of manslaughter. Therefore by only presenting the jury with one option, guilty or otherwise of manslaughter, they could choose to punish them or not. There were three families now devastated because of what had happened on that film set – it would be a brave soul who decided that those in charge should not pay.

Amazingly the film itself was released in June 1983 to the most terrible reviews. One reviewer described it as not worth watching let alone dying for. Neither of the children were shown in the film and the audience numbers were so low that the movie was soon replaced at the box office. After so much pain and suffering it was soon forgotten by the public, whose only real interest in it was the trials which were looming up.

At the preliminary hearings the legal teams came out ready to fight; already there was a clear division between the directors and producers and those who were employed to carry out specific jobs. Landis was still standing by his basic defence that those experts he employed should have acted responsibly in carrying out their jobs. As he wasn't an expert it was impossible for him to pass an informed comment on things like the explosives and the helicopter flying.

Judge Brian Crahan presided over the preliminary hearing before the Los Angeles Municipal Court. He faced the outgoing, rather flamboyant character of Landis' attorney and head of his defence team, Harland Braun. In the court-room the defendants were sat according to their allegiances – Landis, Folsey and Allingham were seated together, while Paul Stewart and Dorcey Wingo were also together. One of the groups would have to take the blame and both parties were keen to pin it on the other.

After Harland Braun had delivered his pitch on why the specialist staffs were to blame, Eugene Trope, acting on behalf of Wingo and Western Helicopters, responded de-fiantly, "The responsible party here is the director-produ-cer, and I think Landis is trying to shift the blame off to anyone and everyone he can."

To gather support for his case and to portray Landis in a positive light, Braun described the movie as a cinemato-graphic statement, explaining that the film was about over-coming bigotry and that the children were there to demonstrate this point in the most poignant way. Most of those listening were more content to think it was just another film, a remake of a 1950s classic, nothing more nothing less.

As Renee's mother was called to the stand the clamour of reporters out in the corridor could be heard all around the court. Talking through an interpreter Shyan-Huei Chen cried as she described watching her daughter die. It was a poignant moment and one which Landis himself could not help being moved by. Talking to a reporter a short time later he said, "This is a terrible, terrible accident and it will cause pain and anguish to all of us for the rest of our lives. I can think of nothing worse than losing a child. The idea that this can be anything other than an unforeseeable accident is not only wrong, it's bewildering." A heartfelt comment no doubt and possibly the only thing to say at that moment. The sheer emotional outpouring at seeing Chen on the stand would have been enough to swing any juror in favour of a guilty verdict – for the sake of the mother someone must pay.

To add more weight against Landis the casting director Marci Liroff testified that she had warned Landis about working the children after curfew and had also pointed out the danger attached to shooting the scene in the way it was planned. In a final shot at Landis, Folsey and Allingham she looked across at them and said they were guilty of wilfully hiring the kids illegally.

As the preliminary hearing was entering its final stages the defence and prosecution argued their cases once more. Braun side-stepped an expert witness who had said the helicopter crashed because of the explosion and instead developed his own theory. He claimed that the helicopter had suffered "heat delamination" which had pared off the rotor blades' protective skin and that it was this which had caused the helicopter to crash. Calling his own expert defence witness Braun put Gary Fowler, a metallurgist, on the stand. Fowler explained that the explosions had created a 180-degree fireball, a temperature much lower than would normally cause heat delamination. On this basis Braun argued that the defendants could not have foreseen the danger as the situation was unprecedented.

Kesselman quickly responded that the exact cause of the crash was immaterial because the helicopter was brought dangerously close to the explosions.

Finally in April 1984, Judge Crahan announced his decision. He dismissed the manslaughter charges against Folsey and Allingham on the grounds that homicide could not be established on the grounds of them hiring the children. He did however uphold the charges against Landis, Stewart and Wingo. Landis as the director had staged the events leading to the deaths, he had gone beyond simply setting the scene, and he had actively sought to direct key staff to push their roles into the danger zone. Paul Stewart had been the man responsible for the special effects and as the expert he allowed the explosive devices to be too large and inappropriately placed. Wingo, an experienced helicopter pilot, had knowingly flown too low through the action scene and had therefore contributed to the failure of the helicopter.

In a final whirl of last-minute negotiations, the prosecution sought to have the charges against Folsey and Allingham upheld, a request which was eventually agreed by Judge Gordon Ringer. So in November 1984, all five were now facing charges, a decision the California Supreme Court decided not to review – it would now go to a full trial.

Once the press were aware that there would now be a full trial there was a race to re-evaluate the case all over again. Landis and the others were in the dock and would now remain the focus of media attention until the final results were through.

Landis, disappointed at having to face a trial at all, decided to replace his legal representative. Braun had despatched a letter without consulting Landis and this spelled the end of the relationship. He was therefore replaced by James Neal, a well-respected and very experienced lawyer from Tennessee. Neal had come to public prominence during the 1970s when he had acted as a prosecutor on the Watergate case. He had also won a number of high-profile media-centred cases representing and successfully defending the Ford Motor Company in the case of the exploding Pinto motor car. When the autopsy revealed the extent of Elvis Presley's drug use his doctor was indicted on over-prescribing medication, a case which Neal won, much to the bemusement of the public who had lost a major national figure at such a young age. Although Braun had lost the role of defending Landis, he did however secure the task of representing Folsey.

The prosecution suffered a shake-up as well. The high-profile nature of the accused meant that all parties were becoming public figures. Kesselman, who had prosecuted the case so far, had to relinquish the task when the media jumped on a story regarding a club in which he had a significant interest. Hostesses at the club had been arrested on lewd conduct charges and several were also illegally resident in the United States. It was thought that the bad press surrounding Kesselman might spill over and affect the prosecution. Now everyone was in the papers for one reason or another.

The new prosecutor had a reputation of her own to protect, being referred to in the press as "The Dragon

Lady". Lea Purwin D'Agostino was a strikingly beautiful, petit and extremely tough prosecution lawyer. She had a string of victories to her name and became something of a media figure herself, always arriving in court dressed in designer clothing and sporting an array of expensive jewellery.

The personality mix in the courtroom demanded as many column inches as the details of the case itself. D'Agostino and the defence attorneys enjoyed what can best be described as an acrimonious relationship. Their styles could not be more different. D'Agostino would often be bold, assertive and arrogant, whereas the defence team often came across as sexist, the whole defence group including the accused often looking like an old boys' club. Neither appealed to the media and neither easily commanded more empathy than the other.

The jury was equally diverse consisting of seven women and five men, amongst them a mix of Asian, black and Hispanic citizens. Their occupations were clearly far removed from the closeted world of the rich and famous Hollywood set, and indeed the wealthy legal teams who were about to confront them. Amongst the group there was a pallet repair person, a chemist and a typist.

In the middle of the opposing teams sat the experienced, well-known judge, Roger Boren. He had made his name as the Judge who presided over the court case against the cousins Kenneth Bianchi and Angelo Buono, better known as the "Hillside Stranglers".

So with four years having elapsed since the deaths on the set of *The Twilight Zone*, the case finally came to court on 3 September 1986. As Landis and his co-accused sat in silence, D'Agostino stood to deliver her opening statement. Her case was simple: Landis had sought to illegally hire the children not only because he wanted to work at night but because he knew the teacher-welfare worker would have objected to the obvious danger the scene presented. She also suggested that Wingo and Stewart were both aware of the danger that they were in, yet proceeded anyway. Then in a shock move D'Agostino announced that the jury would be asked to watch the film footage showing the moment when the scene went terribly wrong. Leaving no one in any doubt she reminded the jurors that the crash and the deaths they were about to witness were real, ironically not Hollywood make-believe.

It would be a hard act to follow but James Neal needed to respond to provide some balance to the arguments. He opened by describing the meticulous planning which had gone into the preparation for the scene. He suggested that if no other events had occurred to change the outcome, then the scene would have been shot successfully and no lives would have been lost. Neal argued that something had happened, something that the director and his colleagues could not have planned for. Pointing the finger of guilt at James Camomile, the man who triggered the explosions, he suggested that he had detonated two explosive devices simultaneously, causing the explosive blasts to combine in an effect much larger than was planned. It was this unfortunate blending of the explosive effects which had caused the helicopter rotors to delaminate. Camomile had also failed to act safely in checking the proximity of the helicopter before allowing the devices to explode.

The prosecution now called their first witness, Donna Schuman, who although a close friend of Folsey confirmed that Landis and Folsey had contrived to employ the two children illegally. In a twist that grabbed headlines, Schuman now added some detail which she had previously kept quiet during the preliminary hearing. She now recalled a conversation between herself and Folsey during which she had asked Folsey if he knew the penalty for working the children after curfew, to which he replied, "A slap on the wrist and a little fine – unless they find out about the explosives." A ripple of shock ran through the courtroom and the defendants visibly blanched at hearing the statement given in such a damning way.

The case descended into legal technical detail at this point. When asked why she had not disclosed the nature of this conversation before she maintained that Kesselman had suggested she keep this quiet on the basis that you never reveal your full case until you are in front of the jury. The defence were quick to point out that under the rules of discovery it was incumbent upon the prosecution to make the facts available to the defence prior to commencement of the case. In a dramatic gesture James Neal pointed out to the jury, "We either have a witness who is a liar or a prosecutor who is withholding information."

In a series of bizarre twists Kesselman was asked to take the stand and then D'Agostino was asked to take the stand, each arguing a particular angle. These hearings were in the presence of the Judge only, as neither defence nor prosecutor could be called as a witness. By undertaking this unusual strategy the defence were successfully able to give the impression that the prosecution had a problem and if nothing else had drawn the jury's attention away from the cold facts of the case. Even the press followed the diversion, entertained by the infighting and quarrelling the two legal teams indulged in.

When the prosecution asked Colleen Logan, Deputy Labour Commissioner, to take the stand, it was their turn to get the case back on track. After Logan confirmed the laws on employment of children within the movie industry, she whacked another nail into Landis' coffin when she confirmed that her office had already levied fines on Landis and Warner Bros for infringing the strict child labour rules in respect of Renee and My-ca.

Although the Judge ruled against D'Agostino being allowed to ask the hypothetical question as to whether she would have granted the waiver for the children, Logan was able to confirm that she would have taken a dim view of allowing the children to work in such close proximity to the explosives and the helicopter.

The media waited intently for the most moving of the eyewitness testimonies, that of the children's parents. My-ca's mother was the first to take the stand and under questioning from D'Agostino she denied knowing that a waiver was required for her children to work, or indeed that there would be explosives or a low-flying helicopter. She also claimed that Folsey had suggested she needn't come back for the second night's shooting, saying, "I'll treat them like my own." Although My-ca's father attended the next night's shooting, My-ca's mother would never see him alive again, a fact that D'Agostino brought home with high emotional impact.

When it was time for the jurors to watch the scenes they were taken down to the Samuel Goldwyn Theatre on Wiltshire Boulevard. As the scenes from the first night's shooting unfolded the jurors were able to see Vic Morrow pick up the children and run towards the river, the village burning behind them. When Landis calls for the scene to be halted he is seen waving his arms, indicating the helicopter should move away. As the helicopter turns away the audience could clearly see the downdraft blowing the children's hair around, a stark reminder of how close the chopper actually was.

The audience were quiet and nervous as the final scene was about to be shown – other than the outcome they were not precisely sure just what they were about to see. Nobody wanted to watch the deaths of the three actors in beautiful Technicolor. Luckily the explosions around the water were so strong that a wall of spray was thrown up so high that hardly anything else could be seen. When the spray dispersed the helicopter could be seen lying at an awkward angle in the river and before the filming actually stopped rolling crew and staff could be seen running down towards the river.

Other cameras around the set caught the terrible scenes from other angles; one clearly showed Morrow struggling against the downwash of the rotors before the helicopter hit the water, its rotors whipping up a spray of water which thankfully hid the moment of death.

As the shocked audience sat in stunned silence D'Agostino took the opportunity to ram home the facts of what they had just seen. "The jurors are not supposed to make up their minds until they have heard all of the evidence, but they can't not see what they have just seen. They've just seen three people killed. And for what? A lousy movie."

D'Agostino had made a perfectly good point and in the process had pulled at the heartstrings of all of the jurors – no one can deal easily with the death of a child – and the members of the jury were swept away with the graphic nature of the evidence they had seen.

Back in the courtroom Shyan-Huei Chen took the stand and added to the concept of a cover-up when she reported the details of a conversation she had on the night Folsey visited her in the trailer, when he had said, "If the fire department people come over and ask what you are doing here, just tell them you are friends helping us. Don't mention anything about money."

Chen poured more petrol on the flames when she described the moments just before the crash. She explained that Landis was standing behind her with his bullhorn. As the helicopter came into view, ready to enter the scene, Landis was shouting, "Lower, lower." The words now sounded more like an instruction to cause death than a directorial instruction intended to improve the scene.

Harland Braun, now acting for Folsey, had a difficult task – he now needed to cross-examine Chen. Gently enquiring about the conversations she had held with Folsey the week before the filming, he was able to draw out some small admission that maybe she couldn't remember the full details of their discussions, therefore Folsey maybe had pointed out some of the dangers. A hollow win for Braun but at least something.

When D'Agostino cross-examined George Hull, the chief fire safety officer for the location shoot, he too claimed he had been kept in the dark about the details of the special effects. He claimed he did not realize the explosions were going to be so huge, or that the helicopter would fly just 24 feet above the river. And in a final swipe at the defendants he claimed he did not know that real actors would be used in the final scene, and that he had never been on a film set before where children had been used in the same scene with special effects explosives.

The jury saw 71 witnesses take the stand in as many days; one juror claimed that it was overkill. Many did not like the aggressive manner in which D'Agostino cross-examined the witnesses. When Camomile took the stand, although D'Agostino adopted a more relaxed style of questioning; he was clearly under stress and had suffered much anxiety since the deaths. Camomile's cross-examination by Neal proved an even bigger ordeal for him. Neal wanted the blame for the crash pinned on Camomile and pursued him mercilessly. He asked why Camomile had not looked for the helicopter before setting the explosives off. "You were not looking at the helicopter, were you?" Camomile was resigned. "I don't believe so," he responded in a whisper. Neal was on a roll now, he had Camomile almost admitting guilt. "Isn't it a fact that the special effects man on the firing board is supposed to look at the set before setting off any of the special effects to determine at that particular point whether it is safe or not?" Camomile answered in the affirmative, appearing to concede at least some of the responsibility for the accident. But Camomile was immune from prosecution; anything that was pinned on him wouldn't matter, though it would serve to draw the responsibility away from Landis. The danger would be that in a world where someone must pay for a mistake, if it couldn't be the person responsible then it would have to be somebody else, and that someone might turn out to be John Landis.

The defence eventually called Landis to the stand. Looking more like a college professor in his tweed jacket he sat upright and looked carefully at his lawyer. After Neal had painted Landis as a perfect family man, he moved gently into the details of the film. Landis confirmed without exception that he had chosen to break the labour laws. He had done so because he didn't think he would get the waiver, he regretted it now but at the time it seemed to be just a technicality. He said he explained this to the children's parents and they all understood the deal. When asked if anyone had suggested there was anything dangerous about the action scene they were going to shoot he said, "Absolutely not."

Neal was trying to establish that if Landis had never been asked to consider any level of danger then he should not be found criminally responsible. Landis also denied joking with members of the crew in respect of losing the helicopter, claiming that the scene had been planned in great detail.

Landis often had tears in his eyes, especially when talking of the children, but the hard-hitting D'Agostino tried to suggest that he was merely acting in order to curry sympathy from the jurors. In a bout of questioning which left the jurors wondering what was happening, D'Agostino pursued Landis for a gruelling twenty minutes on how actors could conjure up tears, before deciding the attack was not yielding any beneficial results.

When Dorcey Wingo, the helicopter pilot took the stand he looked visibly drawn and stressed – he had been under the care of a psychiatrist since the accident and had been diagnosed with post-traumatic stress disorder, a condition often associated with soldiers who experience the trauma of battle. After an initial introduction Wingo's lawyer, Eugene Trope, sought to present the pilot's experience. Wingo had clocked up hundreds of flying hours; he had been a helicopter pilot in Vietnam and when he returned had flown as a firefighter, attacking forest fires and carrying out rescues for hikers who were stranded. He had expected that flying for the movie business would be easy by comparison to his most recent flying history. When Trope began enquiring about the work on *The Twilight Zone* his questions were well thought out and calculated to draw the finger of blame away from his client. Wingo claimed that Dan Allingham often used the phrase "Safety first", and confirmed that on the night of the accident he and others had indulged in several safety meetings. He claimed to have told Paul Stewart, the man in charge of the special effects, "The helicopter and the special effects cannot occupy the same airspace at the same time," and that as the pilot he should have the last word before anything went ahead, especially if Stewart was planning to throw any debris into the air. Wingo also affirmed that he thought Stewart, the expert, would certainly know a lot more about pyrotechnics than he would, so ultimately he would have to take his word for it when it came down to the explosive details.

When Strope enquired about the accident itself Wingo lost his composure, the stress of recalling the night and the three deaths clear for all to see. When D'Agostino took the floor she was once again less considerate of the witness's feelings. Without delay she suggested that Wingo was looking to protect both himself and John Landis. Asking if the two had become close Wingo rather pompously responded, "Propinquity has set in, yes." D'Agostino ridiculed the word by repeating it slowly as if trying to fathom its meaning.

Pursuing Wingo further she homed in on the one opportunity he might have had to prevent the accident, namely the 11.30 p.m. shoot during which the explosions had already caused a stir. D'Agostino asked, "Didn't you feel it was absolutely mandatory that you express your dissatisfaction to Landis or Stewart?"

"No," Wingo responded.

And in an opportunity not to be missed D'Agostino quickly came back with, "You hadn't developed propinquity by then?" Nervous laughter quickly passed through the courtroom.

Wingo later appeared to lay some of the blame at Vic Morrow's door when he suggested that the actor had let himself and the children down by not running from the scene. When cross-examined by D'Agostino, Wingo claimed to have had a discussion with Morrow before the scene during which Wingo had advised Morrow to keep his eye on the helicopter. The cross-examination became heated when D'Agostino asked how on earth he thought the actor would be able to keep his balance in the river, hold the two children and keep looking up for the helicopter. Flustered and now under more pressure Wingo explained how he had told Morrow to listen for changes in the helicopter's engine sounds, saying it was a plan of what to do if he was forced to bring down the helicopter. After both parties had become somewhat angry D'Agostino asked him directly if he thought Morrow was to blame. Staring back defiantly at D'Agostino and clearly searching for the right words, Wingo said, "I am saying it is extremely – it distresses me to the max that he never looked up after having had that conversation with him."

Following an afternoon recess it was D'Agostino and Wingo who were back on centre stage, she still looking to challenge Wingo's view of what Morrow should have done. Eventually it all boiled down to the few seconds between the helicopter faltering and when it finally fell into the river.

Asked where he thought Morrow might be able to run to with the children, Wingo responded, "Away from the helicopter. He had over five seconds between the time that the sound of the helicopter changed and it impacted. I would hope to god he could have used those five seconds to his advantage and the children's."

The debate continued when D'Agostino repeatedly pressed Wingo on what might have reasonably been expected of Morrow; he was an actor not an aviator, so could he have been expected to recognize the change in the pitch of the engine?

As Wingo fluffed his way through the answer D'Agostino changed tack and suggested that Wingo had the same five seconds as Morrow. The beleaguered Wingo flatly refused to agree that his five seconds were the same – as far as he was concerned he was in a crashing helicopter and one that could not be flown.

After such a fast-paced onslaught Wingo was naturally tiring of the unrelenting questions when D'Agostino caught him off-guard with a particularly pertinent question. "How did you brief the children on what to do for this flight, sir?"

Without delay, Wingo flatly answered, "I never talked to the children." D'Agostino let the words linger in the air.

When Wingo left the stand the defence called a technical witness, one who was prepared to discuss the highly technical nature of delamination and the fact that when it happens due to excess heat the helicopter usually crashed. Under cross-examination D'Agostino simply refused to accept the delamination theory, pressing home her view that it was flying debris which had caused the crash. It was in these subtle differences that the lawyers hoped to make their case. If the defence could show delamination had caused the accident then they could also claim that no one should have expected it to happen and if no one knew about the possibility then the prosecution could not attach blame. The Judge though had already instructed the jury that the precise cause of the accident need not be foreseeable for a manslaughter conviction.

The media had since given up examining the detail of this

long-running court battle; they now simply described the daily battle of the lawyers and more importantly what D'Agostino was wearing or doing, her heavy duty attacks often making more news than the progress of the trial. Many media commentators were now basing their prognosis for the defendants on a feel for who seemed to be winning the war of words. Mostly this appeared to be the tough D'Agostino. With the Judge instructing that unforeseeable events did not make for an adequate excuse, even the Judge seemed to be indicating his view of who was to blame.

In keeping with her commanding performances D'Agostino's closing statements were equally tough talking. She had prepared well and was keen to have this last opportunity to quash any lingering sympathy the jurors might have with the defendants.

She began with, "There is no motion picture that was ever made, or that will ever be made, that is worth risking one human life for, much less three. The utterly senseless, needless loss of three lives for a motion picture is what makes what these defendants did so barbaric."

With this backdrop D'Agostino went on to describe the defendants' defence as lacking any true credibility, saying that they had based their whole situation on three main defences, "The SODDI – some other dude did it. The red herring defence – confuse the facts with technicalities. And the BEE defence – blame everyone else."

But the comedic attack on the defence's arguments quickly disappeared when D'Agostino turned hard again in ramming home the facts regarding the children's employment. Landis and the others had known it was illegal to work the children after curfew. They had wilfully chosen to bypass the rules because they anticipated the welfare-teacher officer would have stopped the children working with the explosives, and they knew this would happen because to anyone with sense the explosives presented a clear danger to life.

After what seemed an eternity of powerful arguments it was Landis' attorney who stood to make the first of the closing statements for the defence. By contrast James Sanders' words lacked the hard-hitting appeal that D'Agostino had managed to deliver. Sanders' style was one of the quiet man asking for nothing more than a consideration of what he was about to impart. In his view the most important consideration the jury had to make was whether they genuinely thought Landis believed the scene presented an obvious danger and therefore had acted in a reckless manner.

James Neal followed Sanders and used his time to attack Camomile once more, asking how he could have failed to carry out the proper checks when he was using the highest level of explosive device allowed by the state of California.

Arnold Klein, closing for Paul Stewart, reasserted his view that Stewart had done all he could to prepare for the scene properly; he could not though be held responsible for the actions of Camomile.

Eugene Trope, closing for Dorcey Wingo, made a simple statement. No pilot wants to die, therefore the jury must assume that he flew with safety in mind and was caught by debris which was the result of a badly organized special-effects explosion.

Dan Allingham's team tried to appeal to the humanity of the jury – everybody can make a little mistake from time to time, but no one would expect the result to be death. Leonard Levine explained that his client thought that the production team might be convicted for the illegal hiring of the children, but that he would never have done it if he had thought there was any danger at all.

In terms of the children being hired George Folsey seemed to have gathered the most bad press, his reported conversations with Donna Schuman making him seem totally guilty, not just of the hiring but of joking about the nature of the explosives. With potentially the worst case to answer Harland Braun used his closing speech to attack Schuman, claiming that she was psychologically imbalanced and was keen to see someone convicted because she herself felt some sense of guilt.

The prosecution were to have the last word before the jurors would be asked to retire in order to consider the verdict. D'Agostino took to the floor once more and in a scene more reminiscent of a courtroom drama started to deliver a badly calculated and highly dramatic scene of her own. Walking so that she was directly in front of the jury, D'Agostino held out a potato in one hand and a straw in the other. She then pushed the straw into the potato before saying, "If a straw can do that to a potato, imagine what a piece of bamboo can do to a helicopter's rotor blades." With that she handed the potato to a juror and sat down.

The jury may have been confused by this last-chance antic of the prosecution but it made great copy for the headlines. As the reporters went back to their offices to write the last report before the verdict, the Judge dismissed the jury and asked that they make their verdicts accordingly.

The jury went away and deliberated the details of what they had heard over the course of the long trial. On 29 May 1987, the jury had concluded its decision making and was ready to tell the world. The world's associated press gathered like flies on the dead and impatiently sat while the verdicts emerged.

The verdicts were first passed to Judge Boren who then passed the details to the court clerk in order that they could be announced.

She began, "We the jury in the above-titled action find the defendant John Landis not guilty of involuntary manslaughter." And for each and every count the same verdict had been agreed. There was a stunned silence in the court; D'Agostino looked visibly shocked. She then shook her head making it clear to all she was disgusted by the outcome.

Landis' wife, Deborah, hugged each juror in turn, tears of joy streaming down her cheeks, the pressure finally over.

Both Landis and D'Agostino immediately went on a round of television talk shows. D'Agostino made it clear that she felt Landis walked free because the jury were in awe of his celebrity status. During one show the jury foreperson rang in to dispute the claim that they had let Landis off because he was famous, claiming the majority of the jurors had not heard of him before the trial.

In a poll taken at the time it appeared that most Americans thought Landis guilty of manslaughter, but the twelve Americans who counted most did not.

From Manhattan Millionaire to US Manhunt

Robert Durst

Robert Allen Durst, a rich New York real estate heir, became America's first billion dollar fugitive after jumping bail while awaiting trial for the murder of Morris Black. This, however, was just one startling event in the life of Durst who had over the previous 20 years had other brushes with the law and lived a very peculiar lifestyle.

Durst was born into privilege, his grandfather Joseph Durst having built a fortune out of developing real estate in the New York area. On his death the business was passed on to his son Seymour, Durst's father, and he continued to build the empire into a multi-billion-dollar concern called the Durst Organization. Durst's earlier life, along with his siblings, was one of luxury, being brought up in plush surroundings and wanting for nothing. He lived in the upper-crust surroundings of Scarsdale, New York and attended Scarsdale High School, before completing his undergraduate degree at Lehigh University. In contrast to Durst's obvious good fortune at being born into wealth, an episode in his earlier life was to shake him to the core and cause him no end of psychiatric problems, which some think explain his behaviour in later life. At the tender age of seven Durst witnessed his mother's suicide at the family home in Scarsdale when she threw herself off the roof of the mansion. This terrible trauma caused the young Durst to endure many hours of counselling, during which the doctors revealed that he had a deep-seated anger which if left untreated had the potential to turn into schizophrenia. After a while Durst was able to move on with his life and after completing his undergraduate studies at Lehigh went on to UCLA to conclude his graduate training. Friends from those days reveal a strange personality, quite intense and prone to outbursts of anger if provoked; he was also a habitual marijuana smoker. The extent of Durst's ability to be angry became more apparent when it was time for him to join the world of work. As the older brother he expected that it would be he who would ascend to the top job in his father's business and was taken aback when his father announced that it would be his younger brother Douglas who would now head the operation. In a fit of anger Durst walked out of the building, out of the business and never returned – he was not about to play second fiddle to anyone. His anger had got the better of him and it could have proven a costly mistake – alienating himself from his family could have cut him off from his inheritance.

As a prominent New York family the name Durst was as well known in its heyday as the name of Trump in the 1980s and 1990s and as such their activities were widely reported in the press. It is not therefore surprising that Durst felt humiliated when news of his brother's appointment became public knowledge.

For all of Durst's quirkiness he was never short of beautiful women to accompany him on his busy social schedule – he would think nothing of jumping on a plane and jetting off to Europe, Asia or anywhere he wanted, all in the name of fun. And his fun always included a diet of marijuana. In the 1970s he frequented New York's well-known celebrity disco, Studio 54, although he was never quite comfortable in such public surroundings. He never really acquired a pure playboy persona being equally interested in sculpture and architecture. He counted amongst others in his social circle Jackie Kennedy Onassis, Mia Farrow's younger sister, Prudence, who he dated for a while, and John Lennon, with whom he enjoyed primal scream therapy, at the time the latest innovation in handling anger and fear. Eventually Durst married a young woman who he met in one of his offices. Kathleen McCormack was a fourth-year medical student when she called into a Durst Organization administrative office to pay the rent which was due on her apartment, one of a number in a building which was owned by Durst. They got to know each other and initially Kathleen quite liked the eccentric charms exuded by Durst, but by the time they had been married a while these eccentricities were to wear thin.

Once they were married McCormack graduated as a nurse and decided she would pursue her dream of becoming a paediatrician. Her time now was spent studying for her chosen career, a situation which Durst was not always sympathetic towards – they were after all well off and neither in reality had to work. But unlike Durst McCormack did not come from a monied background, she was the product of a middle-class Irish Catholic family from New Jersey and her work ethic was strong.

In line with their wealth and status the newly married couple maintained three homes in the New York City area: an apartment on the Upper West Side of Manhattan, another on the Upper East Side and a plush house in the small Westchester county town of South Salem. Durst was a man who seemed intent on moving about and lived at the three addresses in equal measure, which meant that much of their time was spent apart, often not seeing each other for days at a time. For McCormack this was not necessarily a bad thing as their marriage had deteriorated to the point where Durst's anger would often boil over and result in violence – she had visited the hospital on more than one occasion to have bruises looked at. Although to some extent McCormack lived in denial of her husband's temper she did not hide his behaviour from her friends, who had come to despise him for it. Many of them pleaded with her to flee the family home before anything terrible happened and although she was now considering her options, she had signed a very biased pre-nuptial agreement which would have left her with not more than she arrived with, and she was not about to let him get away with that.

Over time Durst apparently felt that he was losing control over his wife and became more preoccupied with her where-abouts. A friend of McCormack's, Gilberte Najamy, threw a party one evening in January 1982 at her apartment in

Manhattan, which McCormack attended. Not long after she arrived Durst called on the telephone and demanded that she return home. She explained to Najamy that she had to leave because her husband was upset and added prophetically, "I'm afraid of what Bobby will do."

She was never seen again. Four days later Durst walked into the 20th precinct on the Upper West Side of Manhattan and reported that his wife was missing. Suspicion was immediately aroused when it was noted that Durst had waited four days before calling in the authorities, a point he was able to explain away as being down to their multi-location existence which often meant they did not come across each other for days on end. Durst admitted that they had argued and that during this time McCormack had consumed a bottle of wine before he took her to the Katonah New York train station, where she had taken the 9.15 p.m. train back into the city – he had not seen or heard from her since. The police were concerned that she had not been in contact but were equally perplexed by Durst's calm behaviour, which seemed very strange for someone reporting his wife missing.

Witnesses came forward and claimed to have seen McCormack at the Upper West Side apartment the day after the party, and a woman who identified herself as Kathleen called in to the Dean's office of the Albert Einstein School of Medicine that day to say she was sick and unable to attend classes.

A week later Durst announced in the *New York Post* that he was offering a $100,000 reward for information leading to the whereabouts of his wife. McCormack's friends however found this ploy to be nothing short of a diversion – as far as they were concerned Durst had done something quite horrible and this was just a ruse to cover up his activity. Between them they calculated McCormack's movements on the night of the party. Given the train schedules they reckoned that McCormack would have had no more than forty minutes to drink the wine if she had managed to get the 9.15 p.m. train back into the city. The police were aware of the anomaly but were unable to find any other evidence which might point to Durst's guilt. Although the file on McCormack remained open, with no further evidence presenting itself, and with the absence of a body, the police could do nothing about it, however much they suspected Durst of foul play. Meanwhile McCormack's friends collated information and maintained files in the hope of uncovering the truth, and never allowed her disappearance to be forgotten. In another twist to the disappearance Najamy and another friend, Kathy Traytsman, were both burgled and the contents of those files were taken, presumably to ensure nothing could emerge which might incriminate the perpetrator of the disappearance. Najamy however became fixated on McCormack's disappearance and it pushed her into a deep depression which forced her into alcoholism.

The papers reported the disappearance and the details regarding the reward but were also keen to discuss the mystery. The finger of guilt was pointing straight at Durst but he seemed able to live with the innuendo which surrounded his wife's demise. He never passed comment and seemed keen to let the past just fade away. It was noted that Durst simply got on with his life, dating new women, travelling the world and living the good life. Nearly 19 years after McCormack's disappearance Durst married his second wife, Deborah Charatan, a prosperous real estate broker.

It was long not though before scandal once more surrounded the wealthy Durst. Just days after he was married to Charatan one of his closest friends, Susan Berman, aged 55, was found dead at her Los Angeles home. She had been discovered in a pool of blood with a bullet hole in the back of her head. They had been friends since their days at UCLA and shared a deep common bond – Berman had seen her mother commit suicide too. The murder was initially thought to have been a gangland hit as Berman was the daughter of Davie Berman, partner of the legendary mobster, Bugsy Seigel, and an associate of the Jewish mob boss, Meyer Lansky. Berman was a writer who had already published two books about her father's interests in Las Vegas, but neither had sold well and neither particularly gave away any big secrets – children of the mob never got to know any of the details. The police therefore concluded that it was unlikely Berman had been killed to avoid any embarrassing exposés. Besides, she had been shot from behind and there was no sign of forced entry into the apartment. It was therefore concluded that Berman knew the killer well enough to let them into the apartment and also felt comfortable enough with the person to turn her back on them.

Berman did not enjoy the security of a wealthy background – her father's involvement with the mob had not left his family great wealth. With her books not selling well Berman was living on the breadline and she frequently ran out of money, unable to pay bills and needing to borrow off friends, promising to settle up when she was on a more even keel. In 2000 her old car finally gave up the ghost and she wrote to Durst requesting a $7,000 dollar loan for a replacement car. She had reason to believe he would respond positively – apart from their close friendship it was Durst who had given her away at her own wedding. It was four months before she finally received a reply – inside was a cheque for $25,000 and a brief note to say it was a gift not a loan.

Although Durst was not considered a suspect in Berman's murder it is coincidental that in the weeks before her death she had been contacted by the New York State police who intended to interview her over the 1982 disappearance of Kathleen McCormack, Durst's first wife. She had also told *New York* magazine that she had information which would "blow the top off things", although she did not expand upon this claim. Did the killer of McCormack act to prevent Berman spilling the beans? It is also interesting to note that shortly before Berman was murdered she had received a second cheque from Durst, again for $25,000.

With Berman ready to blast the case wide open, the media once again prepared to feast on the scandal which all expected to surround the Durst family, particularly Robert. More theories emerged regarding the disappearance of McCormack, and also the murder of Berman. No one missed the link between Berman being ready to divulge information likely to lead to the killer of her friend Kathleen McCormack and her own sudden death; surely whoever had dealt with McCormack had dealt with Berman. Things were hotting up again for Durst and being under pressure was not his strong point; he had found in the past it could push him over the edge.

Another friend of McCormack, Ellen Strauss, also believes that it was Durst who killed Berman. She claims Berman was very particular about who she would let into her house and that in terms of men, Durst was one of the few who would be allowed in. Strauss believes that the motive for Berman's killing was that she assisted Durst in the cover-up of his wife's disappearance.

As more and more stories emerged regarding the two crimes it was Najamy, McCormack's close friend, who cast further suspicion on Durst. In a magazine article she theorized that she thought it was Berman who had called into the Dean's office the day after her disappearance, not McCormack, and that the money Berman received from Durst was nothing short of hush money for keeping the events secret. Why would anyone call into the Dean's office to report such a non-event as a missed day through sickness? Her murder arose out of the fact that Berman was pushing for more money to keep the deadly secret. This explains the fact that the killer did not have to break in and why he was able to shoot Berman in the back of the skull. It was a fine theory but one for which once again there was no supporting evidence.

Since his marriage to Charatan, Durst had expanded his real estate portfolio, buying and renting houses in all parts of America, including Texas and a number in New Orleans; he had also started cross-dressing and living as a number of alter egos. His marriage had become one of convenience and it afforded him the freedom to travel and live as he wanted. The continual media intrusion had left him tired and he wanted to live in obscurity for a while, out of the police and public gaze.

One of Durst's many bolt holes was a modest four-unit apartment on Avenue K in Galveston. When in residence here he adopted the name Dorothy Ciner and dressed accordingly, with cheap dresses and a wig. To avoid having to speak he had lead people to believe that he had a bad throat infection and insisted on communicating via written notes.

The landlord who looked after the apartment noted that the woman wore a wig and had glasses which were held together with sticking plaster, and although he hadn't seen her frequently at the apartment he was aware she had a male visitor called Robert Durst, although not surprisingly he had never seen them both at the same time.

Across the hallway from Durst, alias Dorothy Ciner, lived a 71-year-old man called Morris Black. Known to be a bit cranky and a bit fast with his temper, he should have fitted in well with Durst. Black had been estranged from his family for years and had lived in various parts of the United States, but now he seemed more content by himself, having few visitors. He had a conviction for threatening to blow up a utility company after they had presented him with what he thought was an excessive bill. He did, on the other hand, have a charitable nature – when he found a cheap source of reading glasses on the Internet he purchased five cases of them and then gave them to the Jesse Tree, a Galveston-based charitable organization, instructing them to distribute the glasses to those who most needed them. During the time that Durst occupied the cheap apartment in Galveston he and Black became acquainted, a move which would cost Black dearly.

On 30 September 2001, a 13-year-old boy fishing from a jetty near his home overlooking Galveston Bay, spotted something unusual floating in the water. He called to his father who initially thought the object was a dead pig, however on closer inspection it became obvious that it was in fact the headless, limbless torso of a man or woman. Later the same day other residents in the area saw bin liners being washed up in the surf, which on police inspection were seen to contain the legs and arms which belonged to the torso, the head however remaining strangely elusive. On emptying the bags they revealed other items of interest: a plastic sheath for a bow saw, a receipt from a local hardware store and a local newspaper with a mailing address of 2213 Avenue K, Galveston. A matter of days later another bin liner was washed up on the shore, this one containing a .22 calibre automatic pistol with two loaded clips. With the arms of the man now in the hands of forensic experts the police were quickly able to establish from fingerprints that the man whose remains had been washed ashore was Morris Black, a fact which tied in nicely with the mailing address on the newspaper. If Black had not been convicted of a minor misdemeanour his identity may never have been established. His head, which remains missing, would have been the only other piece of the jigsaw which could have conclusively determined his identity.

The police department immediately despatched officers to Black's address at Avenue K where they found an apartment covered in bloodstains. On closer inspection the bloody smears led out of Black's apartment and across the hall to an adjacent dwelling, the home of one Ms Dorothy Ciner, alias Durst. Inside the apartment they discovered a pair of bloodstained boots and a bloody knife. Other traces of blood could be seen on the kitchen floor and on the living-room carpet. The elusive Ms Ciner was nowhere to be seen, although police checks revealed that there was another Ms Ciner who lived in another state – not the one they were looking for but one who had known Durst while at school, but had not been in contact with him for years. The police were now suspicious of the Dorothy Ciner who lived in Galveston – everyone who knew her believed there was something not quite right about her, not to mention her strange association with Durst, a famous, wealthy, New York real estate magnate.

The police ran a check on Durst's name and established that he was the driver of a silver Honda CRV mini SUV, registered under his own name in Texas. Just nine days after Black's body had been discovered a cruising police patrol car spotted the silver Honda and pursued the car until he was able to get the driver to pull over. From descriptions provided the officer realized that the driver was Robert Durst and as he leaned in towards the car he chillingly noted the bow saw lying in the passenger side foot well. The patrolman concluded a speedy arrest and back at the station Durst was officially charged with the murder of Morris Black. Durst was not a co-operative detainee and refused to answer any questions without the presence of his lawyer. After much debate the charges against Durst were officially listed and the police authority intended, on the evidence they had secured, to pursue a prosecution against Durst. Surprisingly, given the nature of the crime – the suspect had after all dismembered the body after the murder – Durst was given bail of $300,000, a lot of money in Galveston terms but loose change in Durst's world. His estranged wife Deborah Charatan posted the bail money through a bond agent. The arraignment was set for 16 October 2001, and with the date set Durst was allowed to leave.

During Durst's detention the police examined the Silver Honda and found a 9mm pistol hidden in the boot space, the same calibre as the weapon used to kill Susan Berman.

The prosecution and the police were in no doubt that Durst was guilty of Black's murder, but what they could not fathom out was a motive. They speculated that Black may have established that Ms Ciner was in fact Durst and had threatened to expose him. They were both known to have short tempers – perhaps there was a clash of personalities. But neither these nor any other theories seemed sufficiently good enough reasons for someone to indulge in the type of crime and cover-up that Durst was suspected of. The prosecution would now have to spend a significant amount of their time trying to establish Durst's motives for murder.

For the media this was another major story – not only was Durst part of one of New York's most prestigious families, he also had history. His wife had gone missing and had never been found, and his so-called best friend, to whom he had paid several instalments of money, had been murdered in the most mysterious of circumstances. Susan Berman had been murdered and it was assumed by all, including the police, that Kathleen Durst had met the same fate, except that her body had been better disposed of. Durst's lawyers would have a difficult time defending these latest charges – the jury, who were still out there waiting to be selected, would have to have been living in a sealed box not to have read and seen the reports on Durst's complex history.

For a while though this would not be a matter anyone

would have to worry about, for on the day of the arraignment Durst simply did not show up – he had jumped bail and disappeared again. The hunt was back on and this time the police and the media were keen to see him apprehended – he had almost certainly killed one person and was suspected of a further two. Durst most certainly could be dangerous.

The prosecution meanwhile were able to review the results of Black's autopsy. It revealed that 71-year-old Black had endured a particularly violent attack and although he had suffered a heart attack during the assault it was not that which had killed him. He had been severely beaten, as evidenced by the extensive bruising on his chest, elbows, back and shoulders, and had also suffered four breaks to the bone in his upper right arm. The cause of death was established as being brought on by a large amount of blood which had entered his lungs, the trauma of which led to his heart attack. The autopsy also revealed a more chilling side to the murder – the killer had attempted to chop off Black's fingers, presumably in a bid to avoid his identity being revealed. For whatever reason, the killer then changed his mind and decided to remove the arms, the legs and the head, which to this day has never been recovered.

With Durst on the loose the police were painfully aware now of just what type of person they were dealing with. A shooter can perform his task at a distance, it is impersonal and the perpetrator need not necessarily face the results of his actions. Black's murder demonstrated that the killer was unaffected by the sight of vast amounts of blood and was happy to dispense violence in close-quarter combat. Durst's erratic behaviour and propensity for sudden bouts of anger meant he was very much a potential danger to the public; he had to be found before he exploded again.

The media ran story after story and his face was plastered across the screens and newspapers of America, but there was one flaw in this high-profile manhunt – there were no photographs of Durst dressed as woman, the disguise he had favoured while trying to blend into the background. In a bid to further enhance their own chances of a scoop the newspapers began to indulge in investigations of their own.

The *Galveston County Daily News* hired a private investigator to track him down, or uncover any reportable facts. As well as having residences all across the United States Durst was also prone to using aliases, amongst others Robert Deal Jezowski. His residences were identified as being in Los Angeles, Pasadena, and a number in New York, Coral Gables, Florida, San Francisco and Trinidad, California. Investigation of phone records revealed that Durst also had places in Dallas and New Orleans. The investigator visited New Orleans and interviewed the landlord of the property there who said the occupier of the property was a man who dressed as a woman and who called himself Diane Winn, again claiming to be mute, either to avoid having to get into potentially awkward conversations or to avoid being identified as a man. Although it would appear that Durst did not pass easily for a woman; most people who came across him while cross-dressing seemed to see through the disguise immediately.

The investigator acting on behalf of the newspaper made sure that whatever he found he passed to the police authorities immediately. The New Orleans property was subsequently raided by the police who found a number of items of interest, including a wig, a video tape recording of a news program regarding the disappearance of Kathleen Durst and a silver medallion which had been bequeathed to Durst in Susan Berman's will. The medallion had once belonged to Davie Berman and therefore one imagines that it was of great sentimental value, perhaps a small indication of the real friendship that existed between the two. Also found in the apartment were the keys to the silver Honda in which Durst had previously been arrested. Other information soon came to light which showed that after Durst had jumped bail he had made his way to Mobile, Alabama, where he had rented a red Chevrolet Corsica, and in a further twist to the story, Durst was now using the name Morris Black, using both Black's driving licence and Medicare card as identification. In order to make himself look like a 70-year-old man he had now shaved his head and his eyebrows.

The trail ran cold after it was shown that Durst had moved on from Mobile, Alabama, to Piano, Texas, where he visited a friend who was able to confirm that Durst was now dressing as a woman again. Where he went after Texas is not known but when he did eventually resurface it was in typical Durst dramatic style.

On 30 November 2001, security guards at a supermarket in Hanover township, Pennsylvania, were drawn to the suspicious movements of a man wearing a brown wig and acting strangely. Security cameras followed the man closely as he wandered around the store. Eventually the man took a sticking plaster from a strip and went to the rest room, emerging shortly afterwards with it placed over what was clearly a shaving cut. Then while still under scrutiny the man took a chicken sandwich from a refrigerator cabinet and was seen to hide it inside his coat. Heading down towards the checkouts the man picked up a newspaper and again slid it inside his coat, before walking past the cashiers and out of the store. Having been under surveillance the whole time the security guards were ready for the task of apprehending the thief, followed the man out to the carpark and grabbed him just as he was about to get into his red Chevrolet car. Meanwhile security in the store had already called the police who were on their way.

When the police arrived they were not aware of who they were being called to, although on arrival they could see they had an older man who was obviously dressed as a woman, with a poor looking wig. When they asked the man his name he replied, "Robert Durst." The social security number he provided matched his name and Durst was arrested and taken into custody. He did not resist arrest but once again he refused to answer questions without his lawyer being present. Meanwhile examination of the red car showed that the licence plates did not belong to the car, the Maryland plates had been stolen. In the rear of the car the police recovered an amount of marijuana, two .38 calibre handguns and $37,000 in one hundred dollar bills. The need for cash was paramount if Durst was to remain on the run – since he had jumped bail the courts had frozen all of his bank accounts. The police were puzzled as to why he had attempted to steal what amounted to less than ten dollars worth of goods – when his pockets were turned out at the police station he had $500 on him. If he had paid he might still have been on the run. For an intelligent man it was these inconsistencies which demonstrated Durst's often detached thinking – having gone to what must have seemed like great lengths to prevent detection he then put himself in a totally unnecessary risk situation.

The media once again jumped on the case and reported in detail how the cross-dressing billionaire was arrested for stealing some meagre goods from a supermarket, they too feeling it reflected the insanity of the man. The press gathered for the day Durst was due to be extradited back to Texas where he would face trial for the first-degree murder of Morris Black. Once again the press bandwagon rolled and Durst seemed to endure nothing but bad publicity, a situation which the defence were rightly worried about. But if nothing else, being Robert Durst meant he could afford the best defence money could buy. As the press reported at the time, if O.J. Simpson had been defended by the "dream team", then Durst had employed the "supreme team". And supreme they would certainly need to be, for there were few Americans who believed that Durst could explain away his actions in a way that would allow him to walk away a free man – he had after all butchered his victim and allowed his remains to be washed up for all of Galveston's public to view; there could therefore be few expectations of sympathy. His money could buy him a great deal of skill, but the public don't react too well to murder and dismemberment, especially when it is carried out by a member of the exceedingly well-off club.

On 28 January 2002, Durst was placed in the back of a secure vehicle and without incident was driven to Texas, the media pack in pursuit and ready to report any little incident. After much deliberation and discussion Durst finally entered a guilty plea at his arraignment, but claimed that he acted in self-defence. The news astounded everyone but Durst and his assembled team of lawyers; the media and the prosecution found it hard to believe that the defence were going to go ahead on the basis of self-defence – Black after all had suffered substantial injuries, more than anyone would need to inflict if they were simply trying to defend themselves. The outcome of this particular trial seemed pretty much a forgone conclusion.

John Springer of Court TV asked Ron Gold, a Morristown, New Jersey, lawyer what he thought of the self-defence claim. "I could see how they could try a case of self-defence, particularly if there are no witnesses. But when you have a ton of aggravating factors – concealing what happened and throwing the body parts in the bay and things like that – insanity and self-defence are the last resort."

Ron Gold amongst many other qualified commentators all passed their opinions and most seemed to agree that whichever way the defence tried to play it, the outcome appeared obvious.

Meanwhile the Judge who was set to try the trial, Judge Susan Criss, had a major challenge on her hands to ensure a fair trial. If the media were allowed to run amok, if details relating to the case were aired too early, then she would face the defence team trying to claim that their client could not be guaranteed a fair trial. Bobbi Bacha, a private investigator who was involved with members of Black's family in a civil case against Durst, was under the restrictions imposed by a gag order which officially prevented them from talking to the press. Others who were seen to be acting in a way likely to reduce the opportunity of a fair trial were also warned by the Judge.

The trial was certainly high profile and the amount of media attention it was receiving meant that the Judge was under increasing pressure to allow the media to cover the proceedings in a more direct way. She finally ruled that she would allow a single television camera to film parts of the trial, namely the reading of the charge to the jury, the final arguments and the reading of the verdict. She would also allow one still camera to be present throughout the trial, which had been set for 25 August 2002, which would be her 212th Judicial District Court.

The proceedings and preparations did not get off to a trouble-free start for Durst; having paid a $1.2 million dollar advance to his legal team he subsequently asked permission from the Judge to sack them as they had requested a further $600,000 to cover additional expenses. The Judge called them together and was able to bring both parties to agreement with no one apparently best pleased.

As the defence team prepared for the impending day in court they began a frantic round of requests aimed at the Judge. They were hoping to suppress certain pieces of information they believed could prove damaging to the defence of their client, but essentially they were out to question everything in the hope of strengthening their otherwise weak position.

Jury selection expert Robert Hirschorn recommended that certain changes be made to the questions used to select the jury in an attempt to have people selected who have been less predisposed to Durst's guilt, but more importantly people who were less likely to want to impose the death penalty.

Durst's team then attempted to suppress the identification of Durst by a Galveston resident, Lorre Cusick, who claimed she had spoken to Durst a few days before Black's body was washed up – he had apparently asked her if the fishing was good in the area. The resident picked Durst from a photo line-up, but Durst's team questioned that the photo used had in fact been one which had been in the media already, making her selection less dependable.

Chip Lewis, another member of the "supreme team", requested that the blood found at the scene, the paring knife and other evidence found at Durst's apartment and in his trash cans should be suppressed because the police did not have an official warrant for the searches. They had instead encouraged the landlord to instruct them to carry out the checks on the grounds of safety. Assistant District Attorney Joel Bennett rebutted the request stating that the landlord had requested a search be made to check on the safety of Dorothy Ciner and that the trash cans were the property of the city and therefore would have been emptied by city staff anyway. This was a blatant attempt to hide from the jurors the fact that Durst had a pistol and a butcher's saw in his possession at the address where the murder took place.

The situation really could not have looked much worse for Durst although his defence team were trying every trick in the book to suppress the evidence which would surely place Durst behind bars. In spite of the fact that many people were barred from speaking to the press and media, they had all the facts and information they wanted and painted a very black picture for Durst, who was still in custody and unable to get bail again – not because bail had been denied, which would not have been surprising given his recent bail-skipping antics, but because the Judge had now set the bail at a staggering $2 billion dollars, making Durst America's first billion-dollar inmate. Even Durst's wealth could not stretch that far.

To make matters worse for Durst the New York District Attorney Jeanine Pirro began to re-examine the disappearance of Kathleen Durst. As news of this spread again through the media making him look every inch the killer, it was left to nobody's imagination that the authorities believed that Durst had indeed murdered the woman and disposed of the body, albeit more effectively this time. A new book written by author Matt Birkbeck, called *A Deadly Secret*, revealed for the first time a possible motive Durst might have had for killing his wife. In the book Birkbeck claims that a friend of Kathleen Durst had urged Kathleen to blackmail Durst into giving her a fair divorce settlement by threatening to expose his embezzlement of funds from the Durst Organisation. On the night of her disappearance Kathleen Durst had allegedly taken two grams of cocaine and drunk two bottles of wine at the party before going home to confront her husband. She vanished that evening or very soon thereafter.

Meanwhile more details of Durst's personal life were emerging and again they did not paint a particularly pleasant picture. Galveston Police Department uncovered a long history of deceptions. Long before his cross-dressing days Durst had been taking other people's names and social security numbers, and using them to hide his own identity. Dorothy Ciner, the alias he used in Galveston, was a real person, someone who he had known previously; he also used his wife's identity and the name Jezowsky. His legal team would eventually try to depict a man who was particularly uncomfortable and who simply wanted to become part of the masses, embarrassed at being so wealthy and wanting to be out of the limelight. The prosecution had another version.

When the court case began certain details were not allowed to be used by the prosecution, including the facts relating to his wife's mysterious disappearance, because although the authorities had their suspicions he had never been charged as there was nothing to bring a charge for. His wife's body, if she was indeed dead, had never been recovered. The murder of his friend Susan Berman would also be suppressed – the defence did not want to have their client found guilty by too many coincidental associations. It was unlikely however that the jury were not already aware of the eccentric Mr Durst's past. All of the other evidence was laid before the court and by and large both the defence and the prosecution were agreed that Durst had in fact murdered and then butchered his victim – what they did not agree on was the plea of self-defence. It was therefore incumbent upon the prosecution to prove that Durst had acted intentionally, but this was proving more difficult to achieve as there were no witnesses to the actual crime itself.

The defence counsel spoke glowingly of their client's good pedigree, of his otherwise clean record. Although their client had admitted his involvement in the crime that he had fought with Black over a gun, which had gone off accidentally, and had shot Black in the head, the autopsy did not reveal this wound as the head had never been recovered. Durst claimed Black, whom he had known quite well, had gone over the edge one day – he was prone to bad temper and the two had got into a heated dispute which resulted in a struggle. Durst claimed that Black had lunged for the gun and he had been forced to respond.

In terms of Durst's disposal of the body in such a macabre way the defence described this as the actions of a scared man desperate to avoid detection. It was proof of his desire to cover his tracks rather than proof of murder.

The prosecution described the conditions under which the accused was arrested, stealing goods from a supermarket while on the run from police. His character therefore was one of a bail-jumping criminal who had illegally used aliases to avoid being caught. He had also considered the disposal of the body in detail and had planned his actions meticulously.

As the opposing teams began there summing up there were few people who believed that Durst would not be committed for first-degree murder, except for the jury that is. When the Judge asked each jury member in turn what their verdict was a stunned silence spread throughout the court as each in turn declared "Not guilty".

Outside the courthouse the press and media fed their stations and offices with the result, which was described as a shock outcome, a victory for money over justice. Everyone questioned the outcome and wondered aloud what it would have been if the accused had been a truck driver or a shop worker instead of the wealthy real estate mogul he actually was. It was into these claims and headlines that Durst walked following his November 2003 acquittal. The acquittal in court did not however result in his release, for he had been retained on charges of bail jumping and tampering with evidence, namely the dismemberment and disposal of Morris Black's body.

The jurors themselves became the target of media pressure when it was suggested that the only reason Durst was found not guilty was because they were swayed by the sheer style of Durst's legal team. The jurors however responded by stating that the prosecution failed to persuade them that Durst had acted intentionally and without this proof they were prepared to accept that Durst had acted in self-defence.

Just as Durst might have been thinking he could now move on with his life another twist was added to the already long-running saga – nearly a year after his shock victory on murder charges Pennsylvania authorities indicted him on two counts of interstate gun transportation. At the time of the indictment Durst was just days away from release for the bail jumping and evidence-tampering charges when he was taken into custody by Federal marshals for transfer to Pennsylvania to face the gun charges.

Durst's defence team had already managed to secure him a

low tariff for bail jumping and evidence tampering. The team had successfully managed to remove the trial judge, Susan Criss, after she had publicly expressed regret over the jury's verdict. Subsequently the defence team struck a deal with the prosecution whereby Durst would receive a five-year prison term, most of which would be covered by credit for time already served.

Durst's lawyers, who were not expecting there to be any additional suits, claimed that their client was now being pursued for vindictive reasons. Dick DeGuerin, a member of Durst's defence team, described the action as a "malicious prosecution".

When Durst faced the charges in Pennsylvania his lawyers began a round of plea bargaining intended to minimize the effect of the prosecution; without this it was possible that Durst could have faced up to 15 years in prison had he chosen to go to trial.

Durst was finally sentenced to nine months imprisonment, a $30,000 fine plus a further two years supervised release. United States District Court Judge Timothy Savage agreed to a deal whereby Durst would be given credit for time already served which means that he should finally walk free in April 2005.

Robert Durst remains the wealthiest man in the United States penal system, his wealth appearing to have bought him a significant amount of skill in terms of his defence team, skill many others could not have afforded.

Rather than wanting a break from all of the costly legal wranglings which have dogged his life for the past few years, Durst is now involved in a legal dispute with his brother Douglas and one his cousins who have sought to change the rules governing the family trust fund, of which Durst is one of thirteen benefactors. Durst is fighting to ensure that he can bequeath his share of the wealth to his estranged wife Deborah, a situation other members of the family are not pleased with.

There are now active investigations on both coasts of America, with authorities saying they can prove that Durst was in Los Angeles at the time of Susan Berman's death, something which Durst has always denied. This alone would not provide sufficient evidence of guilt, interesting though it is. No charges have been brought but the police do not rule out further interviews with anyone they think might be able to help with their enquiries.

In the Family

Marvin Gay v Marvin Gaye

I heard it through the grapevine. It is virtually impossible to read those words without adding to them the melody which has become famous the world over as Marvin Gaye's signature song. The man who would be an icon began his all-too-short life from very meagre beginnings. Marvin Pentz Gaye Jr, one of the most gifted and visionary musical talents was born 2 April 1939, in Washington DC. The second of four children born to Alberta and Marvin Sr, an ordained minister in the House of God, a Christian sect bringing together parts of Judaism and Pentecostalism, a mixed religious environment with very strict values. It would be the hands of his father who would, some 45 years later, take the gift of life from this singing legend. To understand the person that Marvin Gaye became, you really need to understand the feudal father–son relationship he was to suffer throughout his life.

Marvin Gay Sr was born in 1914, the third of 13 children of poor farm parents in Jessamine County, Kentucky. It was an unhappy childhood which was to be repeated in Marvin Jr's own home later in life, and like his father, Marvin was to become a strict disciplinarian, abusive and totally in control of his household.

In 1919, with the farm work unable to provide enough money to keep the large family going, George and Mamie Gay moved to Lexington. Shortly after arriving in Lexington Mamie and her son, Marvin Sr, began attending a storefront church, affiliated to a religious sect which was strangely, yet proudly named "The House of God, The Holy

Church of The Living God, The Pillar And The Ground of
The Truth, The House of Prayer for All People". Marvin Sr
was to prove a good religious scholar, absorbing the mor-
alistic stories and taking them all very seriously. Years later,
in 1934, he moved to Washington DC, as a House of God
preacher.

It was while preaching in Washington DC that Gay Sr met
Alberta Cooper, a regular member of his congregation. After
a brief but proper courtship they were married in July 1935.
Marvin and Alberta had four children: Jeanne, in 1937,
Marvin Jr, on 2 April 1939, Frankie, in 1942, and Zeola,
known as Sweetsie, in 1945.

Marvin Sr continued to preach, popular with the congregation but poorly paid. The family managed to survive
on Alberta's wages as a maid and made do with subsidized
housing. In 1950, Marvin Sr left the church when he was
overlooked as a candidate for the role of Chief Apostle of
the House of God. His working life never really took off
and he spent the majority of his adult life out of work.
Unfortunately for his children he had plenty of free time
and focused much of his attention on them, his penchant
for the strict application of his rules never far away.
Although he had given up his church role he still held
many of its beliefs and forced these upon the family. Not
only were their strict rules about what you could and
couldn't do, discussing certain subjects was also considered
a sin. The Gay household was no place to discuss athletics,
dancing, movies, television and popular music. His daughters had to dress demurely and he strictly enforced a no
lipstick or nail polish rule. The children were routinely
tested on biblical passages, and had to always obey Gay's
firmly set curfew. If rules were broken or disobeyed then
there were consequences to be paid, namely a beating, and
there were many. To add to the children's problems they
were all bed-wetters, no doubt the result of some deep-
seated psychological problems, yet this too prompted the
unwanted attention of their father.

Marvin Gaye Jr claimed that living with his father was
something like living with a king – a very peculiar, change-

able, cruel and all-powerful king. The children were made to seek Gay Sr's favour, something which Marvin would refuse to do, spending much of his time defying his father, resenting his dogmatic and cruel attempts at child rearing. His father would take pleasure in the punishment of his children, sending them to their bedrooms to await his belt, often leaving them for up to an hour, giving them plenty of time to sweat it out. They were terrified of the door opening as they knew he didn't make idle threats when it came to a whipping. If Gay Sr was overzealous in his pursuit of punishment, Alberta Gay would provide the soft centre of the family. Marvin Jr relied on his mother to lift his spirits – it was she who would console him and praise his singing.

A contradictory facet of Marvin Sr's character was his penchant for dressing in his wife's clothes, even her wigs and shoes. Later in life Marvin Jr was at pains to admit that he also had developed a fascination with women's clothes, although he was quick to point out that he had no attraction for men, although interestingly, five of Marvin Sr's siblings were homosexual.

Wasting no time at all, Marvin's singing career started at the tender age of three, when he first sang in church, a role he enjoyed and excelled at, so much so that he was soon elevated to a soloist in the choir. Singing was not his only musical accomplishment for he was also able to play the church organ and the family piano, an old but reliable instrument which was kept in the family's living room. He was self taught and played by ear, never feeling the need to learn how to read music; he was a natural. His father encouraged his son's passion for music, himself a self-taught pianist, but Marvin had to keep in mind that he was only allowed to play religious melodies, at least when his father was in the house. Music was a great source of enjoyment for Marvin and he would use this pleasure to take away some of the pain of a very unhappy home life. He attended Cardozo High School where he had many musically talented friends and together they formed a band in which Marvin played piano and drums. Along with his pals he enjoyed going out to see musicians, especially rhythm and blues bands, his favourites being James Brown,

Jackie Wilson and Sam Cooke, the inspiration for the extra "e" in his surname, which he added in 1957.

With increasing pressures at home Marvin dropped out of high school in 11th grade and at 18 joined the American Air Force. But military life did not suit – he had escaped one dictator only to find another, he was still being ordered around and found he still wasn't enjoying himself. The Air Force gave him only menial jobs to keep him busy – instead of flying jets, which he thought was the whole idea of joining, he found himself peeling potatoes. Having concluded that he had "jumped out of the fat and into the fire", he feigned illness and managed to get an honourable discharge, leaving because of his inability to adjust to regimentation and authority. With the swift end to his military career, Marvin was now ready to pursue the only thing that really mattered to him and fulfil the passion in which he had always sought refuge – his music.

He returned to Washington and began singing in several street-corner "doo-wop" groups, forming a singing group called The Marquees, in which Marvin was lead tenor. The group played local events and competitions where, by a stroke of luck, they were spotted by Bo Diddley, himself a local musician and one just on the cusp of gaining popularity with his amazing guitar melodies. It was with the assistance and enthusiasm of Diddley that The Marquees recorded their first double-sided single, containing the songs, "Hey Little School Girl" and "Wyatt Earp". The record did moderately well, encouraging Marvin to audition for the lead in another band, The Moonglows. The band loved him and offered him the lead singer's role. Finally making some progress the band moved to Chicago, where Gaye came across other musicians, occasionally providing back-up vocals on songs for Etta James and Chuck Berry. After relocating to Chicago, The Moonglows recorded a selection of singles for Chess Records, including 1959's "Mama Loocie", which along with other recordings did rather well, enough for them to start touring. It was while on tour that the group performed in Detroit, where Gaye's graceful tenor and three-octave vocal range won the interest of fledgling impresario Berry Gordy Jr, who, in 1961, signed him to the Motown Record label, marking the beginning of a long, productive career with one of the best-known labels in the US.

Gordy had a fantastic talent for blending rock 'n' roll, gospel, and rhythm & blues into very popular, commercial tunes, which appealed to a vast audience. As Marvin himself once put it, "We produce black dance music that white kids want to buy." It was while at Motown that Marvin met Gordy's sister Anna, the namesake for one of his record labels, Anna Records, who became a major part in Marvin's life for several years. The couple met when Marvin was only 20, whereas Anna was already 37 years old. Despite the age difference, the friendship blossomed and they fell in love, marrying in January 1961.

During his early Motown years Marvin produced many minor hits including, "Stubborn Kind of Fellow", "Hitch Hike" and "Can I Get a Witness", but his first top ten hit, "Pride and Joy", was the one which launched him, earning him great adulation from his ever-growing fan base. The hits just kept on coming – both as a solo artist and as one half of a duo – and by the mid 1960s he had secured three top ten hits, "Ain't That Peculiar", "I'll Be Doggone", and "How Sweet It Is (To Be Loved by You)". These great songs were shortly followed by another big hit, "It Takes Two", a duet which hit all the right notes commercially. Marvin was now a worldwide singing phenomenon, his face adorned the covers of countless magazines and his voice rang out from juke boxes and radio speakers, but with the success came the money, the glory, the temptations and the gradual slide into drug abuse.

Throughout these early years of Marvin's success, it was Anna who provided the guiding force in his life. He often said, "I sang all these songs for Anna," but by now Marvin Gaye had started to mirror some of the behaviour he had learned from his father. Anna Gordy was a very strong-willed woman, characteristics which Marvin found difficult to cope with so that from the beginning the couple's relationship was tempestuous and fiery, with Marvin often resorting to violence. He confessed, "We came to blows on more than one occasion, and I'm going to tell you something, Anna could hold her own."

Despite the turbulance within the marriage, the couple longed for a child, but after years of hoping and waiting they eventually discovered that Anna was unable to conceive. Reminiscent of Marvin's childhood, his father added to the grief by taunting his son, claiming he wasn't man enough to produce him a grandchild. In 1965 desperation kicked in and the pair came up with a plan whereby Anna would fake being pregnant – she told all her friends and family that she was pregnant, even giving the date the baby was due, as well as wearing progressively large maternity clothes. On the due date the Gayes took delivery of an adopted child, a son, and decided to name him Marvin III.

The child, though a welcome addition to the Gaye household, did nothing to quell the growing rift between Marvin and Anna, who having rowed to the point of physical attack on many occasions, split up frequently. As their marriage crumbled they each took lovers, both having many sexual partners during their ten years together. Marvin had more than ample opportunity to indulge in extramarital sex and spent the majority of the 1960s recording duets with a multitude of gorgeous female singers, adding further strain to his already weak marriage.

Marvin was spending a great deal of time with his singing partner, Tammi Terrell and the pair became very close, both in and out of the recording studio. Between them they managed to record some of the best records of the era, records which have stood the test of time – "Ain't No Mountain High Enough", "Your Precious Love", "Ain't Nothing Like the Real Thing" and "You're All I Need to Get By" to name but a few of their hits. Sadly the relationship was doomed for during one of their performances Terrell collapsed into Marvin's arms while they were on stage and was subsequently diagnosed with a brain tumour. Terrell's illness heralded the end of their recording partnership, a real blow for Marvin, although later the same year he released the record for which he became most famous, "I

Heard It Through The Grapevine". With his song a terrific success Marvin was elated, but typical of the singer, his success was to be followed by devastatingly bad news – in early 1970, Terrell died of her illness, an event which sent him spiralling downwards.

Marvin Gaye's public image was that of a confident man who had built up a musical persona as the ultimate lover, but by the early 1970s this was all set to change – his behaviour had grown increasingly erratic and he was now spending the majority of his time working on his own. He had withdrawn from public view, making very few appearances, and seemed on the verge of becoming a recluse. He avoided any work which forced him into the public eye, missing concerts and even studio work. At a particularly low ebb following an argument with Anna, he holed himself up in an apartment, only this time he was equipped with a gun. His depression had spiralled to the point where he was reported to have threatened to kill himself if anybody tried to enter the room. It was Anna's father who came to the rescue and managed to pacify the distraught Marvin, calming the situation down. With all of the pressures, the fame and the public scrutiny, not to mention his violent marriage, Marvin had taken to drugs and was struggling with his increasing use of cocaine, one of the triggers which had caused him to reach such a dangerous low.

His absence from the public circuit and the diminishing output from his record label had the media speculating over his health. The rumours of his drug use, his violence, the womanizing and his preoccupation with guns were now circulating amongst the gossip columns – it seemed that everyone but those closest to him were aware of his life-threatening problems.

In 1973, during the recording of the title track of his new album *Let's Get It On*, Marvin encountered a young girl who was to become his lover, and subsequently his second wife. Janice Hunter was just starting out as a singer and had begged her father, a co-producer of the record, to introduce her to Gaye. Marvin recalled that for him it was lust at first sight, while Hunter had a more romantic description of their initial meeting, describing her first encounter with Marvin as "The figure in my fantasy came to life."

This time he was the older person in the relationship, by now aged 33, whereas Janice was just 16 years of age. Hunter's family however did not seem to disapprove – on the contrary, the girl's parents encouraged the relationship with the famous, wealthy singer. Hunter was totally besotted with the successful older man and he too was totally taken with her, enjoying the flush of a new, very willing, sexual partner. The power of his new sexual relationship seemed to be echoed in the lyrics of his songs, giving him a new lease of life at Motown.

But the strong sexual themes of his music were not overlooked by his father, who by now was disappointed and angry with his son. The years of religious tutoring seemed wasted as Marvin flaunted his sexuality through his records, ignoring his father's rule that sex is only for procreation. The old family conflict was never far from the surface, but Marvin was far too independent, both financially and mentally, to spend any time dwelling on old wounds.

With his success in the record charts, Marvin was on top of the world and was soon to have more to celebrate – Janice was pregnant with his daughter. Nona Gaye arrived in September 1974 and was followed just 14 months later by a boy, Frankie. Anna Gaye had ignored Marvin's newly developed relationship for as long as she could, but news of Hunter's pregnancy triggered a change of heart and in 1975 Anna Gordy Gaye filed for divorce.

The divorce proceedings were long and bitter, with Marvin being as defiant as he could be. He would antagonize Anna at every opportunity, angry that she was seeking to extract what he considered to be too great a portion of his wealth. They finally reached a settlement in which Marvin had to record an album and give all the proceeds to Anna in lieu of alimony. Marvin devoted the next year to the *Here, My Dear* double album, which ended up being an ode to his soured relationship with Anna. Its ironic title, which contained cynical, personal statements clearly referencing their life together were so hurtful to Anna that she considered taking Marvin to court. In some of the lyrics he reflected on the breakdown of his 14-year marriage and of the joy of discovering his new love. In 1977 the couple were divorced, leaving the way clear for him to marry his young lover and the mother of his two children.

After an intensely sexual start to their relationship, things started to change with Marvin's now heavy use of cocaine. History started to repeat itself as the friction which his erratic behaviour caused inevitably triggered the domestic violence which became a new feature in the couple's life. At this stage in his career Gaye was singing romantic ballads, yet in contrast his private life was quite different and he now got his kicks out of degrading Janice. He had found a way to torment both himself and Janice, and in a bizarre twist he forced her into a number of affairs with other well-known singers, including Frankie Beverly, Rick James and Teddy Pendergrass. Still not yet 21 years of age she was used as a pawn to satisfy Marvin's degrading sexual and sadistic tendencies. Hunter was now caught in a catch-22 situation – she was unable to refuse Gaye's demands yet she knew that as a consequence of her actions he would become angry and then of course violent. He was using her to punish himself and would suffer the consequences of his own delinquent perversions. In a rare insight Marvin did share some rather intimate information with his mother regarding his kinky sex life, describing how his first wife Anna had taught him certain sexual tricks, using her body in a certain way, tricks which Marvin then taught Janice.

Marvin had entered another phase of his tormented life. Unhappy in love he continued to torment Hunter, and all the while, the spectre of his drug problem lingered like a dark black cloud. The rumours of his strange existence were perpetuated in the tabloids, no doubt one source being his estranged father.

Later, Hunter described the darker times which she and Marvin shared. She is reported to have recalled, "The dark side of life and the dark side of the mind really fascinated him; there was stuff that I can't even talk about, things that just went so deep, so dark and so bizarre . . .

Forbidden, dangerous, scary, off-the-wall ways of thinking and behaving."

Marvin was very chauvinistic and forbade Hunter from pursuing her own ambition of becoming a singer, saying to her, "I like to see women serve me and that's that." In Hunter's case, serving Marvin meant feeding his evil fantasies. He was completely obsessed with sex, an unstoppable womanizer and a chronic masturbator who watched and read endless pornography. Perhaps it was a psychological problem from his overly restricted childhood, but he was now kicking back, only twice as hard.

With all of the problems which surrounded him Marvin was now tiring of his second marriage; it appeared as though he felt too restricted by his young wife and craved the freedom of being a single man. With his record sales plummeting and tax demands needing to be met, Marvin was starting to drown in a sea of opposing pressures. His poor financial situation meant he needed to sell records and perform at concerts, yet his depression robbed him of the will to work. He was becoming increasingly unreliable and missed concert appearances, claiming ill health as the cause of his cancellations. As the pressure reached fever pitch, Marvin turned to his destructive crutch, drugs. The substances which were destroying his life were becoming the only things which could afford him the temporary pleasure and relief that he craved. Finally in a bid to try and save his marriage and get away from his troubles, Marvin fled the US mainland to Hawaii. Hunter visited him there on several occasions but found that the old wounds were still open – almost as soon as they were in each other's company the arguments would begin. Finally Hunter could take no more and left him and their children, moving in with one of Marvin's friends, Teddy Pendergrass.

When he eventually became bored with his life in Hawaii, he returned to the studio and cut another record, but with poor sales he was forced to withdraw the album. With the small amount of money the record created Marvin was unable to meet the fresh demands coming from the Internal Revenue Service. Desperate for space away from his pressures he fled to Europe where he planned to tour, hoping to re-establish his waning fan base. His concerts were very well received, spurring him to extend the tour, eventually heading to Belgium. It was while in Belgium that Marvin was besieged by demands from the IRS totalling $2 million in back taxes. Having been tracked down and backed into a corner he was forced to declare bankruptcy amid furious rows with Motown.

Gaye cut his ties with Motown and signed a fresh recording contract with CBS, for which they paid the princely sum of $2 million. This focused Marvin's attention and he made a valiant effort to impress CBS and get his career and life back on track.

CBS were not disappointed with their new protégé and in 1982 Marvin provided them with one of the best records of his career, "Sexual Healing". This became one of his best-known records which well received by his critics and was soon selling in volume all around the globe. He followed this with the album *Midnight Love* which was a great boost to Gaye's mental state and indeed CBS, who were very pleased with their new signing. With his career once more back on top, he went all out to fulfil his side of the deal, even agreeing to tour, the thing he least liked. A massive tour of the United States was organized to promote his new album, the result of which earned him two Grammies, eventually selling 1.5 million copies. He was now enjoying the success which he had been craving and it was the first top ten album he had recorded in over six years.

Once more his massive selling hit songs boosted his celebrity status and he found himself back in the press and back under pressure. But the strain of touring was revealing the cracks in his mental state and again he turned to drugs. His cocaine use had grown dramatically and he was now spending a small fortune on narcotics, simply to get him through the tour.

Unfortunately his increased drug use had its down-side – he was often bad mannered, late for rehearsals and was becoming increasingly paranoid that there was somebody out there, watching and following him. He started collecting a large number of weapons, including guns, even a small machine gun, and he took to wearing a bulletproof vest, removing it only when he was performing on stage. The tour itself was running fairly smoothly, but cracks began to surface, the management of the tour had not been good and it soon became obvious that they were heading for financial disaster. This was just too much for the emotionally weary Marvin, who was already convinced that his life was in danger – the strains caused by the failure of the tour had become too much for him to cope with, his recording skills deserted him and he sank to rock bottom. His depression had reached an all-time low – fuelled by his now chronic cocaine addiction he sought emotional support from the only person he could turn to – his mother.

This was to prove a fatal decision, one that would ultimately bring about the end of a legend – perhaps his paranoia had been a warning after all. Desperate and in need of support, Marvin moved home to be with his mother. The house in the Crenshaw district of Los Angeles was one which he had bought for his parents years before. He always made sure that his folks wanted for nothing – throughout his career he would always make sure that they had money, cars and clothes. His mother was immensely proud of her son and was thrilled that the family were able to live so well. His father, on the other hand, although happy to accept the charity from his son, wasn't grateful, expecting his son to pay him back for bringing him into the world.

The house was large and Marvin took up residence in one of the bedrooms. He was reacquainted with family life and enjoyed spending time with his brother Frankie and his wife, Irene, who lived in an apartment which was attached to the main house. Even though he was heavily into drugs he was able to start recharging his batteries and enjoyed a stable home for the first time in a long while. Able to relax, he took time to reassess his life and career. His mother was also recovering as she had recently undergone a serious operation and was able to spend time with her beloved son. Marvin Gay Sr was not at the house when Marvin arrived as he had returned to Washington DC for a few months in a bid to sell his original family home. Marvin was unhappy that his father had not thought it necessary to be with his wife during her recovery period after her operation, but took solace in the fact that he did not to have to face the old man, at least until he had managed to reorganize his life.

Marvin's career seemed to be on the verge of recovery, and it appeared that he was patching his life back together again, when his father returned in January 1983. The men clashed almost from the word go. Arguments erupted with both men throwing hurtful comments at the other. Marvin resented the fact that his mother had been left on her own by the man she had cared for all her life, at the one time when she could have really done with his support. Old family arguments soon surfaced but there were never any winners in their battles, they were just too alike to see the other's point of view. Alberta was often used as a reason to have yet another row, which inevitably became more and more violent, pushing Marvin's life further into the danger zone with each heated attack.

Marvin was still in deep depression and threatened on several occasions to take his own life, absolute torture to Alberta's ears. She would beg her son not to talk of such drastic actions; Gay Sr on the other hand simply kept his feelings to himself. The bitter clashes and resentments continued, during which the 70 year old and the 44 year old would often resort to violence to resolve their issues, leaving Alberta to dole out the tender loving care and bandages when necessary.

Escalating rows were just part of daily life, yet those around the house could see that there would come a point when everything would come to a head, although they could not have guesed what the end result would be.

The day of reckoning arrived on 1 April 1984, ironically April Fool's Day, the day before Marvin's 45th birthday. He and his mother were talking in his bedroom when his father yelled for his mother to come and find some lost paperwork. Of course this irritated Marvin and he told the old man that if he wished to speak to his mother he ought to at least come upstairs and do so in the same room. His father stormed upstairs to confront his son, barging into his bedroom to have his say. Marvin, annoyed at the intrusion, pushed him back into the hallway and a full-scale argument erupted, escalating into a fist fight. As the two men punched each other, Alberta fled the room, listening from downstairs to the all-too-familiar sounds of the two main men in her life locked in hand-to-hand combat. When the noises finally stopped, it was Gay Sr who appeared downstairs, heading for another room as if to calm down.

On his return he was carrying a gun, a .38 calibre pistol, and went back upstairs heading purposefully towards his son's bedroom. Before Marvin could talk him round the old man calmly shot him in the right side of the chest, the bullet perforating his right lung, heart, diaphragm, liver, stomach and kidney before coming to rest against his left flank. The shot caused terrible injuries and forced his son to the floor, blood oozing out of him. Even the most angry parent would have been snapped out of their anger at this point, seeing their son lying in a growing pool of blood, but not Marvin's father – he took a few steps closer and fired another shot at point-blank range. Without any emotion or apparent concern for his son, the old man simply turned and left the room, leaving Alberta distraught as she tried to comfort her dying son. Unable to comprehend the horror of what had just unfolded, Alberta cradled her son, hoping that he would somehow come round. When she realised that all hope was fading she rushed to Frankie's apartment to raise the alarm. With the ambulance summoned Alberta returned to sit with her beloved son, still praying that there was some hope for his survival. When the paramedics arrived they were met with a scene of panic and confusion with people trying to direct them to the gunshot victim – but they had been warned that there could still be a risk from the gunman and were reticent to move ahead until they were sure there wasn't any further danger. They knew that the gunman was Marvin's father and were therefore very surprised to find the man sitting on the front porch, calm as you like.

It was Alberta who gave the all clear to the paramedics when she found the gun and threw it outside. When they entered Marvin's bedroom the medics found him lying in his brother's arms, bleeding profusely. He was rushed to hospital, but having sustained massive injuries, was pronounced dead at a little after 1.00 p.m., just hours away from his 45th birthday. Marvin Gay Sr was arrested by the LAPD.

The police arrived marginally earlier than the media, immediately arresting Gay Sr for the murder of his son. He was quietly taken away for questioning. The popular star enjoyed a resurgence in his music as it suddenly seemed that every radio station wanted to play Marvin Gaye music again. The papers spoke of his tortured life, the great musical talent and the darker side of a family whose anger finally resulted in death. Gay Sr did not enjoy good press, and there were many who were prepared to comment on the harsh life endured by the Gay siblings. Yet this was a strange crime, with the man responsible for bringing one of soul's best-loved singers into the world being his killer. People could only speculate as to why.

Gay Sr was still in custody in the Los Angeles County men's prison when the funeral of his son took place. The autopsy on Marvin concluded that his death was caused by massive trauma occurring as a result of two gunshot wounds, but it also revealed the drug use which affected Marvin's life. Analysis of his system showed that he had indulged in both cocaine and angel dust in the hours before his murder – could this have contributed to the events which resulted in his death? Only those at the house and Gay Sr could shed light on what had really happened, and the police were keen to find out more.

Over 10,000 fans visited Marvin's house to pay homage to the musical soul-man who had entertained them over the decades. They queued for hours to take their turn and get a last glimpse of him in his open casket. He was dressed in one of the outfits he had worn on his last tour, a gold and white military style suit with an ermine wrap around his shoulders. His family, of course, were at the funeral, his mother taking time to kiss Marvin's cheek and say a last goodbye. Both of his ex-wives and their children were there also, despite the often violent lives they led with him. The congregation was led by the Chief Apostle of the House of God, Gay Sr's old church. Stevie Wonder sang at the distressing church service, and Smokey Robinson spoke, as did Dick Gregory. After the service, his body was cremated and his family scattered his ashes at sea.

Marvin Gay Sr was charged with the murder of his son, to which he pleaded not guilty, claiming that he had acted in self-defence after his son had attacked him. He apologized, saying, "If I could bring him back I would. I was afraid of him. I thought I was going to get hurt. I didn't know what was going to happen. I'm really sorry for everything that happened." He then claimed to have fired the gun without realizing that it was loaded. While awaiting trial Marvin Sr was given a full medical examination during which it was discovered that he had a number of bruises on his body; doctors also found a walnut-sized tumour in his pituitary gland at the base of his brain. There was no way of knowing how long it had been there, or if it affected his behaviour. He underwent surgery to have this removed and was reassessed, whereupon he was deemed competent to stand trial.

Gay Sr's legal team entered into a plea bargain with the prosecution – in exchange for his pleading guilty to the lesser charge of voluntary manslaughter with a gun, the prosecution would not pursue a full-blown murder charge. As Gay Sr was now 70 years of age, it appeared that no one had the heart to go for a life sentence, except those who loved Marvin's music and who believed the stories of Gay Sr's tyrannical parenting. The prosecution were also mindful of the bruises Gay Sr had upon his body and could not escape the fact that Marvin had endured a significant amount of drug intake in the run-up to the incident. The manslaughter with a gun charge was deemed by all concerned to be a satisfactory compromise. When the time came for Gay Sr to face the court on 2 October 1984, he entered a plea of no contest to the charge and the Judge delivered a sentence of five years probation. The Judge summed up with: "This is one of those terribly tragic cases in which a young life was snuffed out. But under the circumstances it seems to be agreed by everybody, including the very able and experienced investigating officers, that in this case, the young man who died tragically provoked the incident." Turning his attention back to Gay Sr, in addition to his sentence, he banned the elderly man from drinking or owning a gun.

In an interview from prison, while being held for his son's murder, Marvin Sr explained the killing to a reporter. "I pulled the trigger," he said. "The first one didn't seem to bother him. He put his hand up to his face, like he'd been hit with a pellet. Then I fired again. I was backing towards my room. I was going to go in there and lock the door. This time I heard him say 'Oh' and I saw him going down. I do know that I did fire the gun. I was just trying to keep him back off me. I want the world to know it wasn't presumptuous on my part." After his convoluted and wandering explanation as to how he killed his son, Gay Sr was asked a final question, as loaded as the gun which he had used. Did he love his son, to which he replied, "Let's say that I didn't dislike him."

Not everyone seemed as convinced as the courts that Gay Sr acted in self-defence. He had not been stopped from going downstairs to collect the gun and he fired a second shot, even after the first one had hit his son. One can only assume therefore that the second shot was intended to kill him. These and other arguments have all been discussed through the media over the years since his death, but justice through the courts had already been delivered.

The consensus seemed to be that as Marvin was so depressed and unstable after a lifetime of violence, abuse, failed relationships, financial instability and his terrible drug addiction, he was ready to give up the fight for life. He appears to have backed his father into a corner, belittling the proud old man, not adhering to his strict values and morals and returning to his home when he was clearly not welcome, at least to his father. Ironically it was Marvin himself who provided his father with the gun which eventually ended his life. Only a few months before his death he gave his father the unregistered .38 calibre Smith & Wesson, literally handing him the loaded gun and waiting for him to use it. Some did say at the time that he wanted to end his life, but just didn't have the guts to carry it out himself.

Alberta divorced her husband of 49 years and moved in with her daughter, but her luck was soon to run out – only three years later she died of bone cancer. Marvin's brother, Frankie Gaye – he also added a showbiz "e" – died in 2001 after suffering a heart attack. During his recording career he even covered some of the songs which Marvin had originally recorded. He wrote a book about his brother titled *Marvin Gaye, My Brother*, but he sadly died before it was published. Gay Sr lived until 1998 when he died in the Inglewood Retirement Home, California, aged 84.

Throughout his lifetime Marvin wrote and recorded more than 200 songs, 66 of them Billboard hits, including "Sexual Healing" which was nominated for "Best R&B Song" at the 1984 Grammy Awards. In 1987 Marvin was inducted into the Rock and Roll Hall of Fame. Later, in 1991, Marvin received a star on the Hollywood Walk of Fame – proof that despite his troubled private life, his unique singing abilities, writing skills and versatility throughout his three decades of entertaining, the public really did love and appreciate his talents. He produced brilliant music and he will be forever remembered as one of the greats.

Whether justice was fairly dispensed is a matter of great debate – to take a life which you helped create is a poor defence, yet in this instance no one wanted to examine the details of what really happened. In musical terms, Marvin Gaye has earned his place in the history books; in celebrity murder terms, his father secured his position too.

The Death of a Goddess

Marilyn Monroe

During late Saturday night and early Sunday morning between 4 and 5 August 1962, most of Hollywood was either asleep or making plans to get there. Little were they to know that by the time a new day had dawned, the end of an era would have come about while they had slept. A woman who was adored over the world for her wit, talent and especially her beauty – a true goddess – would be pronounced dead. The icon, Marilyn Monroe – formerly Norma Jean Baker – had died at the age of 36, leaving the world to mourn her and the police to try and unravel the mystery of her death.

On the day of her death Marilyn had received a package from her (at that time) suspected lover Robert Kennedy, the then Attorney General. It contained a soft toy – a furry tiger – and possibly an accompanying note, which seemed to have upset her. She sat on a lounger beside her outdoor swimming pool on that hot early August day and pondered about the message she had just received. She had also learned that Robert would not be attending a get-together at their mutual friends' – Pat (née Kennedy), sister of the President, and Peter Lawford.

It was becoming clear to Marilyn that Robert was making attempts to stop their relationship, possibly at his wife Ethel's request. He had not returned her calls that week and some considered that the gift of the toy tiger could have been a message that it was over. Obviously Marilyn was upset about being ditched by him, and had seemingly threatened to go public on the Monday and hold a press conference if Robert did not contact her to straighten matters out.

She had spent the day contacting her close circle of friends and confidants. She had spoken with a good friend of hers, Jeanne Carmen, to try and arrange a night out with her, but Jeanne had already made plans as it was her birthday. The last time Marilyn spoke with Jeanne was around 10 p.m. Another person who she now relied on quite heavily was her psychiatrist, Dr Greenson; she telephoned him early in the day and he came out to visit her at some point during the afternoon. This was not unusual, as he saw her most days. He arrived at her house at around 6.30 p.m. and recalled that she was rather groggy and seemed somewhat depressed. She had wanted to take a walk on the pier at Santa Monica, and the doctor recommended that she have plenty of fluids before going out. He suggested to her housekeeper Eunice Murray that it might be advisable that she stay the night with Marilyn, which Eunice had done on many previous occasions. The doctor bade them farewell after around a 45-minute stay, as he was on his way to a dinner appointment. He was to hear from Marilyn once more before her death; she called him at around 7.40, when he was preparing to get ready for his night out. He was pleased to hear that Marilyn was sounding much brighter and less slurred. He suggested that she should get a good night's sleep and that he would see her the following day. The next time he was to see Marilyn, she would be dead, but what happened between his last telephone conversation with her and finding her dead is very hazy to say the least.

Marilyn talked with Eunice and decided not to go out to the beach after all; instead she chose to listen to music and call some friends. Eunice Murray said that at around 8 p.m. was the last time she saw Marilyn alive: in her bedroom listening to Frank Sinatra. Eunice said that at around 10 p.m. she passed by Marilyn's room and saw a light shining under her door, but decided not to disturb her.

At around midnight Eunice woke up to use the bathroom; on passing Marilyn's door again she noticed that the light was still on. She decided that she should check on Marilyn and called her, but didn't get a reply. She knocked on the door and still didn't manage to rouse Marilyn. When she tried to open the door, she realized that it was locked.

It was then that she decided she needed help and the first person she called was Dr Greenson. He arrived and also tried to gain access to Marilyn's room but was unable to get in. Eunice then suggested that they might be able to get in through the French doors from outside. Dr Greenson went outside and tried the door, but found it locked. He looked in and saw a lifeless Marilyn lying on the bed. Realizing that he needed to get to her quickly, he smashed the glass and entered the room. He found Marilyn lying face down on the bed, bare-shouldered and with the telephone handset clasped firmly in her hand; presumably she was trying to make a telephone call when she was dying.

Dr Greenson then opened Marilyn's bedroom door and informed Eunice that Marilyn was dead, before calling Dr Engelberg to come and formally pronounce her dead.

During the evening Marilyn made and received various telephone calls. One was from her friend Henry Rosenfeld, at some time between 8 and 9 p.m. He said that Marilyn answered her own telephone and his conversation with her was not unusual; although she sounded groggy, he wasn't unduly concerned. Later in the evening she called Sidney Guilaroff, her hairdresser, probably to arrange an appointment with him – not what you would expect from somebody planning their imminent suicide. Later still, at some time between nine-thirty and 10 p.m., Marilyn received a call from her former lover, José Bolaños; he had a brief conversation with her but was not alarmed or concerned by their brief discussion.

Possibly her final call of the evening was to her friend Jeanne Carmen, to ask her again to come and visit; but by now it was after 10 p.m. and Jeanne declined the invitation, saying that she would call her back the following day.

On reading these "facts" it would be easy to conclude that Marilyn had died due to a suicide bid, whether intentional or accidental. This was the initial finding of the investigation team which had been appointed by the corner, Dr Theodore Curphey. After the initial investigation, it was rebadged "probable suicide". The problem was that the "facts" continued to change and contradict one another, depending on who was being asked to provide details of the order of that evening's events.

The carpet in Marilyn's bedroom had recently been replaced with a very luxurious thick pile, so thick that there could have been no chance that any light could pass underneath it. Therefore it would have been practically impossible for Eunice to have seen that there was a light on in the bedroom. The windows were reported to have been fitted with blackout blinds, therefore Dr Greenson couldn't have seen the lifeless body of Marilyn lying face-down on her bed. But also there were reports that in fact the French doors had been left ajar to let air circulate, owing to the high temperatures in early August.

By the time that the police were eventually called to Marilyn's home, she had been dead for some time – possibly a number of hours. By the time the undertaker, Guy Hockett, arrived to remove her body, she was quite rigid with the effects of rigor mortis; he noted that it was difficult to straighten her body out sufficiently to get it on to the gurney to remove it. It would appear that by this stage she could have well been dead for around seven hours. This would mean that she had died not long after her last telephone conversation, which was at around 10.30 p.m. She was then taken under the cover of a blue blanket to the county morgue in the Los Angeles Hall of Justice.

The timing of events was to prove difficult to tie down, as Mrs Murray was rather confused when giving her description of the events. At one point she said that after noticing that Marilyn was still awake at around midnight, she didn't call the doctor immediately, but instead went back to bed and fell asleep until around 3.30 a.m., when she then called for the doctor.

It was noted by Los Angeles police Sergeant Jack Clemmons that the room was extremely tidy, and that Marilyn's bed appeared to have fresh linen on it. Mrs Murray had indeed been laundering bedlinen before the police arrived, though she doesn't appear to have offered a sufficient explanation for this late-night laundry session. On Marilyn's bedside table there were, among other things, several bottles of tablets, apparently used in her suicide bid: but there was no drinking vessel at hand. How could she have taken a large number of pills with no means of using any water, or anything else, to assist her in swallowing them? When questioned, her friends confirmed that she had difficulty in swallowing tablets, even with the aid of a drink.

Strangely, when pathologist Dr Thomas Nohuchi performed an examination of the contents of Marilyn's stomach, he could not find any trace of the Nembutal capsules (a barbiturate sedative), of which Marilyn was believed to have swallowed in excess of 40. Nor could he locate any of the contents of these capsules, namely the drug itself. He concluded that he could not locate any barbiturates in her stomach, nor could he find any of the tell-tale yellow colouring which is associated with Nembutal use.

Toxicology reports were to prove more successful in locating drugs in Marilyn's system. Expert Ralph Abernathy managed to find high doses of barbiturates in Marilyn's bloodstream; so high was the concentration that the amount she'd taken had been enough to have killed several people. The amount of Nembutal found in her body was around ten times the prescribed normal therapeutic dose, and the chloral hydrate levels were twenty times the usual recommended dose. Either of the doses were high enough to kill her, but both taken together was considered a massive overdose. The precise readings he recorded were four and a half milligrams percent of barbiturates and eight milligrams percent of chloral hydrate (a strong sedative, often used as a treatment for sleeplessness).

Incidentally her blood was also tested for the presence of alcohol, and this gave a negative result – so on her last night alive, Marilyn didn't enjoy her favourite tipple, champagne. Her liver was also examined and it was found to contain 13 milligrams percent of barbiturates. Unfortunately, with the autopsy not being a full one, there were many organs which were not examined and indeed some of her organs were destroyed. Strangely all the medical photographs and slides produced from her specimens were lost, and this impeded any further investigations into the cause of her death.

The problem was deciding how Marilyn had managed to take such high doses of strong drugs without there being any trace of them in her stomach. If they had all been taken at once, there would definitely have been some residues of the gelatine capsules left behind for the pathologist to find. It may have been that she had taken the drugs over the course of the day or even the evening; but the high doses would have prevented this from occurring, as she would have been too overcome by the effects of the drugs to consume them over any sustained period of time.

The next most obvious method of taking such a high strength dose of drugs would be to have taken them intravenously, but after a detailed examination of Marilyn's skin with a magnifying glass, neither Dr Noguchi nor his assistant John Miner were able to find any evidence of the puncture wounds associated with intravenous drug use. As the intravenous method of administration was discounted, it left toxicologists to come up with other suggestions as to how Marilyn may have overdosed. The methods put forward were that they could have been introduced into her body by way of an enema or a suppository, but after investigating these possibilities it was thought highly unlikely that this was how she received the drugs. The corner reluctantly came to the conclusion that Marilyn had acute barbiturate poisoning due to ingestion of an overdose: she must have swallowed the tablets, but this was by no means a satisfactory conclusion.

It was not just the unusual or even unexplained method of the drugs being introduced into Marilyn's system but also the unaccountable time lags in between the events of the evening.

What happened between Marilyn's last telephone conversation and the following morning, when her body was removed from her home? Was her previous relationship with John F. Kennedy and subsequent affair with his brother Robert her downfall? She had threatened to hold a press conference, and this could well have been extremely embarrassing – not only for the famous brothers, but also for their families and friends. There is a very fuzzy picture of events which could implicate the Kennedys; they were definitely sufficiently concerned with her recent mental instability to feel that she might well make life very difficult for them. They stood to lose everything: their jobs and possibly their marriages could be in jeopardy.

Another theory was that this was punishment of the Kennedys, carried out for the Mob, because of Robert's fight against organized crime. It could be that Marilyn's death was a warning to the Kennedys that the Mob meant business, and by murdering the most famous Hollywood star – and their former love interest – the Mob proved their point, quite shockingly.

By the morning of Sunday, 5 August, the press had already been tipped off about Marilyn's death and were starting to congregate outside the front of her home. They were not welcomed by the police, and totally unwanted by the friends of the star who were calling round to her home for reassurance, as they were totally shocked by the rumours of her death. They needed to visit her to put their minds at rest, but on arriving they were goaded by the press, eager to have something to report which would gain an edge on their competition. Pat Newcomb was one such friend who had called at the star's home; she was kindly greeted by the press pack, to whom she gave something to report by calling, "Keep shooting, vultures."

Peter and Pat Lawford were described as being totally shocked and devastated to hear of the death of their mutual friend. Peter, being one of the last people to speak to Marilyn, was overcome with grief. The couple took the opportunity to get away from the whole sorry affair and they decided to take a break away from prying eyes. So too did Mrs Murray; she was surprisingly allowed to go to Europe, considering that she was one of the key witnesses in the police investigation. After police had questioned Mrs Murray they reported that she appeared quite evasive and extremely vague in her recollection of the events leading up to the police's arrival at Marilyn's home on the morning of Marilyn's death. Why then was she not questioned further and cross-examined, to enable her to give a satisfactory picture of what had happened? And more especially how was she able to leave the country while the investigation was still underway? Some felt that she had been scripted and had rehearsed the responses that she would offer when being questioned; the only problem was that she was unable to keep to the prearranged script and would get confused between true facts and the version of events which had been offered to her.

When Dr Greenson was questioned by Deputy District Attorney John Miner, three days after Marilyn's death, he was reported to have aired his opinion that she had in fact been the victim of a murder. Because of doctor–patient confidentiality, his interview was never made public, although this did not stop the press from speculating heavily on what they thought had transpired.

One key witness, Walter Schaefer, who was working for the ambulance service which was called out to Marilyn's home on the morning of her death, claimed that an ambulance was sent out at around 1.00 a.m. and that she was taken to Santa Monica Hospital. He also implied that she was accompanied by Peter Lawford, and that it was he that made the decision to have her body taken back to her home, when it was clear that she was dead. Although Peter never admitted to being at her property on the evening of her death, it was thought that he had even gone to the trouble of tidying up her bedroom before the police were called. Nobody will ever really know what he was tidying away, and whether he removed any incriminating evidence that could have embarrassed his brother-in-law, Robert Kennedy. He may well have come across notes from the Attorney General; possibly there was one with the toy tiger which she had received on 4 August. Peter was not formally questioned by the police until several years after Marilyn's death, and is no longer able to tell his version of events as he passed away in 1984.

Some people believed that Robert Kennedy visited Marilyn on the evening of her death, although he was staying with his wife Ethel at the home of their friends, the Bateses, in San Francisco. Kennedy was believed to be at the ranch until 10 p.m. that night and attended church the following morning a little after 9.30 a.m. so if he did leave to visit

Marilyn he must have made the 60-mile journey during the night. He may well have wanted to clear the air with her and let her know that it wasn't his decision to end the affair, but that of his wife. If she threatened to divorce him, it would end Robert's career and possibly also that of his brother. He may well have wanted to talk her out of going public and holding her threatened press conference, and to explain the gift that she had received earlier in the day. He would have been keen to collect from her any incriminating evidence which she owned – it was highly likely that they had exchanged notes and gifts. More importantly, Marilyn was renowned for keeping a diary, and it may well have been this that Robert was keen to take from her.

It is virtually impossible to guess whether or not he did indeed have one final meeting with his former lover, as Robert too is dead. He was assassinated in June 1968; struck by a gunshot wound to the head in the Ambassador Hotel in Los Angeles. He had just given a speech after winning the California primary election for his campaign for the Democratic presidential nomination. His assassin was named as Sirhan Bishara Sirhan, a Jordanian Arab.

It was believed that after Bobby had left Marilyn, she rang her good friend Peter Lawford for a shoulder to cry on and even talked of taking her life, but Peter must not have considered her to be serious, as he didn't think it necessary to make the journey to visit her. He probably put it down to a cry for attention.

To add even more confusion to the debate, it was heavily suggested that Marilyn's home was being bugged. One theory was that she was being watched by the Mafia, namely by Jimmy Hoffa. He would have gained much if he could collect information from Marilyn, which he could then use to bribe the Attorney General. Another group who could well have been interested in the goings-on of the lover of the Kennedy brothers was the CIA, who may well have considered her a security risk. Lastly was the Federal Bureau of Investigation – the FBI. John Edgar Hoover was just as keen as the next to keep abreast of any situation involving the Kennedys and indeed the Mafia.

It is anybody's guess who would have ordered the termination of Marilyn Monroe, or indeed if anybody did: but owing to the fact that Mrs Murray lived, not necessarily to tell the tale, she must not have been aware of all the facts of the evening. She was obviously well cautioned as to what the implications would be if she ever gave too much away, and she never did give a satisfactory account of her employer's death. It is suspected that she came across Marilyn in a terrible state and then decided to call her close friend Peter Lawford, which was why he was involved in getting Marilyn to hospital – although, with her dying shortly afterwards, Lawford was desperate to get her back home. He was worried that her suspicious death might have bad implications for his brother-in-law and obviously wanted her to be "discovered" serenely in her own bed, after dying in her sleep. He might well have wanted extra time to get his story straight before having to call the police. In the end, he must have decided to leave the scene, after removing private documents in order to protect his friend. He left Mrs Murray to wash Marilyn's nightclothes and bedlinen; possibly if she had been given an overdose by way of an enema, her nightware and sheets might have been soiled.

The scene was then left for the police to pick through, which they did, but they came to unsatisfactory conclusions. The press were not missing the point and wanted answers for readers.

When Marilyn died, she was one of the most famous women who had ever lived but she had been brought into the world in totally unexceptional circumstances. She had been born to single parent Gladys Baker on 1 June 1926 in Los Angeles General Hospital. Her father was listed on her birth certificate as Edward Mortenson, although Marilyn never knew him and was never sure if he was her father or not. Gladys had apparently been married to a Martin E. Mortenson a couple of years before Marilyn's birth, but it was thought that this Norwegian baker had died in 1929 in a motor accident. However, this information cannot be confirmed as definite.

Gladys suffered throughout her life with mental health

problems and, as she was unmarried at the time of her daughter's birth, the baby was taken into foster care. She was placed with Mr Albert and Mrs Ida Bolender and lived with them until she was seven years old. She had a strict early upbringing, as the Bolenders were quite religious, and Marilyn later recalled that they brought her up quite austerely.

By the time Marilyn had reached her seventh birthday, her mother was coping well and was able to take up full-time responsibility for her daughter. Sadly this was short-lived and soon Gladys was readmitted to a mental hospital for treatment in Santa Monica, after a seemingly vicious attack on one of her friends. Marilyn spent the remainder of her childhood between various foster homes. She spent over a year living in the Los Angeles Orphans' Home, returned to foster care and then was appointed to legal guardian, Grace McKee. Marilyn lived happily with Grace for around four years, until Grace had the offer of marriage and moved away. Not really wanting to take her teenage charge with her, Grace took on the role of matchmaker and encouraged the 16-year-old Marilyn to marry one of her neighbour's sons, 21-year-old Jim Dougherty.

After a whirlwind "romance" the two were married on 19 June 1942. Marilyn later admitted that Grace had arranged the marriage and that she felt that she had no choice but to marry Jim. But the pair were not together long before Jim joined the Merchant Marines and was soon sent overseas. He left Marilyn behind and she found work at a local factory called Radio Plane, where she had the job of inspecting parachutes. Marilyn managed to have the odd weekend with her husband when he was on leave. It was while she was at work that she caught the attention of an army photographer, Private David Conover. He had visited the factory to take pictures of attractive girls to send on to the troops to help boost morale.

Conover didn't take long to realize that Marilyn was special, and after photographing her on the assembly lines, in her overalls, he asked her if she would like to earn extra money as his model.

Her modelling success was speedy and she found herself

on the cover of various magazines; her job in the factory was quickly left behind. She found herself on a number of modelling assignments and thoroughly enjoyed the experience. When Jim came back from the Pacific for his leave, the pair had little in common. The marriage was doomed and ended in late 1946.

Marilyn had already signed a contract with Twentieth-Century Fox Studios, and had changed her name to Marilyn Monroe. Monroe was her mother's family name – her grandmother was Della Monroe, who died at the age of 51 in an asylum. Her grandfather, Otis, also died in an institution with a form of insanity.

Marilyn's acting career was underway and she went on to star in over 20 movies; she was to become a household name and a massive Hollywood star. Her early roles were, as you would imagine, small bit parts, but the young actress would dominate the screen whenever she walked on and was soon to take the starring role.

In 1952 she met her next husband, Joe DiMaggio, who had recently retired from baseball. He was 12 years older than the 25-year-old actress, but this was not to stop the pair from forming a close relationship. After Marilyn had finished filming *Monkey Business*, she flew straight to New York to spend time with him.

It wasn't long before Marilyn was back on location, this time to film the brilliant *Niagara*, which was renowned for its amazing scenes and of course its beautiful blonde star.

There were rumours that, while Marilyn was filming *Niagara*, she rekindled an old friendship with Robert Slatzer, a writer and reporter. No firm evidence exists, but Slatzer claimed that he and Marilyn crossed the Mexican border and were married on 4 October 1952. If this is true, all records were quickly destroyed, as the famously jealous Joe DiMaggio wasted no time in confronting the pair and the whole thing was hushed up. This was also to the relief of the studio bosses, who were not keen for their most famous star to be dragged through the gutter press.

At the end of the year Marilyn was back on set. This time she was starring alongside Jane Russell in *Gentlemen Prefer*

Blondes. The two became good friends, and in the summer of the following year they were invited to Hollywood Boulevard where they made imprints of their hands and feet and signed them; the imprints were left to dry and were displayed on the sidewalk.

Joe and Marilyn finally tied the knot on 14 January 1954 at the City Hall, San Francisco. The marriage was presided over by Judge Charles Perry. There were no friends or members of Marilyn's family present at the ceremony; the only guests were the witnesses, Frank "Lefty" O'Doul, one of Joe's old friends from his baseball days, and Reno Barsochinni, Joe's best man and friend. If Joe was hoping for a quiet wedding, he was to be disappointed as Marilyn spent her last couple minutes of singledom calling her media contacts, to enable them to spread the word that she was about to become Mrs DiMaggio. Joe presented Marilyn with a beautiful diamond-encrusted wedding ring, and the couple were declared man and wife. Marilyn signed the register as Norma Jeane Mortenson Dougherty.

By the time the couple emerged from the City Hall as Mr and Mrs DiMaggio, they were greeted by a crowd of hundreds, all wanting the first photograph of the happy couple. After a few short interviews, the pair left for their honeymoon and were not seen for two weeks – quite a feat for Marilyn.

The couple appeared to have different ideas of what married life would entail. Marilyn was hoping to continue with her acting career, but with the stability and protection offered by her new husband. Joe, on the other hand, was looking for a wife to be his partner and his other half; he was expecting Marilyn to tail off her acting work and spend more time with him.

He was soon to be put straight. When they visited Japan for an extension to their honeymoon, they were mobbed, and he was soon aware that whether he liked it or not Marilyn was going to carry on being a hot commodity. This was to cause a great strain between the newly married pair and was a constant cause of arguments. Joe was intensely upset when Marilyn performed before several thousand American troops in Korea. She sang several songs, including *Diamonds Are a Girl's Best Friend*, and the audience went wild. She thoroughly enjoyed the experience of being adored by so many, much to the irritation of her new husband.

At the end of May, Marilyn began filming *There's No Business Like Show Business*, but her performance was constantly interrupted by her medical problems. She was poorly throughout the summer with anaemia and bronchitis. Some put this down to her chronic use of sleeping pills, and she was described as being very tearful and lethargic as well as having difficulty in remembering her lines.

By mid-September she was well enough to be photographed while promoting her recently completed movie *The Seven Year Itch*. Outside the Trans-Lux Theater in New York City, in the early hours of the morning, with an astonishing over 2-000-strong audience of camera crews, media reporters and fans, she performed her world-famous "skirt blowing" scene. To her credit, the shoot was a total success. The triumphant Marilyn didn't ignore her fans and stayed for several hours to pose for photographs and sign autographs.

None of this publicity went down well with her husband, and the marriage was well and truly on the rocks. By October the marriage was declared over and the couple were soon divorced.

Within a year, Marilyn was involved in another romance which was to lead to marriage. Her new beau was Arthur Miller. Again an older man, he was just what Marilyn needed to get her life on track. He was much quieter then her previous husband and was a steadying influence on her. Some would say that this was an unusual match, but the mix of the intellectual playwright and the blonde bombshell somehow seemed to work.

In February, Marilyn returned to Hollywood to shoot her role in the movie *Bus Stop*. As soon as filming was completed, she returned to Miller in New York and they were married on 29 June 1956. Amazingly they were together for over four and a half years. When Marilyn wasn't away shooting a movie, the couple lived in either their farm in

Connecticut or their apartment in New York on East 57th Street.

When *Bus Stop* was released, Marilyn was highly praised for her comic talent, her sense of timing and brilliantly conceived sensitivity. She was triumphant, but also exhausted and was ready for a break.

The couple rented a house at Long Island, where they spent weeks relaxing and Miller was able to complete his play *The Misfits*. Five years later, this play would be turned into a screenplay, the last movie that Marilyn would make. This holiday was described by Marilyn as one of the happiest times of her life. The couple were able to chill out and, in relative anonymity, spent time together like any other married couple, but this bliss was short-lived as Marilyn became pregnant. Initially, the couple were elated – until they discovered that the pregnancy was ectopic and had to be removed surgically. Marilyn was distraught, and suffered from chronic insomnia, seeking solace in sleeping tablets. This could have been the turning point for Marilyn, who now appeared to be on a downward spiral.

By 1958, she was back in Hollywood, filming *Some Like It Hot* with Tony Curtis and Jack Lemmon. Due to her deteriorating health, she was invariably late arriving on set. She also had difficulty in remembering her lines, and her marriage was starting to show cracks. Like the true star that she was, Marilyn managed to pull the cat out of the bag and came up with the goods; again the film was a hit.

By 1960 Marilyn was seeing Dr Greenson on a regular basis. He frequently prescribed her tranquillizers and barbiturates. She was about to embark on filming *The Misfits*, but due to her poor health she was once again irritating her fellow actors. She was to keep her leading man, Clark Gable, waiting around on set for hours. She was constantly late on set, and was still unable to remember her lines – if indeed she had tried to learn them in the first place.

Miller was also on location, but by now they were hardly speaking and were living in separate quarters. By 4 November, thankfully, the filming was completed and everybody breathed a sigh of relief. Despite numerous problems during the shooting, they had managed to produce another success. Unfortunately, the following day Clark Gable suffered a heart attack and died on 16 November. Marilyn blamed herself; she thought the stress she had put him under had contributed to his condition. This then pushed her deeper into despair.

By January 1961 the Millers divorced, and Marilyn took a house in the Brentwood area of Los Angeles. She hired a housekeeper, Mrs Eunice Murray.

By the end of the year, Marilyn was having an affair with the President and joined in his birthday celebrations the following year. She was asked to sing for him at the President's gala birthday celebration in Madison Square Gardens on 19 May 1962. Marilyn glittered in her sequinned dress, which had been designed for her by eminent designer Jean-Louis; it had cost around $5,000. She wore absolutely nothing underneath it and had to be sewn into it just before she went on stage. She performed her own rendition of the Happy Birthday song, which was broadcast the world over and is one of the most famous film clips featuring her. She was by now famously late, and gave a "breathy" tribute to the President – who was not accompanied by his wife, but was with his brother Bobby and Bobby's wife Ethel.

Shortly after the celebrations for the President's birthday, Marilyn returned to Hollywood to resume the filming of her uncompleted last movie, *Something's Got to Give*. She was struggling with the schedule, but managed to create a scandal by removing all of her clothes for a skinny-dipping scene. The shots taken by the closed set were soon worth a fortune. They were bought by Hugh Hefner for a reported $25,000 and immediately featured in *Playboy*.

Marilyn had now resumed her relationship with Joe Di-Maggio, and it was believed that the two were to remarry on 8 August 1962. This was despite the fact that she was believed to be having an affair with the Attorney General, Bobby Kennedy.

Filming was not going well and Marilyn's inability to show up and lack of script rehearsals infuriated production crew. She was told to quit the film and get herself in shape. By

1 August she had managed to negotiate the situation and was rehired with a fantastic salary increase of two and half times the original amount agreed. This was to prove immaterial as, of course, she would die four days later.

The funeral was arranged by her fiancé, Joe DiMaggio. He went to great lengths to keep it a small family gathering, insisting that only her closest friends were invited outside her family. He continued to have flowers placed beside her grave for 20 years after her death, as he had promised her when she told him of the pledge made by William Powell to Jean Harlow when she was dying.

The IRA Bomb

Earl Louis Mountbatten

It is only recently that the people of the United Kingdom and Ireland have to some extent begun to believe that the troubles they have lived through for so many decades, characterized by terrorist bombings and reprisal killings, may finally be drawing to a close. For many years, particularly the 1960s, 1970s and 1980s, the newspapers and television news programmes were dominated by the activities of the paramilitary group, the Provisional IRA and their Loyalist counterparts on the other side. Daily reports of individual murders were punctuated with bomb blasts that killed and maimed members of both the Protestant and Catholic communities. The British Army were there to help keep the peace and to curtail the activities of the warring parties, however, as news reports readily display, they were often the target of discreetly placed bombs, detonated remotely as the targets passed by and often with devastating effect.

To many British people living on the mainland, the historical reasons for the unrest were probably long forgotten; it was for most just a feature of the daily news. There seemed no end in sight for the troubles, just a perpetual tit-for-tat series of attacks on people you didn't know. For those reading or watching the news each day a degree of acclimatization occurred, making people more shock-proof to the news they heard. The quest for Ireland's independence from the UK and for it to be reunited as a single country, however, was a goal for which the IRA were prepared to fight, and across the decades they planned and carried out increasingly horrific attacks.

The activities of the terrorists were mainly aimed at killing each other and in the case of the IRA, the British Army as well, so that to some extent these were the news items which seemed regular events, the "norm" in a country used to hearing daily acts of terrorism. The IRA's ability to shock re-emerged with a vengeance on the morning of 27 August 1979.

Lord Louis Mountbatten had for many years spent an August vacation at Classiebawn Castle, his remote family dwelling in County Sligo on Ireland's rugged north-west coast. Although only a few miles from the Northern Ireland border Mountbatten never used the services of a bodyguard, not wanting the tranquillity of his summer break ruined by the constant awareness campaign which would accompany any manned security measure. The close proximity of the Northern Ireland border was only one issue which should have been noted; the area was also a well known haunt of IRA activists, a safe haven away from the more notorious trouble zones of Belfast and its surrounding towns and cities, where weapons could be hidden and meetings could take place away from ever-prying eyes.

Mountbatten was now 79 years of age and had no formal public duties which would keep him in the public eye. He was nevertheless a senior citizen of the extended royal family, being the uncle of Prince Philip (husband to the Queen of England) and a man who had played a large role in the rearing of Prince Charles, the future King of England. A blow struck against him would also strike a blow against the royal family.

But Mountbatten had made his decision – he would not be held captive by security constraints, not even while in Ireland. He believed his quiet comings and goings on the west coast would go unnoticed, whereas with a security force in place he might draw more attention to himself and his party. This had worked for over 30 years, across a time period when both sides of the Irish question had been active in pursuit of violence. Why should his holiday in this particular year be any different? Besides, the local constabulary kept a low-profile eye on the castle when he was in residence.

However, Mountbatten's annual occupation of Classiebawn Castle had not gone unnoticed and the IRA were now intent on planning an attack which would focus the attention of the entire world on Ireland, and in particular the placid waters of Donegal Bay and Warrenpoint, close to the border with the Irish Republic.

In line with Mountbatten's desire to live a security free existence, all aspects of his stay in Ireland went unchecked, including his 25-foot boat, *Shadow V*, which rocked gently on its mooring in the tiny harbour of Mullaghmore, a small fishing village not far from Mountbatten's residence.

Before sunrise on the morning of 27 August 1979, a dark figure approached the harbour, his associate keeping watch from a safe distance. The man moved stealthily along the front searching for *Shadow V*, which stood out nicely amongst the older fishing boats used by the local fishermen. Without guard and tethered to a small jetty, the man strode along the jetty and jumped onto the boat's deck. He was not familiar with the boat's layout, but he did not need to be; he placed a small package where it wouldn't be noticed, wrapped innocently as it was and returned quickly to the car he had arrived in. The stealthy part of his plan was now complete; the balance of it was simply a matter of waiting and staying close by, but out of view. He parked the car overlooking Donegal Bay and closed his eyes, waiting for the sun to come up.

Mountbatten liked to rise early and on this particular sunny day he was keen to be up and off. He was planning a leisurely fishing trip out in Donegal Bay. He was particularly looking forward to this trip as he would be able to enjoy the company of his 14-year-old twin grandsons, Nicholas and Timothy Knatchbull. After breakfast Mountbatten headed for the harbour with those who were to join him on the fishing trip. In addition to himself and his two grandsons he was accompanied by his daughter, Lady Patricia Brabourne, and her husband Lord Brabourne, his mother, the Dowager Lady Brabourne, aged 82, and a local boy, Paul Maxwell, who would act as a crew member for the day.

Arriving at the harbour at around 11 a.m., Mountbatten's

party passed pleasantries with a number of the locals while they readied themselves for the trip. Mountbatten, dressed in faded green corduroys and a pullover, was a popular man in the village and could often be seen, knee deep in water fishing for shrimp in the bay. He had over the years managed to cultivate a bit of a "folksy" image and would often take local children out on his boat. The assembled group climbed aboard *Shadow V*, and loaded their fishing supplies and lunch boxes while Mountbatten started the motor. It didn't take long before everything was in place and Mountbatten gave the order to Paul Maxwell to untie the boat.

A short distance away, the activities on Mountbatten's boat had drawn the attention of the man in the car. He sat bolt upright, watching the activity on deck, concerned for them to make progress but also that they should not discover the package which had been discreetly hidden on board.

After a short delay *Shadow V* slowly manoeuvred away from the jetty and gently turned towards the open sea, forcing a small bow wave to disturb the otherwise glassy calm of the waters.

In the car, the man who watched them departing with great concentration reached across to the passenger seat and picked up a small device about the size of a transistor radio. He flicked a switch and a small red light glowed to show that the unit was now live; his fingers hovered over the only other button. As he watched *Shadow V* move further away from the shore he allowed his finger to depress the button that would bring disaster to the local community of Mullaghmore – the time, 11.30 a.m. BST.

A second after the remote control detonator button was pressed, a massive explosion ripped through *Shadow V*, completely obliterating the boat and blasting pieces of it high into the sky. Those on shore heard the deafening sound of the 50lb bomb exploding and turned to see the remnants of *Shadow V* falling from the sky; the craft had literally been blown to pieces and now lay strewn across the surface of Donegal Bay.

Other fishermen, who were on the water at the time and quite close by, brought their boats amongst the wreckage looking for survivors. Amazingly they were able to find some of the passengers in the water. Mountbatten himself was dragged aboard one boat, but he had sustained enormous injury, his legs were practically severed and his blood loss was huge. He died shortly after being pulled from the water. Two Belfast-based doctors who were themselves on holiday rapidly made a makeshift first-aid station at the harbour side, using a couple of old doors as stretchers, broom handles for splints and ripped sheets for bandages, while they waited for the emergency services to arrive and transfer the injured to Sligo General Hospital. Sadly though, the bomb had claimed other victims beyond Lord Mountbatten – his grandson Nicholas died at the scene as did Paul Maxwell. The other passengers were found badly injured but alive and were transferred to hospital where they received treatment. Lady Brabourne was one of those who made it to hospital, but she died the following day, having sustained terrible injuries. A member of the local Garda police force accompanied the victims and survivors to the hospital in Sligo and was devastated by what he saw. Detective Garda Eddie MacHale said, "I will never forget looking at the body of Paul Maxwell in the ambulance. There are some things that never leave you and I will never forget what I saw in the ambulance and later at the morgue. The lad was sitting on the engine and didn't have a chance. I was there as a policeman trying to be professional but what I saw would take tears from a stone."

As chaos erupted at the harbour side, few noticed the car with the stranger at the wheel pulling away from the scene and heading back to the border.

The police immediately put out alerts to all police officers operating in the area; they were familiar with the operating style of the IRA. They knew that more than likely the bomb had been exploded remotely and therefore the perpetrator was likely to be in the area and would probably be heading for the border. At the scene, the police saw pure carnage; there was little anyone would be able to do out on the water so emphasis was placed on taking statements and trying to determine if witnesses had seen anyone who might have been hanging around at the time of the explosion.

Within minutes the media had become aware of the story and they broke the news globally. If other events had left the nation unmoved, this particular attack proved to be momentous. The perpetrators had managed to murder several members of the broader royal family and this fact alone seemed to change the feeling of the nation. People everywhere were sickened by what they saw and what they read – if there was any doubt as to who the guilty party were, this was soon removed when the IRA admitted carrying out the bomb attack, an anonymous spokesman stating, "This operation is one of the discriminate ways we can bring to the attention of the English people the continuing occupation of our country."

If the explosion in Donegal Bay and the deaths there were not enough, just a few hours later a number of other explosions occurred. A three-vehicle army convoy travelling along a duel carriageway at Warrenpoint, just 44 miles from Belfast, was caught in the blast from a half-ton bomb which had been hidden under bales of hay on the back of a flat-bed trailer, parked on the hard shoulder. This massive device, which had been detonated remotely, caught the rear vehicle in the convoy, a 4-ton truck carrying a number of soldiers from the 2nd Battalion, Parachute Regiment, six of whom died at the scene. Those who were not injured were deployed to seal the area and take up defensive positions in case of a sniper attack. Within minutes of the first explosion, helicopters carrying men from the Queen's Own Highlanders arrived from Bessbrook base, carrying medical help and more soldiers. As the dead and injured were departing by helicopter another massive explosion resonated around the scene. A further 12 soldiers lost their lives, two Highlanders and ten more paratroopers, including the commanding officer of the Queen's Own Highlanders, Lieutenant Colonel David Blair, the most senior army officer killed at that time in Ireland. In a further sickening twist of this event, two local youths also found themselves involved when soldiers shot at them in the mistaken belief that they were part of the IRA hit squad. The youths were however just coincidental witnesses; one was killed while the other sustained a shot to the arm.

The media found itself reporting on what was now the third and most destructive act of the day – 22 people in total had died in three carefully executed operations, but it would be the death of Lord Louis Mountbatten and members of his family which occupied the press. He was an old man, a member of the British aristocracy with a great history of service to his country during two world wars. His death would also require a state funeral, a media event which would give the IRA another opportunity to remind the world of what they had achieved.

As the media got to grips with whipping the public to fever pitch over the indignation at the attack, Margaret Thatcher planned a trip to Belfast. Aware that it would take little to spark an eruption of greater sectarian violence in the aftermath of this most outrageous attack, she avoided any public display of emotion. She arrived in Belfast, walked through the city's main shopping streets and talked openly with members of the public about the latest attacks. There was much applause and cheers mixed with a small amount of heckling from a group of women whose husbands were in prison for alleged terrorist offences. She then flew by helicopter to visit one of Northern Ireland's most fortified bases at Crossmaglen, a frequent target of terrorist attacks.

The murder of Mountbatten served to reconcile the British people in their resolve to destroy the IRA. Unlike other members of the royal family, Mountbatten had gained a sincere reputation for having given the utmost services to his country. He certainly had a distinguished career, having served in the Navy during the First World War before going on to command the 5th Destroyer Flotilla during the Second World War, eventually becoming the Supreme Allied Commander in South-East Asia. His experience in this region led to his appointment as Viceroy of India after the Second World War, overseeing the granting of independence to both Pakistan and India. Known to the British people as "Lord Louis", he was given the title of "Earl Mountbatten of Burma" in recognition of his services to the Far East. Margaret Thatcher, Prime Minister of the day, remarked,

"His life ran like a golden thread of inspiration and service to his country throughout this century." In India a week of mourning was declared.

Ironically, given Mountbatten's distinguished service to Britain and indeed to a number of serving prime ministers, one area of policy in which he had cast no comment or opinion was that of the troubles in Northern Ireland.

On that fateful day in 1979 the ever-watchful Garda were operating a number of standard check points along the border between Northern and Southern Ireland, hours before any of the attacks had taken place. As cars approached each checkpoint they would be requested by armed members of the police force to stop. The occupants would be asked for identification papers or driving licence details before being allowed to continue. As these border-crossing areas had been themselves the target of attack, additional armed police would be set back from the road block with weapons at the ready should any trouble arise.

When the old Ford Zephyr approached the checkpoint and stopped the Garda officers approached the open-side window and asked a few questions to the driver who calmly responded. As the proceedings were steadily progressing one of the other officers recognized the vehicle as having been reported stolen. The officers asked the men to climb out of the car, where they were duly arrested for driving a stolen vehicle. The bombs had not yet exploded so there was therefore no need to assume the two men who were in the car had done anything other than steal the vehicle they were in. They were arrested and taken to a local police station, where during police questioning, the bomb which killed Mountbatten exploded. Interest in the two men increased and the Garda soon established that they were Thomas McMahon and Francis McGirl.

McMahon was a senior figure in the IRA, a notorious figurehead amongst IRA supporters. He was the leader of the IRA's much-feared South Armagh Brigade, which had reputedly killed up to one hundred British soldiers. He was also one of the first to be sent to Libya to be trained in explosives and remote detonation devices, a skill they had honed for their own terrorist purposes – McMahon was now considered one of the IRA's most skilled explosives experts.

The man with him, Francis McGirl, was not a heavyweight IRA member, but was known to have close connections with the group and was thought to be, if not a terrorist, then a sympathizer. His association with McMahon on arrest would change the public's perception of the man and later hold much sway in the Dublin courthouse where they were both now headed.

When news of the arrest hit the papers there was an undeniable hint of triumphalism – the prospect of yet another attack going unpunished was bad enough, but the murder of Mountbatten brought out the desire for revenge in the British public and those who supported their position in the fight against terrorism. The media reported on the chance arrest of the two men, driving the stolen car just hours before the explosions and for most who read the stories there would be no need for a trial – the two men were guilty. As their faces were spread across the newspaper front pages it would be difficult for anyone to conclude anything other than the fact that the two men had been heavily involved in the destruction that day. Their arrest prior to the explosions served only to suggest one of two alternative scenarios: the first being that the bomb had been detonated by a timer device; or secondly, that there had been others involved in the attack who had actually detonated the device by remote control. The police concluded that the second scenario was the most likely, for no one would know for sure the arrival time of Mountbatten's party, or for that matter if he would for certain arrive that day. A timer device would have run the risk of the boat exploding in the harbour causing unplanned damage and loss of life.

After the explosions were reported McMahon and McGirl were interviewed and their clothing taken for forensic analysis. With lawyers now appointed the two men claimed they had nothing to do with the explosions, they had been given the car and did not even know that it was stolen. Soon after they were removed to a Dublin prison where they would be held pending their court cases.

As the case developed through the media, other more unsettling rumours began to emerge regarding those who lurked in the background to Mountbatten's murder. There had been rumours before regarding the IRA's link to the Russian KGB, the committee for state security. Alleged former members of the KGB claimed they had provided the bomb which wiped out Mountbatten and other members of his group that day. It had been established that a leading member of the Irish Communist Party with connections in the IRA, also had links with senior members of the KGB. The history of these associations can be traced way back; even Joseph Stalin had commented that he thought the Irish movement was a fair and democratic protest against British Imperialism. It was also reported that during the 1960s the IRA had helped the Soviet agent George Blake escape from Wormwood Scrubs; in return the Russians provided further guns and ammunition. It has of course never been fully established just who or what group provided the bomb. The IRA had the skills and a ready supply of Semtex with which to carry out these attacks, but they needed money and a source willing to provide the heavily controlled substances required to make these explosive devices. However, with the media in full swing there was every possibility that this terrorist attack could indeed have caused a major international incident, as the press and the public wanted an equally large target from whom to extract revenge.

McMahon and McGirl had to sit out the period before their trial in jail; there was no way they were going to get out on bail and so had to watch with the rest of the nation as Britain, accompanied by representatives from other countries around the world, prepared to bury Mountbatten. In a state funeral befitting someone of Mountbatten's stature, the nation laid on all the prerequisite pomp and ceremony due to a man who had given so much of himself to his country. Armed forces from around the world, including Burma, India, the USA, France and Canada, accompanied British servicemen escorting the naval gun carriage carrying Mountbatten's body. The procession which commenced at Wellington Barracks, close to Buckingham Palace, travelled along the road to Westminster Abbey where the service was to be held. Lord Mountbatten's horse, Dolly, was led at the head of the parade with Mountbatten's boots reversed in the stirrups. The cocked hat of an admiral of the fleet, his sword of honour and his gold stick adorned the top of his coffin. Above the noise of the crowds which lined the streets, the music of the Royal Marines brass band could be heard playing some of his favourite tunes. Westminster Abbey was packed with all manner of highly ranked members of the royal and political world. The Archbishop of Canterbury praised the earl for his devotion to the Royal Navy during his service and after the public ceremony the coffin was taken to Romsey Abbey, near the Mountbatten family home in Hampshire, where, after a final private service, Mountbatten was buried on 5 September 1979, nine days after he had been murdered.

Just a few months before the trial was due to begin the funeral re-ignited public opinion and once more the papers ran headline after headline, underscoring the public outrage at both the murder of Mountbatten and of the killing of so many British soldiers. The defence counsel for the alleged bombers would have to fight not only the available evidence but also the overwhelming public emotion which was evident, driven to greater heights by the emotive press coverage. The funeral produced many images, including those of Lord and Lady Brabourne, who between them had lost one child, a mother and a father. In one shocking moment, a family had been completely decimated – someone would have to pay, the crime was too huge; the lowest compensation would be a guilty verdict for those who committed the atrocity. In the days that followed the two bombings, thousands of residents, both Catholic and Protestant, gathered in the town square in the nearby coastal village of Warrenpoint and held a vigil for those who had lost their lives. Afterwards they walked in a procession to the scene of the explosion and laid flowers. Covered by newspaper reporters and the television media the scenes seemed to show a community split by religion and politics but united in their view that violence should not be carried out in their name. McMahon and McGirl would have to face all of this in court and it would be a brave judge who would allow them to walk free.

Because of the fear of reprisal, the usual jury system did not apply to trials involving suspected members of the IRA. The long-reaching influence of the various paramilitary groups meant that the courts could not be sure a jury would not be tampered with and as the communities were roughly split in allegiances it had proven difficult to find groups of individuals who could be depended upon to deliver an unbiased verdict.

Presiding over the trial, held at the Anti-Terrorist Special Court in Dublin, were three senior judges, who would examine the evidence provided by the prosecution and then listen to the rebuttals provided by the defence team. The press gathered outside and delivered a constant stream of detail regarding the progress of the trial and of the details submitted as evidence. The accused pleaded not guilty and the trial commenced without further delay; security was heavy and visible, the prospect of a jailbreak a very real possibility.

The evidence presented consisted of four elements, three of which were based on forensic findings and the fourth purely on the fact that the accused, one of whom was a known senior IRA operative, were driving a stolen car on the day of the bombing, in itself hardly the indisputable concrete evidence one would normally require to secure a guilty verdict. The forensic evidence however presented a more compelling story. McMahon had traces of green paint on the sole of his boot, paint that matched that which had covered the decking of *Shadow V*. Sand particles found in the tread of his boots matched the type of sand found around the harbour at Mullaghmore, although as the defence were apt to point out, the sand at Mullaghmore did not benefit from being unique. Perhaps more compelling than anything were the traces of nitro-glycerine which had been found on McMahon's clothing. At any other time it might have been possible to dismiss the paint and the sand as almost circumstantial in that neither constituted irrefutable proof of guilt, while nitro-glycerine and the chemical parts of which it is made can be found in any number of industrial chemicals. The judges, however, were convinced and both McMahon and McGirl were found guilty and sentenced to life imprisonment on 23 November 1979. The media triumphantly announced the verdict and for many, justice was finally seen to be done.

Following his imprisonment, McMahon found himself back in court a short time later, this time bringing charges against those who managed his captivity, claiming that guards had broken his arm while he was trying to resist a strip search. The drama increased to a crescendo as McMahon attempted to escape from the courthouse when he produced a small Browning pistol and managed to fire one shot. Luckily no one was hurt but the question of how he had obtained the pistol became a mystery to which no answer has ever been found. One report suggests it was passed to him by a man with whom he shook hands on the way into court, a possibility, but McMahon was handcuffed to a prison officer at all times. He was, however, released from the handcuffs in order to visit the toilet, where it is suggested he collected the weapon which had been hidden there sometime earlier. It has even been suggested that the weapon was provided by a member of the security forces. The attempted escape involving the pistol reflected badly on McMahon and the press once again vilified the man for his propensity for violence.

McGirl, who had been convicted more or less by association, had his sentence quashed at an appeal hearing in 1980, and died following a tractor accident in 1995.

At the time of writing there is relative peace in Ireland thanks to the Good Friday Agreement, Ireland's framework for peace and political independence. As part of this political process, prisoners associated with the struggles were to be released early and Thomas McMahon was the seventh high-profile prisoner to be released under this scheme. He walked free, amid a flurry of press outrage, in 1998, having served 18 years behind bars. He has since turned his back on the IRA and has become a carpenter.

Beauty and the Beast

Dominique Dunne

Many people have witnessed at first hand, or at least seen the consequences of a person close to them struggle in an abusive relationship. This is often caused by jealousy and when fuelled by personal insecurities, the victim's life can be made a miserable one. They can find themselves constantly trying to reassure their irrational partner, but often these actions are fruitless. This jealous behaviour is usually most common during the teenage years, and diminishes as couples form a stronger and more stable bond. During young adulthood, adolescent men encounter their first experiences of love and can become fiercely protective in defending it. If they are aware of any threats to this new relationship they can go to great lengths in order to ward off predators. These actions alone can be enough to sour their new-found status quo, creating great strains on the romance.

No parent wishes to see their beautiful young daughter spending all her spare time alone in her bedroom, uncharacteristically choosing not to mix with her previously close friends, apparently at her new boyfriend's beck and call. When questions are raised at to why she is no longer seeing her girlfriends, and the reply is that her boyfriend simply does not like them, the situation can be very upsetting for all involved.

Thankfully, as maturity develops, emotions settle down and life becomes much more bearable for most people. Sadly though, for the parents of *Poltergeist* star Dominique Dunne, their daughter's jealous boyfriend could not control his

temper and the beautiful 22-year-old actress paid the ultimate price. After ending the turbulent relationship, Dominique was trying to get on with her life, but John Thomas
Sweeney was not prepared to leave her alone.

Sweeney was desperate for Dominique to give him yet
another chance and for them to reconcile their relationship,
so he decided to call round to the home which they had
previously shared to try and convince her that he was a
reformed character. Dominique had company as she was
rehearsing lines for a new role in the science fiction series *V*,
with her co-star David Packer.

When rehearsals were disturbed by a knock at the door,
Dominique looked through the window and saw that it was
Sweeney, so she told Packer she would be back shortly.
Dominique was determined not to give Sweeney access into
the house as she did not want a full-scale argument in front of
her guest. She decided instead to try and placate him and
then send him on his way as quickly as possible from the
doorstep. Sweeney's previous track record made her well
aware that he would read too much into the meeting with her
co-star and Dominique was not willing to go through another
confrontation, hoping that he would take the hint and leave
of his own accord. However Sweeney sensed that she was
hiding something, or more importantly, somebody, and
demanded to be let inside his one-time home. Dominique
stuck to her guns, waiting for the inevitable argument to
erupt.

The actress had decided that she was not going to be
pushed around by Sweeney, refusing point blank to let him
into the property – she would not entertain the idea of
reconciling such an unhealthy relationship. As the couple's
quarrel became louder Sweeney suddenly grabbed Dunne by
the throat and dragged her to a nearby driveway where he
strangled her for over three minutes; when she no longer
struggled with him he released his grip.

By this time Packer had heard screams and decided he
would go outside to see exactly what was going on; he found
the pair, Dunne, laid on the ground with Sweeney knelt
above her. Packer then summoned the police, who arrived

within five minutes, took one look at the unconscious actress and immediately called for an ambulance to assist. During the journey to the nearest hospital, Cedars Sinai Hospital, her heart stopped, although fortunately the ambulance crew were able to restart it. Medical staff performed a brain scan, which showed, as they suspected, that she had suffered severe brain damage owing to anoxia – her brain had been starved of oxygen – while she was strangled. The doctors tried in vain for five days to restore Dunne's cerebral functions but were unsuccessful. On 4 November 1982, at 11 a.m., her parents made the difficult decision to have her removed from the life-support machine. Their beautiful daughter died almost instantly, just three weeks before they were due to celebrate her 23rd birthday.

The Dunne family were united in their grief and helped one another through the terrible weeks following the shocking death of their loved one. Dominique's funeral arrangements were made and her funeral service took place on 6 November at the Catholic Church of the Good Shepherd in Beverley Hills, the same church in which she had been baptized as a babe in arms. Her funeral was heavily attended and mourners turned up in their hundreds to pay their last respects to such a well-loved young woman. She was laid to rest near Los Angeles at the Westwood Memorial Park.

Public sympathy was virtually overwhelming and nobody had a bad word to say for the promising young star. The same words were repeated by many: "She had her whole life in front of her and had so much to live for."

Meanwhile John Thomas Sweeney was in police custody, having been charged with the murder of Dominique Dunne and was awaiting trial, which was set for early August 1983, nine months after Dominique's death. It would be held at the courthouse in Santa Monica.

During Sweeney's police custody, officers investigating the death never once heard him show any remorse for his actions. In one interview he is reported to have said, "I fucked up . . . I can't believe I did something that will put me behind bars forever . . . Man, I blew it. I killed her. I didn't think I choked her that hard. I just kept on choking her. I just lost my temper and blew it again." Although he was willing to admit guilt, he showed no signs of remorse, appearing to regret his actions only because they had now caused him to lose his liberty.

Sweeney's defence lawyer, Michael Adelson, based the majority of his defence around the claim that the attack was provoked. He said that Sweeney wished to reconcile the couple's differences and try again, but it was Dunne who instigated the physical assault. Sweeney was then said to have lunged for her, after she admitted lying to him when he had earlier suggested that they get back together, which resulted in a violent struggle, although Sweeney had no reported marks on his body at the time of his arrest. Sweeney's recollection of the events immediately after this point in their meeting was very sketchy. He claimed that he could not remember anything until he had knelt beside the unconscious body of his former girlfriend, still with his hands around her neck. He further claimed that he made an attempt to resuscitate her, but to no avail.

It was also claimed that Dominique would "belittle" Sweeney and that she would make him feel inferior, by her seemingly higher social status. This must have been difficult to hear – for her friends and family the reality was that she was nothing like this and was very down to earth and well grounded. Finally, Adelson concluded that the tragedy which had occurred was not a brutal murder, but a sad act of passion, by a man at the depth of despair.

The largest part of the prosecution case, handled by District Attorney Steven Barshop, was formed around Sweeney's physical abuse of a previous girl friend. Her statement was damning as far as Sweeney's defence was concerned. She claimed that the relationship lasted for three years during which she was subjected to physical abuse on several occasions, possibly as many as ten. The wounds which she sustained on two of these incidents were so bad that she was detained in hospital to recover. Besides the usual cuts and bruises she also suffered from a broken nose, a perforated eardrum and a collapsed lung. This testimony surely not only proved that Dominique did not die as a result of a one-off act of passion, but that she was murdered at the hands of a serial abuser. Amazingly Sweeney's defence team were able to argue with the Judge, Burton S. Katz, that this testimony be excluded from the trial as it was deemed prejudicial, and he agreed.

Dominique's friends were called to give a character witness and were asked their opinion of her relationship with Sweeney. They agreed that she was initially very happy with Sweeney, but as the couple became more intimate and started living together, she grew wary of him. One friend described how she was aware that Sweeney and Dominique had on several occasions prior to her death been involved in heated arguments. She went on to say that after the relationship was over, Dominique was constantly fearful of Sweeney returning to her home.

By the end of September the jury were ready to offer their verdict, finding the defendant guilty of voluntary manslaughter. The shocked courtroom went silent – most were surprised to hear that a man could take the life of a defenceless human being in cold blood and get away with a voluntary manslaughter judgment. Several jury members were questioned afterwards regarding their findings and admitted that they would have been able to find him guilty of second-degree murder (with a minimum 15-year prison sentence) if they had been given more information regarding Sweeney's violent past.

Despite Dominique's massive popularity with the American public and the huge press coverage of the case, it appeared that Sweeney had managed to "get through the net".

On 10 November, the Judge sentenced Sweeney to six and a half years imprisonment. As he had already been in police custody for a year, he was looking at only serving another two and a half years, if he was able to sustain his good behaviour. He served the majority of his sentence at the medium-security prison in Susanville, California and was released on 21 June 1986, promptly returning to Los Angeles to resume his career as a chef.

It is such a travesty that a young woman with a promising career in one of the most sought after occupations possible, was killed when she had so much to live for. Her life, up until meeting Sweeney had been a happy one. She was born on 23 November 1959 in Santa Monica, California and her proud parents, Dominick Dunne and Ellen (Lenny) Beatriz Griffin Dunne, named her Dominique Ellen Dunne. She had two elder brothers Griffin and Alex; the couple also had two other children, but sadly they had died within days of their birth.

Her father was of Irish descent and had grown up in Hartford, Connecticut; her mother was originally from Nogales, Arizona, where she had lived on a large ranch. They met by chance in a railway station in Dominick's home town. It was apparently love at first sight and the couple were married on Ellen's parents' ranch in Arizona, in 1954. They lived for a short time in New York, but owing to Dominick's busy working schedule the couple moved to Beverley Hills.

Dominique was destined to have some form of film, television, or acting career almost from birth, as her mother was an actress and her father a movie producer, later to become a journalist and author. Her eldest brother Griffin also became an actor, later moving to producing and directing films. Her parents mixed in celebrity circles and the young Dunne children were unperturbed when introduced to popular movie stars of the day. Indeed Dominique's godmother was the daughter of actor Gary Cooper – Marie Cooper.

Dominique enjoyed, by many standards, quite a privileged life; she was born in the up-market area known as Beverley Hills and started school life at Westlake School in Los Angeles. She was a happy outgoing child and was very popular amongst her peers; she was a very bright pupil and had no difficulties with progressing easily in school. She moved on to high school, initially attending Taft School in Watertown, Connecticut, before moving to a previously all boys school – Fountain Valley High School in Colorado, where she had the privilege of being among the first 20 girls to enrol there when it converted to co-ed status.

The only blemish on a very happy childhood was the separation of her beloved parents when she was 11 years old. But this alteration to her life was only a slight blip as her mother and father continued to maintain a good relationship and the children spent a good deal of time with each of them. Later in life, when Dominique was 16 years old her mother was diagnosed with multiple sclerosis, a chronic and progressive disease of the nervous system, although initially her symptoms were very mild.

After graduating from high school Dominique moved to Europe for a year to study the Italian language and art at the Michelangelo School. She was fluent in Italian by the time that she returned home the following year and immediately wanted to find work.

She initially took a job as a receptionist and translator at the Italian High Commission based in Los Angeles, but this job was short lived as her natural gift was calling her. She longed to take up acting so she quit and returned to education, enrolling at the Colorado State University to study the art of acting, where she stayed for one year.

Her acting career took off virtually as soon as she left the college and Dominique was soon to be on TV screens in several popular programmes, including *Fame*, *Hill Street Blues* and *CHiPs*.

Her first film role was in 1979, in the made-for-television movie, *Diary of a Teenage Hitch-hiker*, where she won the role of Cathy Burke. This was a relatively easy introduction to film as she was to act with one of her friends, Charlene Tilton (best known for her role in *Dallas* as the character Lucy Ewing). Also in this production was Craig T. Nelson, who was later to star beside Dominique in their most famous movie, *Poltergeist*.

In 1980, Dominique had a second television film role in *Valentine Magic on Love Island*, where she played a character called Cheryl. This was, as the title suggests, the story of love on a fantasy island. Dominique enjoyed the experience that she was gaining, and her acting ability was improving with every take.

During 1981, Dominique pushed herself hard and took on two film roles, the first being the lead role in *The Haunting of Harrington House*. This was a stretch as the now 21-year-old actress was to play the part of Polly Ames, a 14-year-old schoolgirl. Later that year she co-starred in *The Day the Loving Stopped* alongside Dennis Weaver (best known for his role in *Duel*), Ally Sheedy, another good friend of Dominique's (from *Breakfast Club*) and Valerie Harper (a household favourite after starring in *Rhoda* and *The Mary Tyler Moore Show*).

Dominique's big break came in 1982 when she successfully auditioned for the role of Dana Freeling in the blockbuster hit *Poltergeist*. The film was destined for success with a brilliant cast, was produced by the infinitely talented Steven Spielberg and directed by Tobe Hooper, of *Texas Chainsaw Massacre* fame. The story is about the haunted Freeling family and Dominique plays the eldest of three children, 16-year-old Dana; the youngest character Carol Anne was played by child star Heather O'Rorke. The film's strong acting cast and fantastic special effects made this the must-see film of the year, and catapulted the three youngest cast members to headline fame.

During her busy working regime Dominique still managed to have some private time, where she enjoyed socializing in with friends and colleagues. One evening while at a party she met a handsome, successful chef from the highly regarded Los Angeles restaurant Ma Maison called John Sweeney. The two got on well and soon their friendship blossomed into a romance. They set up home together, but Sweeney gradually began to reveal a side to his personality which until then he had managed to disguise – he started to become highly confrontational and jealous of any attention which Dominique received when they were out.

On one occasion when they were out together having lunch, a fan of the movie *Poltergeist* recognized Dominique and asked for her autograph. Sweeney was enraged and confronted the unsuspecting man, shaking him and demanding that he leave his girlfriend alone to enjoy her meal, his actions that were too extreme, making other restaurant goers rather embarrassed to have witnessed it. If this was how he behaved in public, many were wondering what sort of life the young actress was subject to when the couple were alone together.

Further incidences, each escalating in violence, eventually and inevitably were directed at Dominique. She decided that she could put up with his behaviour no longer and demanded that he move out of their shared home.

Dominique was wary of being alone in the house, but with each passing day she hoped that Sweeney would find another focus for his attention. Sadly, this was not to be the case and he constantly checked up on her, making her fully aware of this. Regardless of Sweeney's actions Dominique continued with her acting career; she had managed to get the role of Robin Maxwell in the hit television series *V*, and had asked one of the actors back to her home so that they could run through the lines for the next episode.

After being convicted of voluntary manslaughter, Sweeney was released from prison less than four years later, and went back to work as a chef.

Dominick Dunne was so enraged at the appallingly short prison term that Sweeney got, his whole life changed on the day that the sentence was passed. He started a totally new career writing about trials, adamant that the defendant's rights far outweigh those of the victim, who in Dominique's case had lost her life. He was appalled that the jury could believe the lies which were told in court, thus allowing the defendant to get away with murder.

Dominique's mother, similarly enraged, became an activist for victims' rights and founded the organization "Justice for Homicide Victims Inc.". After suffering from multiple sclerosis for over 20 years she died at the age of 64 in early 1997.

The other young female star of *Poltergeist*, Heather O'Rorke, was to have an extremely short life, sadly dying at the age of 12 of an intestinal blockage. She was also buried at Westwood Memorial Park, Los Angeles, just a stone's throw from Dominique's own grave.

I Have a Dream

Dr Martin Luther King

There have been a number of assassinations which have had a worldwide impact: John F. Kennedy in 1963, his brother Robert in 1968 and without doubt, Dr Martin Luther King, also in 1968. Much has already been written about King and his goals in respect of black human rights in America, but even more has been written about his untimely death, on 4 April 1968, and about the man who was imprisoned for it, James Earl Ray. King's murder has, like the murder of the Kennedy brothers, been the subject of much speculation and has prompted an array of conspiracy theories, some of which have a degree of merit; others would appear to be downright ridiculous.

The conspiracy theories persist for many reasons, but perhaps the most telling reason is that King's own son no longer believes that Ray was the assassin. With the approval of King's widow and his siblings, Dextor King met Ray in prison in 1997. Shaking hands to open their meeting the two sat down together to talk. Ray began by stating his position, "I had nothing to do with the shooting of your father," a position he had maintained for over 30 years – only briefly on arrest did he admit to his part in the killing, changing his statement soon afterward. Having talked for a while in calm low tones, King asked the question he wanted to have on record for his own piece of mind, "I want to ask for the record – did you kill my father?"

Ray replied with a sincere and definitive response. Fixing King with a stare he said, "No, I didn't, no, no."

"I believe you, and my family believes you, and we will do

everything in our power to see you prevail," King responded, and with this the whole media machine resumed the debate as to who really lay behind the murder of Martin Luther King.

Once again, decades after the event, the public were reading the details, looking at the facts and considering the alternatives. A whole new generation, familiar with King's legacy, would now be led through the maze of conspiracies and asked to consider if the person who had lived behind bars for all those years really was the man responsible for the death of an icon.

The man heralded as the saviour of black America, King spent much of his time fighting the ingrained racism that persisted across much of American society; wherever he saw injustice he fought to have it corrected. One of the areas he was especially concerned with was the rights of black workers, to share the same pay and conditions as their white counterparts. It was this very subject which had brought him to Memphis, Tennessee, on 3 April 1968. He had planned to march in support of Memphis sanitation workers, who were engaged in a labour strike. The strike followed previous action the month before, during which sporadic outbreaks of violence had occurred, a situation King hoped to avoid; he had arrived intent on a peaceful display of unity.

King and several of his associates, including the Reverend Jesse Jackson, arrived in Memphis and checked in to the Lorraine Hotel, on Mulberry Street, a part of town mostly inhabited by African Americans. King was allocated room 306 at the front of the hotel, overlooking Mulberry Street and the carpark directly in front of the hotel. His room had the benefit of French doors which lead out onto a small balcony overlooking the street and adjacent to the rear of other buildings on the opposite side.

The buildings opposite sat on South Main Street which ran parallel to Mulberry Street; the rooms at the back of these faced the front of the Lorraine Hotel. They consisted of a variety of buildings which housed amongst others, the fire brigade, Canipe's, a record store, a fast food store called Jim's Grill, above which were a number of cheap rooming houses. The back door to Jim's Grill faced the Lorraine Hotel, as did the rooming house directly above. The two rows of buildings were separated by car parks, rear yards and a whole range of overgrown bushes and small trees.

Lloyd Jowers, the white owner of Jim's Grill, specialized in after-work drinking, generally to a mixed group of customers, who would arrive after 4 p.m. and enjoy beer and cheap food until late.

Sometime before 4 p.m. on 4 April, James Earl Ray parked his white Mustang on South Main Street and checked in to one of the second-floor rooms above Jim's Grill, using a false name. His room and the communal bathroom at the end of the corridor overlooked the Lorraine Hotel, particularly room 306, King's own room.

After checking in to the hotel, Ray then went back onto the high street to do a bit of shopping. Peculiarly, the item he wanted was a pair of binoculars which he duly purchased from a nearby shop, returning to his room with them straight away.

At around 6 p.m., King ventured out onto the balcony and engaged in a conversation with some of his colleagues who were in the carpark beneath the balcony. Just after 6 p.m., still engaged in conversation, King was shot with a single bullet, fired by a sniper who was housed in the buildings opposite the Lorraine Hotel. The bullet, fired from a 30.06 calibre rifle struck King from relatively close quarters, severing his spinal column. He died on the balcony, not long afterwards.

The sniper's timing had been lucky – if King had been on schedule for his dinner date he would not have been at the hotel at that time. His colleagues in the carpark below were preparing to leave for a dinner date with another local activist. Knowing that King always ran late, the dinner date was set for 5 o'clock, but true to form, King was only just preparing to depart, one hour after his expected arrival. This late departure, coupled with King's unexpected appearance on the balcony, gave the assassin the opportunity to strike. And he did – with deadly results.

Shortly after 6 p.m. on 4 April 1968 King was dead. Born

in January 1929, the grandson of the Reverend A.D. Williams, he was just 39 years of age. A supporter of African American human rights, King attended Moorehouse College in Atlanta, before moving on to Crozer Theological Seminary in Pennsylvania, and finally Boston University, where he deepened his knowledge and understanding of theology. He married Coreta Scott in 1953 and the following year accepted the pastorate at Dexter Avenue Baptist Church, in Montgomery, Alabama. Just two years later in 1955 he received his doctorate in systematic theology.

King's first foray into black rights came with his support of the bus boycott, in response to Montgomery's policy on segregation on the buses. The boycott continued throughout 1956, bringing King to national prominence. In December that year the United States Supreme Court declared the policy on segregation to be unconstitutional and it was scrapped. Feelings were split in the southern states; many white people did not support the African Americans in their plight, afraid of how the changes might affect them. However, there were many who found the treatment of fellow Americans, under the policies of segregation, to be unpalatable, the split in thinking causing much public unrest, which would frequently erupt into public displays of violence.

In the spring of 1963 King led mass demonstrations in Birmingham, Alabama, where the local police were known to be violently opposed to the integration of the black and white communities. The clashes between the protestors and the police made front-page headlines when the police attacked the group with dogs and fire hoses, to which many members of the protest responded with violence of their own, the clashes prompting outrage from both sides of the debate. The headlines however reflected a passive group of peaceful protestors harangued by local officials for daring to march in support of civil liberties. President Kennedy responded by submitting broad civil rights legislation to Congress, which subsequently became the Civil Rights Act of 1964. Later, more than 250,000 protestors marched on Washington in support of jobs and freedom, at which King gave his now famous "I have a dream" speech.

King was now one of the most well-known, if not well-liked, men in American society. He was awarded *Time Magazine*'s Man of the Year award in 1963 and was the recipient of the Nobel Peace Prize in 1964. Along with the accolades however came the ever-increasing scrutiny from central government officials, politicians and particularly J Edgar Hoover, the infamous FBI director. Hoover in particular went to great lengths to undermine King's power base and influence, especially when King spoke out so strongly against America's involvement in the Vietnam War, giving the Johnson administration yet more high-profile criticism.

The day before he was killed while in support of the striking sanitation workers, King gave his final speech, during which he spoke the now immortal words, "I've been to the mountain top." He was praised by many for his work in support of civil rights but condemned by others for his militant views, even though his non-violent message was often lost on those who fought in the streets.

When news of King's death broke there were riots in many cities across the United States. Many African Americans believed he had been silenced to stop black progress into mainstream American society. As a man revered for his non-violent message, King was held in high regard by a substantial volume of people, both black and white, who supported his cause. When news of his death hit the front pages, most Americans wanted to know who had committed the crime, and right from the off there were those who believed there was more to the crime than met the eye.

When the fatal shot rang out, King's colleagues down in the carpark immediately summoned the police, who arrived within minutes. Spreading out to ensure they had sufficient coverage they quickly found a suspicious "bundle" on the sidewalk outside Canipe's record store. Closer inspection showed it contained a 30.06 rifle, holding a spent cartridge case, with attached scope. The bag also contained items belonging to a petty criminal called James Earl Ray, whose fingerprints were all over the weapon. The hunt was now on.

The fact that the police arrived on the scene almost immediately was mainly because there were already a number of them assigned to keep an eye on King and his party. A couple were already at the fire station, one positioned at the back of the station from where he could clearly see the hotel where King was staying, and in fact had a perfect view of the balcony outside Kings room. When the news of the attack broke, additional police officers raced to the Lorraine Hotel as well as fanning out along the shops and premises of South Main Street, from where it was suspected the shot had been fired. One of the first people to be questioned was Lloyd Jowers, owner of Jim's grill, who had been serving his dozen strong crowd from behind the counter. Describing the man who had taken the upstairs room, he initially helped the police with their investigation, but later added a twist of conspiracy with a claim that he too had been involved in a plot to murder King. But for now the police were intent on finding the one man who all the evidence pointed at – James Earl Ray.

After the shooting Ray went on the run, abandoning his Mustang in Atlanta, where the police impounded the vehicle hoping to secure further evidence against him. From Atlanta Ray headed to Canada, where he had travelled the previous year after escaping from prison having been held on another charge. Throughout this period the papers carried Ray's photograph and once again trial by media was in progress using the basic facts as disclosed by the police as the main evidence. To further cement Ray's likely guilt was the fact that he was a known villain, a prison escapee who was now on the run again. The police ran a massive investigation and media campaign to capture Ray, which finally delivered a breakthrough when he was caught and arrested at London's Heathrow Airport, just two months after the murder. During his brief spell in London Ray had also managed to rob a bank, thus cementing the notion that if nothing else he was a career criminal.

The evidence against Ray would seemingly be beyond doubt. Having escaped from jail he was on the run at the time of King's murder. He was known to hold strong racist views and had been heard to pass comments in relation to King and his activities. He was the occupier of the room from where

the fatal shot was reportedly fired and was seen fleeing the
scene shortly after King's assassination. A bag containing a
rifle he had bought just six days earlier, which matched the
type used to kill King, was surprisingly found on the sidewalk. The gun had Ray's fingerprints all over it and other
material in the bag belonged to him. After the attack Ray
took decisive action to avoid being caught by the authorities,
eventually fleeing to London, where he further enriched his
reputation as a career criminal by robbing a bank. By any
standards it would be difficult to conclude that Ray was not
the killer, yet a lot of the evidence was circumstantial – he
was in the area of the shooting and he did flee the scene, but
this did not prove he did it. The gun of course did have Ray's
fingerprints all over it, but it was never conclusively proven
to be the actual murder weapon. The bag was also con-
spicuously found on the sidewalk; it wasn't even hidden in a
bin or thrown into the bushes but was placed in such a way
that anyone would find it. Did Ray dispose of the bag badly
or did someone else place the bag where it would be easily
found?

These questions and others did not need to be asked in the
initial period following Ray's arrest. There were few who
doubted his guilt, including the lawyer who would have to
defend him and the press and media who had already presented their conclusions. It was therefore of no surprise to
anyone when Ray pleaded guilty to the charge of murder,
avoiding the need for an expensive court case and in the
process winning himself a 99-year prison term, a softer
option than the guaranteed death penalty should he be found
guilty by jury – a verdict that most thought was assured,
should he elect to have his day in court.

So in March 1969 Ray accepted the sentence, knowing full
well that the rules prevented him from appealing against the
decision. Yet this is what he did just three days later,
recanting his confession and pleading to have his case heard
in court. He said that his lawyer Percy Foreman had essentially forced him into the confession, claiming that he had
threatened to withdraw his services if he wished to fight the
case. Initially it was suggested Foreman's actions were those

of a caring lawyer who did not wish to see his client put to death. But later Ray would allege it was a mixture of the lawyer's involvement in a conspiracy to see Ray portrayed as a lone gun man, and also that Foreman was hoping to conclude a lucrative movie deal.

The problem Ray seemed to face was the authorities' refusal to consider reopening the case, always claiming that to do so someone would need to present strong evidence that the man behind bars either didn't commit the crime or did not act alone.

Once again the media machine started to work the other side of the argument. Having lambasted Ray as King's assassin, they were now intent on proving that others, some shadowy group, were also involved in King's death. King's family, in the form of his wife and children, were themselves concerned that King might have been removed for political reasons, by political people, and if this was the case then Ray did not act alone. In a conversation recalled by King's wife, on the occasion of JFK's assassination, King, on hearing the news, remarked prophetically, "That's exactly what's going to happen to me." He too had seen the likes of JFK and RFK assassinated, either during power or on the verge of winning power, in circumstances which presented more questions than answers. Now his family were struggling with the same questions, questions which the press were happy to present on many occasions – was Ray an independent, murderous bigot or was he a patsy for a consortium of people who were playing for bigger stakes than the death of one black activist and the freedom of one small-time career criminal?

Over the years that followed Ray's incarceration there emerged three primary conspiracy theories, all of which assert that Ray did not act alone, but was involved with others in the assassination of King. These theories have been tested and presented in books, newspapers, on prime-time television and even via restricted investigations carried out by the District Attorney's office, but never in a court of law, attended by the man at the centre of the controversy.

The first conspiracy theory which emerged came from Ray himself, who claimed to have been set up by a mystery man named Raul. Ray claimed he had been involved in a smuggling operation with Raul, but that he neither knew the man's last name nor indeed the nature of the smuggling operation. He claimed he was instructed to purchase a gun and book in to the room above Jim's Grill. He had then been told to park his car and await further instructions, which he did. When the fatal shot rang out Raul ran to the car and the two made their getaway. The claims were given plenty of press coverage and some mild degree of credibility when retired FBI employee, Donald Wilson, said he had taken pieces of paper from Ray's car which had the name Raul written on them. He had then stored the papers in his freezer for 30 years before presenting them to the public. His claims however were disputed by the FBI who have said they are "total fabrication", suggesting he was never part of the initial investigation. As to why he would have removed evidence and stored it in a freezer for three decades one can only speculate.

The second theory, and the one to which the King family now subscribe, is that King's assassination was organized by high-ranking members of the government, including President Johnson, but also the CIA, the FBI, the Memphis Police Department, the Mafia and the Green Berets. Whether it would involve all or some of these will probably never be known. But the assertion is that people who held the highest ranking roles in the world's largest democracy had sought to remove King for reasons of their own. It will be noted that similar claims have been made over the assassinations of JFK, RFK, and even the events surrounding the death of Marilyn Monroe and the fatal road accident involving Edward Kennedy at Chappaquiddick, in which Mary Jo Kopechne died in suspicious circumstances, which effectively ended the presidential aspirations of the youngest Kennedy brother. To give credibility to these claims, it was Ray's last lawyer, William Pepper, who claimed that the US government had hired a Mafia hit man to murder King and that the assassin was backed up by soldiers from the Green Berets, who were hiding in the area, ready to finish the job off in the event that he missed. Pepper, who wrote a book detailing his claims, alleges that the CIA, the Memphis Police and army intelligence were also involved in the plot. Adding a twist of incredulity to the claims, Pepper says that the commander in charge of the Green Berets, Billy Eidson, had been killed off to prevent him disclosing details of the plot – although he was found to be alive and well and not best pleased at the accusation. To add another twist to the tale, a military cablegram produced by Pepper as evidence of his claims, was shown to be a forgery. He did however manage not only to have his book hit the book stores during the same month that Ray died, but also managed to persuade Dextor King that his father's murder was the result of a senior government plot that involved the then President of the United States, Lyndon B. Johnson.

The third of the conspiracy theories and the one which has some detail to support it suggests that Lloyd Jowers, the owner-operator of Jim's Grill, was offered $100,000 to hire someone to carry out the shooting. At the time of the initial investigation Jowers claimed he was serving drinks in the bar when King was shot and used a number of his customers to provide his alibi. On the day of the shooting, however, many of his customers had been drinking heavily as usual and could not be relied on to give a reliable testimony. Initially for Jowers this was of minimal importance; once Ray's identity and the facts relating to his recent gun purchase had been established, and that his room overlooked the murder scene, the outcome was pretty much set. The bank robbery in London just prior to his arrest served to confirm further Ray's criminal tendencies and when he was eventually confronted with the crime, he agreed to plead guilty, seemingly to spare his own life.

As we have seen in other cases the media, which initially served to crucify Ray, now started to examine the evidence again. Just days after his imprisonment for 99 years Ray attempted to withdraw his admission, but from this point until his death the authorities would not allow him a retrial, even after other official bodies found that he did not act alone. Over the years since his confinement the press have re-examined the story and presented the various theories which over the course of time have become engrained in a type of folk law.

Conspiracy theory number three, that Jowers, owner of Jim's Grill, played a part in the assassination of King, did however gain further credibility when, after 30 years of claiming no involvement, Jowers suddenly changed his position. In December 1993 Jowers appeared on the ABC's *Prime Time Live* programme and changed his decades-long position, now stating that he was involved with others to assassinate King. Jowers claimed a local produce dealer who was involved with the Mafia gave him $100,000 to hire someone to bump King off. The deal to kill King was agreed with a hit man called Raoul (Raul) – Ray neither shot King nor indeed had anything to do with the planning of the murder.

The gun found on the sidewalk just after the murder was never forensically tested as it was decided that without doubt the man they wanted was Ray. The pressure put on Ray to admit to the crime meant that there was never any need to build a case against him, as it would not be tested in a court of law. And so no further analysis was ever carried out on the weapon to prove that it was indeed the gun from which the fatal shot was fired. Analysis of the rifle decades after the event proved inconclusive. Unfortunately the version of events as presented by Jowers was not examined in a court of law and attempts made later to obtain an official examination of his claims were met with changes to the story. It would appear Jowers was happy to present his version of events, but not in an official way, one that could have seen his own liberty threatened. What is not in doubt is that Jowers attempted to make money from his claims, seeking compensation from the producers of a programme who were aiming to film a "mock trial" of James Earl Ray. This action in itself has served to undermine the credibility of the statements he made, even though his claim of being involved with a man named Raul matches the details provided by Ray himself.

As recently as 1998, the otherwise discredited Donald Wilson, former agent with the FBI, revealed that for the previous 30 years he had been concealing papers that he had taken from Ray's Mustang, which were relevant to the murder of King. Only two documents were ultimately retrieved, one, a portion of a 1963 Dallas telephone directory, had handwritten entries associated with the assassination of President Kennedy, including the telephone numbers of Jack Ruby and Lee Harvey Oswald. Both pieces of paper made reference to the name Raul, but the meaning of the name or the identity of the person behind the name has never been established. Unfortunately, Wilson's evidence has been frequently contradictory, to the point where its reliability must remain in question.

Raul featured prominently in the claims made by Ray and was also echoed by others in their evaluations of King's murder, but the individual has never been found. In recent years a Raul found living in New York State was identified, but he was quickly ruled out of any involvement in King's demise. Thirty years after the crime was committed there is still no additional information that could lead investigators to the shadowy figure called Raul.

Throughout Ray's time in prison, his counsel sought to free him using many and varied legal approaches. As the years have marched by, the conspiracy theories reported in the media and in the many books which have been published serve to maintain interest and confusion in the "who shot King" mystery.

In 1994 Ray filed the last of his several state petitions for post-conviction relief, *Ray* v. *Dutton*. In this last attempt he sought to win a new trial based on the claim that the 30.06 rifle found on South Main Street was not the weapon. Firearms testing carried out pursuant to this claim proved inconclusive and were never satisfactorily tested in court due to Ray's death.

In addition to the post-conviction relief effort taken up by Ray in 1994, his lawyer Dr Pepper also filed a false imprisonment civil suit claiming that Jowers and others had conspired to kill King. That suit, *Ray* v. *Jowers*, was effectively dismissed in 1997.

To many it would appear to be illogical that an individual can make claims to his own culpability in a crime and yet this does not draw the attention of the law. However this is what happened to Jowers, who admitted his own involvement, albeit changing his story on numerous occasions, but because he cannot provide evidence of his own guilt he will never be tried. On the other hand Ray, who did initially admit to murder, was imprisoned without trial and cannot now appeal against the conviction, even though most of the evidence was circumstantial. The effect has been to polarize the opposing camps. The law believes they have their man and do not want to open up the case or re-evaluate Ray's involvement, even though the pressure through the media has been immense and the public, the media and even King's own family firmly believe that King died as a result of a conspiracy. The credibility of Jowers' claims however must be questioned – he has been inconsistent with his version of the events and even members of his own family believe he created his story with the idea that he could make good money out of the media. He never gave his television version of events under oath and now never will – if there is any truth in anything that Jowers has claimed it is lost in the confusion of the various versions of events he has given.

In a twist that the TV world might struggle to come up with, the convicted murderer is now actively defended by the family of the man he is convicted of killing. On 27 March 1997, the week after Ray and Dextor King had held their historic meeting, Dextor appeared on the *Today Show*, opposite David Garrow, author of *The FBI and Martin Luther King*, during which the two argued the case for and against, Dextor fighting all out to prove that Ray was not the man responsible for his father's death. The pair met again just a few days later on CNN's *Crossfire* programme, during which Dextor accused Garrow of being a spook, saying that he had evidence that Garrow was not an agent for the national security and intelligence services.

The media in all of its guises have served to ensure that the assassination of King has never left the public's thoughts. It has also achieved the confusion of the nation, in that the truth as initially described, and as seen to be achieved in court, has now been so severely questioned that over 50 per cent of Americans now believe that King died as a result of a high-level conspiracy, just as they do for JFK and his brother RFK. Whatever the truth behind King's assassination, the media have achieved with millions of people what the lawyers couldn't achieve with 12 people – the conviction that James Earl Ray was not responsible for the death of Martin Luther King.

James Earl Ray died at 10.36 CDT, on Thursday, 23 April 1998 at the Columbia Nashville Memorial Hospital; he was 70 years old. The cause of death was listed as being liver failure, despite never being a drinker or a smoker. Anyone who hoped for a death-bed confession was sorely disappointed, for he just slipped away and with him went any hope of a final outcome. It is unlikely however that his demise will halt the interest in this case, as the media will see to it that the debate continues.

The Killing of a Gangster Rap Star

Tupac Shakur

The world of rap music has endured a tough reputation. Born out of the street gangs which inhabit the darker side of most American cities, gangster rap lyrics are hard hitting, no-holds-barred reflections of life in the urban ghettos. Predominantly a black music culture, the words of the songs often refer to the realities of gang life and the hatred of the police, whose activities at times seem to concentrate on those who live in the deprived black neighbourhoods. White commentators have decried the music as violent and provocative, likely to corrupt young minds. The glorifying of gang life and the money-for-nothing attitude portrayed in the songs certainly presents a very negative picture for the millions of people who have bought and played this new hard-nosed music.

Those stars who have made the music have become millionaires and have enjoyed all the trappings of their success. One of the biggest stars of this scene was Tupac Shakur who recorded under the stage name of 2pac. During his recording career he sold millions of albums, some of which remained in America's top sales charts for months at a time. Like many of the top rap stars to emerge, Tupac's beginnings were back in the ghettos and it is his own memories and experiences which have served his song writing so well. As with many of his contemporaries Tupac had not only had a violent past, but he also lived with violence, or the risk of it, day to day. His fame and fortune did not buy him the respectability and safety one might expect – the world of gangster rap meant always having to prove your own authenticity; it was he who coined the phrase "keep it real". Given the violent nature of many of his records it would appear that no matter how well off he became he couldn't shake off his own gang roots and as such he put himself in the firing line from the countless thugs who inhabit the gangland streets of America. He lived dangerously and died violently, not unlike the many poor teenagers who bought his records and listened to the words which talked of killing police officers, drug pushing, absent fathers and the lack of respect for women. Many of the big stars of rap have had major problems with the law, but when it comes to living fast and dying young, Tupac Shakur was the James Dean of the 1990s.

Tupac Amaru Shakur, whose real name was Lesane Crooks, was born in inauspicious beginnings in New York City in 1971. His arrival in the world could not have been harsher, his mother Afeni Shakur having been released from prison the month before he was born after serving time for her involvement with the militant black group, the Black Panthers. She had been held on bombing charges but was acquitted and was released just in time to give birth. By the time Shakur was born his father had already left and remained absent for most of his life, emerging once again after his now famous son had been shot for the first time. The earlier part of his life was spent in the Bronx, one of New York's toughest neighbourhoods and one where gang life was rife. He eventually moved to Baltimore where he found some enjoyment studying acting at the High School of the Performing Arts. It was here that he wrote his first attempt at a rap record, spurred on by the loss of a friend who had been killed while playing with a gun. The loss brought out a different emotion in Shakur who now wrote of gun control and the problems of gun ownership. His attempts were sufficiently good for him to win opportunities to perform the song on many occasions, and it was this first taste of the limelight that encouraged him to drop out of school and move to northern California.

His pursuit of stardom began in earnest when he auditioned for the band Digital Underground and managed to join them as a member of the road crew. They eventually gave him the opportunity to record with them and he performed on a number of their releases. With a recording now under his belt he struck out on his own and in 1991 released an album called *2pacalypse Now* which managed to sell half a million copies and contained two singles hits. His lyrics had become more aggressive and he wrote of the darker side of human life, unwed teenage mothers and his emerging trouble with the law. Later that year he engaged in a $10 million lawsuit against the Oakland Police Department, stating that he had been assaulted by the police as they tried to arrest him for jaywalking.

His own experience with the police and those who he called friends was that they were always trying to pin something on them. The lyrics to a number of his songs pertained to killing police officers, but always within the context of self-defence. However his lyrics obtained some degree of notoriety in early 1992 when a Texas state trooper was shot and killed by a teenager who had been listening to *2pacalypse Now*. Dan Quayle, Vice President of the US at the time, demanded that the album be withdrawn from sale, but Interscope, the label who had released the album, refused – for a gangster rapper the exposure couldn't have been better and soon Shakur was rising up the charts.

At about this time Tupac's acting career was also beginning to blossom, having previously played the violent bishop in Ernest Dickerson's film *Juice*. In 1993 he played opposite Janet Jackson in the film *Poetic Justice* as well as releasing the multi-million selling album *Strictly 4 My N.I.G.G.A.Z*, which contained more messages of violence.

By this stage Shakur had become the focus of the media who vilified his work as encouraging the worst type of behaviour and which portrayed negative images of women, a fact not lost on the jury who indicted him in 1993 on charges of sodomizing a female fan. The fan had claimed that Shakur and a number of his associates had sexually assaulted her in a Manhattan hotel suite, a charge which earned him a prison stretch.

During the trial Shakur endured the first of his many

violent encounters – while entering a recording studio he was using he was shot twice and robbed of $40,000 worth of jewellery. Although he survived the ordeal he was sentenced to serve four and a half years for the sex attack, with the potential of early release for good behaviour. The shooting of Shakur was widely reported and the press had a field day linking the attack to his violent songs, exposing the star as a shady character who, although successful, still had links to the seedier characters who lived a life of criminality, a claim that could never be entirely justified, even though he was at the time serving a sentence for sexual assault, which many thought a reflection of his low opinion of women.

In 1994 Shakur appealed against his sentence and was released on $1.4 million bail, the money being posted by Death Row Records, his new recording label and the one with whom he would enjoy great success. The enigmatic owner of Death Row Records was Marion "Suge" Knight, another man with a gangland reputation who also looked after other famous rappers such as Snoop Doggy Dog amongst others. Knight had built the label to its $100 million position and had dreams of it becoming the Motown of the 1990s, an opportunity lost when his main star finally lost his life.

On his release from prison in 1995 Shakur concluded the album he had started before his prison stretch, adding one of the songs he had written while in jail. *Me Against the World*, another album concentrating on ghetto violence, entered the Billboard album chart at number one and managed to sell over two million copies. Now rich and infamous, Shakur started acting like the moneyed gangster rapper he always wanted to be. His sales success was anchored in the fans' belief that Shakur was the real McCoy, a fact that Shakur was intent on proving and his public behaviour became more aggressive.

Straight off the back of his latest album success Shakur immediately started working on his next album. No one could describe Shakur as anything other than totally committed as he worked night and day perfecting his particular brand of hip-hop. His next release reflected the new Shakur

– opulent and flash, enjoying the things in life his money could now buy him. *All Eyez on Me* sold nearly 2.5 million copies and again was a number one hit, the first double album of its type to do so. This time the songs saw Shakur flaunting his new wealth; fast cars, night clubs and loose women were now the lyrics of the day.

It was around this time that Shakur and the CEO of Death Row Records, Marion Knight, started to feel the competition that was being exerted by other rap stars recording on other labels. The competition would often flare up with threats of violence being made and comments of a derogatory nature in the general media. Most of the rap stars had a similar background in that before their musical success they had come from a strictly poor background, and like Shakur, still had that street-fighting mentality that no amount of money could eradicate. The stars formed their own gangs mainly around their label and cultivated relationships with other celebrities with a reputation. Shakur and Knight were both friends with the boxer Mike Tyson, who as well as having a fearsome reputation within the ring, had a bad-man image out of it. Tyson had written Shakur an uplifting letter while he was languishing in jail on sex charges. Reciprocating, Shakur wrote Tyson a song which he played as his walk-out music for his title fight against Peter McNeeley in August 1995.

It would be Mike Tyson who would be one of the last men to see Shakur on the evening of his death, as he went to watch his latest title fight against Bruce Seldon. Excited at seeing the boxing match and of being able to be seen publicly with Tyson, Shakur and his entourage arrived in Las Vegas at 2.30 p.m. on Saturday, 7 September 1995. Shakur and Tyson were later due at a night club called Club 662, where they were to promote the negative side of gang life. The queue at the club was already growing at the door in preparation for the arrival of the stars who were to attend.

Tyson fights were a grand affair and tended to attract a lot of stars from the world of rap; his bad-boy image seemed to fit in well with the theme they promote. The fight was due to commence at 8 p.m. and so Shakur and his party arrived around 7.30 to ensure they were all seated in time. As usual the atmosphere was electric in anticipation of Iron Mike's performance.

With the usual pre-fight build-up Tyson finally approached the ring, flanked on all sides by the numerous helpers he employed. The fight though was short lived as Tyson despatched a flurry of blows which ended the fight in just 109 seconds. As Tyson left the ring Shakur was the first to congratulate him with a hug and they had a brief chat agreeing to meet later at Club 662.

At roughly 8.30 p.m., Shakur and his group began to file out of the MGM Grand and were heading through the hotel's Grand Garden when they ended up in an argument with an individual. Whatever was said between them is not known, but hotel security cameras caught a group of about eight men rounding on the lone man and giving him a severe kicking. The man was left on the ground as the group calmly strolled away. The security footage does not show clearly who were involved in the scuffle but later an MGM employee claims to have seen Shakur and Knight in a brawl with the lone black man. Following the incident Shakur's party walked away, preparing to visit a nearby house where they intended to change their clothing before leaving for Club 662.

Later that evening Shakur and his group set off in an impressive convoy consisting of five executive-class cars. Shakur and record boss Marion Knight were alone in Knight's BMW 750 at the head of the convoy, with the other four cars, one of which contained two professionally employed body guards, following on behind. It was just after 11 p.m. when the convoy turned eastbound on Flamingo Road; Knight was driving and Shakur was playing the music; he was in a good mood and was looking forward to getting to the club.

As the convoy slowed to a halt at the intersection of Flamingo Road and Koval Lane a white Cadillac pulled alongside. The car contained four black men, one of whom opened fire with a semi-automatic weapon. Knight's BMW was sprayed with thirteen bullets which ripped through the passenger door. Shakur was hit four times in the chest and abdomen, while Knight, who was farthest from the gunman, was struck in the head by a bullet which was thought to have ricocheted off Shakur.

The drive-by shooting was over in seconds; the Cadillac sped away, turned onto the Strip and away into the night. Knight, who had not yet realized that he was injured, spun the car around and headed in the opposite direction from where he had travelled; it is thought he was simply trying to head away from the direction of the Cadillac. Police officers who had been operating in the area had heard the shots and could see that the target was the BMW sedan which was now u-turning and fleeing back up Flamingo Road. A patrol car pursued Knight and Shakur, who by now was slumped over in the passenger seat, losing blood from the four shots he had taken. As the traffic slowed on Flamingo the pursuing patrol car finally managed to close in on the car and bring it to a stop. Having already radioed the emergency services a para-medic team were already making their way to the injured duo, who by now were in severe need of assistance. Shakur was incoherent when the paramedics pulled him from the vehicle and started to prepare him for a rapid trip to the University Medical Centre, where medical staff were pre-paring themselves for a major trauma victim.

The rest of the convoy had become ensnared in the traffic and surprisingly the car containing the bodyguards did not try and pursue the Cadillac – later all of those who travelled in the cars behind would claim they had seen nothing of the incident, even the bodyguards whose job it was to provide the protection. The events though did have many witnesses, including two police officers who were directly adjacent to the shooting, as they were dealing with a stolen vehicle misdemeanour. The road that evening, like most nights, was full with motorists and those on foot, as was the Strip, the escape route taken by the gunman. Yet other than the basic facts as described by the police officers, no one else came forward to assist in the investigation that followed, including those who were a part of it.

Shakur was rushed to the University Medical Centre

where his condition was described as critical. He underwent the first of three operations, one of which removed his right lung which had been hit three times, causing extensive damage to some of his major blood vessels. After the operations were complete a hospital spokesman said that Shakur's chances of survival were now 50–50. The first 48 hours were critical, as the damage to the major arteries needed to be repaired and the vital signs stabilized. His initial 80–20 against prognosis looked like it had improved significantly, although doctors now warned that the second danger phase was about to be entered. The week following the operation would tell if Shakur's wounds had suffered any infection during the operations, his life still hanging in the balance as he was held in suspended animation, the subject of a drug-induced coma. Breathing apparatus pumped blood around his body, while tubes automatically fed nutrients into him and took the waste away. It would now be a matter of time.

As for Marion Knight, he was released later the same night. Shrapnel had hit him in the head, but had caused little damage; Shakur had taken most of the impact. Knight immediately disappeared, not wishing to be interviewed by the police, who were keen to receive his eyewitness testimony.

Meanwhile the University Medical Centre had become the scene of large crowds as fans and the media crowded round the entrance looking to talk to anyone who could offer them an update. Inside the centre, Shakur's mother paced the floor waiting for a breakthrough having been joined by the head of the Las Vegas Nation of Islam. Reverend Jesse Jackson had called in to wish them luck, cautioning youngsters who listened to his music not to treat the glorification of the gangster scene as anything other than a waste of life. Other stars of the rap scene called in and all passed their own comments in relation to the events.

The media gathered from both the east and west coast, TV cameras were placed all around the entrance to the Medical Centre and reporters from all of the national newspapers were in evidence, the *Los Angeles Times*, *Washington Post*, *New York Daily News* and a large contingent from Black

Entertainment Television. At one point friends of Shakur and fans turned on the press, claiming it was their interpretation of Shakur's work that had given him the gangster image. There can be no doubt that no good news was ever printed about Shakur; it was overwhelmingly bad, and as far as the press were concerned Shakur had reaped what he had sown. It was clear then that they were there to highlight the outcome of gang culture, not to publicize the crime with a view to catching the perpetrators, and the fans seemed to sense this.

If the press didn't see the positive side of Shakur then those fans who couldn't make it to the University Medical Centre certainly did – the switchboard was taking up to 10,000 calls per day from fans wanting an update. A spokesman for the hospital said this was the most calls they had ever received for a single person.

The press though had their own angle to pursue – what they were intent on discussing was Shakur's criminal past rather than his impressive record collection. The fact is that both were worthy of note – Shakur had been involved with the law on a number of occasions, all of which fitted in nicely and supported his persona as the hard man of gangster rap.

Shakur had over time had his run-ins with the authorities. In 1992 while attending a festival in Marin County he was involved in an incident which resulted in the death of a six-year-old boy from a stray bullet. The year after he was charged with the shooting of two off-duty Atlanta police officers, charges which were subsequently dropped. In the same year he pleaded guilty to misdemeanour assault charges after attacking a fellow rapper with a baseball bat.

Shakur was arrested in November 1993 and charged with sexual assault after a fan claimed she was attacked in a Manhattan hotel room and sodomized by Shakur and a number of his friends. The investigation into these events were carried out over a number of months before finally coming to court in 1995.

In April 1994 Shakur and his brother Maurice Harding were stopped on Hollywood Boulevard and found to be in possession of two 9mm pistols. The pair were arrested and later charged. Just one month later in May 1994 Shakur commenced a 15-day jail term for attacking the video director Alan Hughes, while they were preparing to make a music video. As a result of his previous misdemeanour assault charge Shakur also had to carry out civic duties by reporting to a Caltrans work crew, an obligation he failed to comply with and one which would later have him back in court for failing to follow his parole rules. In October 1994 Shakur incurred another misdemeanour assault charge, this time from the authorities in Michigan.

In early 1995 Shakur was imprisoned having been found guilty of the sexual assault charge and was jailed for up to four and a half years; he was sent to a prison in upstate New York.

There were many other minor offences which never reached court – in the week prior to his shooting he and a number of his group were involved in a fracas with other attendees at the MTV awards, a scuffle ensued but no real damage was done. The events were reported, but once again it seemed that Shakur was simply living up to the image he had created. For those who revered him his actions were part of who he was; for those who loathed him, he couldn't be any lower than he already was in their opinions.

It was this image that the media had presented over the years and it was still this image they were presenting as Shakur lay in his hospital bed, unaware of anything that was going on about him.

What had been a critical injury unfortunately turned to murder just six days later when Shakur died at 4.03 p.m. on 13 September 1995, which by chance was a Friday, unlucky for some. Later that evening the coroner performed an autopsy on Shakur before releasing his body to the Davis mortuary, which had been instructed by Afeni Shakur to cremate him. A day later his remains were passed to Afeni, who left Las Vegas heading back to California.

The fans who gathered around the Medical Centre were in shock – only days before the word had been that Shakur's position had improved slightly; they were therefore expecting him to pull through. The official cause of death was described as respiratory failure and cardiopulmonary arrest; the damage caused by the bullets had been too great.

Mourners at the hospital, including Knight, lingered together even after Shakur's body had been removed to the mortuary. From those who had been at Shakur's bedside during the six days since he had been shot, including the members of his back-up band Outlaw Immortalz, whispers began to emerge that those in Shakur's closest circle knew who had carried out the attack.

The police, however, just like the press, were not being fed information. Those who had been in Shakur's company that night couldn't remember what had happened or claimed not to have seen the events – it was as if all those in the cars following, including the drivers, were looking in the opposite direction. It appeared that the underworld code of not co-operating with the police was being enforced. The media fared even worse – when any of them was spotted by fans an alarm would be raised and the individual warned off. Although the bad press was finally coming home to roost, it didn't change their reporting style – Shakur's death was simply the conclusion to a life bordering on perpetual criminality. His contribution to the world of music was either overlooked or overshadowed by his violent death.

From the moment Shakur was hospitalized the police hoped that he would be able to shed light upon or even identify those who had shot him, but with his death this particular opportunity was lost and no one else seemed to be coming forward. Knight, who had gone to ground in the days following the shooting, eventually came forward to the police flanked by three lawyers. As someone who had suffered some small injury during the shooting Knight was not considered a suspect, however it was hoped that he might be able to identify the perpetrators or suggest a reason for the attack; but like all the others who had been there he maintained a grim silence.

Through the press it was common knowledge that a strong element of gang loyalty existed between the various known gangs. Knight for instance was thought to be affiliated to the Los Angeles based Bloods, as he wore an expensive ring with the letters M.O.B across the centre, standing for Member of the Bloods. The police believed that the shooting might have been linked to some gang feud, although they were quite certain that the intended target was Shakur – his side of the vehicle had been peppered with bullets and no obvious attempt had been made to hit Knight.

As the police tried to reconstruct the events, they began by looking at the group's activities before the fateful car journey. Investigations at the MGM Grand uncovered the security tape which showed the violent altercation between Shakur's group and another black man. Investigations found that the man who had taken the beating was Orlando Anderson, a notorious member of another Los Angeles gang called the Crips. Los Angeles police were able to confirm that the gangs were indeed warring and had investigated a number of incidents between them.

As the world of hip-hop and leading members of the black community gathered to mourn the passing of Tupac Shakur, the police and the press prepared for the expected retaliation, the tit-for-tat murder that would be needed to settle the score. And they were not to be disappointed, for around 12 shootings occurred in the Compton district of Los Angeles in the days following the attack on Shakur. Compton seemed to be the epicentre of the gang culture in LA and it was here that police thought their killer might lurk.

It appeared then that 22-year-old Orlando Anderson might have had a double motive for the attack on Shakur – he had suffered at his hands just after the Tyson fight when he was knocked to the floor, and he had allegiance to the Crips gang. Two Metro homicide detectives from Las Vegas arrived in Compton where they joined members of the LA Police Department in a special round-up operation of gang members. Officers who were dressed in military style uniforms and sporting black masks set off flash-bang diversionary devices as they stormed houses in the Compton, Long Beach, Lakewood and Paramount areas of the city. Kicking in doors they dragged individuals from their beds in the early morning raid. Anderson, who had previously been detained over a murder in 1994, was one of those arrested in the raids and was immediately taken in for specific questioning, although police were at pains to point out that he was detained for questioning over a murder in Compton, although he would also be questioned about the events in Las Vegas. During the early morning raid the police were able to round up 21 gang members from both factions, who were suspected of involvement in the dozen shootings which had occurred in Compton since Shakur's murder, three of which had been fatal.

As the police began the arduous task of interviewing those who had been arrested, it was Anderson who let slip that he believed it was Marion Knight who was the target of the assassins, not Shakur, information he claimed he had heard on the grapevine. Other than this the gang members denied all knowledge and involvement in either the Compton shootings or Shakur's murder, providing in-built alibis for each other. Meanwhile the investigation in Las Vegas was proving equally fruitless. No trace of the new Cadillac which had been seen leaving the scene could be found and nothing had emerged from the many members of the public who had witnessed the incident. No one it would appear wanted to get involved, like the media claimed; this was gang business, not some innocent member of the public who had been killed.

With the police unable to solicit help from either the public or the gang world their investigation essentially ground to a halt. Their enquiries had been unable to unearth any facts which would assist in a conviction and all the while rumours and accusations gradually filtered through to the police and the press.

The world of television eventually turned its more positive focus on the case when the show *Unsolved Mysteries* aired details of the drive-by shooting in the hope of jogging people's memories. The producer of the show was surprised when the switchboard took more than 250 calls regarding the events from members of the public, many more than other similar incidents had generated. For days following the programme's transmission the show had been forwarding tip sheets to the Metro homicide unit, who said they were meticulously following each lead up. The show had invited members of the Metro unit to join switchboard staff but unlike other times, they did not attend, a fact which was noted when members of Shakur's family claimed the police were not working as hard to solve their case as they might have been for someone from a good Las Vegas home. The show has a 28 per cent solve rate but in this instance many of the tips were from people unwilling to give their identities; one lead which appeared to be quite hot was unable to be followed up effectively as the informant refused to provide contact details, presumably afraid of reprisals. For a serious programme and one whose track record is helping to bring criminals to justice, it is perhaps surprising to hear that around 70 per cent of the callers claimed to believe that Shakur was still alive and had simply gone to ground to avoid further violence.

It was apparent that the only people who could possibly assist in the investigation were members of Shakur's entourage that night. One man the Metro police did want to question again was Yafeu Fula, aged 19, and a member of Shakur's backing group. He had been in the car directly behind Knight's BMW when the attack took place and had been briefly interviewed after the event, as all of the entourage had – his close proximity to the attack meant that it was almost impossible to conceive that he had not witnessed the entire proceedings. To the officers' chagrin Fula returned to his home in New Jersey and remained elusive, communicating via Knight's attorney. As the police were making progress to have Fula returned to Las Vegas for questioning they were faced with another problem – Fula was found dead in the third-floor hallway of an apartment building, shot once in the back of the head. The New Jersey Police Department were confident of an arrest almost immediately and within days arrested a 16-year-old boy whose name could not be revealed for legal reasons. Shortly after this a second youth turned himself in but after prolonged questioning it could not be established if Fula's murder had been connected to the Shakur investigation. Either way, the Las Vegas police had lost the one person who had indicated in his first interview that he might be able to identify the murderer. The two youths were later charged with murder and weapons offences.

And so without the evidence needed to pursue the case, the police, like members of the media, were left to speculate over the question of who had murdered Shakur. Two main theories emerged, one of which alleged that another big-time rap artist, Notorious B.I.G., real name Christopher Wallace, had planned the attack after the two had been involved in arguments. Once close friends the two had since fallen out and had taken to insulting each other in public. Shakur had written lyrics in one of his songs which suggested he had slept with B.I.G.'s wife and that he wanted to kill him. Nothing short of hatred now existed between the two. A *Los Angeles Times* article claimed that Biggie, as he was often referred to, had met with members of the Crips gang in Las Vegas and offered them one million dollars to kill Shakur, even offering his own gun as part of the deal. When the story emerged friends and family of the star closed ranks to discredit the story and provide alibis for the night Shakur was shot. Documentary evidence supported Biggie's claim that he had been holed up in a New York recording studio during the day and had then returned home with friends to watch the Tyson fight on pay per view.

Sadly Biggie suffered the same fate as Shakur just months later when gunmen opened fire on his vehicle as he was driving home. The star's driver drove him to a nearby hospital where he was pronounced dead from multiple 9mm bullet wounds. One of Biggie's entourage in the car behind tried to pursue the shooter but was unable to keep up. Frustratingly the police were unable to connect the killing of Shakur with that of Notorious B.I.G.

The second theory and the one given most prominence by the police and the media was that Orlando Anderson, one of the men picked up in the early morning raids in Compton, lay behind the attack. He and fellow members of the Compton Crips gang had attacked and robbed one of Shakur's bodyguard's months earlier in Los Angeles. It was by chance that the bodyguard spotted Anderson leaving the MGM Grand after the Tyson fight and pointed him out to Shakur who confronted Anderson with his group and extracted the revenge which was caught by the security cameras. It is known that Anderson was then approached by MGM staff who tried to persuade him to press charges, something he refused to do. Shaken and bruised it is then thought that Anderson headed to the Excalibur Hotel where he had a room booked with his girlfriend. News of Anderson's beating spread through the gang underground and before he got to his hotel his phone and pager had started to ring with messages from his Crips gang associates. He arranged to meet a group of them at the nearby Treasure Island Hotel which had served as Crips headquarters during many profile boxing matches. Here in a marijuana smoke-filled room the gang members planned how they would extract their revenge, the most hotly disputed topic being who would get to pull the trigger. The gang initially planned to shoot Shakur after his performance at Club 662, by placing armed snipers across the road from the club's entrance. As it turned out they were unable to carry out the attack in this way and had to revert to a back-up plan when Shakur and his entourage managed to get in cars and head away. A car containing Anderson and three associates followed the convoy down the road until they had the opportunity to attack when halted at traffic lights, which resulted in Shakur's eventual death.

The man the police thought most likely to be the culprit and the man Shakur's mother filed a wrongful death suit against subsequently claimed to be one of Shakur's biggest fans, a claim others vehemently denied. Again though, just two years after Shakur's death, Orlando Anderson went the same way, killed by a gunshot in the Compton district of Los Angeles.

Afeni Shakur has always claimed that the investigation carried out by Metro Police was less thorough than it might have been for any other citizen, a situation she bitterly despises. As she has pointed out herself, when Ennis Cosby was shot, son of the television actor Bill Cosby, the press and the police searched high and low for the perpetrators, yet for Shakur, the bad man of gangster rap, they ran a lacklustre investigation supported by a media machine intent upon presenting only the bad side of her son's music and reputation.

Shakur was a complex individual and someone who is only now getting the recognition he deserved for his musical ability. His fifth and last album, *Makeveli*, went on sale after his death and became an immediate number one selling success. Shops sold out in hours and even his previous albums enjoyed a second wind. Radio stations coast to coast were inundated with requests to play Shakur's music.

In a final twist, the video made by Shakur just a month before his death depicts the star being ushered into heaven following an ambulance ride in which he is seen riddled with bullet wounds. He is met in heaven by the comedian Redd Foxx who is seen hosting a jam session with Jimi Hendrix, Louis Armstrong and Billie Holiday – a case of life imitating art.

A Callous Roadside Shooting

Ennis Cosby

Anyone would be annoyed if they got a flat tyre, especially if it was dark and cold outside. So who would ever guess that what should have been just an inconvenient delay could actually lead to murder. Yet this is exactly what happened to Ennis Cosby, son of the famous Hollywood television star, Bill Cosby, when he was driving towards a friend's house one evening.

As soon as Cosby realized that the car was in trouble he pulled over and walked around the side of it to see what the problem was. He soon found that he had a flat and that he would need to change it before he would be able to continue. But before he could finish the job he was dead.

William H. Cosby Jr was born on 12 July 1937 in Philadelphia, Pennsylvania. As a young boy he enjoyed listening to comedians, including Fred Allen, Gracie Allen, Jack Benny, George Burns and Jimmy Durante. He left school after tenth grade to join the Navy where he stayed for four years as a medical corpsman, during which time he completed his High School education. By his twenties he had already appeared in television and film shows and was proving to be extremely popular. During the 1960s he received six consecutive Grammys and in 1984 his situation comedy *The Cosby Show* began, making him a household name, his character known to millions of fans as the loving dad of the house, Mr Cliff Huxtable. At its peak the show had in excess of 70 million viewers, running from 1984 to 1992. Throughout this period of huge television success he was still a fantastically popular, witty comedian, using family life as the basis for his material.

Bill Cosby was enjoying a truly successful life. Happily married to his wife Camille Olivia Hanks, a direct descendant of Nancy Hanks, Abraham Lincoln's mother, they had four daughters, Erika, Erinn, Ensa, and Evin, followed by one son, Ennis. This well-regarded Afro-American, famous as an actor, stand-up comedian, singer and author, wrote a wonderful book entitled *Fatherhood*, which became a number one best-seller, in which he recounts many amusing stories associated with becoming a parent, managing to persuade the reader that he thoroughly enjoys the experience.

Sadly for the Cosby family, on 16 January 1997, the worst fears of any parents were realized when news reached them that their beloved son Ennis had been murdered, apparently while changing a flat tyre at the roadside in Los Angeles. As a child Ennis had struggled with dyslexia, but with great determination had fought to deal with the problem, confident that it would not hold him back. As an adult he had managed to cope with his disorder and was planning to become a teacher of children with special educational needs, spending his free time helping children who were suffering with the disability he knew so much about. He was studying at Columbia University for a Master's in special education and would no doubt have gone on to inspire other youngsters with the disability to achieve all they could. It was while enjoying a vacation in Los Angeles that Ennis Cosby was killed, the apparent victim of what was described as a roadside robbery.

Ennis had been driving his dark-green convertible Mercedes down the 405 Freeway in Los Angeles when he was forced to pull over due to a flat tyre. Realizing that he could not continue he decided to phone a friend, Stephanie Crane, whose house was relatively close by. As it was too dark to change the tyre he was hoping that she might drive out and help. She arrived a short while afterwards, parking her car a small distance behind his and using her headlights to provide the much-needed illumination. After a brief chat Ennis got down to the task of changing the tyre while Stephanie sat in her own car to keep warm. She had only been there a short while when from nowhere, a white man appeared next to her door with a gun. The gunman threatened to shoot Crane if she did not get out of the car, but spurred by a sudden rush of adrenalin, and taking advantage of the already idling car, she locked her door and accelarated away, leaving just the gunman and poor Ennis on that dark and lonely road. Once Crane had put enough distance between herself and the gunman she bravely turned the car around and headed cautiously back to the scene, where to her relief she saw the man running away. As she pulled in to the edge of the road again to check on her friend, she was met with a scene of pure horror – where only minutes before Ennis had been changing a tyre, he was now sprawled out on the ground in a pool of blood.

Kneeling next to Ennis, Crane saw immediately that he needed help, his blood loss seemed huge and she was unable to see exactly where his wound was. Panicking, she managed to stop a motorist who advised her that his condition did not look favourable. Rushing back to her car she then called the emergency services, quickly describing the situation, but by the time they arrived, 27-year-old Ennis Cosby was already dead, the victim of a single gunshot wound to the head. Fame and fortune are simply no defence against a callous murderer, especially when you happen to be in the wrong place at the wrong time. And from this brief encounter on a dark Los Angeles road, Bill Cosby lost his only son.

The motive for the murder was not clear – Ennis was holding a packet of cigarettes when he was shot, was still wearing an expensive Rolex watch and had some $20 bills in his pocket.

Stephanie described the man she saw as white, approximately 5 feet 10 inches, about 160 pounds and between 25 and 32 years old. Another witness was questioned by police but was unable to offer any useful description of the attacker. A police sketch artist provided an interpretation of the killer's features using the details provided by Crane. Once the sketch was confirmed as being a close fit to the man Stephanie saw it was widely circulated.

The media jumped on the case and offered their support

by publishing the artist's sketch on the front page. The TV news channels also ran the image, with every communication channel coast to coast joining in, a real boost to the manhunt which was now under way. Obviously everybody wanted to know as much about the case as possible and newspaper sales rocketed.

After Ennis' body was discharged from the County Coroner's Office a funeral was held at the Cosby home in Massachusetts, on Sunday 19 January 1997. He was later buried on the family estate on Bardwell Ferry Road, in Shelburne. In March, Bill Cosby visited the scene of his son's murder to place a white cross with a message reading, "Thank you, friend".

By now several multi-national companies were offering large rewards for information on the case. This was to prove crucial in finding the assailant. The *National Enquirer* and *America's Most Wanted* offered a $100,000 reward for information leading to an arrest. Every effort was being made to catch the man who had killed the son of America's best-loved, and at one time highest-paid, television star. The police authorities devoted a massive amount of manpower to the case, the rewards were geared to draw someone out of the woodwork and the television coverage was unprecedented. It wasn't long before they received an all-important call from a man claiming to have information on the Cosby killing; his name was Christopher So and he was prepared to inform on an associate in return for the reward, claiming that one of his colleagues had been bragging about murdering a black man. The name which he was to put forward was Mikail Markhasev, a 19-year-old Ukranian immigrant.

On 12 March, just a couple of months after the killing, the police were informed that a call had been received offering the name of a potential suspect, and shortly afterwards Markhasev was arrested on suspicion of the brutal murder of Ennis Cosby. Markhasev lived at Magnolia Blvd in Los Angeles, he already had a police record and was associated with local gangs who were involved in drugs. The police immediately suspected that Markhasev was seeking money for drugs when he allegedly killed Cosby.

The trial was set to commence on 22 June 1997, some six months after the murder. Bill Cosby stated that he would not be attending the court as he did not wish to interrupt or take the focus away from the legal process, although many family members and friends did attend, keeping him informed on all aspects of the trial as it unfolded.

Allocating the jury members was to prove a difficult task – there had been so much information about the case in the press and on the news that to find people who could demonstrate that they had not already been influenced by media reporting was difficult. Potential jurors were made to complete large questionnaires to reveal how much they knew about the case, with many carefully versed questions to assess whether they had already started to develop a bias. They were asked, for example, how much television they watched and indeed if they had watched any Bill Cosby shows. They were also asked to declare what if anything they already knew about the defendant, particularly if they were aware of his past and his involvement in gangs. After completing the questionnaires, the jurors were then interviewed separately and informed that they should only use the information that they were presented with in court. It was later reported that some of the prospective jurors were shown to have already formed the opinion that Markhasev was guilty, and the only way this could have happened was through the general media, who once again were keen to present their story, irrespective of the impact it might have on the trial. Eventually a jury was chosen, an even match of men and women, four of them black, one mixed race and the others white.

America had by now entered the era of the televised trial, in principle the method by which the public could see justice being done. However, not all judges believed that the cameras helped promote fairness, most believing it would enhance the circulation of the newspapers or the viewing figures of a particular channel, but not the prospect of a fair trial. There was a distinct feeling that the presence of the media simply promoted the prospect of "trial by body language" – great for actors, but a challenge for an average citizen. Cameras were therefore banned from the courtroom by order of Superior Court Judge David Perez, who feared that to have the daily court proceedings fed to the public via television would more than likely turn the case into a television drama. The Judge also turned down chief prosecutor Anne Ingalls's request for the jurors to remain anonymous, the prosecution's request being denied on the grounds that under Californian law the jury's identifications must be known except in extenuating circumstances, conditions which Ingalls could not satisfy.

When the case of *California* v. *Markhasev* began it was Anne Ingalls who opened for the prosecution, giving her version of events for the night that Cosby was murdered. In a bid to capture the jury's attention and sympathy Ingalls set about constructing the events, making sure that she never lost sight of the shock value attached to the murder itself. She explained how Cosby pulled in after suffering a punctured tyre, that he called his friend because it was so dark, going on to describe the chilling situation Crane found herself in when she was confronted by the gunman. Ingalls spoke at length about the fear Crane felt as she pulled away from the scene, leaving her good friend at the mercy of the killer. Then as Ingalls was about to portray the final moments of Cosby's life she handed out a series of photographs, each graphically and horrifically showing the young man lying in a pool of his own blood. To add weight to the already gruesome pictures, Ingalls described Cosby's last moments – how Markharev demanded money from Cosby, but when he didn't act fast enough, had shot him in cold blood at close quarters.

With the jury now sufficiently shocked at the sheer violence of the crime, Ingalls went on to provide the evidence that she hoped would prove Markhasev had committed the murder. The first person called to the stand was Stephanie Crane, who supported Ingalls's version of events – when asked if the culprit was in court, she pointed at Markhasev, who sat stony faced in the dock. Ingalls then produced letters allegedly written by Markhasev while he was in prison awaiting trial, and to read passages, which were apparently intended for Markhasev's friend, Michael Chang. From the letters she read that the defendant had intended to go out and commit a robbery, but that it had gone horribly wrong. The letters had been checked by a handwriting expert, Karen Chiarodit, who testified that those produced did match samples of writing provided by the defendant. What followed must have been a blow to the defence, for Ingalls then called the second of her first prosecution witnesses, one Michael Chang, the man to whom Markhasev had written. Chang did not hold back; speaking directly to the jurors he described how Markhasev had told him, "I shot a nigger. It's all over the news." Then to finish her annihilation of the defendant she offered the first piece of irrefutable DNA evidence. When the murder weapon was found it was wrapped up in a knitted cap, examination of which proved that the cap had been worn by the defendant at some point. The DNA link to the cap would be a significant nail in Markhasev's coffin. DNA never lies and jurors are not normally swayed by the argument of coincidence.

Markhasev had entered a not guilty plea to the charges of murder and attempted armed robbery. Henry Hall, the man called upon to defend Markhasev, appeared to have his work cut out, however he slowly began to piece together a different story, claiming that the court had got the wrong man and that it was an acquaintance of Markhasev, Eli Zakaria, another man allegedly present on the night of the murder, who was in fact responsible for the shooting of Ennis Cosby. Hall was at pains to point out that the gun – found one month after the event in a field – did not have the defendant's fingerprints on it, yet no one had suggested that Markhasev had been wearing gloves. Hall then went on to dismantle Crane's earlier identification of Markhasev, describing how she had failed to identify the defendant in a police line-up. When it came to the letters that Markhasev had allegedly written, Hall simply denied his client had anything to do with them, asking the jury if they honestly thought that his client would write such incriminating notes while under the noses of those who would gladly exploit such information.

Gabe Drapel, a loose associate of Markhasev, was then called to the stand. He testified that on the night of the murder he had visited Markhasev at his house and that he was wearing a knitted cap, identical to the one recovered by the police. Forensics had shown that the gun which was found was indeed the murder weapon and the DNA examination of pieces of hair showed that the chances of the hair not belonging to Markhasev would be as low as one in 15,000.

Susan Brockbank, a criminologist, was also called to the stand. She was questioned in a friendly manner by Ingalls, who simply wanted to reinforce in the jury's mind that the DNA evidence was nothing short of conclusive. She reiterated the slim chance which existed for the hair sample to belong to anyone other than the defendant.

The murder weapon itself was not a chance find, having been found after Christopher So had indicated to the police where Markhasev had said he had thrown the gun. The police discovered the .38 calibre revolver, wrapped in the knitted cap, just yards from where it was described to be. If Christopher So wasn't the killer then the court was asked to believe that he knew of the weapon's whereabouts only because the actual murderer had told him. The revolver was produced in court and criminologist Diana Paul was called to the stand to compare the bullet that had killed Cosby with the bullets found in the alleged murder weapon. She confirmed that the gun must have fired the shot that killed Cosby, saying, "The bullet was fired from that gun and no other."

Prosecutors called Michael Chang to the stand, but he refused to testify, taking the Fifth Amendment, the position one takes if there is risk of self-incrimination by giving evidence.

Christopher So was called to the witness stand but was very reluctant to appear, claiming that he was endangering himself by doing so. In his testimony he recalled overhearing a conversation between the accused and Michael Chang, during which he recalled Markhasev saying, "I shot a nigger. It's all over the news." He also testified that Chang and the accused had spent time looking for the gun, some five or six days after the shooting, but it had been thrown into some bushes and the pair were unable to find it. When they returned from the unsuccessful hunting trip So recalled another statement: "Well, since we can't find the gun, you know, I'm going to have to come back and look for it again later." It was during this conversation that So learned of the area in which the gun had been discarded, the area in which the police did eventually find the gun and the incriminating knitted cap.

So remained on the stand while the defence team tried to undermine his testimony. Hall directly claimed that So was purely motivated by the reward money, of which he had already been paid $40,000 by the *National Enquirer*, with more to come if Markhasev was found guilty. Hall then asked So, "How much is the reward that the *National Enquirer* are offering?" To which he replied, "A hundred thousand dollars." Allowing the value to hang in the air a little, Hall then enquired, "Did the money motivate you in part or wholly to make the call to the police?" So, looking uncomfortable, responded, "Yes."

The defence then called Los Angeles police detective, Bert Luper, to the stand. He confirmed that when he interviewed So before the arrest of Markhasev, So concluded the interview with the question, "Does my story sound good?" The defence concluded that this provided proof that So was motivated to provide his statement, purely to get his hands on the reward money, and that it was thought he might be prepared to say anything which enhanced his chances in that respect.

The prosecution's next witness was the man who the defence claimed was the real killer of Ennis Cosby, Eli Zakaria. His presence in court gave the jury a chance to compare his likeness with the sketches of the alleged Cosby killer. It was an ingenious move on the part of the prosecution as the defence team were unprepared for the appearance of Zakaria, dressed in prison clothing and having been brought directly from jail where he was serving a sentence for an earlier misdemeanour. Faced with the collapse of their main strand of defence, Hall requested a recess for a few days, he needed to reassess his client's position. Judge David Perez granted the request and the court recessed.

The prosecution tried again to get Michael Chang to give evidence, but when he eventually took the stand he simply repeated his last statement and again took the Fifth Amendment. The prosecutors were disappointed at Chang's refusal to co-operate, for it was Chang's evidence that could give So's testimony the backing it needed. In a strange way Chang's refusal to testify gave weight to the idea that Markhasev was a violent man, capable of revenge. When another potential witness also refused to testify on grounds of personel safety, the prosecution had managed to make a point anyway, even if they did not get the eyewitness testimony they were after. These men were either very loyal friends or were worried that their testimonies might provoke the accused to seek revenge on them.

The defence then pulled out their one and only witness who was prepared to provide Markhasev with an alibi – his mother. Vicktoria Markhasev took the stand and testified that her son had been with her on the night of the shooting, helping her family move house. Her statement was well meant, but the prosecution pointed out that she had in fact already told the police that her son was at a party on the night of the shooting and that she hadn't seen him. Prosecutors got her to admit she had originally given police a different story, that Mikail was indeed headed to a party and that she hadn't see him.

The defence team then called a witness, Kathleen Bias, who claimed to have seen Markhasev and Zakaria at her house just hours after the murder. Bias, who lived in the Los Alamitos area of the city, said that the two men had called by on the night of the shooting. She described Markhasev as being calm and acting pretty normal, while describing Zakaria as frantic and out of control, acting very weird and moving very fast. The defence team used the men's behaviour as a reflection of guilt, claiming therefore that the police had arrested and charged the wrong man. Unable to contradict Bias's version of events, they instead sought to undermine her on a personal level, claiming that she had been trying to sell her story to a tabloid newspaper and that her sole goal in coming forward was to make money out of her association with the case.

By 6 July 1997, the court was ready to consider the closing statements of the opposing teams, and for the first time since the trial had began Bill and Camille Cosby took their seats in court, fully prepared to hear the summing up.

Anne Ingalls summarized the key factors that for the prosecution proved Markhasev's guilt. Markhasev had boasted to his friends about killing a black guy, which was nothing short of a confession. The letters he had written while in prison confirmed that he was privy to information about the case, information which only the murderer could have known. She also pointed out that the jury had seen the handwriting, and that they, along with the handwriting expert, could see that it matched sample writing provided by Markhasev. Christopher So had been able to help in the guns retrieval only because Markhasev had given him the location, and when the gun was retrieved the knitted cap provided the DNA evidence linking the accused to the gun, which was forensically proven to be the murder weapon.

When the defence attorney Henry Hall took to the floor he had what can only be described as an uphill struggle; the weight of evidence against his client seemed overwhelming. He initially suggested that there was reasonable doubt regarding Markhasev's guilt, claiming that many of the witnesses were more interested in securing the reward money than a correct verdict. He repeated his original objection to Stephanie Crane's identification of his client, saying she had been unable to identify Markhasev in the police line-up. After offering little in the way of additional convincing evidence Hall concluded his last defensive statement and handed the reigns back to Judge Perez.

Judge David Perez then began his summary of instructions for the jurors, reminding them that they could only consider the one charge against the accused – whether Markhasev was guilty of felony murder during an attempted robbery, not the lesser offence of second-degree murder.

The newspapers and media were running at full tilt as the

entire country awaitied the verdict. Everyone wanted to see Ennis Cosby's killer go to jail, and perhaps as importantly, to allow "America's dad", Bill Cosby, the opportunity to move on. The headlines were conclusive – the killer was indeed on trial and the evidence was overwhelming.

The following day the jury returned its decision, finding the accused, Mikail Markhasev, guilty of first-degree murder, attempted robbery and the illegal use of a firearm. As the prosecution had not sought the death penalty the prescribed sentence was predetermined, a mandatory life sentence without the opportunity of parole.

After the sentencing, Bill and Camille Cosby released a simple statement through a family spokesperson. "The Cosby family is satisfied with the judicial process that has led to this conviction, they have no comment regarding the sentence."

Defence attorney Henry Hall blamed the media for poisoning the jury and convicting his client before he even went to trial. On 7 August 1997, he filed a motion claiming that despite a court order, prosecutors had repeatedly referred to the accused's alleged gang affiliations throughout the trial. Hall also claimed that one juror had indicated that she had determined Markhasev's guilt before final arguments were completed. Another juror had reportedly said that Markhasev should be hung for Cosby's murder, a statement made before the deliberations had begun. Hall complained that with all these influences the jury must have been prejudiced against Markhasev. When asked how his client felt, Hall responded sharply, "He was just convicted of murder and he's going to spend the rest of his life in prison without the possibility of parole. He's nineteen years old, so it doesn't take a rocket scientist to figure out how he feels about it." Hall went on to say, "There is still a reasonable doubt in my mind that he was the person who pulled the trigger."

With all of the media pressure and headlines it is difficult to conceive that the jurors were not affected, and must have found it difficult not to pre-form some opinions on the case prior to the trial taking place. Even Bill Cosby was aware of the media circus which would surround the trial of his son's killer, one of the deciding factors which kept him and his wife from attending the trial. He along with everyone else involved in the trial knew that if he had attended he would have been the focus of every news programme and every newspaper's front page headlines. With cameras capturing every tortured expression on his face and the headlines guessing at how he would be feeling and how he would be coping with the trial, his presence would surely have affected the proceedings, although clearly not the outcome. Bill's actions in keeping out of the public eye were a vain attempt to enable his son's killer to receive a fair trial, despite the fact that the press were serializing the court proceedings and the television stations were broadcasting regular bulletins. The jury had been well screened prior to the court case but it would be fair to say that they came into the court with a predetermined opinion as to what they thought had happened.

Despite Hall's claims, on 11 August 1997, Mikail Markhasev was formally sentenced to life in prison without the possibility of parole. As the sentence was read Markhasev showed no emotion while his family wept silently.

After declaring his innocence throughout the proceedings and beyond, Markhasev did eventually admit his guilt and in doing so gave up his right to appeal. He reportedly wrote to prosecutors apologizing for the killing of Ennis Cosby, saying he felt it was the least he could do. In his letter he went on to say that more than anything, he wanted to apologize to the victim's family, saying it was his duty as a Christian, and apologised for the great wickedness for which he was responsible.

In a rare interview following the death of his son, Bill Cosby related the difficulties of coping with the death of an only son, explaining the frustrations in trying to accept that his son had been killed and the ensuing realization that nothing he could do would bring him back. He described his son as his hero, referring to the respect they shared for one another and how he could always rely on him to be honest, because that was the way he had been brought up. He went on to add that his relationship with his son, rather than that of a father and son, was very much one of friends, and as friends they shared many interests.

The confession of Markhasev proved the jury right in bringing in a guilty verdict, any predisposition to this outcome beforehand clearly proving that the power of the media should never be underestimated. The celebrity status which surrounded Ennis Cosby before 17 January 1997 was unable to provide protection from a ruthless killer who acted on impulse after seeing Cosby's car in trouble, however it did contribute to his killer been brought to justice. The case had the undivided attention of both the police and the media, with Markhasev's picture everywhere, but perhaps more important was the reward money as it was this that coaxed Markhasev's so-called friends out of the shadows.

Sweater Girl in a Tight Spot

Lana Turner

On the evening of Good Friday 1958 the shouting had reached a crescendo. Fourteen-year-old Cheryl Crane had abandoned all efforts to continue with her homework, the television in her bedroom having long since failed to drown out the raised voices coming from her mother's bedroom across the hall. Cheryl had, on previous occasions, unwillingly overheard Lana Turner, her beautiful mother, quarrelling with current boyfriend, Johnny Stompanato. She sat on the edge of her bed, wishing that the arguing would stop, when she was alarmed by the sound of breaking glass, followed by more raised voices. At the point she could resist no longer, worried for her mother's safety and only too aware that Johnny could and would resort to violence. The week-old bruises on her mother's face were already fading, but Cheryl's memory of the events leading up to that fight were still fresh in her mind. She ventured out of her bedroom and padded across the landing. Standing with bated breath she paused outside her mother's room.

In a bid to put an end to the argument, Cheryl decided to knock on her mother's door, whereupon her mother called out asking her not to enter the room, adding that Johnny would be leaving soon. She stood there a little while longer before plucking up courage to call to her mother again to let her in to the room. Again, Lana asked her daughter not to enter the room and to go back to her own bedroom until Johnny had left. Unable and unwilling to leave her mother's door, Cheryl decided to stay there until she had seen her mother. The arguing resumed and the child overheard threats from Stompanato, telling Turner that he would cut her face and spoil her world-famous good looks. He then continued to threaten Lana that he would kill both her and her nosey daughter. Cheryl was terrified for her own safety and desperate to assist her mother. She raced downstairs to the kitchen where the first thing she found on the counter was a knife; in need of some physical protection she instinctively picked it up and hurried back up to her mother's bedroom door.

The door flew open and Cheryl saw Stompanato coming towards her with one hand raised. The terrified Cheryl assumed that he was about to attack her so she lunged forward in order to get to the protection of her mother. Stompanato stopped in his tracks and fell to the floor, dropping the hangers and clothing that he was carrying. Lana looked to her daughter, thinking that she had punched and winded him, but suddenly realized that it was much more serious. "Oh my God, Cheryl, what have you done?" she called as it dawned on her that her daughter had just stabbed her lover, who was by now gasping for breath on the floor. Lana asked Cheryl to go and get some clothing or sheets to soak up the blood, while she tried to administer mouth-to-mouth resuscitation. It wasn't long before she became aware that Stompanato was not making any effort with his breathing, and that she was fighting a losing battle. She shouted for her daughter to help her, but the devastated Cheryl dared not go back into the room and decided to call her father, Stephen Crane, who only lived a few blocks away. Lana realized that she was unable to deal with the situation on her own and called her doctor who arrived, but it was already too late, Stompanato was dead.

Lana made the decision to call her lawyer Jerry Geisler, her mother and the police, so that the house was soon busy with people trying to calm down the devastated mother and stunned daughter. Outside Lana's home the press were already gathering, obviously after a tip-off by somebody in the neighbourhood who had heard the argument. Stompanato was pronounced dead at the scene by the doctor and shortly after was taken to the morgue. Cheryl was escorted to

Beverly Hills police station, accompanied by her mother where the pair were questioned by police officers. Cheryl spent the night in a police cell and the following morning she was fingerprinted and interviewed further, later that day being transferred to a juvenile hall where she stayed for almost a month.

The month when mother and daughter were separated felt the longest of their lives. Lana had seldom been separated from her only child, and the time they were apart was difficult for them both; Lana was especially protective of Cheryl, as she was her only child. When Cheryl was born Lana was diagnosed with rhesus haemolytic disease, which can affect subsequent pregancies, so she decided that she would carry on the family tradition of having only one baby.

She had been born Julia Jean Turner on 8 February 1921, to John Virgil and Mildred Frances Turner at the Providence Hospital in Wallace, Idaho. John had served as an infantry platoon sergeant in the First World War, receiving several medals for valour, shortly before the couple met. John and Mildred were delighted to learn that their daughter was fit and well after her birth. Lana enjoyed a quiet, happy childhood, and as with many only children, was the apple of her parents' eye. They spent much of their spare time enjoying her company, entertaining one another by singing and dancing with her. Indeed John was reported to have a talent for dance and singing – possibly where Lana inherited her own talents.

After a failed attempt to run a dry-cleaning business Lana's father returned to his old trade, mining – a dirty, dangerous, poorly paid job. He was proficient at cards and would supplement his wages by gambling as he often won. Unfortunately, one particular night his winning hand was to be his downfall; he had experienced a particularly profitable evening and was boasting about how he would treat his beautiful daughter to a new tricycle with his winnings. On his way home he planned to surprise his family with his winnings, but he was brutally robbed and beaten – he never even got home as his assailant killed him before he could get there. The murderer was never caught, which weighed on Mildred's mind for many years to come.

After the death of her husband Mildred decided to move with her child to California in the hope of better job prospects. Lana continued her education at Hollywood High where she was a very popular, lively member of the school. She enjoyed spending time with her friends and on Saturdays she loved to go to the movies which she watched intently, marvelling at the wonderful costumes which the actresses wore.

As a very attractive young lady, she caught the eye of the publisher of the *Hollywood Reporter*, Billy Wilkerson. He couldn't help noticing the beautiful 15-year-old girl and took the opportunity to give her a card, advising her that she should contact Zeppo Marx, a local talent agent. She did contact him and was soon introduced to director Mervyn LeRoy.

LeRoy recognized that her good looks and fantastic physique could take her far – the only thing he was unhappy about her was her relatively plain name of Julia Jean, with her nickname, Judy, being not much better. After a name-suggesting session they came up with Lana – and Lana it was, Lana Turner.

The first role she was offered was in a film called *They Won't Forget*, in which Lana had the small part of a murdered schoolgirl, Mary Clay. She took her mother with her for support but soon realized that she was confident in front of the camera and was declared "a natural", finding the whole experience both exciting and relatively easy. When the reviews came in Lana was delighted with them; one newspaper read, "Short on playing time is the role of the school girl. But as played by Lana Turner it is worthy of more than passing note. This young lady has vivid beauty, personality and charm." After the release of the film it wasn't long before Lana found herself with yet another name – owing to the tight blue sweater which she had worn in the film, she was known as "The Sweater Girl", not a label that Lana ever really cared for, but nonetheless she couldn't shake it off.

At this point in her career Lana had no expectations of becoming a famous actress and would have been satisfied with just the one role to her credit. But LeRoy had other ideas and was soon preparing her for her next film, *A Star Is Born*, in which she managed the minor role with ease. She took similar roles in several other films during the late 1930s including *The Great Garrick*. Almost as soon as filming had ended she found that she was being sent on loan to Samuel Goldwyn to take a part in *The Adventures of Marco Polo*. One of the requirements for the part was that she had to have her eyebrows removed, to be replaced by fake, thick black ones; unfortunately for Lana her eyebrows never recovered and she spent the rest of her life having to have them falsely applied, rather like false eyelashes, or having them drawn on.

In early 1940, Lana married her first husband, Artie Shaw, the band leader, on the set of her current film. When she first met him she had just broken up with her boyfriend and Shaw appealed to Lana, as he was a handsome, confident, almost arrogant man; she later admitted that if she hadn't been at a low ebb following the break-up with her boyfriend, she probably would have never married Shaw. The marriage was in trouble from the start, with Shaw insisting that Lana dress more demurely when not filming and that she should spend more time around the house, preferably without makeup. At this point of her life the last thing Lana needed was a jealous, insecure husband to be reining her in and calling all the shots. She was not averse to airing her views and the two clashed often. The marriage managed to limp on for just under seven months when the two parted as they were no longer able to tolerate one another.

A big financial advantage came Lana's way when LeRoy left Warner Bros and moved to MGM, taking Lana with him – she found that her wages of around $50 per week practically doubled, enabling her to provide some financial stability for both her mother and herself. The two ladies found themselves a house, which they shared, and as Lana's movie career continued to blossom so too did her salary.

In July 1942, Lana was married for the second time, to restaurateur Stephen Crane, who owned the famed Laua Restaurant on Rodeo Drive, Beverley Hills. Shortly after the marriage, the tabloid press were quick to point out that

Crane's Mexican divorce from his first wife was not valid as it was not recognized in the US. In a bid to quell her public embarrassment, Lana's marriage to Crane was quietly annulled in February the following year, the couple being legally married in March 1943. This was Lana's third marriage and she was only a month past her twenty-second birthday. They were tremendously happy when they found out that Lana was expecting their first child, and wasted no time in telling Mildred that she was to become a grandmother. Lana's mother was pleased for the couple as she could see the excitement and anticipation in their faces, but reminded Lana to be careful and look after herself during her pregnancy.

In 1944 Lana gave birth to a beautiful daughter who was named Cheryl. Lana was once reported to have said that she would have liked one husband and seven children, but Lana's dreams for a large family were dashed and she would only have Cheryl – although she did manage to notch up seven husbands, eight if you count Stephen twice. During the Second World War Lana did what she could for the war effort, giving speeches to the troops and even offering to kiss any man if he would buy a war bond for $50,000. She did keep her promise and later claimed that she managed to increase the defence budget by several million dollars.

By the end of the war Lana secured a new contract with MGM, which saw her salary rise to a then staggering $4,000 a week. Her next role was that of Cora in the movie *The Postman Always Rings Twice*. It was a fantastic role for her and she was delighted, feeling that she had proved herself to be a first-class actress. Lana played the sexy, adulterous wife quite breathtakingly in the film which was a massive success and she became really big news. She was often adorning front pages of fancy magazines and newspapers, the model that every girl was envious of and that every boy dreamed about.

Her successful working life unfortunately proved to be a great strain for Lana and Stephen's marriage. Her punishing filming schedule forced the couple to spend extended periods apart, inevitably the marriage was soon in trouble and the couple were divorced in the summer of 1944.

In 1948, at the age of 27, Lana was now an accomplished actress and was ready to take on her first technicolour movie, playing Lady de Winter in *The Three Musketeers*. Her leading man was Vincent Price who played Cardinal Richelieu. She found Price to be a great mentor and as she watched him perform she noticed that he would add his own touches to his character, which gave an extra dimension to his role. She managed, with some success, to copy this style and thoroughly enjoyed the whole process. The elaborate costumes, and her inspiration from Price, made this one of Lana's all-time favourite movies. After the release of the movie the reviews came in – Lana was praised beyond her wildest dreams, with quotes like "she is unreal" and "a proper goddess" in some of them.

As she celebrated by enjoying an evening with her mother and young daughter Cheryl – Mildred was so proud of her daughter – the trio enjoyed a special toast to Lana's success, but there was also a tinge of sadness that John, Lana's late father, was not able to share their joy.

In April 1948 Lana married husband number three (marriage number four), millionaire socialite Henry J. Topping Jr, who despite his formal name was known as Bob. Bob was a tinplate millionaire and the proud owner of the Yankee Stadium. The couple's marriage lasted for four years before they chose to go their separate ways and were divorced in December 1952.

The following year she married again, this time her husband was Lex Barker, the star of the Tarzan movies. Once again Lana was front page news with congratulatory photographs which sold newspapers by their thousands, but after three years this marriage was to end bitterly when Cheryl confided in her grandmother that Lex had sexually molested her when she was only ten years old. Sadly it took Cheryl three years to pluck up the courage to tell her as she was terrified at what the consequences would bring. With the help of her grandmother Cheryl was able to tell Lana her devastating news.

Lana was to marry three more times: firstly to a rancher, Fred May, then a businessman Robert Eaton and finally to a night-club hypnotist, Ronald Dante, all of which inevitably ended in divorce, with none lasting longer than four years.

She continued to star in many movies although she became less satisfied with the roles, each one a sure-fire sign that her career was slowing down, although she did enjoy one last shot at the big time. In 1958 she starred in *Peyton Place* which turned out to be a phenomenal success and for which she received an Academy Award nomination for Best Actress.

Believing that her career was once again in the ascendancy, Lana was pleased to enjoy the attentions of a new admirer, John Steele, an extremely handsome man with wavy hair and olive-skinned good looks. He was very charming and attentive, commencing his courtship of Lana with regular telephone calls, before inundating her with an array of romantic gestures, even taking the time to discover her taste in music so that he could buy the songs she liked best. Under the weight of such heavy duty romancing the flames of passion were soon ignited and Lana was swept away by the attention her new lover was bestowing on her. Cheryl was also included in the fabulous gifts from Steele, who presented her with every child's dream – a stunning Arabian horse.

Lana's friends were keen to find out more about her new love; the rumour mill had already produced a number of unsavoury stories regarding the new man's background and if the stories were true, Lana would need to know – and fast. By the time Lana and Steele had fully established their relationship it had become common knowledge that his business dealings brought him into contact with the seedier side of the LA underworld. When Lana's friends found out the truth they were quick to inform the now besotted actress that the man she was with was not who he claimed to be. John Steele was in fact the cover name for one Johnny Stompanato, a man whose background held a number of dark secrets. With a career which was full of twists and turns, he had at one time or another been a Marine war veteran, a night-club bouncer and a bodyguard who allegedly carried money for gangsters. Police records showed that he had once been stopped and was found to be carrying several tens of thousands of dollars, the owner of which was never fully established. He had established himself as something of a gigolo, often seen in the company of older, wealthier women. He had been married a number of times, once to a Turkish woman, but more notably to an actress called Helen Gilbert, who admitted that it was her wealth that supported the couple. Stompanato certainly had expensive tastes, loved to frequent expensive restaurants and would ingratiate himself with his chosen target, usually an older woman who might be more receptive to his obvious charms. He would invariably indulge in a relationship with them, fleecing them gradually, until they eventually discovered his true intentions, then, as the relationship fell apart, he would simply move on.

For Lana, still in the first flush of love, all of these cascading facts were uninvited and she sought initially to ignore them, not prepared to admit that all the facts were true – her new lover was, in her eyes, a wonderful, considerate, handsome man, just what she needed. She believed the lies he told her and described him as "utterly considerate" – even the news that his real name was Stompanato, and not Steele, seemed to appear irrelevant.

When Lana was on location in England filming *Another Time, Another Place* she found that she was lonely and missing Stompanato quite badly, so she decided to call him to see if she could persuade him to come over and join her, hoping to enjoy some discreet sightseeing together. Keen to accept, he was soon on an aeroplane and heading for a romantic reunion.

Initially they enjoyed each other's company and spent quiet evenings together at small night spots. Lana was all too aware of the British press and made every attempt to keep her new lover out of the limelight, determined not to make the front pages. Unfortunately Stompanato wasn't happy with being kept in the dark, even though Lana tried to explain that she was trying to protect him from the media who would surely envelope them if they were seen out in public. Stompanato didn't take the news well and for the first time the couple argued, only it didn't end there – as the argument escalated the couple had their first physical scuffle, during which Lana sustained a number of injuries. Unable to visit the set as her face was obviously bruised, she was shocked by his aggression and wished that she had never invited him over to join her. She confided in a friend, explaining how Stompanato had turned nasty during what she thought was just a quarrel. After talking the whole thing through Lana realized that he had entered Britain with a false passport. The authorities were informed and a furious Stompanato was returned to the United States where he simmered, his anger never far off boiling point.

Lana was no fool and was well aware that Stompanato would be biding his time, awaiting his chance to force a confrontation. She was exhausted after filming and decided that she could do with a rest; she needed to recharge her batteries before the inevitable showdown with him. As Cheryl was being well cared for by her father and grandmother, Lana decided to secretly book a trip to Acapulco, hoping to have a few days to clear her head before returning to Los Angeles. To her horror, when she arrived in Mexico she was surprised to walk directly into a media storm – and if the cameras and microphones weren't bad enough, things got worse when Stompanato emerged from behind the glare of the flash bulbs, seeming very pleased with himself. She had told nobody about her arrangements and assumed that he must have used some high-level contact to have tracked her down so easily. Stompanato's actions no longed contained the thread of romance which were evident early on; his shock appearance in Acapulco only added to her worries and she now felt that she could go nowhere and confide in no one as he appeared to have eyes and ears everywhere. Years later she admitted that she never did find out how he learned of her trip and conceded that his ability to uncover her whereabouts confirmed to her that he had the power to do almost anything he wanted.

The couple stayed in Acapulco with Stompanato continuing to be abusive and sometimes violent towards Lana, although by now she was so scared of him he rarely had to become physical to get what he wanted. When the "holiday" was over the couple flew back to Los Angeles where they were reunited with Cheryl. By chance a photographer was on hand to snap the happy moment, although the headlines the following day painted a less glossy picture. When the papers hit the news-stands the headlines were less then complimentary – rather than reporting the happy reunion they declared, "Lana Turner Returns with Mob Figure", just the kind of press reporting that she had been trying so hard to avoid.

Amid the torment of the scathing headlines Lana had managed to secure some good news – her role in *Peyton Place* had resulted in an Oscar nomination. Stompanato was thrilled and looking forward to accompanying her to the star-studded event, but the recent tabloid reports had made her more guarded and she was determined not to have a repeat performance. She decided to put her foot down – no matter how much Stompanato tried to coerce her into letting him join her, she was adamant that she did not want to be seen out with a known gangster.

With her mind made up, Lana decided that she would take her daughter Cheryl with her to the awards ceremony. The pair went on a wonderful shopping trip and enjoyed choosing their outfits together. Lana chose a beautiful strapless white lace gown which moulded perfectly to her famous curves, while Cheryl opted for a more modest green taffeta dress. On the day of the event mother and daughter had their hair coiffured to perfection and Lana had a makeup artist add the finishing touches. The early evening was fraught with tension. Stompanato was still furious at being denied his rightful place next to Lana, but soon they would be able to forget their stresses as they mingled with the celebrity A-list and the money men who constituted the Hollywood top brass. Kissing Lana's mother goodbye, they left her to watch the ceremony on television, hopeful that by the time they returned home Stompanato would be in a better mood.

The evening was wonderful and Lana introduced her now very grown-up looking daughter to all the stars. Although she didn't win the award she was a gracious loser and commended the winner, praising Joanne Woodward for her role in *The Three Faces of Eve*. Cheryl was sent home before the real party began, still buzzing with the awesome experience. For Lana the night was young and she continued to party with her friends and colleagues. Unfortunately Stompanato was left to reflect on what he considered to be a public snub and by the time that Lana arrived home he was in a rage.

He laughed at her for not winning and made snide comments regarding the amount of alcohol she had drunk, wanting to know who she had been talking to and to hear a blow-by-blow account of all the men who had shown any interest in her. He added that she would never be allowed to leave him as he simply would not allow it. He continued pushing her around and finally took out his anger by slapping her around the face. Lana was knocked to the ground only to be yanked back up again, whereupon Stompanato continued to dish out more of the same. Staring intently into her eyes, he announced how things would be from that point on, insisting that she would never leave him out of anything like that again.

When Cheryl saw the state of her mother's face the morning after the award ceremony she was devastated. Lana pleaded with her not to tell anyone, especially her mother, and God forbid, her ex-husband, – her embarrassment at being the battered partner was too great to bear. Lana now felt that she had been too trusting of Stompanato and should have known better, realizing that he was too good to be true and only out for himself. She told Cheryl that if she could keep the secret, she would finish her relationship with him, promising that he would bother them no more.

True to her word, on Good Friday, 1958 she boldly told Stompanato that it was over and that she no longer wanted him around. Although he didn't live with her Stompanato had left some clothes at her place and she asked him to come round and collect them. Lana was no fool – she knew that he wouldn't leave without an argument and had mentally prepared herself for the final goodbye. The only thing she hadn't prepared for was how out of hand things would become.

Stompanato threatened that he would cut her face and spoil her good looks for ever if she ended the relationship and threatened to have her mother and daughter killed. As he continued his diatribe of threats, neither he, nor Lana, were aware that just outside the bedroom door Cheryl had been listening to everything. She was terrified for her mother's safety, had heard enough bad things about Stompanato and had witnessed the results of his handiwork at close quarters. Frightened yet determined to protect her mother, she armed herself with a kitchen knife. Inside the bedroom Stompanato was taking a break from his tirade of threats; sensing he was on his way out he started to collect his clothing, pulling out the heavy wooden hangers from inside the wardrobe. With his hand up to his shoulder he let the clothing hang loosely down his back, he glared at Lana one last time as he headed for the bedroom door where he was surprised to bump into the now petrified Cheryl, who was stood facing him. Before he could register the change in Cheryl's demeanour, or spot the dangerous-looking knife, Cheryl lunged forward, sticking the kitchen knife deep into his abdomen. Lana, thinking that Stompanato had been winded, turned to Cheryl and asked her what she had done, but before she had a chance to respond Lana saw the knife on the floor. Without thinking she placed it in the marble sink. Turning her attention to Stompanato, Lana was shocked to see him bathed in an expanding pool of blood, panting in short shallow breaths. As the horror of the situation dawned on them, they were suddenly aware of the real risk to Stompanato's life and of the implication for themselves. In a bid to help the now dangerously ill gangster, Lana dispatched Cheryl to the bathroom in order to bring towels, but by the time she returned the situation seemed much worse. In a panic, Cheryl called her father, Stephen Crane, and rapidly explained what had happened. Not long afterward Lana made a number of calls of her own, the first to her doctor, who immediately made his way over, and then, as if recognizing the predicament she was in, made another call to her lawyer.

When the doctor arrived, Stompanato was slumped on the

floor, his body lying amid the expanding crimson tide. In what would clearly be a last-ditch attempt at saving the man, the doctor injected his heart with a large dose of adrenaline, but it was too late – his blood loss was too great. The doctor pronounced Stompanato dead at the scene.

As the flashing blue lights of the LA police force headed up to Beverley Hills, so did the press, only in much bigger numbers. By the time the police arrived the scene looked more like the setting for a press conference. Cameramen and reporters were already warming their ever ready audiences with speculation of murder at the Turner residence. The headlines the next day would have been even more annoying for Stompanato – he was dead, and at the hands of a 14-year-old girl, daughter of a major Hollywood star.

It fell to LA District Attorney, William McKesson, to brief the press on the incident at Lana Turner's house. During the press conference he explained that it was Cheryl who had been arrested and that she would not be receiving special treatment as a minor; she had been jailed overnight and then transferred to a juvenile hall, pending an investigation. She was not allowed bail, McKesson believing that she was in danger of attack from the mob.

In the weeks leading up to the inquest, Lana's lawyer, Jerry Geisler, worked hard on the case, ensuring that Cheryl didn't have to testify, declaring that she had been traumatized by the events and was still only 14 years old. The inquest was held at the Hall of Records in downtown Beverley Hills, a large courtroom by anyone's standard, with around 160 seats. Of these three-quarters had been reserved for the media; two television stations had already announced that they would broadcast updates live from the inquest. There were only 40 seats left for members of the public, far too few considering the massive queues which had formed that morning. Lines of people had started arriving before sunrise, gripped by the new Hollywood scandal which had already been dubbed "Lanagate".

Just before 9 a.m. Geisler, Lana and her former husband, Stephen Crane, arrived at the inquest and were besieged by the waiting press. The trio did their best to make their way

inside as quickly as possible, but were jostled by the eager
news hounds, who were keen for a comment.

The jury, consisting of ten men and two women, were also
well aware of the press contingent in the court, and like the
rest of America were familiar with the facts – as presented by
the press at least. Lana and Stompanato had been hot gossip
for several months; the headlines had screamed their discontent at the Hollywood actress's choice of suitor. Before
the facts had emerged, sympathies had been formed – it
wouldn't take Perry Mason to bring home the right verdict in
this case. Stompanato had become the victim twice, once at
the hands of 14-year-old Cheryl and once at the hands of the
press. His mobster connections and known penchant for
brutality all served to present the dead man in a bad light,
and even though he had been stabbed to death there were few
who had any sympathy for him.

The first person called to testify was Mickey Cohen, an
aquaintence of Johnny Stompanato and the man called to
identify his body at the morgue. On a short visit to the stand
he confirmed that the body he had identified was that of his
friend, before being dismissed.

The autopsy report was produced by the coroner who
confirmed that Stompanato had died as a result of a single
stab wound to the abdomen. During the course of his
testimony the coroner passed comment on the general physical health of Stompanato, highlighting the poor condition
of his liver.

The next person called was the doe-eyed Lana. Impecca-
bly turned out, she had obviously put a lot of thought into
her appearance and was looking stunning, dressed in a silk
grey suit, her hair neatly set and her makeup as flawless as
ever. In a role she was well suited to, Lana would need to
give an Oscar-winning performance if she was to ensure her
daughter's freedom. She was on the stand for over an hour,
running through the events leading up to the night of
Stompanato's death, including her violent quarrels with
him. She went on to give a detailed account of their final
argument and the events shortly thereafter. She maintained
her strength throughout the questioning, breaking down just

twice, before composing herself and carrying on with her testimony.

After hearing her statement the coroner called for a recess and Lana was allowed out of the courtroom, walking headlong into a crowd of reporters who were gathered all around the building, desperate to detect any sign of strain on her beautiful face. She became trapped in the centre of the press pack who were determined to hold on to her; feeling faint, it was Geisler who manoeuvred her away from them to allow her the opportunity to compose herself.

When the session resumed, the police investigators who had attended the scene took the stand, pointing out some of the facts which had caused them confusion. The knife which had allegedly been used to kill Stompanato had been devoid of fingerprints, a possible sign that the murder weapon had been cleaned. The officers also reported that there was little sign of an affray in the bedroom, or elsewhere in the house; they could not therefore prove that Stompanato had become violent or aggresive in the minutes before he was stabbed.

As the inquest was drawing to a close an anonymous man shouted from the gallery, "Lies! All lies! This mother and daughter were in love with Stompanato! Johnny was a gentleman!" Stompanato had enjoyed little support up to this point in the proceedings – nobody was sure if the man was working on behalf of someone or if he was just voicing his own opinion. Nevertheless, support for Stompanato was short lived.

The jurors took only half an hour to come to their verdict and concluded that the death of Johnny Stompanato constituted justifiable homicide. They deemed that Cheryl was literally terrified – concerned for her life and that of her mother – and was therefore justified in using deadly force to stop Stompanato from killing them.

Mickey Cohen was the first to voice his opinion after the verdict, announcing to the press, "It's the first time in my life I've ever seen a dead man convicted of his own murder. So far as that jury's concerned, Johnny just walked too close to that knife."

Johnny Stompanato's family were also unhappy with the

verdict and brought a wrongful death lawsuit against Lana Turner and Stephen Crane. The case was eventually settled out of court. The press reported that Lana had given a performance which she could never match. It was unbeatable, containing everything a great romance should have – love, hate, laughter, tears, glamour and heartbreak, not to mention the tragic death scene.

Cheryl walked free from the court and back into her parents' arms. Lana's popularity seemed undamaged by the court case; on the contrary, during the trial interest in the movie *Peyton Place* soared, with box office takings once more going through the roof. *Peyton Place* proved to be another case of life imitating art – in one scene Lana is interrogated during a courtroom cross-examination regarding the crimes with which her on-screen daughter is accused.

Lana died of throat cancer on 29 June 1995, aged 74, one battle that her daughter couldn't fight for her. Cheryl was at her bedside when the curtain finally fell.

Christian Brando

On 16 May 1990 Dag Drollet was enjoying an unusually quiet evening at Marlon Brando's sprawling luxury home in Mulholland Drive, Los Angeles, unaware that his life was in grave danger and that he would soon be breathing his last breath. He had enjoyed a long warm bath and was now relaxing, flicking through the television channels and chilling out. His heavily pregnant girlfriend, Cheyenne Brando, and her brother Christian were out for the evening, having dinner at the well-regarded Musso & Frank Grill. Drollet was not aware that the majority of the conversation between brother and sister was focused on his behaviour. Cheyenne was painting a picture of a violent and abusive bully of whom she was scared, not just for herself but for her unborn baby also. As the evening wore on the pair consumed large amounts of alcohol and the description of Drollet's behaviour became more and more elaborate. Christian had not met Drollet before that evening and even then only to exchange brief pleasantries, so he was ignorant of the true situation between Cheyenne and father-to-be Drollet.

The truth is that Drollet was unhappy in his relationship with Cheyenne and had told her that if her violence continued he would have to leave her, this being the probable catalyst for the outpouring of emotion to Christian. Cheyenne was obviously seeking sympathy from her older brother and may well have wanted him to teach her boyfriend a lesson. Unfortunately the lesson would be hard taught as Cheyenne had managed to wind her brother up into such a rage that the totally unaware and unprepared Drollet would not stand a chance.

At around 10.30 p.m. Cheyenne and Christian returned to their father's home to find that Marlon was in his private quarters and that Drollet was relaxing in the den. Christian wanted to have it out with Drollet and so he went straight there to confront him. Having been revved up by Cheyenne all through dinner he was now angry and ready to exact revenge, believing as he did that Drollet had apparently been abusing his little sister. Christian stormed into the room shouting "Are you slapping my sister around?" Even before Drollet could reply Christian added, "You will not do that anymore." Drollet was completely puzzled, staring in amazement at the man in front of him, then his eyes widened as he realized that Christian was holding a gun and that it was pointing directly at his face. At that moment something tipped Christian over the edge and he fired one shot, hitting Drollet in the head.

The unmistakable sound of a gunshot startled the whole household and Marlon soon entered the den to find his son staring at Drollet, who lay on the floor, blood pooling around him from an obvious head wound. Reality soon kicked in and Marlon, though stunned, took control of the situation, immediately requesting that the authorities be summoned. He tried to comfort the dying man but could see at once that his words were of little help; it was also apparent that he was not sufficiently skilled to administer the type of help which Drollet badly needed. Closer inspection led Brando to the conclusion that even if help arrived immediately, Drollet's injuries were likely to be fatal.

Marlon then turned his attention to his son, who on cursory inspection had obviously been drinking heavily, although the reality of his actions had sobered him up somewhat. Marlon tried his best to calm his son down, and also managed to dissuade him from trying to leave the house. His son was now panicking, and in his dilemma had considered making a run for it in an attempt to avoid being caught at the scene. Even as a young man Christian was never that keen on facing the music for any of his wayward actions, large or small. What he had achieved that evening was, however, very much on a new level. On this occasion Marlon was not prepared to let his son leave, any thoughts of leniency would depend on his co-operation, whereas running away would only imply more guilt – if more guilt was possible. Marlon talked him round, pointing out that he should stay and deal with the situation – whatever happened he would have his father's support, even though Brando himself did not know why Drollet lay dead in his house. Marlon escorted Christian and Cheyenne into his own bedroom to cool off and ordered them to stay put and await his further instructions. Christian took this short amount of time to apologize to his horrified sister, who couldn't believe that the evening had ended so tragically. She may have set her brother up to teach her boyfriend a lesson, but did not expect to lose the father of her unborn child in the process. With a mixture of alcohol and terror her brain struggled to see how her discussions earlier had somehow created the bloody havoc in which they were both enmeshed.

When the emergency services arrived it was Marlon himself who answered the door, immediately rushing the officers into the den. Upon entering the room LA Fire Department Captain Tom Jefferson described the scene as eerie, observing that Drollet "was lying back on the couch, kind of like he was watching TV". He stated that the victim was holding a remote control in one hand and a cigarette lighter in the other; in the moments before being shot the young man had clearly been engaged in a spot of channel hopping. The only difference between him and any other television viewer that night was the fact that he had just sustained a fatal gunshot wound to the head.

When the police searched the property they found Christian talking with his distraught sister, the pair still in their father's bedroom. The couple were separated by the officers, Christian was put in handcuffs and escorted from the property to a waiting police car. He was still under the influence of alcohol, a reading of his blood alcohol level was taken and the result showed that it contained 0.19 per cent alcohol, almost twice the drink-driving level.

He was initially interviewed by Steve Osti from the LAPD who described him as chatty but erratic. He was told that he had the right to remain silent and had the right to an attorney. Christian did not take up either offer and immediatly confessed to shooting Drollet, claiming, "I did it because he hurt my sister. He was lying on the couch. He was fighting with my sister. I told him to leave my sister alone. We were both in a rage. The fucking gun went off." Although his statement was full of inconsistencies regarding the actual events which had occurred in the den, he never at any point denied the fact that he was the one who had pulled the trigger. However many questions remained. Why had he got the gun in the first place? Was it for self-defence, believing that Drollet was beating his sister? Or was it to commit murder? Had Christian been aiming to scare Drollet when the gun accidentally discharged? These were all questions which would have to be answered if Christian Brando intended to maintain his liberty.

With a big Hollywood star involved in such a controversy it was only a matter of time before the tabloid press got wind of the hot new story. The announcement of Drollet's death was on television before Marlon had managed to call his long-time friend Jacques Drollet, Dag Drollet's father, and break the sad news that his son was dead – let alone admit that it was his son who had dealt him the final card. Marlon needn't have worried, for in a world where television news travels faster than a speeding bullet, Jacques Drollet had already seen the headlines and was now aware that his son had been killed at Marlon Brando's house. He just didn't know why.

A media frenzy, the likes of which had never been seen before, took everyone involved by surprise. There were stories that reporters had scaled the high walls surrounding Brando's house on Mulholland Drive and, managing to evade the high-level security system, had got into the grounds, where they rummaged through the garbage in a bid to beat their rivals to "bag" an exclusive. To their disappointment the reporters had succeeded in selecting the wrong garbage and instead of sifting through Brando's rubbish they were scouring through his neighbour's discarded trash. The neighbour was none other than Jack Nicholson, not press friendly at the best of times, whose rubbish turned out to be no more incriminating than anyone else's.

The whole area around Brando's home was swarming with the media. News reporters were already making their television links from outside Brando's main gates, which were guarded by a multitude of uniformed officers. Photographers and press agents had decamped to the area in their hundreds, not wishing to miss any vital clues as to what was happening. Several news stations had taken to the skies and were recording anything and everything from their "eye-in-the-sky" helicopters – although only the basic facts were known, the amount of police activity in the grounds and the heavily policed security cordon around the perimeter, meant that something very newsworthy had occurred at Brando's house that evening. And when the police outnumber the ambulance men, murder seems like a likely option.

Marlon Brando sat in his home and struggled to make any sense of the unreal situation which he now found himself in, a far cry from his humble beginings. He was born 66 years before Drollet's death, in Omaha, Nebraska, to proud parents, Marlon Brando Sr and Dorothy Pennebaker. He was the Brandos' only son and the third of three children – his sisters being Jocelyn aged four and Frances aged two. He was the son that the parents had hoped for and who now made the family unit complete. But by the time Brando had reached the age of 12, Marlon Sr and Dorothy had started to have marriage problems and the couple separated. Dorothy was then left to bring up the three children alone, so with them in tow she moved to Santa Ana, in Orange County, California.

Marlon Sr and Dorothy had been separated for around two years before a reconciliation was achieved and the couple reunited. With their relationship now back on track they decided that a new start would be helpful, so they moved house once again, this time upping sticks to Libertyville, Illinois, just north of Chicago, near Lake Michigan.

When Brando reached his mid teens he attended the

Shattuck Military Academy boarding school in Fairbult, Minnesota. But the headstrong young man was already exhibiting signs of his uniquely independent character, even in military collage, and did not take to the discipline there, so they eventually expelled him for misconduct.

By 1943, Brando moved to New York, where he attended the Dramatic Workshop of the New School for Social Research. He took the work very seriously and was a natural student. His teacher Stella Adler had lived in Moscow in the early 1930s, and had studied with Konstantin Stanislavsky at the Moscow Arts Theatre. Stanislavsky taught the "method", which is where actors have to try and develop every part they play using their own emotions. On passing on her interpretation of the "method", she found the young Brando was an excellent student and that this technique suited his acting style. Later in life this lesson was to prove invaluable to him as he used the method style of acting for every character he portrayed throughout his long career.

Brando's acting career enjoyed a number of great highs and he will always be known as one of Hollywood's legends. By his early twenties he was already proving to be such a competent actor that he auditioned for and managed to secure the role as Stanley Kowalski in Tennessee Williams' *A Streetcar Named Desire*, a role for which he won many plaudits. Throughout the movie Brando gave a brilliant performance and was nominated for Best Actor in a Leading Role at the Academy Awards – quite an achievement by anybody's standards. He was now wealthy beyond his wildest dreams and a recognized star the world over. Enjoying the benefits that his fame brought him, he indulged in his many passions, including food and women. The Oscar was well deserved but he would need to draw on his geat emotional strength more than ever when he would eventually have to go before the most demanding of all audiences – just twelve true men, not handing out awards, but rather jail sentences.

He met his first wife when he was 33 years old while filming *The Young Lions*. His young bride, Anna Kashfi, an Indian actress, was formerly known as Joan O'Callaghan.

Already pregnant and showing, the wedding ceremony was held at Brando's aunt's house in East Rock. By May the following year Anna gave birth to their son, Christian Devi Brando, named after a close friend of his father, Christian Marquand. The marriage was rocky from the start and was not helped by the fact that Brando was openly seeing other women. Anna's own problems with alcohol and barbiturates abuse caused their relationship to flounder, inevitably the marriage was turbulent and the couple divorced when Christian was still in nappies.

Brando soon went on to marry his second wife, a Mexican actress called Movita Castaneda, and in 1960 they had a child, another son for Brando, called Miko. This marriage also floundered – Brando's womanizing ways had not left him – and two years later it all ended in a bitter divorce. Brando's third wife was already in the wings and once again he was quick to make an honest woman of her. The latest Mrs Brando, another actress, Tarita Teripaia became pregnant and blessed her husband with his third son in as many women. Simon, the youngest of Brando's boys, was soon followed by two daughters, Cheyenne and Rebecca.

Brando, quick to marry, was equally quick to adopt the favours of a string of other beautiful women, many content to play second fiddle to the official Mrs Brando. Back in the saddle and up to his old tricks, the eclectic Brando family continued to grow.

It is true to say that the Brando ran an open house, with a diverse range of people constantly coming and going. In line with his A-list status, he also maintained the trappings of his success, with various homes both in America and elsewhere, even buying a private island where his family could relax away from the media's prying eyes and long-range lenses. The whole Brando clan were constantly shuttled between the various family homes and the private family island near Tahiti.

Brando was able to secure custody of Christian although his busy filming schedule meant that he did not spend a significant amount of time with the boy. Instead, Christian was primarily brought up by a small army of ever-changing nannies and helpers. Although they both apparently enjoyed the small amount of time they did manage to have together, the time slots seemed few and far between. Like most maturing boys, however, the need for a strong male influence, a guiding hand, was evidently required, but sadly lacking.

One may have supposed that to have a tremendously successful father like Brando would have meant that life would be easy, and that the son might expected his every whim to be pandered to. In reality Christian, like many kids growing up, only craved the love and closeness of his parents. Even with good role models the offspring of famous people can often go off the rails when they reach young adulthood. With the confidence bestowed through their parents' shimmering stardom they are keen to experience life for themselves, and clearly have the financial ability to enjoy all that the world has to offer. Inevitably, having famous parents can make you popular amongst your peers and Christian happily found himself in this position, never short of friends who were always ready to party. He spent the majority of his time travelling between Hollywood and Tahiti where he became the favourite older brother to Cheyenne who was 11 years younger than Christian, a fact which did not stop the pair from spending a great deal of time together, chatting and confiding in one another. Cheyenne enjoyed the support that Christian offered, and he in return became a father figure to her, providing a level of protection which would later reveal itself in a more dramatic and bloody way.

As Cheyenne grew up she blossomed into a true beauty, very popular amongst her peers and with a demonstrably high intelligence, not to mention a keen competitive streak. Her favourite subjects at school were science and art, she was a keen dancer and in her spare time she was an accomplished horse rider. Sadly though, the trappings of her famous father's success brought her into contact with alcohol and drugs, but unlike other Hollywood children, Cheyenne indulged in adult levels of intake. The same self-destructive habit which characterized Brando's food intake appeared to have been passed to his eldest daughter.

Occasionally, to the surprise of those around her, Cheyenne would erupt into fits of rage, often at the drop of a hat. These outbursts were the first indications that she was suffering from some form of mental illness. When she was 19 years old, her father was, as usual, away filming. On this occasion he was in Toronto shooting the movie *The Freshman*, with Matthew Broderick. Cheyenne, in desperate need of her father's attention, wanted to visit him on the set. Seeking his permission to make the trip, she was refused, a decision which angered the feisty Cheyenne. Never happy when refused something, for she was used to getting what she wanted, the rebuttal hit her more heavily than might have been expected. Furious at her father, she decided that the best way to burn off some steam was by going for a drive. Her boyfriend, Dag Drollet, had parked his car in Brando's driveway; when Cheyenne came looking for the keys he knew better than to refuse and allowed the obviously furious girl to take the car. The writing was on the wall, but Drollet could not read it. The mixture of instability and a deep-seated anger could be a potentially lethal combination, as Cheyenne was soon to find out and as Drollet would a few months later. While she was driving away her anger rose and as her blood boiled the speed of the car gradually increased, soon far exeeding the speed limit. Unfortunately she was unable to handle the car at such high speed and lost control of the vehicle on a bend. The car crashed and she sustained terrible facial injuries in the process, including breaking her jaw, losing part of her ear and lacerating her face.

After having plastic surgery her scars faded and the surgeons managed to restore much of her good looks – but Cheyenne was devastated with the results. She blamed her father for the accident, insisting that if he had allowed her to join him when she asked then she would still be beautiful. Her mental health deteriorated dramatically and she came to rely more and more on drugs; she was struggling to keep on an even keel. With her father more absent than present, Dag Drollet became the centre of Cheyenne's attention and in return he became the rock against which she could lean. During her recovery, Cheyenne discovered that she was pregnant with Drollet's child – the timing couldn't have been worse, for her mental health was at an all-time low and her drug use was at an all-time high.

The couple had been together for around a year, but the relationship was not a stable one. Drollet and Cheyenne would often argue, usually fuelled by drink, and would at times come to blows. Drollet confided in his parents who, wanting the best for their son, encouraged him not to antagonize his pregnant girlfriend and instead try to make a go of it. He eventually explained to his father Jacques about Cheyenne's violent mood swings and her drug and alcohol abuse. It was during one of these discussions that Jacques realized the gravity of his son's situation and urged him to be very careful, warning him that there was no way of knowing what the outcome of their fights might be. Shortly before Drollet's death his father made a final plea to his son to leave Cheyenne, fearful that the drugged and alcoholically charged youngster might at any time explode into a fit of violence. Now more than ever before, Jacques was concerned for the safety of his son. Sadly Drollet did not take his father's advice – time would show that he was to pay dearly for his mistake.

By now Cheyenne was at rock bottom. She was taking much longer than expected to recover from the car crash, was depressed, pregnant and on top of all that she was upset that the situation with her boyfriend was precarious and that he might, as he had threatened in the past, decide to leave her.

Brando was aware of his daughter's psychiatric problems and decided that she should leave Tahiti and return to Mulholland Drive prior to having the baby. He wanted her to have the benefits of a Los Angeles birth, worried that the Tahitian facilities might be a little primitive and with all of the added complications his daughter had brought upon herself, she more than anyone might need access to the latest medical technology.

Drollet moved with Cheyenne to her father's house, hoping that the steadying influence of the patriarch may settle his pregnant girlfriend down. But this would not prove to be the case for Cheyenne had now come to resent the fact that her father had spent so little time with her as a child and actively displayed her annoyance at any given opportunity. She was also no longer comfortable with the pace of life in Los Angeles, much preferring the peace and quiet she enjoyed in Tahiti. Brando encouraged his daughter to attend psychological counselling, but her moods did not improve and she became more erratic and violent. Drollet knew that the relationship could not survive after the birth of the baby, but was determined to stay with her to offer what support he could until the child was born.

The enormous house was constantly busy – as well as Drollet, Cheyenne, and her parents, a team of servants were constantly coming and going. Another frequent visitor to the property was Christian. He had already been married, had a home of his own and occasionally worked as a welder. There were similar family traits emerging between the step-siblings – Christian was no stranger to drugs and was also noted for his hot temper, especially after he had consumed a lot of alcohol. He was finding it difficult to be his own person; constantly recognized as his father's son he felt overpowered by the Brando image. He had a large number of acquaintances, but like many people who have famous relatives, he found himself surrounded by friends and hangers-on, all keen to mix with the legendary Brando.

As a gun enthusiast Christian owned a selection of firearms. He was once reported to have suffered a blackout, during which it was suggested that he managed to shoot one of his friends. Luckily the man's injuries were only superficial, the bullet merely grazing his face, but had it been a couple of inches in the other direction Christian might well have found himself charged with his death. After the blackout he was totally unaware of what had occurred and apparently had no recall of the events.

Less than ten days after Cheyenne and Drollet had moved into Brando's palatial home Christian turned up and met his sister's boyfriend for the first time. He considered him to be a decent sort of guy and they got on reasonably well, although they did not find much to say to each other after their initial introductions. Christian invited the pair out for a meal, but Drollet, happy to spend time alone, suggested that it would be nice for Christian and Cheyenne to go out together and catch up.

The two happily went off leaving Drollet in the den and Brando in his own room. By the time they returned Christian's mood had completely altered and he was ready to avenge his sister's apparent violent treatment by her boyfriend – for his alleged abuse of Cheyenne, the price was to be his life in full and final settlement.

The news of Drollet's death and the ensuing court case was to dominate Los Angeles tabloids with front-page news for almost nine months, the reading public being fed every ounce of information they could stomach.

Drollet's parents were understandably heartbroken at the news that their son had been killed. Aware that his girlfriend was unstable, they did not expect that her half-brother would be the one to take their son's life.

Brando was devastated too; he was a very private man, some would say almost reclusive when he wasn't working. But he was all too familiar with how the press worked and was aware that his family's deepest secret would soon be splashed on the front of every newspaper in America, if not the entire world.

He wasted no time in contacting his friend and attorney, William Kunstler, and told him, "The messenger of misery has visited my house." Kunstler, who handled the press during the early part of the investigation, advised Brando to use the high-profile criminal lawyer Robert Shapiro to defend his son.

On examination of the den, and later during the autopsy of Drollet, a picture emerged as to what had transpired at the Brando house that evening. It started to become apparent that the evidence didn't point to a struggle, but rather it appeared that the victim was shot in the back of the head while relaxing. It was initially thought that the pair had engaged in a face-to-face confrontation, resulting in Drollet suffering a shot to the front of his head, but this clearly wasn't the case. The evidence suggested a cowardly attack from behind, not one intended as a lesson, but one intended to kill – no discussion required.

After being questioned by police Cheyenne was exhausted and her mental state was in crisis. On 15 June, her father took the unusual decision to have her hospitalized back in Tahiti. The flights were personally organized by Brando and some felt that he was trying to manipulate the legal process. Cheyenne had confirmed on numerous occasions while being questioned that the death of her boyfriend was not an accident and that Christian had collected his gun with the intention of shooting Drollet. The reason for her relocation then became more apparent – Tahiti is under French jurisdiction and as such the American authorities would be unable to subpoena her to testify in court. Her absence would therefore hinder the prosecution's case, and in doing so would not only spare Cheyenne the stress of the trial, but might also aid Christian Brando's defence. Cheyenne's movements, and more particularly her escape to a foreign jurisdiction, were not lost on the press and media. Brando's claim that he was looking after his daughter's mental well-being was lost in the headlines claiming Brando was simply orchestrating his son's defence by removing a witness who might prove awkward.

On 26 June, not long after arriving in hospital, Cheyenne gave birth to a sickly child named Tuki. Shortly after his birth he began showing signs of solvent withdrawal and had to be detoxified to clear his system. His mother was in such a state following the birth of her baby boy that she took a drug overdose, but was luckily discovered in time and survived this particular suicide bid.

Christian on the other hand was in jail, his father unable to raise the $10 million bail which had been set by the municipal judge. Over the coming weeks his defence team compiled their case, as did the prosecution, and throughout the pre-trial preparations the press were hot on their tails, reporting anything and everything which was thought to be of interest and which might help them sell a few extra copies.

By early August the Judge decided that there was enough evidence to try Christian with first-degree murder. He also reduced the bail request to $2 million, a sum Brando raised by using his house as collateral. Grateful to get his son out of jail he personally handed over Christian's passport and took the opportunity to talk to the media who were encamped outside the courtroom. He announced, "I have a hide this thick." He held out his hand with his fingers wide apart before going on, "But when it comes to my son and my children, you're speaking to someone with a different impulse."

He took his time and spoke to the reporters for more than half an hour. One asked, "Could anything have been done to prevent the May 16 tragedy?" to which he replied, "Where is a feather dropped by a seagull on the heads of two thousand persons going to land? There are too many unknowns."

The prosecution's first-degree murder case was weakened by the fact that they were unable to subpoena Cheyenne back to the United States. In addition the Judge had informed them that unless Cheyenne was present in court her statements could not be used. As she was in poor health both physically and mentally it became obvious that she would not attend the trial, statements collected from her doctors in Tahiti having recommended that she was too unstable to be allowed to testify. To add to their problems the prosecution were informed that they would not be able to use the police tape recording of Christian's confession, as the police had neglected to make him aware that he was entitled to have an attorney present with him free of charge. The police had assumed that the "free of charge" element of his rights were not necessary considering his father's immense wealth.

The Municipal Court Judge, Larry Fidler, informed prosecutors, "It's a clear error and I will not allow the statement to be used." Disappointed but undeterred the prosecution pressed on with the original charge of first-degree murder – the rest of the evidence, including the autopsy, told its own story.

Robert Shapiro was able to secure a plea bargain with the District Attorney who agreed to reduce the charge to voluntary manslaughter if his client was willing to admit his guilt. On 14 January 1991, Christian Brando entered a guilty plea to the charge of voluntary manslaughter. This was not well received by the press, public and even less by Drollet's father, Jacques Drollet, who was quoted as saying, "Marlon Brando is rich, well known and his lawyers are very clever. They will find a way to get Christian out." The public opinion at the time was that Marlon Brando could afford to somehow pay for his son's freedom, do a deal which would lessen the charges and maybe even allow him to walk free.

Christian used the time he had before the trial to try and get some kind of sanity back in his life. He had been through detox, was regularly attending Alcoholics Anonymous and had started to resume his work, although it seems that he was resigned to his fate – the charge of voluntary manslaughter had a maximum of 16 years imprisonment. He was not well received when he ventured out and complained that he would be better off in prison serving his sentence rather than receiving abuse from members of the public. He was reported to have complained, "I did plead guilty to a man-slaughter, it's a tragedy and I do feel bad. If I could give my life to have him come back I would do it, but there's nothing I can do. But are people going to spit on me all the time? Can't I just go to jail? Is that OK?"

By March the case was ready to be conducted. Christian's character was first to be dragged through the mud, a psychological report describing him as being prone to violence, a dropout and a threat to society, concluding that his violent outbursts were escalating.

His defence psychiatrist Dr Saul Faerstein had assessed him and claimed that Christian was chronically depressed with a somewhat diminished capacity due to drug abuse, saying, "He is a tempestuous kid from a tempestuous family, frustrated and angry about his life." He put some of the blame on Christian's parents. "Neither of them provided a stable, protective, safe emotional environment for Christian to grow up in."

By the second day of the hearing Marlon Brando was called to the stand to defend his son. The courtroom was packed, and so too were the streets outside. Everybody wanted to get a glimpse of the star and wanted to see how he was bearing up under the stress of his son's ordeal.

Marlon Brando was first questioned by his son's defence council, Robert Shapiro starting by asking him a range of questions, during which he displayed a whole range of emotions and was, on occasions, reduced to tears. He testified that he had not always been there when his son was growing up, but he felt that he had not neglected him and didn't consider himself to be a bad father. He did however lay some of the blame for Christian's upbringing on his mother, Anna Kashfi, saying, "She was probably the most beautiful woman I've ever known, but she came close to being as negative a person as I have met in my life." He then turned his thoughts to himself and admitted, "I led a wasted life, I chased a lot of women. Perhaps I failed as a father, the tendency is always to blame the other person. There were things I could have done differently, I did the best I could." Then Brando's demeanour changed, maybe because he felt that he had opened his heart too wide. He suddenly became angry and said, "This is the Marlon Brando case. If Christian were black, Mexican or poor, he wouldn't be in this courtroom. Everyone wants a piece of the pie."

Turning to where Dag Drollet's family were sitting he apologized to them in French, their native tongue, "I cannot continue with the hate in your eyes. I'm sorry with my whole heart," before going on, still in French, to say that if he could exchange himself for Dag Drollet, he would gladly do so.

Unfortunately his sentiments were lost on the grieving Jacques, who was unimpressed by Brando's "performance", later admitting that he didn't believe a word of it and was still so angry he could have killed him.

After being on the witness stand for several hours he was able to stand down. Tired, he tried to make a quick exit via the back entrance, not wanting to face the mob of reporters who were eagerly awaiting his exit at the front of the courthouse. The swarm of media men and women who staked out the courthouse day by day wanted a piece of Brando's performance for themselves. They had heard of his "Oscar winning" display of emotions, the crying, then the anger, the apology in French, all of which would make great copy. The headlines came thick and fast – this certainly was a major production and Brando, as usual, found himself playing the lead part.

On the third day Christian took the stand. Appearing remorseful he pleaded, "If I could change places with Dag, I would." He also used his time on the stand to apologize to Drollet's family and added, "I'm prepared for the consequences."

Christian's admission of guilt in exchange for the lesser charge of manslaughter meant that the prosecution could only hope to pursue the longest sentence available. They fought hard to show Christian as a man who had lived a life of contented luxury, spoilt beyond any normal measure, and who believed he could have anything he wanted and do anything he wanted, without impunity. The prosecution set out to make an example of this young man – what he had done was to shoot a defenceless man in cold blood; in any other court it would have been first-degree murder. In their view Brando had already been shown leniency, his charge had been reduced, so the least that Drollet's family could expect was a proper prison term, one which reflected the enormity of the family's loss.

After both sides had summed up and presented their final statements all that was left was for the Judge to pass sentence. The packed courthouse was silent as he spoke about the sad loss of Dag and the dreadful effect the whole situation had inflicted upon both families. He summed up by stating, "The only thing everyone can agree on is that this was a tragic situation for everyone it touched." And with these words still resounding in the ears of those gathered in the court, the Judge declared that he was handing down a sentence of just ten years to Christian. A murmur of discontent swept through the gallery, although the defence team breathed a deep sigh of relief.

Christian was immediately taken away to start his sentence at the California Men's Colony in San Luis Obispo. With an amount of time already served while in custody, if he kept a clean record while in prison, there was every chance he would be freed within four years. The Drollet family were unhappy with the sentence, claiming that it was far too short.

They also knew that after Christian's comparatively short incarceration, he would be a young man, with plenty of money, enjoying the life that he had denied their son. Public opinion mirrored that of the Drollet family, but within weeks their mood softened as their daily fix of gossip on Christian slowed down. It seemed that the tabloids had run out of exclusives from his "friends" and former lovers, he was able to serve his time quietly and would be a free man in just four years.

While Christian was serving his time his sister was struggling – by now she had been formally diagnosed with schizophrenia and was on daily medication. Her friends in Tahiti had all but turned their backs on her, some claiming to be afraid of her. She was still mourning the loss of Dag Drollet and no doubt felt at least partly to blame for his death at the hands of her brother, confessing that when her thoughts turned to Drollet, she wished she could join him. Five years later she hit rock bottom when she lost custody of her son, the point of no return. In her mother's home in Tahiti on Easter Sunday, 1995, 25-year-old Cheyenne took her own life and hung herself. Her father was so devastated to lose his beautiful, troubled daughter, he was unable to travel to attend her Tahitian funeral. Also missing from the service was Christian, who was still serving his sentence.

When he was informed of his sister's fate he was distraught, having never had the chance to see her one last time, to say his goodbyes and make his peace. Tarita, Cheyenne's mother, applied for custody of her grandchild Tuki, which was granted and he continues to live in Tahiti with her.

After negotiations between Marlon Brando and Jacques Drollet it was decided that Cheyenne could have her last wish – she wanted to be buried with her former love, Drollet, permission was granted and she was buried in the Drollet family crypt next to him.

Marlon Brando went on to appear in more blockbusters, but when not filming he became increasingly reclusive – obviously the strains of his son's incarceration and the death of his daughter had taken their toll. On 1 July 2004 he died in hospital from lung failure, and was cremated, as he had wished, in a strictly private funeral, only attended by close friends and members of his family. He was prepared for death and had even taken time to write an address to be read at the service.

He left behind a dynasty of children and grandchildren, and will always be remembered for his astonishing acting ability which will live on for generations to come.

Christian was released from prison in 1996 after serving his sentence. He initially led a quiet life, until his name hit the headlines once again when he was involved in yet another murder trial, this time involving the death of his former lover, Bonnie Lee Bakely. Bonnie was drawn to stardom, the rich and the famous; her dream was to become a movie actress and she moved in those circles most likely to assist with her ambitions. Another unhinged personality, she had married a number of times, always to those with money. She had become pregnant at the time that she was involved with Christian, but after having DNA tests it was confirmed that the child was that of her husband, Robert Blake. After discovering the true father of the child, she and Blake married in November 2000. Not long afterward, having eaten out in Los Angeles, Bakely was shot and murdered while she sat in the car waiting for her husband who had returned to the restaurant to collect something he had left behind. Christian's name was associated with the case but he was exonerated when he was able to provide a satisfactory alibi. Blake is still awaiting trial at the time of writing.

Whether Christian's sentence was long enough has been hotly disputed in the media – if the court got nothing else right at least the Judge's final comments were accurate, for this tragic event certainly did touch the lives of both families. In the end Brando lost the most, and ironically the man who committed the crime became the last one standing, enjoying his liberty, life and a good portion of his late father's estate. The press believed there was one other victim – justice.

William Desmond Taylor

Hollywood in the swinging twenties, the era of the silent movie, was as loud and abrasive as the Hollywood of the twenty-first century, just as packed with characters and with no less gossip and scandal. Hollywood film-making was in its infancy but the actors and actresses who adorned the silver screen earned plenty of money and learned quickly how to enjoy themselves. The rules and expectations though were different to those enjoyed in today's Hollywood. Prohibition meant that alcohol was not always readily available, not through the normal channels at least, and drug use was a pastime only the rich and famous could indulge in. Sex was a subject much practised but a little less discussed and one's sexuality, if different from the norm, was a secret that needed to be guarded. Secrets, however, were not always easily hidden, even long before the advent of *Hello* magazine; Louella Parsons was the biggest gossip columnist of her day, a friend and foe to the stars in equal measure.

One of Hollywood's most respected directors from the silent era was William Desmond Taylor, who directed such stars as Mary Pickford and Dustin Farnum, and won many plaudits for his screen work. Amongst the films he directed were such great titles as *Davy Crockett, Tom Sawyer, Huckleberry Finn* and the especially notable *Anne of Green Gables.*

In line with Taylor's status as a top Hollywood film director he had the living arrangements to match, with a large house in the then fashionable West Lake Park area of California. His home on a private-gated community at Alvarado Court was of Spanish design with an elaborate landscaped garden. The houses, all of which were built around a U-shaped road, were mainly occupied by other members of the movie-making fraternity; Charles Maigne, another big director lived next door. Among his other neighbours lived the actors Douglas Maclean, Agnes Aires and Edna Purviance, a real upper-class social scene if ever there was one.

It cannot be doubted that Taylor was certainly enjoying the fruits of his success, both in material terms and in his social interactions. However the enjoyment of his well-earned status came to an abrupt end on 1 February 1922 when he was gunned down within the relatively safe confines of Alvarado Court.

Taylor had enjoyed a close relationship with the actress Mabel Normand, although reports differ as to the nature of their friendship. Some said they were in love and others that they were merely friends. What they certainly shared, in addition to a joint interest in books, was a fascination with mind-altering drugs, not unlike many of the Hollywood A-listers of the day. For Normand though the interest had turned into a deep-seated dependency, a reliance which risked her life. Taylor was aware just how on the edge she was and was concerned for her well-being, determined to help her kick the habit.

On the day of Taylor's murder Normand had visited Alvarado Court to pick up a book on German philosophy, leaving at around 7.45 p.m. Taylor had walked her across to her car where he noticed a copy of the *Police Gazette*, a tabloid gossip magazine, on the back seat. They laughed as Taylor commented on the extremes of her reading material, from gossip to philosophy, and kissed cheeks as Normand jumped in the car before setting off down the horseshoe lane to head home.

Taylor turned and headed back indoors and within minutes, sometime around 8 p.m., he was shot in the back with a single bullet and killed. Douglas Maclean and his wife Faith, who occupied the house nearest to Taylor's, heard the sound of the shot and went to their window to look out. Faith saw a stranger, aged around 20, outside Taylor's residence; for a moment they looked across at each other before the man turned and unhurriedly walked back into Taylor's house. The man's calm behaviour made Faith less suspicious and eventually she and her husband put the noise down to a car backfiring. They had seen Normand's car outside Taylor's house earlier and assumed it had come from her vehicle as she left. A short time later Faith saw the man again as he emerged from the house and strolled across the piece of land that separated Taylor's house from the MacLeans', his calm composure allaying any fears that he may have been up to no good. As the stranger disappeared into the night Taylor lay dead in the hallway of his house and the opportunity to call the police had gone.

The following day Taylor's butler and general helper, Henry Peavey, arrived at 7.30 a.m.; he had with him the director's breakfast as well as a bottle of milk of magnesia which Taylor had requested. Letting himself in with the key he walked headlong into the bloody scene, in the middle of which lay Taylor, a chair peculiarly astride one of his legs. Reeling back from the scene Peavey began to scream until a small group of people had gathered round the doorway. Taylor was found to be fully clothed with his wallet, which contained 78 dollars, still in his trouser pocket. His jacket pocket contained a silver cigarette case and an ivory toothpick, not to mention an expensive Waltham pocket watch. His finger sported a rather obvious two-carat diamond ring, a present from the studio, and above this on his wrist, the latest in fashionable timepieces, a wristwatch. If the motive of this cowardly murder had been robbery then the perpetrator had bungled the crime completely. Further inspection of the house also indicated that the killer had neither taken nor disturbed anything in the process of looking.

As the crowd gathered on Taylor's porch a number of other individuals arrived on the scene, presumably despatched from the studio, their motive an apparent cleanup operation. Even as Hollywood was emerging as a major centre of film-making excellence it had already begun to reel from a number of scandalous revelations marking the beginning of the media's obsession with celebrity. As if these overpaid, overindulgent actors didn't have enough bad press already, the newspapers had been thriving on a couple of recent episodes which had left a severe blemish on Hollywood's not quite untarnished reputation. The first of these scandals was the affair between Fatty Arbuckle and the ironically named Virginia Rappe. Arbuckle had carved himself out a lucrative career as a silver screen comedian whose talent had made him popular with the public for many years. Unfortunately Rappe had died at one of Arbuckle's many parties. When the police arrived they arrested Arbuckle on rape charges, suggesting he had raped her in such a way as to cause her death. It was assumed the overweight actor had somehow managed to rupture the young woman's bladder, although much more gross versions of events were circulated in the press. Although Arbuckle was tried three times he was eventually acquitted, but not before the press had dismantled his reputation. Among some of the worst headlines a person could endure, Arbuckle's fame and public acceptance were lost and his career effectively ended.

Hot on the heels of the Arbuckle headlines came another scandal which would rock the world of Hollywood. The popular actor Wallace Reid, blonde hair, blue eyed and athletic, died of a drugs-related illness. Long before it was commonplace or even fashionable to have an addiction, let alone be seen to be cured of it, Reid was a morphine addict. The studio had kept it as quiet as they could and enlisted the help of a sanatorium to help break the addiction, but his addiction was much stronger than anyone could have expected and the stress caused by being denied the drugs brought on a fatal heart attack. Once again the press jumped on the story and criticized the whole of the Hollywood set-up for its hedonistic behaviour.

It was to this backdrop therefore that colleagues of Taylor entered the house to remove any incriminating evidence, apparently even if this meant interfering with the scene of the crime – the show must go on. It is now alleged that it was Charles Eyton of Paramount who led the clean-up operation at the time of Taylor's death. In her book *The Honeycomb*, Adele Rogers St John claimed that her husband Ike had also been dispatched to Alvarado Court as part of the clean-up effort; she also claimed that he picked up a pair of mono-grammed knickers from the bedroom with the initials M.M.M on them, which it was thought stood for Mary Miles Minter. She further states that the instruction for Ike to attend came from the mayor of Hollywood, who could not stand the thought of yet more bad publicity for his city.

When the police did arrive they themselves started to examine the scene and begin making enquiries. One of the many mysteries surrounding Taylor's death concerns a man who was at the scene who claimed to be a doctor, but who did not give his name. Before the police entered the house he told a police officer, Tom Ziegler, that he had examined the body and that Taylor had in fact died of natural causes, although when inspecting the crime scene it was patently obvious that Taylor had suffered a major trauma. The would-be doctor was never found and no motive has ever been established as to why this individual provided this unsolicited and incorrect diagnosis.

When the police arrived in their cars it is thought that a variety of studio cars were just leaving, having removed a quantity of bootleg booze and a large number of Taylor's private letters, some of which appeared to have been burned in his fireplace. The police now had a murder on their hands. William Desmond Taylor, whose birth name was William Cunningham Deane-Tanner, had been shot, presumably with murder in mind, because although the studio had obviously removed many items, the killer had not.

When news of Taylor's murder emerged the press were naturally keen to pursue the story – here was another high-profile member of the Hollywood elite who had been killed. Stories and rumours circulated immediately, many of which the press were happy to report; none of it made great reading for Hollywood and very few reporters were keen to treat it as a plain murder. The lack of a robbery clearly presented a dilemma for the police and for the press – if Taylor had been singled out for murder then there must have been something which caused it. If the police could find the reason they might then find the person.

For all his apparent wealth Taylor's recent history before

he died had not always been plain sailing. While he was on a trip to England recuperating from an illness, his first valet, Edward Sands, had taken Taylor's car out and had wrecked it; he then forged cheques for over $5,000 and took clothes and jewellery. Sands was never caught; he simply disappeared before Taylor's return and no trace of him could be found.

Taylor's choice of replacement for Sands also looked on paper to be a strange decision for he elected to employ a known felon called Henry Peavey who was later arrested for vagrancy and indecent exposure, a charge often associated with cruising homosexuals. Rather than sack Peavey it was Taylor who put up bail money for his beleaguered valet. Taylor's behaviour in respect of his home help did not go unnoticed by the papers or by the police when it came to searching out the motive for his killing, and Peavey became the first name on their list.

Taylor was born in Ireland in 1872, the second of four children. His father, Kearns Deane-Tanner, was a major in the British Army and by all standards they lived a fairly affluent lifestyle. Like most families at that time the father was the source of most discipline and Major Deane-Tanner was never slow in delivering what was needed to keep his large family on the straight and narrow. Taylor left home in his teens and managed to find work on the stage – it was 1890 when he landed a bit part in a production of *The Private Secretary*. When his father learned of his son's occupation he felt he could take the disgrace no longer and enrolled him in a place called Runnymeade, an institution in Kansas aimed at sorting out young miscreants. The only good thing to come out of his stay in Kansas was his fondness for horses, an interest which stayed with him throughout his life and which also came in handy when he took acting roles in a variety of Western movies.

In 1901 he moved to New York City where once again he found himself on the stage, and it was here in the same year that he married Ethel May Harrison, an aspiring actress. As his acting career struggled and he failed to get better parts he could no longer afford to support his wife and their new baby, so he decided to go into the family antique business, financed by his father-in-law. As the years ticked by Taylor became bored with the business and bored with his marriage – he still longed to be an actor. It was in September 1908 that he asked staff at his antique business to give an envelope to his wife containing $500, took the balance of their wealth, some $100, and fled the family home without a word of goodbye.

Roaming from state to state and taking on a number of menial jobs he eventually ended up in San Francisco where once again he found work on the stage. Changing his name he gravitated towards the burgeoning film industry, shooting a few westerns before winning his first starring role in the film *Captain Alvarez*, his experience with horses once again proving very handy. After a few years acting Taylor finally made his move to the other side of the camera with his first directorial role, when he was asked to direct a movie for the Balboa Studio.

It was while directing the film *The Awakening* that Taylor fell in love with Neva Gerber, his lead actress, who was married but separated. She had one daughter from her marriage and although she no longer wanted to live with her older husband the rules on divorce meant getting the appropriate approvals were prolonged and difficult, so Taylor and Gerber maintained a close though unofficial relationship.

When the Balboa Studio went into bankruptcy in 1917 Taylor and Gerber ended their relationship and Taylor moved to the American Film Company, often referred to as the Flying "A". It was here that he first hit the big time when he was asked to direct the remaining episodes of a serial called *The Diamond from the Sky*, after its initial director, Jacques Jaccard, was lured away to Universal. The serial was a box office smash and the cast and crew presented Taylor with a two-carat diamond ring as a mark of their appreciation. He followed this with a number of highly successful films which earned himself and the studio a great deal of money.

America's entry into the First World War came along and

temporarily interrupted Taylor's rising star, although he never saw combat as the war ended before he could be posted. His talent was in demand straight away and he immediately returned to directing, having more hits with *Anne of Green Gables* and *The Green Temptation*, the latter being the last film he made before meeting his tragic end.

The murder of a well-known Hollywood player brought the attentions of both the police and the media in equal measure. With the media torn between a desire to find the killer and a wish to disclose the scandal they thought had caused the murder, the police simply followed procedure – it was well known that one ex-employee had already robbed Taylor, maybe he had simply come back for more. The fact that Taylor had not been robbed could have been put down to a number of things, panic being one of them.

The police therefore focused their attention on Taylor's first butler, 27-year-old Edward Sands, the short, fat, ruddy faced man who impressed most who met him with his easy-going manner and impeccable English standards. Although he spoke with a Cockney accent, it was presumed this was false as Sands – real name Edward Snyder – was in fact a citizen of Ohio. The police also established that he had more of a troubled history than Taylor was obviously aware of, for having joined the Navy in 1911 at the age of 17 he was court-martialled for embezzlement and served 12 months in a navy prison before being dishonourably discharged. Strangely Sands then enlisted in the Navy again, deserting just a few months later after which he applied to the Army under the rather grand false name of Edward FitzStrathmore. Securing a job in the finance department of the Columbus, Ohio, army depot he soon found himself in a position of great temptation. Unable to resist, he soon passed a forged cheque before once more deserting his post.

It was during his employment with Taylor that Sands once more suffered great temptation when his boss went on a trip to England, effectively doing a house swap with his friend and playwright, Edward Knoblock. Taylor used Knoblock's home in London and Knoblock came to stay in Alvarado Court. Concerned that his friend might have additional requirements while he was in London, Taylor gave Sands a blank cheque and asked him to use it should Knoblock need anything. Sands cashed the cheque for $5,000 and, telling his new house guest that he had been recently married, he asked for time off to go on honeymoon, to which the unassuming Knoblock agreed. Sands packed his bags and disappeared, taking a number of valuables with him.

When Taylor returned in August 1921 and found Sands, his money and valuables gone and his car wrecked, he contacted the police who searched in vain – Sands was nowhere to be seen. The police continued to search for Sands after Taylor's death but were unable to trace him, and no charges were ever brought as there was no evidence to connect him to the crime, let alone to suggest he was even in the vicinity at the time. The police though felt that Sands was more of a crime-for-gain type of a criminal and to leave Taylor with obvious money and jewellery on him would not have been his style. Sands had never been mistreated by Taylor – if anything the opposite was true – indeed Taylor had the highest regard for him and had even told his friends that he was the best valet in the world.

Although the police were satisfied that Sands was an unlikely murderer, Taylor's friends and certain members of the media always had their doubts. However Sands' departure left the way open for Henry Peavey to step in as valet number two. Black, tall and muscular, Peavey was quickly ruled out of the investigation by the police, although it was known he had a police record for vagrancy and indecent exposure. The police's belief in Peavey's innocence was not shared by everyone, and a reporter named Florabel Muir was totally convinced that he was the killer. Taking investigative journalism to new heights Muir believed she could trick Peavey into a confession and set about creating the trap. It may have been a sign of the times for Muir did not engage in a complex plan but rather staged a simple trick geared to extracting a simple confession. She enlisted the help of two friends, Frank Carson and Al Weinshank, who would aid and abet Muir in the execution of the little plot. Approaching Peavey, Muir and Carson explained that they did not know where Taylor's grave was in the cemetery and asked if he could show them for the sum of ten dollars. Peavey readily agreed and began walking towards the area of the cemetery but as they approached the grave Weinshank, who had draped a white cotton sheet over his head, jumped out of a bush and stood there trying to look ghostly. He then said, "I am the ghost of William Desmond Taylor. You murdered me, confess Peavey," to which the shocked Peavey burst out laughing, soon realising what the trio had been up to and vented his fury at them for attempting such a sick trick.

Although their play didn't work certain members of the media continued to suspect that Peavey was the murderer. Stories and rumours continued to circulate about Peavey – it was even suggested that Peavey and Taylor were having a gay liaison and that Peavey might have killed his boss in a jealous rage. There was certainly some evidence to suggest that if he wasn't gay Taylor may have been bisexual. Art director George Eyton, who was gay, knew Taylor quite well, and had told a reporter he was one of the people dispatched to Alvarado Court on the day Taylor's body was found. When the reporter asked what his job at the house was, Eyton said he had to collect all of the letters from upstairs. When asked why the letters were so important, he replied that Taylor slept with men. Eyton also claimed that Sands had blackmailed Taylor over his relations with men and suggested that Peavey was gay, his indecent exposure charge supporting this claim. It was also suggested that Peavey used to visit the park with a view to soliciting young boys, unless of course this was one of the duties he performed for Taylor.

None of the allegations relating to either Taylor or Peavey were ever substantiated, although the papers acted as judge and jury for Peavey, convicting him in the absence of evidence. In those long-forgotten days it must be remembered that segregation was a part of daily life, so it could have been that Peavey was merely urinating, unable to gain entry to a whites-only toilet. Peavey died in 1937 just seven years after he had given an interview in which he claimed a famous actress and her mother killed Taylor, although he did not name either.

The lady in question was Mary Miles Minter, a young actress who was thought to be in love with Taylor. Born Juliet Reilly in 1902, her mother Charlotte was the original pushy mother. Her goal was to make the young girl a star and from an early age she would dress her to make her look first older than her years, and then later younger than her real age. Charlotte's plan worked and she soon renamed the child using the birth certificate of a dead niece. After many stage roles Minter finally met Taylor in 1919 when he was aged 50 and she just 16. It is thought that Taylor may have become intimate with the young girl, a crime in those days and one punishable with a severe prison term. Whatever the truth of the matter the press established that they had enjoyed more than simple friendship and the resulting headlines caused a wave of public revulsion, resulting in Minter's films being boycotted. Having never enjoyed the role of actress Minter was happy to fade away and lived to the ripe old age of 82. The loss of her daughter's career is what is thought to have provoked anger in Minter's mother and it is thought that she may have pulled the trigger in a fit of anger, although the police never pursued this angle.

Adele Rogers St John, in her book *The Honeycomb*, claims that it was Minter's mother who committed the crime – Taylor had ruined her daughter's career and she was out-raged at his exploitative behaviour. In explaining away the man seen at the time of Taylor's death it is suggested that Minter's mother simply cross-dressed to avoid detection.

Later in an interview in her old age Mary Miles Minter emotionally told a reporter, "My mother killed everything I ever loved". The precise meaning of this statement has never been fully explained, although the media have interpreted this as meaning Minter's mother did in fact kill Taylor.

As with most Hollywood stars who have met a tragic end the media reported all of the various options in relation to the killing of Taylor and there have been a variety of other scenarios which have got their supporters.

One of these involves the actress who had been with

Taylor on the evening of his death, Mabel Normand. A good-looking girl with a mass of brown curly hair, Normand had enjoyed success at a number of studios before finding her niche as a scantily clad swimmer in a number of Mack Sennett productions, gaining herself the rather grand title of "The Queen of Comedy" and "The Female Chaplin". In 1912 Normand became the lead actress in the now much acclaimed Keystone comedies and ended up in a relationship with Mack Sennett, but this came to an end when Normand found Sennett under the covers with another actress. After much turbulence Normand finally quit Sennett for the Goldwyn Motion Picture Company where she found solace in narcotics and in the arms of Taylor. It is within this tangled web that a number of other theories emerge – some believe that it was Normand herself who committed the murder, jealous of Taylor's relationships with other women. Others suggest that Mack Sennett, who had tried to win Normand back, both on a personal and professional level, murdered Taylor, again jealous of their relationship. And the third version of events suggests that a drug dealer had extracted his revenge on Taylor when he refused to cover the bills run up by Normand. Whether there is any truth in these propositions will never be known; what is known is that Normand had spent the earlier part of the evening with Taylor before he was killed not long after she claimed to have left Alvarado Court.

For all of the theories proposed no one has ever been brought to book for the murder of William Desmond Taylor. This is one crime where the power of the media, in all its forms, could not shake out an answer, and so the mystery and the murder remains unsolved.

The Silent Movie Legend

Ramon Novarro

Having spent many millions of dollars already, the MGM studio executives were more than a little disappointed when their latest film, *Ben Hur*, ground to a halt, amid bitter disputes over the quality of the work and the skill with which the film was being assembled. After long talks the studio executives took the tough decision to scrap what had gone before and to remake the film from scratch. In doing so they once again created a vacancy for the most coveted of Hollywood acting roles – the lead part in the film.

The role was awarded to Ramon Novarro, a 27-year-old Mexican actor who brought smouldering good looks to the silent cinema screens of the 1920s. It is still this role for which he is best remembered – this and his brutal murder at the hands of two male prostitutes many years later.

Novarro was born on 6 February 1899, in Durango, Mexico and christened Ramon Samaniegos. His family was relatively prosperous, his father was a dentist and he enjoyed a cultured upbringing until the 1910 Mexican revolution forced them to flee to the United States, where his father was unable to work as a dentist, and the family lived on the verge of poverty. The young Novarro enjoyed a happy family life; a strict Roman Catholic, he was a regular church attendee and loved to sing in the choir. His voice was considered so good that his family saved the money to provide him with professional voice coaching, an investment which would pay off handsomely in due course.

The impoverished young Novarro was forced to take menial jobs to help support his family and moved to New

York City where he took a job as a singing waiter. He also worked as an usher in a local cinema where he could watch the films, getting his first taste of the acting bug. One evening, while singing the latest menu offerings, Novarro was spotted by a talent scout and offered a short-term contract; his break had occurred by chance and now he was now more determined than ever to become an actor.

By 1918, Novarro had broken into the silent movie industry, starring alongside Mary Pickford in *The Little American*. It was, however, during the making of the film *The Prisoner of Zenda* with co-star Alice Terry, the wife of the director, Rex Ingram, that it was suggested he should change his birth name to something more pronounceable. After a little thought the two men agreed on the name Novarro – easier to say, while still maintaining the flavour of some exotic mystery, it matched his dark, Latin good looks.

Novarro's arrival on the silver screen couldn't have been better timed as Hollywood was enjoying a "Latin lover" phase, a role for which he was best placed. He was soon compared with other noted Latin types of the day and at one point was even thought to be the "new Valentino", the original silent screen lover and the epitome of the dashing Latin hero who swept women off their feet. Novarro and Valentino's careers overlapped slightly and they became firm friends – and more – though it would be Novarro who would make the jump to talking movies in due course.

After a string of successful movies starring alongside some of the best actors and actresses of the day, including Greta Garbo, with whom he starred in the 1932 film *Mata Hari*, Novarro had become MGM's most important leading man, challenging Rudolph Valentino to being the number one Latin-lover actor in the world. Along with these great plaudits also came amazing wealth – at his highest point Novarro had a contract with MGM which paid him $10,000 per week, a massive amount in the 1920s and 1930s, though a great testament to his huge audience-pulling power. In 1923, Louella Parsons, the most powerful gossip columnist in Hollwood, wrote a piece on Novarro for the *New York Morning Telegraph*, in which she said:

And come to think of it, why shouldn't Ramon be an optimist. At 23 he is earning a salary of $1,250 a week, with the possibility of increasing to $4,000 and $5,000 next year.

Parsons went on to comment on Novarro's refreshing lack of ego and his personal commitment to those who had helped him. Having asked if he had been offered óther roles from other studios, he replied that he had, but would not be so ungrateful as to accept them. Parsons continued her piece in mock surprise:

We looked about for smelling salts after this noble declaration; it was so unusual. The average motion picture male star who has reached the top in a few bounds usually spends his time telling the interviewer what a bum his director is and how little he knows and what a raw deal he got with his company, but Ramon is not following the usual prescribed path. He is grateful and doesn't care who knows it.

Novarro's endearing character had won the heart of the one person who could have damaged him, Louella Parsons, whose gossip columns were full of stories blowing the lids off the lives of those men and women who called Hollywood home. Novarro though was a true gentleman and his emotions and feelings were real.

He was also an intelligent man who recognized the transient nature of the acting business and unlike other actors who squandered their wealth, he invested wisely, buying a portfolio of properties which would secure his income long after his acting days had ended. At the height of his career and with wealth beyond his wildest imagination, Novarro was, however, a troubled man. His on-screen performances as the dashing hero who always got the woman could not have been in more contrast to his real life, for Novarro was homosexual, and had even enjoyed a romantic involvement with Valentino, the other great Latin lover who was able to fake it on screen.

As well as the contrast with his on-screen performances, Novarro was also a devout Roman Catholic, making his sexuality a problem all round. Although it was common knowledge among most Hollywood celebrities, the rest of the world were unaware of Novarro's true desires. The heads of the studios were only concerned with one thing – profit – and so long as Novarro could continue to draw the audiences, what he got up to in his own time was his own business; most successful actors had one or more scandals to keep out of the public eye and he wasn't any different.

Novarro was of course a life-long bachelor and although he mixed socially with many female friends and colleagues, he was never romatically linked to anyone of them. There appeared to be little of interest for the likes of Louella Parsons – Novarro had carefully cultivated his image as a deeply devoted family man and someone who took his religious responsibilities very seriously. It was perhaps one of his greatest performances, his character remaining stain free right up to his tortuous death, after which every tawdry detail of his personal life was dragged through the courts and the newspapers. Until then, Novarro was considered a class act, a cut above the rest of the Hollywood pack, who would flaunt their excesses unashamedly. Novarro preferred to keep his private life just that – private.

Even at the height of his stardom, when the newspapers and Hollywood rag-mags were awash with his image, he still managed to portray himself as just an actor, devoid of anything other than a normal social life. The reality was, however, quite different, for Novarro had maintained a number of homosexual relationships – as well as his sexual interactions with Valentino, he also enjoyed a long-standing relationship with the publicist and entertainment journalist, Herbert Howe. It is not known exactly when Novarro began to actively pay for the company of young men, but the act of hustling for men did become a feature of his life, one which ultimately lead him directly into the arms of his killers. In pre-1960s America, before the dawn of the sexual revolution, Novarro's sexuality would have been kept under wraps. Blatant relationship-building was a risk and not one to be taken lightly, whereas the company of rent boys, or male prostitutes, provided a safer way to feed his sexual needs, away from the glare of publicity.

His career continued to soar and he eventually made the transition to talking motion pictures, a move which propelled him to Hollywood superstardom. Although best known for his role in *Ben Hur*, the most expensive silent movie ever made, Novarro went on to perform in some highly memorable talkies. As well as his performance with screen goddess, Greta Garbo, he also starred in *The Cat and the Fiddle* with Jeanette MacDonald, and in 1935 he starred alongside the English actress, Evelyn Lane, in *The Night is Young*. His films were a great success and he continued to perform well at the box office, though throughout the middle and later part of the 1930s a sea change was sweeping through Hollywood. It had been recognized that movie-going audiences had started to prefer a less exotic type of leading man and the roles for which Novarro was best known began to dry up. With films now demanding the more "testosterone-fuelled heroes" who had become the vogue, MGM decided not to renew Novarro's contract when it expired in 1935. Even before the advent of the American hero type of leading man, Novarro's career had began to wane – after starring in a number of MGM musicals and having been miscast in a number of films he too had started to realize that his film days were drawing to a close. When MGM didn't renew his contract he wasn't surprised; he had already started to consider his options and had a few plans of his own.

With the best of his film-acting days behind him, Novarro turned to his first love – the stage. He tried his hand in a Broadway production, though by now the name which had guaranteed takings at cinemas all over America was struggling to pull in the crowds for his stage production. The play received terrible reviews and the show closed after a depressingly short run. With the exception of a few cameo roles, Novarro's acting career seemed to be over. A "has-been" before the start of the 1940s, he now turned his attention to his investments, expanding his business horizons instead.

But Novarro could never quite quench his thirst for acting

and continued to accept cameo roles, eventually making his last film in 1960. With television emerging as the new entertainment medium Novarro even managed a few fleeting scenes on some of the new programmes, although these were the death throes of his career. Thereafter he slid into practical obscurity, though he had earned and invested so well that he was able to continue to enjoy a fabulously wealthy lifestyle.

Looking back over his career in a late 1960s interview with Dewitt Bodeen, for *Films Review*, he claimed that he didn't like any of the talking movies in which he had appeared. Just as before he seemed refreshingly frank and honest, without any hint of ego. Novarro forged great friendships on the strength of his normality, always being thought of as a gentleman; it was to come as a great shock to those who loved him when they discovered the horrible details of his death.

He continued to live a lavish lifestyle, the evidence of his wealth plain to see from his cars to the luxurious Laurel Canyon home in which he lived in North Hollywood. The address alone bore witness to Novarro's financial credentials and in due course it would attract the men who would tragically end his life.

With Novarro's new-found obscurity came the freedom to enjoy his life more, and enjoy it he did. He craved the company of young men and found that buying their services presented a better solution to the fulfilment of his sexual needs. The deal was always clear cut – money in exchange for sex, no complications and no attachments, though visitors to the ageing actor's home always enjoyed a warm welcome and were invited to make themselves comfortable. He would supply food and drink, providing a more cultured environment in which to conduct bought-in pleasures. As always Novarro was a true gentleman, asking for nothing other than to be treated in the same fair way that he treated those around him.

To secure the services of the young men whose company he desired, Novarro would often have to risk cruising in his car along the streets and lanes of Hollywood and Los Angeles. He was always careful for his heavily protected private life would have suffered enormously if he had endured the ignominy of arrest. He was certainly lucky as he was never caught procuring sexual services and managed to find many willing partners. In order to minimize the amount of kerb-crawling required to find partners, Novarro often gave out his private telephone number to those young men who he trusted and who he thought he might want to see again. It was through this naive openness that his killers were able to secure an invitation to the old man's home.

On the evening of 30 October 1968, the night before Halloween, 68-year-old Ramon Novarro awaited the arrival of two male acquaintances who had phoned him and asked if he would like to share an evening with them. He knew what they meant and it was the kind of invitation he liked to extend. Dressed in a red and blue robe, looking every inch the tanned older movie star, he sat in excited anticipation.

The two men who had arranged the visit, brothers Paul and Tom Ferguson, both hustlers and both used to taking money off men in exchange for sexual favours, had a different agenda that evening. They were aware of Novarro's wealth and were intent on taking more than the fee for sex, having been told, wrongly, that Novarro was known to keep a large stash of cash at his house and it was this they were after. Their victim was a closet gay, he was old and frail and neither of the young men envisaged anything other than an easy night's work. If they were successful it would be unlikely that the rich old man would want to involve the police as the lost money would be small in comparison to the man's wealth and the potential publicity of a police investigation would be hugely damaging.

When Novarro opened the door to his Laurel Canyon home he was pleased to see the strong-looking young men. He greeted his guests warmly, welcoming 22-year-old Paul and his 17-year-old brother Tom into his home.

Despite his occasional sexual urges, Novarro often simply sought company; he was in effect a lonely old man. Having never married he had no children or family to share his twilight years. His contemporaries in the field of acting had either passed away or were too frail to socialize; he was therefore left to his own devices.

Once his guests were ensconced in the living room he poured drinks and indulged them in easy conversation. Moving to the piano Novarro played them a song, one he had written himself; to his delight the younger of the two brothers showed great interest and asked if he could try to play it. Novarro spent time showing the young man how to play the notes and for a while was happy to pretend that he wasn't paying for the two men's company. After a while he showed them a photograph of himself dressed in a toga, one of the publicity photos for the *Ben Hur* movie. The photograph prompted more casual conversation with Paul joking that the man in the photo didn't look like Novarro, who was by now keen to impress his young friends even more. Somewhat out of character and possibly intent on showing his young guests that he still enjoyed some clout in Hollywood, he phoned a film publicist and instructed him that he wanted to arrange a meeting for someone who he thought had star potential – one of the boys.

As the drinks continued to flow Paul and Novarro moved to the bedroom where the two men engaged in a sex act. With Novarro naked on the bed and young Tom still downstairs, Paul dressed quickly and turned his attention back to his client – his mood had changed in an instant, the tender affections of the well-built young man now replaced by a sudden cold stare. As Paul stood above the old man he demanded the $5,000 that he had heard were kept in the house.

Novarro, shocked and frightened at the sudden change of behaviour of his guest, was at pains to point out that he never kept that type of money in the house. He reassured Paul that his information was incorrect, adding that he would be happy to pay more than normal for the services.

The exact sequence of events is not known, nor at what point the two men decided to take matters much further. Paul's anger was rising, he wanted the money and he wanted it now. When Tom arrived upstairs he too joined in the demand for the cash, pushing and shoving the naked

Novarro, who lay squirming on the bed. When Novarro still didn't provide the cash the two men began to pummel the old man with their fists, at one point knocking him off the bed and onto the floor. With blood now running from his face, Novarro was yanked to his feet only to be slapped back down again.

The Ferguson brothers seemed to be warming to their theme, although whether they still thought there was money in the house is not clear. They were now intent on delivering as much pain as possible to the old man. When the punishment beating resulted in Novarro losing consciousness, Tom retreated downstairs while Paul yanked the naked old man into the bathroom, where he splashed him with cold water in a bid to keep him awake.

For some reason Tom decided to use Novarro's telephone. He phoned a girlfriend up in Chicago, one who he had recently beaten up, and tried to mollify her. During the conversation he explained where he was and what he and his brother were trying to do, at one point breaking off the conversation to see what progress his brother was achieving. Later, the girl told police that she could hear the elderly man screaming.

When Tom arrived back in the bedroom, Novarro lay bleeding on the floor, his brother standing above him. Looking in the old man's closet Tom found a cane, like a ceremonial baton, along with a pair of gloves. Putting the gloves on he danced around the floor twirling the baton, threatening the old man with even worse humiliations if he did not hand over the cash. With the last of his strength Novarro pleaded with his tormentors, continuing to deny that he had the cash. The brothers though were in no mood to be denied and what had been a severe beating now escalated into torture. Holding the man down the two men used the cane to inflict more pain and suffering, hitting him in the genitals and about the head, drawing even more blood. To stop the old man from protecting himself they then bound him with electric cord before resuming their gruesome task. They continued to hit him with the baton until he drifted off into unconsciousness again. In a fit of anger of madman proportions, Tom knelt beside the dying Novarro and scratched his face, leaving a trail of tramlines etched on the old man's already contorted features.

With Novarro now incapable of talking even if he wanted to, the two young men started a systematic search of the house. When drawers and cupboards did not reveal the hidden stash, they pulled each and every painting off the walls, trying to locate a hidden safe or some other secret storage place. Everything was thrown on the floor; Novarro's collection of photographs remembering his glory days were discarded without a second glance. Meanwhile, unbeknown to the two men, what had been a tortuous beating had now escalated into murder. Novarro, left unattended in the upstairs bedroom, had choked to death on his own blood.

When the Ferguson brothers became aware of the results of their handiwork, panic set in. Still fogged by booze the two men decided to try and leave a few false clues for the police, who, when they discovered what had gone on, would arrive by the car load. In a bid to make the attack look like the work of a woman one of the brothers scrawled a message across a mirror: "US GIRLS ARE BETTER THAN FA-GITS", a weak attempt to put the police off their trail. Novarro was gay, a fact that would surely emerge and the crime had been so violent that the thought of a woman carrying out the attack was beyond comprehension. Without the money and with a murder under their belts they now fled the house, hoping that they had not left any clues which might lead the police to them.

The following day, Halloween, Novarro's butler made the grim discovery and called the police who arrived in large numbers, scouring the grounds, taking statements and trying to protect the murder scene. A breakthrough came surprisingly early on when, in an attempt to piece together Novarro's movements on the night and in the days prior to his murder, the police checked the actor's phone records. One call stood out, an outgoing call from Novarro's number, not only on the night of the murder, but surprisingly close to the time of death. When the police called the number a young woman answered the phone and explained how her boyfriend had called from the old man's address. Chillingly she recalled the man's screams as he suffered at the hands of her ex-boyfriend and his older brother.

The Ferguson brothers were soon arrested and charged with Ramon Novarro's murder. Their prints were found at the Laurel Canyon address and with the ex-girlfriend's statement, the prosecution's case looked watertight; the only question which remained was why they had carried out such a brutal attack.

The press and media lost no time in reporting the crime and were just as quick at speculating on the circumstances surrounding the Hollywood actor's demise. Gradually the facts emerged as Novarro's homosexuality became public knowledge and his preoccupation with male prostitutes hit the headlines. At the height of his obscurity Novarro's name was once more heading the bill, though this time for all the wrong reasons. His highly cultivated image was trashed as the press and media dismantled his glossy, ladies' man Hollywood charade. And in an era of non-tolerance towards the gay community, the defence were determined to use Novarro's sexuality as a weapon against him.

As soon as it dawned on the two killers that serious repercussions would result from their actions, they immediately colluded to foil the courts. Paul Ferguson persuaded his younger brother to make a statement to the effect that he had killed Novarro. Their logic was simple yet flawed – Paul believed that the courts would not pursue his younger brother in the way they might him as the boy was still only 17. The prosecution were, however, ahead of the game and convinced the Judge that young Tom should be tried as an adult; he too would face a murder charge standing along side his brother. When Tom discovered his fate he immediately retracted his statement and blamed his brother for the murder, the two young men now fighting each other as well as a waiting jury.

The defence team had agreed to enter a guilty plea, hoping to persuade the jury that the old man had somehow asked for the beating. It was not uncommon at that time for crimes of violence against non-prominent homosexuals to be left unreported, nor was it uncommon for an aquittal to be won purely on the grounds that the victim had made a pass at them. In essence this was the bedrock of the brothers' defence – even the lawyer representing them referred to Novarro as "an old queer". The derogatory remarks continued when the brothers' mother confirmed that Tom had written to her, claiming Novarro had tried to molest him, calling him "an old faggot".

The trial also exposed the sad existence of Paul and Tom Ferguson, both brought up in extreme poverty and forced at an early age to start menial jobs, both progressing rapidly to stealing and hustling to earn extra cash. The compassion which these descriptions might otherwise have created was lost the moment the prosecution described the barbarity of the murder, alleging the accused had tortured the old man with a prolonged beating and had then left him to choke on his own blood.

It did not take the jury long to reach their verdict: both men guilty of first-degree murder and each sentenced to life in prison. The newspapers and media reported the outcome with relish; not only had they scooped a murder story, they had uncovered a long-standing Hollywood scandal. Novarro had at least enjoyed his privacy while alive, but in death, every detail of his gay existence was scrutinized, examined and reported, overshadowing his original fame and forever changing the reason why people would remember him.

The Ferguson brothers served their sentences and were released early on the grounds of good behaviour. Tom, the younger one, disappeared, blending into American society, never to be heard of again. Paul though did not disappear – he moved to the Missouri area and enjoyed basking in his notoriety as a hardened ex-con who had survived the extremes of life in one of America's toughest jails – San Quentin. On his release Paul Ferguson made a successful attempt at getting into the construction business, making himself a lot of money on the way. In 1989, during one of his many drunken nights, he crashed his car into a ditch. Approaching a darkened house looking for help, he discovered instead a lone woman who later claimed that Ferguson had raped her. With his previous record the Judge handed down a 60-year term which on appeal was reduced to 30. Paul Ferguson is just seven years into his latest stretch.

Novarro had suffered two assaults in the end – the fatal beating meted out by the Fergusons and the attack he endured at the hands of the media, who, in one swift move, had transformed his golden movie legacy into a life of sordid gay sex with male prostitutes.

If the media exposed him for the truth about his personal life, the Hollywood movie industry remembered him for his work. They awarded him a star on the Hollywood Walk of Fame in recognition of his contribution to film, his place in the history of movie making now secured, the proof of which is etched into the pavement at 6350 Hollywood Boulevard.

The Intriguing Lucan Case

Lord Lucan

Richard John Bingham was the seventh Earl of Lucan and was born into an elite lifestyle. He had been brought up in the upper echelons of society, with all the privileges that this could offer. So why on 8 November 1974 did he vanish from the face of the earth, leaving a trail of clues linking him to the murder of his children's nanny, Sandra Rivett, and the horrific but not fatal attack on his estranged wife, Lady Veronica Lucan? To this day, some 30 years on, there has never been any contact with any of his three children, nor any firm corroborated reported sighting of him. How can a man with so much disappear, taking so little?

The alarm was raised at around quarter to ten on the night of 7 November. The local public house the Plumber's Arms, in Lower Belgrave Street (a very upmarket district of London), was lucky to be having a busy night with its usual clientele enjoying a few drinks. The atmosphere in the bar immediately changed when a lady, dressed in her nightgown, burst through the doors covered in blood. She staggered forward and shouted out, "Help me, help me, help me. I've just escaped from being murdered. He's in the house. He's murdered the nanny!" She added, "My children, my children, please help me!" She then collapsed and was comforted by the staff from behind the bar. It was obvious that she had suffered a serious assault and the police were called immediately. An ambulance was summoned for Lady Lucan and she was soon on her way to have her injuries treated at St George's Hospital at Hyde Park Corner.

Two police officers, Constable Bedick and Sergeant Baker, were at 46 Lower Belgrave Street at around 10.10 p.m. When they arrived the front door was locked. They wasted no time in battering the door down and found the house to be in complete darkness. They used their torches to illuminate the scene and it was soon apparent that a vicious attack had taken place. There were bloodstains on the walls in the hallway. The basement door was open and they used their torches to light the staircase as the light was not working. At the foot of the basement stairs they saw a large pool of blood. They rushed upstairs to the second floor, where they noticed a room with a shaft of light emanating from the gap where door meets threshold. Inside they found the three children, Lady Frances, aged ten, Lord George, aged seven, and Lady Camilla, aged four. Although they were absolutely terrified, they were physically unharmed.

Relieved at the children's safety, the policemen continued their search of the house. They went back downstairs into the breakfast room, and again found the walls splashed with blood. On the floor was another pool of blood; they were able to see footprints in it, probably those of a man, judging by their size. From the breakfast room, they moved gingerly on to the kitchen and found a large canvas sack with "US Mail" printed on the side. On closer inspection, it was obvious that blood had seeped through the thick material.

The sack was not secured tightly; the top was merely folded over. When the police officers looked inside, they found the battered body of Sandra Rivett. Initially they thought she may have been alive, as her skin was still warm, but they soon realized that she had no pulse and was already dead. She appeared to have been battered around the head with a blunt instrument. After this grim discovery, the officers resumed their search of the premises. In the hallway they came across a 9-inch length of lead pipe which had been wrapped in tape and was covered in bloodstains. It was noted that the piping was badly bent out of shape. There were obvious signs of a struggle, with several pieces of broken crockery strewn around the floor. They also came across a lightbulb on one of the basement chairs – possibly removed by the attacker, to enable them to remain unidentified, or so they might have been able to lie in wait in the darkness. The police also noted that the back door of the property was not locked.

That evening, Lord Lucan was assumed to have paid a visit to Madeleine Floorman, who lived close to the Lucans, and was considered to be a good friend. At a little after 10 p.m. she was napping in front of the television and was quickly woken when her doorbell chimed. It rang several times, and she thought it was probably a youngster playing a prank, so she chose to ignore it and dozed off again. She was awoken again by ringing. This time it was the telephone. When she answered it, she was certain that the caller was Lord Lucan, although he sounded distressed and wasn't making sense. After failing to understand his ramblings, she put down the receiver and continued with her sleep.

Lucan's mother, the Dowager Countess of Lucan, was the next person he made contact with. He called her at around 10.30 in the evening, telling her that there had been a "terrible catastrophe" at his house and that he needed her to go there and collect his children. Realizing that her son was in a frantic state, she immediately left her home in St John's Wood and went to his family home in Lower Belgrave Street to collect the children, as requested. When she arrived, she was shocked to find a full-blown police investigation taking place. She informed the officers that the couple had been living apart and that her son was living in a flat which was close by. She then collected the children, who were by this time relieved to see a friendly face, and took them back to her own house.

Lucan made a third telephone call – this time to his friend Bill Shand Kydd, who was married to Lady Lucan's sister – but he could not get any reply. He then decided to make the journey to Uckfield, Sussex to the home of his long-time friends, Ian and Susan Maxwell-Scott. That night Lucan was driving the Ford Corsair which he had borrowed from his friend Michael Stoop, as he was having trouble with the battery in his Mercedes. He arrived unannounced at around 11.30, looking rather dishevelled, which alarmed them as he was usually fastidious about his appearance. Apparently he had spilled something on his flannels; Susan recalled that he looked quite damp around his hips, as though he had tried to sponge them clean.

They invited him in and offered him a drink. While he was with them, he explained that he had had an unbelievably nightmarish experience and went on to tell them that when he was passing by his wife's home he looked in through the basement window and was horrified to see that she was being attacked by a man. He raced into the house and the surprised attacker took flight and left the property. Lucan then said that his wife became confused and blamed him for hiring somebody to attack her. When he had gone to fetch towels to dress her wounds, she too ran out of the house. Lucan said that he was worried that she would blame him and tell the police that he was the person responsible for her injuries. He then said that he wanted to lie low for a while, hoping that the police would find the real attacker. When he had regained some composure Lord Lucan again tried to telephone Bill Shand Kydd, but was still unable to get a reply. He then telephoned his mother to ask if she had managed to collect his children. She confirmed that they were with her and that they police were also there. She asked if he wished to speak with them but he said that he would contact them the following morning.

He wrote two letters, both addressed to Bill Shand Kydd at his Bayswater home. They were postmarked 8 November. His first one reads:

Dear Bill,
   The most ghastly circumstances arose tonight, which I briefly described to my mother, when I interrupted the fight at Lower Belgrave St and the man left.
   V. [Veronica, his wife] accused me of having hired him. I took her upstairs and sent Frances up to bed and tried to clean her up. She lay doggo for a bit. I went into the bathroom and left the house.
   The circumstantial evidence against me is strong in that V. will say it was all my doing and I will lie doggo for a while, but I am only concerned about the children.

If you can manage it I want them to live with you –
Coutts St Martin's Lane will handle school fees.

V. has demonstrated her hatred of me in the past and
would do anything to see me accused.

For George & Frances to go through life knowing
their father had stood in the dock for attempted murder
would be too much. When they are old enough to
understand, explain to them the dream of paranoia
and look after them.

Yours ever,
Lucky.

In the second letter, he seems to be more interested in his
financial situation. This letter reads:

There is a sale coming up at Christie's Nov 27, which
will satisfy bank overdrafts. Please agree reserves with
Tom Craig.

Proceeds to go to:

Lloyds, 6 Pall Mall

Coutts, 59 Strand

Nat West, Bloomsbury Branch who also hold an Eq.
and Law Life Policy. The other creditors can get lost
for the time being.

Lucky.

After he wrote the letters, his hosts asked him if he would like
to stay the night and get some sleep, but he refused their
hospitality and at around a quarter past one in the morning
set off, saying that he needed to "get back". He was not seen
again, and it wasn't until Sunday 10 November that the
police located the abandoned Ford Corsair. It was found
within 20 miles of his friend's home in Sussex, close to the
docks at Newhaven. On examination, the police noted that
the car was heavily bloodstained. In the boot they found a
large piece of lead pipe, similar to that found at the murder
scene. There was also a notepad, which it appeared Lucan
used to write a note to his friend Michael (from whom he had
borrowed the car). The note reads:

My dear Michael,

I have had a traumatic night of unbelievable coincidences. However I won't bore you with anything or involve you except to say that when you come across my children, which I hope you will, please tell them that you knew me and that all I cared about was them.

The fact that a crooked solicitor and a rotten psychiatrist destroyed me between them will be of no importance to the children.

I gave Bill Shand Kydd an account of what actually happened but, judging by my last effort in court, no one, let alone a 67-year-old judge, would believe – and I no longer care, except that my children should be protected.

Yours ever,
John

As there has not been any further contact with Lucan, what happened to him can only be conjecture, but if he was an innocent man, and did come across an assailant attacking his estranged wife, his actions did appear rather bizarre. He was obviously a well-known figure as he had been photographed numerous times and his face was instantly recognizable to anybody in Britain who had ever read a tabloid paper. Could it be that he considered public opinion would be set against him before he had even had a chance to have his say? He knew only too well that mud sticks and the tabloid press would be only too eager to start throwing it. In his letter to Michael, he made clear his views on the judicial system and didn't seem to have much faith in receiving a fair trial. This story would be big news and with his famous face he would not have stood a chance of going into hiding in the UK. Surely he would have considered himself to be safer in a place where he was anonymous, if such a place existed?

A few days after the attack, Lady Lucan was able to give a statement to the police in which she described, in her own words, the events of the evening of 7 November. She pointed out that Thursday was usually Sandra Rivett's night off, but the two had come to an arrangement where Sandra had taken the previous night off to go out with her boyfriend. Sandra was 29 years old, quite small, around 5 ft 2 inches (the same height as Lady Lucan) but slightly larger in build than her employer.

As usual, the two youngest children were put to bed at around 8.30 p.m. Ten minutes later, Frances went to her mother's bedroom to ask where Sandra was and her mother explained that she had gone to make her tea a little earlier than normal (usually, Lady Lucan made her own tea at around 9 p.m.). After a while, Lady Lucan started to wonder why Sandra was taking so long and decided to go and investigate. She went downstairs to the basement kitchen, but noticed that the light was not on. She called the nanny's name but didn't get a reply. She tried the light switch but it didn't work. She then walked towards the cloakroom, as she thought that she could hear noises coming from that direction.

She was suddenly aware of a heavy blow to her head and cried out in pain. She remembered a deep voice commanding her to keep quiet, while the blows to her head continued. She was struggling to escape from her attacker when a gloved hand grabbed her by the neck, trying to strangle her, and gloved fingers were forced down her throat. She also recalled that her attacker tried to gouge out her eyes. She was a small woman but was not prepared to be defeated easily, as she was well aware that she was fighting for her life. In a frantic bid to incapacitate her attacker, she grasped his testicles and squeezed them for all she was worth. This did the trick and her assailant fell to the floor.

She was sure that her attacker was her husband. She said that he had admitted killing the nanny, as he had mistaken her for Veronica. She tried to calm her husband down and talked to him, trying to gain his confidence, implying that it would be a long time before anybody missed Sandra. She said they discussed hiding the body and concocting a story that her injuries were those sustained during a failed house burglary. Lucan said that she should get some sleep and recommended that she took some sleeping tablets. Feeling that she was in no position to argue, she agreed, adding that she might be better off in her own bedroom. The two made their way upstairs. When they arrived at her bedroom, Lady Frances was still there, and she was instructed to return to her own bedroom. Lord and Lady Lucan went into the bathroom to assess her injuries and decided to use towels to act as a bandage. When Lord Lucan went off in search of more towels Lady Lucan seized her chance and raced downstairs and out of the front door to raise the alarm.

As it became apparent that Lucan had managed to amass gambling debts, it was suspected that he had planned his wife's death so that he could claim the insurance money and alleviate his money problems. He may well have mistaken Sandra Rivett for his wife, as he was unaware of the change to the usual night-time routine. If he was sitting in wait in the darkness of the basement, he would not have been expecting the nanny to be there at all that night, and could have murdered her in error. He had already been bad-mouthed in the tabloids for leaving his wife with three children, while he apparently continued to enjoy his own hobbies – notably gambling. He had been pictured in virtually every tabloid at some time or another over the last 20 years and was aware that they would not hold back in naming him as a suspect in the murder case. He would have not been able to face the humiliation of having to go to trial, accused of murder, and would not wish his family name to be dragged through the news and tabloid press, with all the shame that this would cause to his family.

Richard John Bingham had up until this point enjoyed his privileged life. He was born on 18 December 1934, to George Bingham, the Sixth Earl of Lucan, and Countess Kait Lucan. He preferred to be called John. He had two older sisters and a younger brother soon followed him. During the Second World War, John and his brother and sisters were all moved to the United States, as it was considered to be much safer for them there. They lived in New York and Florida in beautiful luxurious houses and were attended by many servants and nannies. When the war was over and England was again deemed safe, the family returned and John began his schooling in the elite public school, Eton.

In 1953 he joined the armed forces and was commissioned in the Coldstream Guards. While serving in the Army he became well known for his love of gambling and would spend much of his "R and R" in casinos; he earned himself the nickname of Lucky. His love of gambling continued and after leaving the forces he joined a merchant bank; but he found that he could make much more money as a professional gambler, so he resigned from his post.

It wasn't until he was almost 30 that he met his bride-to-be, Veronica Duncan. At a golf tournament she was introduced to him by Bill Shand Kydd, as Veronica was his wife's sister. The couple hit it off and they were soon married. Within a couple of months of their marriage John's father died, making them the new Seventh Earl and Countess of Lucan. They were by now living in Lower Belgrave Street and the couple were soon a trio as on 24 October 1964 their first child was born, Lady Frances. By September 1967 Veronica gave birth to a son, George, and in June 1970 he was followed by Camilla.

The strain of having three young children was difficult to bear and Veronica found herself suffering from post-natal depression. With the encouragement of her husband, she sought help and was prescribed drugs to help alleviate her symptoms. By the early 1970s the relationship was in trouble. John seemed obsessed with the notion that Veronica was unfit to look after the children and she was becoming increasingly concerned with the amount of money he appeared to be losing on a regular basis in the casinos.

It was decided that the couple should part and in January 1973 they separated. Veronica stayed in the family home with the children and John took a flat in Elizabeth Street in Chelsea, but by May he had hired private detectives to snatch his children from his wife. They were successful and Lucan kept the children with him until a custody hearing in June. Much of the hearing was based on Veronica's mental state, which she argued was not an issue until after giving birth to her children and was diagnosed as post-natal depression. She believed that the medication she was prescribed did not necessarily help her symptoms and at times she considered them to be inappropriate for her condition. She felt that her husband had discussed her health with the doctors and had exaggerated her mental state. The Judge found in favour of Veronica and ordered that the children be handed back to their mother. Lucan must have been incensed as a peer of the realm had rarely lost a custody battle, and it had cost him in the order of £40,000; with his already mounting gambling debts, it was money he could ill afford.

The strain of not having his children and his financial problems were weighing heavily on him. He thought that if his wife was out of the picture his life would be much happier. He could be back with his children and he would be able to sell the house, which was worth around a quarter of a million pounds. It was suspected that his mental state had declined with his financial pressures and family stress and he concocted a plan to rid himself of his wife. He thought that he could blame her sudden disappearance on her depression and could claim that she had just wandered off and may have lost her memory. He was well aware that he could easily overpower her, as he was over a foot taller than her and he had been trained in combat when he was in the Army. The plan might have been a success if he hadn't made two crucial errors. Firstly, he killed the wrong woman; and secondly, he failed to kill the right one.

In June 1975, at Westminster Coroner's Court, an inquest was opened into the death of Sandra Rivett. Coroner Dr Gavin Thurston and the coroner's jury listened to testimonies and the evidence relating to the nanny's death and the attack on Lady Lucan. At this time English law was very restrictive over a wife giving evidence against her husband, unless he is charged with an assault against his wife. After much debating, it was agreed that Lady Lucan should give the jury her account of what had happened, as this was an inquest and not a trial.

Lady Lucan's evidence was only to give an account of the attack on herself. She described how on the evening in question she was waiting for the nanny to return upstairs, as she had been longer than usual. Her curiosity got the better of her and at a little after 9 p.m. she went downstairs to the ground floor and stood at the top of the basement stairs. Realizing the light would not work, she simply called out to Sandra, but got no reply. She thought that she heard noises coming from the cloakroom so she turned to go and find out what was causing them. As she did so, somebody rushed out of the room and started attacking her, hitting her on the front of the head, very hard, many times. She recalled being told to shut up and recognized the voice to be that of her estranged husband, Lord Lucan.

She described a struggle, with her attacker forcing three fingers from his gloved hand down her throat, also the attempt to strangle her and gouge her eyes out. Finally she recounted her attempt to free herself from her attacker when she grabbed him by the testicles very hard, he soon gave in and lay on the floor exhausted. Then she persuaded her husband to assist her and he took her upstairs to tend to her wounds. She said that her daughter saw them and that she asked Frances to return to her own bed. While her husband was getting towels, she managed to summon her strength to get out of the room and then out of the house to raise the alarm. She also confirmed that she hadn't seen any strangers in the house and that she had never seen the sack which Sandra Rivett's body was found in.

A casualty officer testified to Lady Lucan's injuries, confirming that on his examination of her he found her injuries to be consistent with those sustained in the described attack. Namely, he noted seven lacerations on her scalp, injuries to the palate and on the back of her throat and bruising to her eye.

Frances Bingham, the Lucans' 10-year-old daughter, had given a statement to the police and this was read out in court. It described that she was in her mother's bedroom with her mother and that they were waiting for the nanny to return upstairs with tea. She described how, after waiting for a little while, her mother went downstairs to see why Sandra was taking so long. Frances said that she heard her mother scream, but was unconcerned as she assumed that she had been scratched by the family cat. She says that the next time she saw her mother was when Veronica entered the room with Lord Lucan. Frances noted that her mother had blood on her face and that her father was wearing an overcoat. She was then sent to her own room to go to bed. After a time she heard her father calling for her mother and then she heard what she assumed was her father leaving.

Pathologist Dr Keith Simpson performed the post-mortem on Sandra Rivett and confirmed that she died as a result of choking on her own blood, and said that with her wounds she probably died a few minutes after being attacked. He also testified that the injuries to the two women were similar in nature, and would probably have been inflicted by the same instrument, by the same attacker.

Also called to give evidence were friends of Lord Lucan. These included Bill Shand Kydd, who described his friendship with Lucan and discussed the letters he received from him shortly after the 7th; Michael Stoop, who was questioned in detail about the car which he loaned to Lucan and the subsequent letter he received from him; and Susan Maxwell-Scott, who described the visit that Lord Lucan had paid to her on the evening of Sandra Rivett's death. Dowager Countess Lucan testified that she received two telephone calls from her son that evening; the first time she was asked to collect his children from their home, and the second time to check that the children were alright and to ask that she did not speak to the police.

Over 30 witnesses gave testimonies at the inquest, including those from police officers who gave detailed forensic reports based on information gathered at the murder scene. It was noted that there was a large amount of blood in various areas in the house, and it was pointed out that Sandra Rivett was blood type B and that Lady Lucan was blood type A. In the basement was the most concentrated source of the blood type B, which was where the body of Sandra Rivett was discovered in the mail sack in the breakfast room. There were numerous blood splashes with a large area of blood-staining near the piano. The blood type A was more prevalent in the hallway at the top of the basement staircase, which was on the ground floor; also in this area there were many hairs matching Lady Lucan's. The hallway was considered an obvious site of attack, with a pattern of radiating blood splashes showing that a victim had been battered.

The lead pipe had a mixture of both blood types on it; so did the blood samples found in the Ford Corsair. The letters which Lucan had sent to Bill Shand Kydd were examined and the envelopes were found to have type AB bloodstains on them. Forensic experts confirmed that type AB blood can be a result of mixing together quantities of type B and type A.

A man's bloody shoeprint was discovered in the basement of the house. The police were unable to identify who had left the print, but they were able to confirm that the blood was that of the murder victim.

A trail of matching fibres were found throughout the murder scene. These were of grey-blue woollen material and they were present in the basement, in Lady Lucan's bathroom in the sink, on her towel, on the lead pipe which was used in the attack and in the Ford Corsair. This provided critical evidence that linked the murder scene with the car and the attacker.

Lucan's explanation to the Maxwell-Scotts of seeing a man attacking his wife in the basement was found to be very flimsy. There was no blood found in the basement which matched his wife's; plus, the view into the basement was very limited from outside, showing mainly the bottom few steps. Also, as the light bulb had been removed on the evening of the murder, the view into the basement would be practically nil.

After four days of statements and evidence, the jury was sent to come to a verdict. After little over half an hour they returned to the room with their verdict. Their verdict was that Sandra Rivett's cause of death was murder by Lord Lucan. As this was a coroner's court, the verdict was to determine the cause of death, unlike that in a criminal court which would be to prove innocence or guilt. This was the last time that such a verdict could be made by a coroner's court; the following month, as a direct result of this hearing, the Criminal Law Act of 1977 abolished the coroner's court's ability to name the suspected murderer.

The theories on this case can be debated for ever.

Some Lucan sympathists believe he did see his wife being attacked and rushed to her aid, promoting him as a hero figure turned fugitive, as he feared that he would not be believed. After all, he was very wary of the press and was aware that they were extremely powerful and had a massive audience at their disposal, keen to read what they reported as the truth. Also, Lucan had been to court earlier, fully expecting that he would gain custody of his children, only to be refused. He had lost all hope of having an impartial judge to hear his version of the events regarding the death of his children's nanny and the beating of his wife. He also felt that his wife would do her best to keep him from taking the children from her and did not expect her to assist at his trial. His best defence would have come from his many friends, who simply could not believe that Lucan would do such a thing. Especially out of character was the way in which the murder and attack took place. They would never imagine that he could use such a crude weapon; it was simply not the John that they knew and loved.

Another theory was that Lucan was the killer, as the coroner's inquest had concluded. The facts regarding hard evidence are too strong, especially as Lucan claimed that he saw his wife being attacked in the basement, when there was no trace of her blood found there, and her attack took place on the ground floor. Also the blood found in the car, and on the envelopes for the letters he had sent to Bill Shand Kydd, all point to Lucan. Add to that his recent unhappy court case, and his debts: he had become a desperate man, and desperate men take some pretty unexpected, drastic actions.

Could Lord Lucan have hired a killer? He might well have wanted his estranged wife to disappear and in his letter to Bill Shand Kydd he mentioned that his wife had accused him of hiring a third party to take her life. Also in the letter he referred to his children and says that he would not want them to see him in court accused with attempted murder. This points to the fact that he felt that he would have been blamed for the act, and as previously mentioned he didn't hold out much hope of receiving a fair trial, due to his public persona. If he had hired somebody to do his dirty work, then surely a hired hit-man would use a better weapon than a piece of lead piping? This is one of the messiest and ineffective ways to extinguish a life; the death would not be instantaneous and would probably take several minutes at best, and the victim might well have time to call for help and raise the alarm. This form of execution would no doubt bring attention to the murderer when leaving the murder scene, as it is virtually impossible to beat somebody to death around the head without transferring some blood to the murderer's clothing.

The final question remains: what happened to Lord Lucan? Many believed that, after abandoning the Ford Corsair, he took a speedboat (some suggested that he may have already left one docked there, ready to dispose of his wife's body, if his original plan had been a success), or bought a ticket on a ferry to cross the Channel from Newhaven. He could well have decided to end his shame and his life and jumped overboard into the cold waters.

Considering that Lucan's passion was for gambling, I find it hard that he would take his own life. I would more easily believe that he managed to get to mainland Europe and has lived an anonymous life. I am sure that the doting father would have followed the lives of his children with great interest, and that he would have been fascinated to learn that on 11 December 1992 he was officially presumed dead, and that the title of the Eighth Earl of Lucan was passed to his only son George, although George prefers not to use the title.

Since his disappearance there have been countless "sightings" of Lord Lucan, literally spanning the world: to name but a few, France, Ireland, Sicily, the Netherlands, Australia and most frequently Africa. The police have received so many Lucan sightings in South Africa that they started to keep a close eye on the frequency of Lucan's children's visits to this area, but after all this time there is still no hard and fast proof as to whether he is alive or dead.

Mark David Chapman

The Murder of John Lennon

Monday, 8 December 1980 was a typical winter's day in New York, crisp and cold, with blue skies and a strong hint of Christmas. If any day was typical for John Lennon then this was one of them. He and Yoko Ono had enjoyed a late morning and had then set off for the recording studio by early afternoon, acknowledging the usual crowd of fans who gathered on the sidewalk outside of the Dakota Building, even signing a copy of John's latest album, *Double Fantasy*, for one eager, if a little intense, young fan. The pair spent the rest of the afternoon and the early evening preparing new material for a follow-up album to *Double Fantasy*, before deciding to return home. John collected his tape recorder and a few tapes and joined Yoko in the back of their white limousine, ready for the journey back across New York City. They chatted as the limo took its usual stops and turns, weaving its way in and out of the famously busy New York traffic, pulling up outside the Dakota Building at 22.48 p.m. Yoko could see a number of people loitering as Jose Perdomo, the Dakota's doorman, walked across to open the door for them. She climbed out of the car, quickly followed by John, who was still carrying the tape recorder. Yoko maintained her lead, saying "Hello" to a man who was standing slightly away from the building, as she reached the front door, while John followed on, noticing the young man who he remembered from earlier in the day. He stared at the man intently as he walked by, but then prepared to enter the building, before hearing a voice behind him say, "Mr Lennon". As John turned to see who had called him, he caught sight of the familiar-looking young man crouched down, one knee on the ground, and pointing a snub-nosed .38 calibre revolver directly at him, with outstretched arms, one hand supporting the other hand's wrist. Recognizing immediately his dilemma John whirled to make his escape, but was caught with two shots, the force of which spun his body round. With blood already spurting from the entry holes, the would-be assassin calmly took aim again and fired three more shots, two of which slammed into John's shoulder blades, exiting his body and smashing into the glass frontage of the Dakota Building; the third missed him completely and ricocheted off the wall. Amazingly he was not yet dead and managed to stagger into the foyer, passing Jay Hastings, the Dakota's security guard, who had pressed the security alarm button to summon the police. "I'm shot, I'm shot," John managed to say as he collapsed onto the floor, blood oozing out of his shattered body. Jay Hastings could hear the sirens wailing in the distance and willed them to get there faster, as Yoko stood looking down at John, screaming, "He's been shot." Hastings knew John was bleeding to death and wanted to apply a tourniquet, but did not know where best to apply it. Removing his jacket he placed it over John in a bid to keep him warm, but could see that the blood loss was substantial and his efforts were of little consequence. Outside, Perdomo had knocked the gun out of the man's hand and kicked it away shouting, "Do you know what you have done?" but the young man wasn't listening. Calmly the killer removed his hat and coat and threw them away from himself onto the sidewalk; he knew the police were very close and did not want to risk being shot, the likely outcome if he were still considered armed. Nobody seemed a bit concerned that he had not tried to escape – he could have made a dash for the subway on the Central Park side of the street, but instead paced up and down the pavement reading from a book he had brought with him, J.D. Salinger's *The Catcher in the Rye*. As the first police car arrived on the scene, the officers quickly ran towards the Dakota Building, still not aware that someone had been shot. When the two officers entered the small foyer they could see that a white male had been shot a number of times and a small lady was standing over the man, terrified; they immediately put out a distress call, "Alert . . . shots fired . . . 1 West 72nd Street", which summoned further police assistance. The police could see that the man was losing his battle and decided to take decisive action. Turning him over, they grabbed his arms and legs with the intention of speeding him to Roosevelt Hospital, on 58th Street. As they lifted him his bones cracked sickeningly and more blood oozed from his lips, his eyes were open but now unable to focus as his life drained out of him. Back outside another police car had arrived and Perdomo pointed out the young man reading the book indicating that he was the shooter. As the policeman made his approach the young man put his hands in the air and declared, "Don't hurt me, I'm unarmed," and as the policeman spread-eagled him against the wall, "I acted alone." The man was handcuffed and put in the back of the police car where he then apologized, "I'm sorry I gave you guys all this trouble."

In the police car carrying John Lennon, the driver looked into the back seat at the bloodied mess that had, just minutes earlier, been the healthy other half of the 1960s song-writing genius of Lennon & McCartney, of Beatles fame. "Do you know who you are?" the driver shouted. Lennon's throat was thick with blood and he was unable to respond, but managed to nod his head. With still a chance of saving Lennon the police car raced with its sirens blazing, jumping red lights and weaving past traffic, eventually pulling into the hospital's emergency entrance. The trauma team were waiting and immediately transferred Lennon to a mobile stretcher, racing him through to the emergency room. Once in there it was established that he had virtually no pulse; a team of seven medical staff, using everything at their disposal worked hard to stem the loss of life, but with such significant blood loss the battle was futile. After much effort the medical staff had to accept that they now had on the table in front of them the lifeless body of John Lennon, one of the greatest writers of modern music the twentieth century had produced. The official cause of death was shock, caused by severe blood loss – he had lost nearly 80 per cent. Dead at just forty years of age, he left his wife Yoko Ono, their son Sean, Julian, John's son from a previous marriage and of course millions of adoring fans from around the world.

The man the police had in custody called himself Mark David Chapman and was in no way trying to distance himself from the crime. Indeed he was happy to point out that he had stayed at the scene with the intention of being caught. He was apologetic at having caused the police such a problem that evening and appeared quite calm, if not a little detached. He had been brought in clutching his copy of *The Catcher in the Rye*, in the belief that he was one part Holden Caulfied, the book's main character, and one part the devil. He was booked and held in custody ready for questioning and the ensuing investigation. Chapman had been surprised at Lennon being able to climb the stairs after he had been shot but never enquired as to the health of his victim once he had been apprehended.

It did not take the press long to get hold of the story and most papers were able to make it their front-page headline the following day. In an age of high-speed telecommunications the word of Lennon's death spread around the world, and as the sun rose in each country in turn, people heard the terrible news. Tributes poured in from fans and well-wishers; other musicians, including the Beatles members Paul McCartney, George Harrison and Ringo Starr, all praised Lennon's life and works. As the emphasis on Lennon's life and times passed, the world now wanted to know who had prematurely taken away the life of this peace-loving super songwriter.

Mark David Chapman was born on 10 May 1955, near Fort Worth, Texas, the first child of David and Diane Chapman. It was not a happy home life; his father and mother argued frequently and often came to blows. This aside, as Chapman grew into a small boy neighbours reported what a friendly character he was and quite clever too; at high school he was later assessed as having an IQ of 121, higher than average for his age group. Unfortunately his intellect did not stand him in good stead in the relationship stakes, his peer group disliked him and he became the target of bullies. His father, who had been a staff sergeant in the Air Force at the time of Chapman's birth, was discharged and won a place at Purdue University, using the GI Bill to get a degree in engineering. With things looking up, the Chapman family moved to a quiet Atlanta suburb, where Mr Chapman took a job in the credit department of the American Oil Company. Things continued to look up when shortly afterwards the Chapmans' second child was born, a little girl, whom they named Susan. As Chapman continued to suffer at the hands of his fellow pupils he gradually withdrew into a world of make-believe, creating an imaginary world in his head. In this world, where he was the only big person, he was surrounded by "little people", who lived in the walls of his house. He was their king, and in his mind they worshipped him; he would be on the front page of their imaginary newspapers and all over their little television sets. He was god in this world and could do no wrong. He entertained the "little people" when he was in a good mood, by playing them music, often the Beatles, one of his favourite groups. He wasn't always in a good mood though and would press an imaginary button on the sofa which would, in his mind's eye, blow up many of the "little people", but he was always forgiven and things would just go back to normal afterwards.

Chapman continued through this period to suppress his anger towards his father, who would have his mother screaming with his bursts of violence. She would be yelling "Mark!" and he would go running in to halt the attack, often pushing his father away. It is no surprise that Chapman came to hate his father, and would, much later, admit to prison psychiatrists that he often dreamed of shooting his father dead. He was quoted later as saying his father never gave him the love or emotional support he needed. "I don't think I ever hugged my father. He never told me he loved me."

His lack of prowess on the sports field contributed to his fellow pupils' disdain for him, calling him "Pussy", but his school work was of a good level, and like other children of that time he maintained normal interests for boys of his age: rockets, UFOs and modern music, which he played pretty much non-stop, especially the Beatles. He was also hooked on the film *The Wizard of Oz*, and looked forward to its showing every Christmas season.

Chapman's life took a turn for the worse when he reached the age of 14. As a freshman at Columbia High his entire persona altered when he started using drugs, initially marijuana, but ultimately heroin. He skipped school, grew his hair long and defied his parents, stopping out late and hanging around the streets with his new-found druggy friends. It was at this point that Chapman first had a brush with the law, being picked up by an Atlanta police patrol while high on LSD. When his mother found out she locked the doped-up Chapman in his bedroom, but he just took the door off its hinges and fled to a friend's house, staying there for the next week. After this he disappeared again, this time running off to Miami where he lived on the streets for a while, before he was given shelter by a man who subsequently bought him a one-way bus ticket back to Atlanta.

And then the "bad" Mark Chapman disappeared as fast as he had arrived. Now aged 16 he went to see a visiting California-based evangelist and claimed to have enjoyed a moving religious experience. It was out with the old and in with the new; gone was the long hair, the Army jackets and the drug-laden bad attitude. Chapman now spoke softly and was calm; he also sported a large wooden cross around his neck. With his new character Chapman found his first girlfriend, Jessica Blankenship, with whom he handed out religious leaflets, his school work improved and he now joined the YMCA, becoming a counsellor at that year's summer camp.

Tony Adams, a senior member of the YMCA on the summer camp, watched Chapman enjoying the company of the younger ones. "They really liked him, he was a real Pied Piper, always had a bunch of kids hanging round his neck." Chapman did indeed have a lot of time for the kids; he enjoyed their love and attention and repaid it with his time and care. The kids called him "Nemo" after the Jules Verne character and chanted his nickname after he won the award for outstanding counsellor, shouting, "Nee-mo, Nee-mo".

Chapman had found a group of people with whom he felt right at home, but as his recent history had shown, he was a man drawn to extremes. His first negative thought in respect of John Lennon came about when the Beatles front man proclaimed, "We're more popular than Jesus Christ now," a comment which infuriated the one-time Beatles fan and turned him against his hero. Chapman and his friends now sang Lennon's "Imagine" to different lyrics, ones in which John Lennon was dead and Chapman replaced Lennon with Todd Rundgren as his favourite musician.

It was around this time that Chapman's friend Michael McFarland gave him the book *The Catcher in the Rye*, the story of a mixed-up teenager who comes to the conclusion that everyone is a phoney and runs away to New York. The book became a massive hit with Chapman, who found a new soul-mate in the book's main character, Holden Caulfield, and dreamed of a new world in which he would fit in.

After graduating from Columbia High, Chapman and McFarland spent a brief period in Chicago where they entertained the congregations in churches and Christian meetings with their new comedy act. Chapman played the guitar and McFarland did impersonations, much to the joy of their audience, but the act was not to be, they couldn't earn enough money and the two soon abandoned their show business careers.

The two returned to Atlanta, Chapman initially doing odd jobs down at the YMCA before deciding to return to college, enrolling at South De Kalb Community College, hoping to get a degree that would qualify him for a career with the YMCA full time. Life really began to look up again for him when he was selected for a place on the YMCA's international programme, working in the Lebanon. Unfortunately the disruption caused by the war there soon had the disgruntled Chapman shipped back to the US along with all of the other YMCA staff. On return he managed to get a placement looking after Vietnamese refugees at a resettlement camp at Fort Chafee, Arkansas. Again Chapman excelled at his work, becoming another big hit with the Vietnamese children and winning further acclaim by becoming an area co-ordinator and key helper to David Moore, the programme director.

The resettlement programme was short lived but before Chapman departed he left an indelible message on the minds of those who were there: "We're all going to get together again one day and one of us is going to be somebody. About five years from now, one of us will do something famous and it will bring us all together." That was December 1975, exactly five years prior to Chapman's murder of Lennon, just one of a number of strange coincidences which the media have used to create further mystery and intrigue.

For now though Chapman was on the top of his game, he enjoyed being with the kids and was generally getting along fine. His girlfriend, Jessica Blankenship, had been out to see him at Fort Chafee and the two were sufficiently positive to discuss the possibility of marriage. He rejoined her in the spring to study religion, at a strict Presbyterian college in Lookout Mountain. Although they both studied together most nights, Chapman found that he was unable to keep up with the demanding workload and was slipping behind in his studies. He had also become depressed over a liaison he had allowed himself to indulge in while he was stationed at Fort Chafee, although he was not about to admit his guilt to Jessica. The guilt did however hang over him like an axe, causing him to slip further into black moods, a state of mind that would ultimately have him teetering on the brink of suicide.

Life was once again changing for Chapman – after his success at the YMCA summer camps, he was now failing at his religious studies, causing him to drop out of college at the end of the first semester; Jessica decided to break off their engagement. In a bid to regain some of the life he had once enjoyed he rejoined the YMCA as assistant director of the summer camp but quit after an argument with one of the swimming instructors. With his life spiralling down once more he managed, with the help of a friend, to find a job as a security guard; he was even offered promotion but turned it down, afraid of the responsibility. He now had the chance to pick up a firearm for the first time. Initially he had joined as an unarmed security guard, but now enrolled on a week-long course that would qualify him as an armed guard, scoring 80 points on the pistol range, well above the 60 required for a pass.

Yet Chapman was now floundering in black despair, unable to shake the thoughts of suicide that plagued him. He dreamed of another life, one in which he would be "a man to be reckoned with", somebody who others would admire. It was while sat in his local library that he came across a map of Hawaii, which he pored over until he could almost see each street in his mind, conjuring up a new life for himself.

And so Chapman finally concluded what he must do. He bought a one-way ticket to Honolulu with what was left of his savings, some $1,200, and booked himself into the Moana Hotel, planning to have one last bash at the high life before killing himself. On arrival he spent the next five days enjoying himself, drinking and eating the best foods, cruising the islands and lying around on the sandy beaches. Life was so good in fact that he thought it a shame to end it prematurely; instead, he checked out of the hotel and booked into a YMCA room to make the most of his money. With life now providing some enjoyment he decided to phone Jessica and tell her of his intentions to kill himself, suggesting that if she would say she still loved him and that she wanted him home, he would call off the suicide and return forthwith. Fearful that she would have his death on her hands if she didn't, she asked him to return. Now reprieved, he bought another one-way ticket back to Atlanta, looking forward to a tender reunion.

Sadly, on his return he quickly established that Jessica had acted solely out of pity for him, she did not want him back and there was to be no romantic reunion. Annoyed and depressed he once again found himself headed back to Hawaii, on yet another one-way ticket. It was May 1977 and with little money, he checked himself back into a room at the YMCA; he felt nothing but empty despair and once again his thoughts turned to suicide. Over the days that followed he spent hour after hour on the phone to suicide help lines, before he could not stand the thought of life any more. He bought a vacuum cleaner hose and drove a rental car out to one of the secluded beaches. Pushing the hose into the car's exhaust pipe, he climbed into the driver's seat and promptly fell asleep. His life was once again spared, this time due to poor planning on his part – the plastic vacuum cleaner pipe had melted in the exhaust and had all but closed up, so that the noxious fumes did not get into the car. When he awoke to a man tapping on his window, he was amazed to be still alive and took this as a sign from God that it was not his time to go yet. He therefore pledged to God that he would try and make better use of the chance that he had been given, checking himself into a mental health clinic the very next day, where the resident psychiatrist put him on an immediate suicide watch.

After only a week Chapman was feeling much better again, his depression had lifted and he was soon discharged from the hospital. Taking a job at a nearby petrol station, Chapman filled his spare time by visiting the staff and patients at the hospital where he impressed the staff so much that they offered him a maintenance job. He fitted in well, delighted his bosses and was a hit with the patients, some of whom hadn't had a conversation in years. He took time to sit and indulge the older ones in lengthy chats, listening to their stories and never once looking disinterested. The doctors and nurses who he worked with looked upon him as a colleague, and were pleased to socialize with him. He had now found a new place to live and was once again looking at himself as a success; with this his mind he dreamed up new and more exciting things to do.

Just as he had once dreamed of coming to Hawaii, he now dreamed of travelling to the Far East and thought he might be able to arrange this through his job. The hospital ran a credit union for staff and he would be able to take up to six weeks extended leave with the approval of his manager, which he was sure to get. With the plan firmly fixed in his mind he began checking out the travel arrangements with a young Japanese-American woman named Gloria Abe, who worked for one of the local travel agents. With his renewed vigour for life, Chapman showed an interest in Gloria, who was keen to reciprocate his affection. But for now Chapman would see some of the world, visiting Japan, Korea, China, Thailand, India, Iran, Israel and then through Europe to Geneva, his final destination Atlanta, where he called in to see his family and friends before heading once more back to Hawaii to meet up with Gloria.

Gloria, who was a practising Buddhist when they met, now ditched her own religion in favour of Christianity, they spent all of their free time together and for a long while the black thoughts that had plagued Chapman faded as he enjoyed his new-found relationship. In January 1979, in a rare romantic gesture, Chapman wrote the words "Will you marry me?" in the sand, to which Gloria wrote "Yes". They were both deliriously happy and planned the wedding for June of the same year, Chapman changing jobs at the hospital to the printing department in order to set aside more money. But again the change proved hurtful to his tender mind. Now working alone and without the happy chatter of the patients to keep him company, his mind soon drifted back to the dark days and his temper re-emerged. Over a brief period he was fired from his hospital job, then got rehired, but walked out after an argument with one of the nurses. He managed to get himself in yet another shouting match, this time with Gloria's boss at the travel agents, and insisted that she quit the company.

With life once more changing for Chapman he took a low-paid job as a security guard at a luxury apartment block, but began secretly drinking. Always one to jump on a band-wagon, he could develop a full-blown obsession in a short space of time, and indeed did do during this short period. His first obsession was for works of art, buying a Salvador Dali for $2,500 and then changing it for a Norman Rockwell painting which cost him $7,500, money he borrowed from his mother. As this phase concluded Chapman marked the date, 13 March 1980; in his diary, as the day he decided that he must completely clear all of his debts – his next compulsion – making sure that every penny he and Gloria earned were saved. He spent hours and hours going over the plans with his advisors and by August 1980 they had reached his goal. Now free of debt, Mark was still unable to relax and felt under constant pressure; and there was now another development – the little people were back, and he was talking to them again.

Life became unbearable for Gloria; her only escape was to lock herself in the bathroom, where she would cry uncontrollably. Chapman's behaviour was more erratic than ever – he would have a sudden compulsion to sell all of his records, and then would go out and buy them all over again. After watching the movie *Network*, he sold his TV, like the character in the film. He then bought new speakers for his stereo but smashed up the turntable in a fit of anger, watched by a terrified Gloria, who now believed Chapman was off the rails.

His interest in Holden Caulfield soon resurfaced when he bought two more copies of *The Catcher in the Rye*, one for himself and one for Gloria, which he insisted she read. He even talked of changing his name to Holden Caulfield, at one point writing to the Attorney General to ask about the procedure. During this period he wrote to a friend proclaiming, "I'm going nuts", and signed the letter "The Catcher In The Rye".

Chapman was sinking faster than ever into a deep depression, his mind was certainly stressed, his grip on reality was lost and he had withdrawn further into the world of the "little people", venting his anger on them and sparing them when he felt happier, a state of mind he was achieving less frequently than ever. He was also visiting the library where, scouring the book shelves for meaningful books, he found Anthony Fawcett's *John Lennon: One Day at a Time*, an account of Lennon's life. Chapman read the book from cover to cover and developed a loathing of what he saw as Lennon's double standards, preaching love and peace yet rich beyond comprehension. As negative thoughts became set in Chapman's mind he spiralled further still. Now praying to Satan, he would sit rocking back and forth, naked, in the dark, just him and his tape recorder, putting the logic of his need to kill Lennon on tape, with a jumble of Beatles lyrics and words from *The Wizard of Oz* and quotations from *The Catcher in the Rye*. When Chapman announced to the "little people" his plan to visit New York, to kill Lennon, they apparently remonstrated with him, begging him not to go through with it, but he, the President, had made an executive decision.

In October 1980 Chapman read an article about the release of Lennon's album called *Double Fantasy*, on which he and Yoko Ono shared vocals. It was yet another sign of what he must do, so, quitting his job, he signed out for the last time under the name John Lennon, which he then crossed out. On 27 October Chapman entered a Honolulu gun store and bought a .38 Charter Arms Special, five-shot, short-barrel gun, for $169; ironically the salesman was named Ono.

A day later he boarded a plane for New York with the gun wrapped in clothing safely inside his suitcase. He had bought a new suit and overcoat for the trip and looked every inch a travelling businessman. He had on him the balance of a $5,000 loan from his father-in-law, having decided once more that he would live the high life before concluding his own life and that of John Lennon. With the end in sight, he booked a room at the Waldorf and enjoyed a meal in their restaurant.

In the days that followed Chapman spent much of his time walking around the perimeter of the Dakota Building, trying to locate the sixth-floor window where he hoped to see Lennon. He masqueraded as a fan, chatting to the Dakota's security staff and trying to get some information on Lennon's movements, information they knew better than to give out, the standard response being, "I'm not sure if Mr Lennon is in town at the moment." His plans hit a snag when, having forgotten to buy the bullets for his gun in Honolulu, he now discovered that New York's Sullivan Laws prevented him from acquiring them at all in that state. His plans now on hold, he called his friend Dana Reeves, a deputy sheriff in Georgia, saying he would be passing through and that he was hoping to have a get-together with his old friends. Reeves invited him to stop at her apartment in Atlanta and he promptly arrived a day later. During one of their conversations Chapman explained he had bought a gun for his own personal protection while he was in New York, but that he couldn't get the bullets for it. Reeves accepted the story and delivered to him five hollow-point cartridges, the type which expand as they pass through their target, delivering maximum damage and stopping power.

On 10 November Chapman was again back in New York, his intention murder, when his life intervened to change his plans once more. On his first night back in the city he had decided to take in a movie, *Ordinary People*, starring Timothy Hutton as a suicidal youth trying to come to terms with his dysfunctional family. The film seemed to strike a chord with Chapman, who, emotional and confused, left the cinema and phoned his wife Gloria. He calmly explained his purpose in New York – to kill John Lennon – but that her love had saved him; he was coming home.

His grip on reality slipped almost the minute he arrived back in Hawaii, the "little people" were talking to him again and the pressure he had felt before he had visited New York was back on him. He started making random harassing calls and bomb threats; he was angry and explained to Gloria that he needed to establish a new career, something to work at, and to this end he was going back to New York to try and do just that. Living with Chapman was a massive stress for Gloria and his return to New York would relieve the pressure, although this time the results would send shock waves around the world.

Chapman returned to New York on 6 December 1980. In the taxi bringing him from the airport he told the driver he was a sound engineer, visiting to assist Lennon with his latest album. Once in the city he checked himself in to a cheap room at the YMCA, before walking the nine blocks to the Dakota Building, where he intended to check out the site and get a feel for his quarry's movements. On the way there he bumped into a couple of girls with whom he struck up a conversation. Jude Stein and Jerry Moll said that Lennon knew them by sight and that he would often stop and talk to them outside the Dakota Building. Chapman, once again taking this chance encounter as a sign, hoped that he could benefit from their relationship with Lennon and invited them to have lunch with him – his treat – if they came back later. Meanwhile Chapman bought a copy of *Double Fantasy*,

Lennon's album, and headed off to the Dakota Building, the revolver tucked inside his coat.

Chapman spent the next three hours pacing up and down outside the Dakota Building but to no avail, Lennon was nowhere to be seen. Now hungry and feeling the chill of the winter day, he set off back towards his hotel, stopping at a book store on the way to buy a copy of *The Catcher in the Rye*, having strangely forgotten to bring a copy with him to New York. While he was collecting the book he noticed Lennon's face on the front cover of the December copy of *Playboy* magazine; it was his first interview in five years. Chapman bought the magazine and read the interview in detail while he had his meal. The magazine reminded him of something that Holden Caulfield had done while he was in New York – when he returned to his room he telephoned for the services of a call girl, choosing only to talk; she left at 3 a.m. $190 better off.

Chapman had by this stage removed himself from the YMCA and had checked in to the Sheraton; it was 8 December and something told him that this was to be the day. Dressing himself smartly and setting aside the gun, his treasured book and Lennon's album he then turned his attention to preparing his hotel room. Taking out the bible he opened it at the start of "St John's Gospel" and wrote the word "Lennon" after "John", before spreading an array of photographs and letters he had received along the bedroom dresser.

With the hotel room laid out as a makeshift shrine, Chapman concealed the gun in his coat pocket, grabbed the *Double Fantasy* album, the book and headed out of the hotel, sure that this time he would see the task through. He arrived at the Dakota Building and once more engaged the doorman in polite conversation for a while, before taking up a position a little further down from the main door, where he settled down to read a few pages of *The Catcher in the Rye*. By concentrating on the book he missed his first opportunity of catching Lennon when he noticed him gliding through the main door.

Continuing his "stake-out", Chapman was soon joined by

the photographer, Paul Goresh, who frequently took photographs of Lennon and Oko, and then by Jude Stein. After a while they noticed five-year-old Sean Lennon leaving with his nanny and Jude was able to introduce Chapman, who later commented, "He was the cutest little boy I ever saw. It didn't enter my mind that I was going to kill this poor young boy's father and he won't have a father for the rest of his life. I mean, I love children. I'm the Catcher in the Rye."

Over the course of the next few hours Chapman would recall that he saw many famous people entering or leaving the Dakota Building, including Paul Simon, Mia Farrow and Lauren Bacall, but not John Lennon. And then out of the blue Chapman heard a familiar voice, he turned and saw John and Yoko amid a small entourage exiting the building. The photographer, Paul Goresh, had to push Chapman into action, whereupon he mutely thrust out his album for Lennon to sign, passing him the pen in the process. Lennon looked at Chapman and replied, "Sure", signing and dating the album before passing it back to him.

Chapman was still in shock when Lennon asked, "Is that all you want?" Still in awe Chapman nodded and thanked him, but for some reason Lennon asked him again, "Is that all you want?" Chapman simply smiled and replied, "Yeah, thanks, that's all." And with that they climbed in the car and were whisked away. When asked later why he hadn't taken the first opportunity to kill Lennon, Chapman explained that he couldn't just shoot him, not when he had signed his album. Expecting Lennon to just brush past him and away, he was taken aback by his sincerity – but not enough to call off the plan. As he stood there in the chilly air, Chapman was enthralled and offered Goresh $50 if he would give him the picture he had taken of them both.

Fighting his inner demons, Chapman nearly left the Dakota to head back to his hotel but he lost the fight, deciding to stay and wait for Lennon's return.

After what had been just another day at the recording studios, John Lennon's white limousine pulled up outside of the Dakota Building. As he walked towards the front door he stared intently at a familiar-looking young man who was standing to one side. As he was about to enter the building a voice behind him called his name; he turned to see the young man knelt on one knee, his outstretched arms aiming a short-barrelled gun directly at him. Turning to run he heard the loud bang of the first shot and felt the searing pain of the bullet's entry. After four more bullets had been fired the deed was done.

Outside on the sidewalk Mark David Chapman opened his book and began to read – the police would come and arrest him and soon he would, for a short time at least, be as famous as his fallen idol.

In the days that followed, the sidewalk at the front of the Dakota became a Mecca for fans looking to pay homage to the lost Beatle. At one point, Central Park housed 50–100,000 mourners who had travelled from all over the US. Not since the murder of President Kennedy had the world been so shocked; people would later define Lennon's murder in terms of where they were or what they were doing at the time of his death, just as they had done over the President's killing 18 years previously.

The world media engine pumped out a perpetual diatribe of Lennon stories before eventually settling on the murderer. Who was he? Why had he done it? And of course the conspiracy theorists moved in – Lennon had been unpopular with the government; they had tried to have him removed from the US; maybe it had been the work of the secret service.

In reality it was just a deranged quasi-fan, Mark Chapman, a man under pressure, a man who spoke to the "little people". It was a senseless death, carried out by a man who claimed he just wanted to be an "average Joe", but who was now despised by all those people who had adored John Lennon. Chapman was charged with second-degree murder, the most serious charge that can be brought beyond the killing of a police officer. Herbert Adlerberg was appointed to Chapman's defence team but soon resigned the post when he realized the difficulty of the job. Alderberg had a strong reputation for taking on impossible odds, but with this case he could endanger himself just by association, such was the strength of public opinion. The police took the risk of a public lynching so seriously that a round-the-clock guard was posted outside the hospital room where Chapman had been taken for psychiatric evaluation. His windows were blacked out in case of a sniper attack. During his court appearances, Chapman would be dressed in two bulletproof vests, bundled into the back of a bulletproof van and driven to the courthouse, flanked on all sides by an armed motorcade.

During his evaluation Chapman told the doctors everything, about the "little people", his suicide attempts and his consideration of other potential high-profile victims. After hours of observation the authorities concluded that although delusional, he was competent to stand trial, if a trial was possible – Lennon was dead and the public were baying for blood. The board of psychiatrists were, however split, with six doctors prepared to testify that Chapman was psychotic, while three others believed that he did not measure up to the medical definition of psychosis.

Chapman's new legal representative, Jonathan Marks, was preparing his case hoping to present his client as ill, rather than bad, and on this count win a spell in a secure hospital rather than the more severe prison, where it was feared he would be killed. In January 1981, another idea occured to Chapman – he would use the trial to promote *The Catcher in the Rye*, by reading it during his trial. His prison guards even bought copies which they asked him to sign, which Chapman eagerly agreed to do.

Then in June 1981, as the case was being brought to court, Chapman had a change of mind – he would, as directed by God, now plead guilty. Marks tried to dissuade him, but when he failed he challenged Chapman's competency to change his plea via the courts. In a private chamber, devoid of both the public and the press, Chapman confirmed his decision to plead guilty and that he understood the implications of his decision. Impressed by Chapman's calm and collected demeanour, Judge Edwards accepted Chapman's plea and on 24 August, amid a packed courtroom, Edwards sentenced Chapman to from 20 years to life.

The world had got what it wished for – Chapman to be imprisoned in the inhospitable confines of a US prison cell, not cocooned within the relative comfort of a secure hospital. The question of his sanity had been answered, his talking to the imaginary "little people" apparently the action of a warped mind, not of a mad one. It is an important distinction – revenge on a person who is mentally ill is not as sweet as that extracted from a sane person and the world wanted to feel avenged.

In the first few years of his imprisonment Chapman went through a series of violent outbursts, smashing his TV set up, blocking his toilet and ripping his clothes. He would later say that the evil spirits inside of him had emerged, hissing and screaming as they retched from his mouth, following which he finally found God again. He has served his time, locked in his 10 foot by 6 foot room in the Attica Correctional facility, in Buffalo, New York. Accepting little in the way of psychological counselling, Chapman is able to review his own life and the crime he committed, claiming that by the time he had served six years the demons that tortured him had finally left.

In October 2000, nearly 20 years after his imprisonment, Chapman was refused parole for the first time. At the hearing he read the following statement:

> I will not appeal against any decision you have. If it's a decision to keep me here in the prison, I will not appeal against it, and I never will. I'd like the opportunity to apologize to Mrs Lennon. I've thought about what it's like in her mind to be there that night, to see the blood, to hear the screams, to be up all night with the Beatle music playing through her apartment window . . . And there's something else I want to say. I feel that I see John Lennon now not as a celebrity. I did then. I saw him as a cardboard cut-out on an album cover. I was very young and stupid, and you get caught up in the media and the records and the music. And now I – I've come to grips with the fact that John Lennon was a person. This has nothing to do with being a Beatle or a celebrity or famous. He was breathing,

and I knocked him right off his feet, and I don't feel because of that I have any right to be standing on my feet here, you know, asking for anything. I don't have a leg to stand on because I took his right out from under him, and he bled to death. And I'm sorry that ever occurred. And I want to talk about Mrs Lennon again. I can't imagine her pain. I can't feel it. I've tried to think about what it would be like if somebody harmed my family, and there's just no way to make up for that, and if I have to stay in prison the rest of my life for that one person's pain, everybody else to the side for a second, just that one person's pain, I will . . . Again, I'm not saying these things for – for you to give me any kind of consideration for letting me go. I'm saying that because they are real, and it happened to me, and I felt her pain then, and I can honestly say I didn't want to feel it up until then. It's a horrible thing to, you know, realize what you've done.

In October 2002, Chapman was again refused parole; coincidentally the parole board sat on what would have been John Lennon's 62nd birthday. At a point when many offenders are released – after 22 years behind bars – the parole board acknowledged Chapman's exemplary prison record but proposed that his release would "depreciate the seriousness" of the crime.

At the time of writing, October 2004, Chapman has again been denied parole on what is his third attempt and his 24th year behind bars. No further comment or justification was issued by the board on this occasion.

Chapman committed a callous murder and deserved the severest of penalties, yet the question remains, would he have been back out by now if his victim had been a truck driver and not one of New York's most famous residents?

In memory of the music and life of John Lennon, the city of New York selected an area of Central Park, just over two acres, and gave it the name "Strawberry Fields" after Lennon's song of the same name. It is adjacent to the spot outside the Dakota where he was slain.

Helter Skelter

Charles Manson & The Family

For many people the middle months of 1969 were the summer of love. On the east coast of the United States, Bethel, in upstate New York, was preparing for the largest music festival that had ever been staged, on a 600-acre site called Woodstock. It would become an iconic legend which would symbolize the hippie, free-love movement and the generalized acceptance of drug use among a generation of young people who believed their parents had tried and failed. Rebellion was rife as young Americans took to the streets to show their disapproval of the war in Vietnam. Scott McKenzie wrote music to match the mood and beckoned the young to don flowers in their hair and join the thronging crowds at the epicentre of this new free for all in San Francisco. The new sense of freedom was symbolized further as man reached Earth's nearest neighbour in space and walked for the first time on the moon – a new era had arrived and hope sprang eternal.

For one small group however the summer of love would become a period of hate as they turned their drug-fuelled disenfranchisement into an orgy of killing, aimed at those who epitomized the opulence they so dearly despised – the rich and the famous of Hollywood.

Charles Miles Manson was the head of a bunch of hippies who held him in such high esteem as to almost be their messiah. The "family", as it was known, had formed around this charismatic, small-time crook, who had spent a significant amount of his time, both as a youth and as an adult, in one form of correctional centre or another.

In 1959 Manson had been given a ten-year suspended sentence for forging a treasury cheque, but was called back to commence the sentence in 1960 on Federal Mann Act charges. He had conned a young woman out of $700 to invest in a non-existent company, and to make matters worse he made her pregnant, and then drugged and raped her room-mate. The judge handling his recall commented, "If ever there was a man who demonstrated himself completely unfit for probation, he is it." Just prior to this he married for the second time, fathering a child, Charles Luther Manson, before divorcing in 1963 whilst still serving his sentence. Aged just 26 Manson was transferred from California to the Federal penitentiary at McNeil Island, Washington, and it was during this stretch that he became obsessed with the English pop sensation, the Beatles. He learned to play the electric guitar and dedicated most of his time to writing music, a task which generated some modest success. As the years ticked by new prisoners informed Manson of the latest culture sweeping across the United States – free love, girls in mini-skirts and the emergence of new drugs. It was of no surprise therefore that on release in 1967, having spent the previous seven years behind bars, Manson was now ready to join in the fun in San Francisco.

On 21 March 1967, now aged 32 and having spent half of his life in one form of correctional centre or another, Manson was released from jail and travelled to San Francisco. Although he apparently resisted release, preferring instead to remain in prison and play his music, the prison authorities once more set him free, this time to devastating effect. Manson was at best ill prepared for life on the outside and the new counter-culture drew him like a magnet. Moving into the Haight-Ashbury area of San Francisco he was easily able to blend in to the hippie scene, busking for money on the streets whilst getting to grips with the new drugs which were available and which most of the hippies he mixed with seemed to be taking. It was during this period that Manson first saw how drugs could be used as a way of exerting great influence over people, a factor that did not go unnoticed.

Manson was now starting to attract hangers-on, mostly women, many of whom were young, impressionable and rebelling against their parents or society in general. He found it easy to dismantle their inhibitions and question the validity of their ideals – good or bad. He was now using a blend of his own distorted biblical verses, mixed with his limited knowledge of scientology, much of which he had acquired whilst in prison, to groom his disciples and present a tainted view of the world. The constant questioning and grooming when mixed with a staple diet of drugs, mainly LSD and marijuana, created an environment in which Manson became all powerful and was soon the accepted head of the group. As well as the drugs Manson would also insist on having sex with all the female members of the "family", further enhancing his superior position. These weak-willed and gullible individuals thought they had found a true leader, one whose understanding of what was needed was beyond doubt. Thus the "family" was born and Manson became its cult leader, for now sex and his general bidding would be sufficient, but soon he would expect more from his followers.

In the spring of 1968 Manson and his followers, who by now had acquired an old school bus, left San Francisco and travelled around northern California, he still writing his particular brand of music and they all still enjoying the drugs and sex lifestyle they had by now become accustomed to. Eventually he and a small group of the family struck up a relationship with a music teacher, Gary Hinman, with whom they lived for a while at his house in Los Angeles. It was through Hinman that Manson came across Dennis Wilson of the Beach Boys, another relationship he tried to manipulate, using the girls to maintain Wilson's interest. Wilson was initially interested in Manson because of the hypnotic effect he seemed to have over his female followers, but soon began to feel uncomfortable in his presence. Aware that Manson was trying to use him to further his musical aspirations he eventually asked them to leave, a request Manson did not receive gracefully.

The family once again needed a base and it was at this time that Manson came across a collection of old ranch buildings once used as a movie set. The Spahn ranch was owned by the elderly George Spahn who was persuaded by Manson, with the help of some of his female followers, that they should be allowed to use the ranch in exchange for cleaning services and other more personal services that might be required by the old man from time to time. With the family now ensconced on the ranch they set about making the place into their very own commune, stealing and scavenging food from supermarkets and shops as a way of survival.

People would drift in and out of the group for one reason or another, but by now a core of lieutenants had formed around Manson. Although men were drawn into the group, mostly because of the women, Manson himself preferred to cultivate a female entourage, keeping the male competition to a minimum. It is not clear if Manson had always intended to organize a killing spree or indeed if he ever intended to become a cult figure for his followers. What is known is that he was still hell bent on breaking into the music industry and becoming a rock star. Although he had not been able to manipulate Dennis Wilson he had at least picked up another potential contact in the form of Doris Day's son, Terry Melcher. It was through the pursuit of this contact that Manson first came across the mansion at 10050 Cielo Drive, in the Benedict Canyon area of Los Angeles. Melcher had been persuaded by Dennis Wilson that he should have a listen to Manson's music, which he duly did. Unfortunately for Manson, who had by now started to feel that he was about to break through, Melcher didn't rate it and told Manson that he didn't want to record it. Manson was angry – he had gone all out to impress Melcher, playing live for him, with some of his girls providing backing vocals and playing tambourines. It is thought that this act of denial on Melcher's part was one of the key incidents that pushed Manson over the edge.

Manson had for a long while been preaching a mix of religion, peppered with song lyrics, all of which pointed to an inter-racial war concluding in the extermination of modern white and black society. He was certainly racist, but the deep-seated hatred may well have been formed during his period in jail. At 5'2" tall Manson was an easy target in jail and it is reported that he had been raped by a number of black prisoners on more than one occasion. Whilst the seeds of Manson's prophecies were being sown in jail, the Beatles released their White Album, containing the song "Helter Skelter", the lyrics of which seemed to fit nicely with the Armageddon Manson was forecasting. He was not aware that the "Helter Skelter" referred to in the Beatles song was merely a reference to a British fairground ride. With the future labelled as "Helter Skelter", Manson began building his plans around it, spreading the word among his followers. His vision was an inter racial war which would commence following a spree of killings carried out by black people on white people in their own homes. The war would result in the annihilation of both blacks and whites and finally only the family would be left – and they would then take power and build a new future for themselves. These ramblings were going on well in advance of the final acts of savagery, so if he was always planning to start the war himself then he was playing a long game – the indoctrination of his followers by means of drugs, sex, threats and the mixed-up sermons he would serve up had taken many months to hit home. But in Melcher's rejection, Manson felt the searing anger that needed revenge – and his followers would need to prove themselves worthy of their positions, by committing the ultimate of criminal acts.

At one time or another the family had numbered as many as 35, but many simply drifted in and out, leaving a core group who Manson modelled into a form of death squad. They had been persuaded that they were special and that they would be the beneficiaries of the new life after the war, along with himself. They had been taught how to break into properties, cutting telephone wires to prevent the police being called, and above all how to subdue people – anyone standing in their way would be killed.

The core group consisted of a number of females, Susan "Sadie" Atkins, Patricia Krenwinkle, Leslie Van Houten, Linda Kasabian, Lynette Fromme, Mary Brunner and just a handful of men, Charles "Tex" Watson, Bruce McGregor

Davis and Bobby Beausoleil. They were a varied bunch and many had come from normal middle-class backgrounds. Susan Atkins, whose real name was Sadie Mae Gluts, was brought up in San Jose, California, where she sang in her school choir and led a normal life until the death of her mother from cancer. Things took a turn for the worse when she moved to San Francisco and became a topless dancer and a bar-room hustler. She had already had some dealings in Satanism when she came across Manson in 1967. At a low ebb she described Manson as providing her with the faith she was looking for and committed herself to him. Patricia Krenwinkle had a good job with a major insurance company, with a car and a smart Manhattan Beach apartment when she walked out leaving it all behind, including her last pay cheque. Seeking thrills she had come across the family and joined them in September 1967, travelling round the West Coast area bingeing on sex and drugs. Leslie Van Houten was considered the least committed to Manson. She had enjoyed a positive childhood, but was considered a "spoiled child" who was impulsive, easily frustrated and liable to outbursts of temper. Linda Kasabian, by contrast, was from a broken home and had a strained relationship with her stepfather. From New Hampshire, she headed west looking for God, but instead found herself caught up in the sex and drugs culture of San Francisco, joining the "family" in July 1969, just weeks before the murders. Charles "Tex" Watson was described by a neighbour from his youth as "the typical boy next door". An "A" student in high school he also enjoyed great success on the sports field, holding the state record for the low hurdles. Watson's problems began when he started taking drugs as a college student, finally dropping out and heading for San Francisco in 1966, meeting Manson and joining the "family" in 1967.

By now Manson was probably already intent on murder, but he still hankered after a music career and decided to take his latest offering to the well-known, West Coast musician and piano teacher, Gary Hinman. Trading on his previous connections with Dennis Wilson and others, Manson persuaded Hinman to listen to his new composition and managed to ingratiate himself into Hinman's house for a short stay. Hinman now made the mistake that would cost him his life. Managing to remain non-committal on the music, he was able to let Manson down gently, but let loose the fact that he had recently come into a small inheritance of some $20,000. Still feeling dejected from the Melcher rebuff, and with Hinman looking likely to deny him a chance too, Manson decided that he would console himself with Hinman's little nest egg, and planning to have his troops call back at a later date – the "family" did after all still need money to run their cars and buy the drugs they were taking.

Manson had in mind another couple who he thought should pay the ultimate price. The new residents of 10050 Cielo Drive were the movie actress Sharon Tate and her movie director husband, Roman Polanski who had rented the house from Melcher after they had got married earlier in the year. In another twist Manson had returned to the house on Cielo Drive in March of that year once again looking to enlist Melcher's support for yet another music project. On approaching the house Manson could see there were others now in occupation, but was annoyed at the frosty reception he was given. Tate's photographer intercepted Manson on the drive and instructed him to get off the property, and worse, that he should leave by the rear entrance, lest anyone should see him. As he strolled away, looking every inch the vagrant, Manson glanced back and caught sight of the "Hollywood types" who had treated him with such disdain. They could never have guessed how this brief interaction would cost them so dearly. After the event the police presumed that Manson had harboured a grudge against the new occupants on Cielo Drive and this became the basis of the motive for the murders that Manson was to orchestrate.

On 27 July 1969, Manson dispatched Mary Brunner, Susan Atkins and Bobby Beausoleil to Hinman's house at 964 Old Topanga Canyon Road. Their mission was to extract the $20,000 that Manson had become aware of earlier. Although it has never been fully proven it is thought that he also instructed the team to murder Hinman for not helping his musical career. The three "family" members managed to gain entrance to Hinman's residence and Beausoleil immediately took the lead. He tried initially to persuade Hinman to simply hand over the money, but was told that it was not in the house. For around two hours Beausoleil kept up the pressure before finally losing patience and produced a Radom 9mm pistol. Threatening the now terrified Hinman, Beausoleil handed the gun to Atkins whilst he ransacked the house looking for the money. Whilst Beausoleil was pulling the house apart upstairs Hinman attempted the first of his escapes, but was persuaded back when Atkins let loose a shot which ricocheted around the kitchen before embedding itself in one of the kitchen cupboards. On hearing the shot Beausoleil ran back into the room and grabbed the gun off Atkins, hitting Hinman around the head with the butt to subdue him. With little progress being made in finding the money Beausoleil phoned Manson to get advice. Expecting more after the three had been gone so long, and now angry at the lack of progress, Manson decided to call in himself. Entering the house he sought to terrify Hinman into submission; taking a sword he cut a slice out of his ear and again ordered the others to check the house for the money. Having been there only a short while he instructed Brunner to clean up Hinman's wound and to bring him out to the ranch after they had completed the search, following which Manson disappeared into the night once more. Hinman had his ear stitched with dental floss and was then bound hand and foot, and laid out on the hearthrug. With Hinman now pretty much under control the gang proceeded to check every drawer and cupboard in the house, but there was no money to be had. What they did discover were the two pink registration forms belonging to the two vehicles on the drive. As morning approached Hinman was untied solely for the purpose of signing over the vehicles. His final mistake was a second attempt to escape – as the ropes loosened he made a dash to the window and began screaming for help. Panicked by this sudden turn of events, Beausoleil pursued Hinman, plunging a knife twice into his chest. Not yet dead the others let him slump to the floor in a pool of blood. As Hinman's life ebbed away Atkins ran her fingers through the still warm blood and daubed messages on the walls. The words "Political Piggies" were discovered later, along with a crude drawing of a panther's paw, an attempt at laying the blame for the killings at the door of the militant black separatist movement, the Black Panthers. A scene of pure destruction was now cleaned up by the gang, the blood-soaked clothes were removed and the surfaces wiped clean of fingerprints, before they left, locking the door behind them. As they were hot-wiring one of Hinman's cars it occurred to them that no one had checked to make sure he was dead. With the door locked they gained access again through a window at the back and smothered him. With the task now fully complete and the scene set up to lay the blame elsewhere, they stopped off at the Topanga kitchen cafe and enjoyed coffee and cherry cakes, before returning to the ranch to give Manson the details.

All in all it was a job poorly carried out and with a bit more luck the crimes for which Manson and his "family" were to become infamous might never have happened. Just four days after the murder Hinman's body was discovered by friends and the LA police department were informed. Sergeant Whiteley and deputy Charles Guenther of the Sheriff's Office were dispatched to the bloody scene and were easily able to identify a number of strange fingerprints, one of which was quickly confirmed to be that of Bobby Beausoleil. A few days later when Beausoliel was picked up the police found the knife that had been used on Hinman and a blood-soaked T-shirt in the back of his car. Beausoleil was charged and subsequently convicted of murder – if only he had implicated the others that would have been the end of the story, but instead he went to prison leaving the others in the clear.

Emboldened by the loyalty of his followers Manson now wished to pursue his murderous activities further and began to plan more shocking crimes. The new occupants on Cielo Drive would be the next targets, their deaths sounding a wake-up call to the overindulgent, rich and famous residents who occupied the big houses around LA and Hollywood. And this one would set the US on the path to the race wars Manson had predicted; this one would be "Helter Skelter".

On 8 August 1969 Manson assembled his chosen gang for the evening's work – Charles "Tex" Watson, Susan "Sadie" Atkins, Pat "Katie" Krenwinkle and Linda Kasabian. Instructing them to get knives and a change of clothes, he announced, "Now is the time for Helter Skelter." Sending them on their way his final piece of advice was to "leave a sign . . . something witchy", and with this the death squad headed away from the Spahn ranch towards Benedict Canyon.

Polanski's home at 10050 Cielo Drive was the perfect location for him and his new bride Sharon Tate. Hidden away in the canyons above Hollywood, the property provided the right mix of privacy and distance from the mayhem of Hollywood. Not a fortress by modern Hollywood standards, the house was entered via big heavy gates and past guest quarters in which a fairly well-built caretaker lived. Polanski was away filming in Europe on this particular night, but Sharon had the company of her young sophisticated friends, Abigail Folger, the coffee heiress and her boyfriend, Voytek Frykowski, and international hair stylist Jay Sebring, who was himself Tate's ex-boyfriend. Eight months pregnant by Polanski, Sharon and her guests were enjoying a low-key evening, not an uncommon event at this particular address. A real looker, Sharon had won beauty competitions both as a child and as a young adult, but really harboured a desire to become a movie actress. In 1963, aged just 22, this goal was finally realized when she landed a part in the US TV series *The Beverley Hillbillies*, which was quickly followed by other TV parts. In 1965 the switch to movie-making was established when she played opposite David Niven in the film *The Eye of the Devil*. She met Polanski in London in 1966, at which time she was dating Jay Sebring; Polanski offered her the lead role in the comedy horror film, *The Fearless Vampire Hunters*. It was during the shooting of this film that Polanski and Sharon became lovers, causing her to break off the romance with Sebring; they were subsequently married in early 1969 after Polanski concluded the shooting of *Rosemary's Baby*, taking the house at Cielo Drive when Terry Melcher moved out. Although Sharon missed Polanski when he was away filming, especially at this late stage of her pregnancy, she was by all accounts deliriously happy. Abigail Folger hailed from a very privileged background, being the heir to the Folger coffee fortune. Aged just 25 she was very much a woman of the era. Having graduated from Radcliffe and with money at her disposal she looked for a meaningful occupation with which to spend her time, much of it involving social work. Along with her boyfriend Voytek Frykowski however, she had become quite heavily dependent on drugs, which had started to cause her some concern. It was through Frykowski that she was introduced to Sharon and Polanski and eventually invested money in Jay Sebring's hairstyling business. Sebring, an internationally renowned hairstylist, had a string of Hollywood customers including Frank Sinatra, Paul Newman and Steve McQueen. He was a known ladies' man who had escorted Sharon for a while before she broke it off to move in with Polanski. They were a close group and a good mix, but above all they all enjoyed Tate's company – she was so different to the normal Hollywood starlet types who were shallow and insincere.

The four gang members sat in the heady atmosphere of the white and yellow Ford, high on marijuana and excitement. After the Hinman killing they knew what to expect and were now thoroughly ready for anything that might lie ahead of them; only Linda Kasabian had feelings of doubt. She had heard the stories of how Hinman had finally met his end – the sheer bloody mess – and it was not lost on her that Bobby Beausoleil was now likely to serve a life sentence because of it. As the Ford slowly turned into Cielo Drive Kasabian had just a little time to consider these facts, before Watson switched off the lights and let the engine idle as he let the car roll along to the end of the road. He pulled into the shadows of a large oak tree and killed the engine. They sat there for a few moments making sure there was no one around. The time was just after midnight on the night of 8/9 August and it was dark and quiet. Watson and the others climbed out of the car and stood in the shadows for a moment; when they were sure there was no one around they spread out along the pavement while Watson climbed up a nearby telephone pole and cut the wires. Before the advent of mobile phones, this act now effectively cut the household off from the outside world. Pushing open the heavy wrought-iron gates, the gang were immediately surprised by the approaching headlights of an oncoming car. While the girls lingered in the shadows, Watson positioned himself in the road and aimed his .22 Bluntline Special revolver directly at the driver. Eighteen-year old Steven Parent, who was driving a sporty two-seater Nash Ambassador, hit the brakes as a feeling of panic embraced him. He had been at the gatehouse visiting the caretaker and had not expected to see anyone at that time of the night, especially someone with a gun. Parent had just graduated from school in the summer and was working several jobs in preparation for starting college in the fall. He had everything to live for when Watson motioned him to open the side window of the driver's door. Parent may have been aware of others moving in the shadows as Watson thrust the gun through the window at his face. As he asked for his life to be spared he was shot at point-blank range four times in the chest. The time was now around 12.30 a.m. At Tate's neighbour's house about a hundred yards away, the Knotts thought they heard the sound of gunfire, but after listening intently for a few more moments decided to go to bed.

By now Linda Kasabian had lost her nerve and would not enter the grounds, electing instead to stay by the car and keep watch, knowing that the shots she heard heralded the start of a bloody massacre that evening and she for one could not face it. She could have left the scene at any time but for reasons best known to herself she stayed and waited for the others to return.

The three remaining "family" members now fanned out across the lawn and stealthily skirted the perimeter of the Polanski house looking for an entry point. When it became obvious that there would be no easy route into the house Watson started to cut through one of the window screens which guarded an unused room at the front. Working quickly but quietly he soon opened the screen and had forced the window ajar. One by one the three of them slid in through the window and stood silently in the dark room, listening for any signs of life. When they were sure they had not been detected they moved along the corridor and into the main living area where they found Frykowski asleep on the couch. Watson nudged Frykowski and he awoke to find the barrel of the gun just inches from his face. Asking what the intruders wanted, Watson responded somewhat poetically, "I am the devil. I am here to do the devil's business. Give me your money." With this Watson sent Atkins off to find some towels with which to tie Frykowski up. As she was returning from the bathroom she passed a bedroom and could hear Sharon, Abigail Folger and Jay Sebring talking. She reported her find to Watson who sent her back to bring them into the front room and to tell them it was a robbery. When Atkins returned with them she set about tying them up but Sebring managed to break free and launched himself at the gun hand of Watson – he was not fast enough and was shot once through the armpit and stabbed four times. With the blood-letting now underway, Frykowski became convinced they would all die; the intruders had already used the gun and a knife on Sebring, so he too made an attempt to pull the gun off Watson. Watson beat Frykowski with the butt of his gun so severely that one of the handle grips broke off. With blood streaming down his face he staggered to the door and screamed for help but it was too late – Atkins and Krenwinkle raced across the room and stabbed at him ferociously. As he fell to the floor they continued to puncture his body with stab wounds. The room was now in chaos as fear and panic spread into the other two captives and it was now Abigail Folger's chance to make an escape bid. She too had wriggled free and headed past Krenwinkle and Atkins onto the lawn where she ran into the darkness, pursued by the much faster Watson who caught her before she got halfway, knocking her to the ground and plunging a knife deep into her chest. Folger now lay dead on the lawn. The terror was now in full flow and could not be stopped, adrenaline pumping through the killers as they began a frenzied attack on Frykowski's dead body, stabbing him a pointless 51 times, although he had already suffered numerous blows to the head and two gunshot wounds. The house was a scene of pure carnage and Sharon Tate had endured watching it unfold mercilessly in front of her. As Atkins and Krenwinkle turned their attention to her she must have known that nothing she could say or do would prevent them from killing her, except perhaps her pregnancy, which at nearly full term was clear for all to see.

From evidence to emerge after the group's arrest. Tate's murder was particularly awful. Pregnant as she was, she had been tied up and had watched the blood flowing all around her. When Krenwinkle pinned her to the floor and Atkins positioned herself next to her, Sharon could only beg for mercy. Atkins later reported to a cell mate whilst on remand that Sharon had indeed begged, "Please don't kill me, please don't kill me. I don't want to die, I want to have my baby." Atkins now high and beyond mercy, looked directly at Tate. "Look bitch, I don't care about you. I don't care if you are going to have a baby. You had better be ready, you're going to die and I don't feel anything about it." With that Atkins thrust the knife into Tate's heart killing her, and continued to stab her a further fifteen times. When the frenzy was over they dragged Sharon's body over to lie next to Sebring's and tied them together, looping a bloodied rope around their necks and throwing it over a rafter on the ceiling. Watson wandered amongst the bodies and kicked at them, whilst Atkins and Krenwinkle spread a flag across the couch. Atkins had run her fingers through Tate's blood and had tasted it, saying afterwards, "It was such a high." With her bloodied fingers she daubed the word "Pig" on the front door. Later Atkins would say that she had wanted to cut out the baby, remove the victims' eyeballs and mutilate their fingers, but thankfully they were running out of time. As instructed by Manson they now quickly changed out of their soiled clothes and collected their weapons before making their way back to the Spahn ranch, throwing a number of weapons out onto the Hollywood hillside as they went.

Back at the ranch Manson took in the details of the night's orgy of killing, annoyingly noting that the team had not cleansed the house of fingerprints and more importantly,

Atkins had lost her knife. He decided that with what little time was left he would drive over to the house with another "family" member and tidy things up a bit. On arrival Manson took in the bloody scene but was not shocked at the devastation his murderous crew had caused. They first wiped Parent's car over to rid it of fingerprints and then returned to the house to do the same there. They used the towels that had been used to hold Frykowski, throwing them over Sebring's face before leaving.

At 8 a.m., still on 9 August, Winifred Chapman, housekeeper to Sharon Tate, reached the main gate and noticed what appeared to be a fallen telephone wire draped across the heavy gates. Walking towards the house she saw Steven Parent's car parked up on the main drive, but did not have any reason to approach it, other than the fact that the car was not known to her. Heading round to the back door she found the key in its usual hiding place and let herself in; picking up the phone she confirmed that it was indeed a downed telephone line she had seen at the gates. The house was not unusually quiet for the time of day as the occupants did not rise too early, especially if they had enjoyed a good evening the night before. Heading through to the main room, Chapman became aware of flashes of red everywhere but it was not until she looked through the open door onto the grass that she began to scream – she could now see the outline of a body on the lawn, the blood in stark contrast to the otherwise green and very neatly manicured lawns. Chapman, now hysterical, ran across to the Knotts' house, passing the unfamiliar car on the drive and this time seeing that there was what appeared to be another dead body in it. When it became apparent that the Knotts were out she finally managed to raise the alarm at the next house, presumably not approaching the caretaker's house because the phone line would have been down for him too.

Jerry DeRosa was the first of the LAPD officers to arrive at the Polanski household and it was he who looked into Steven Parent's car and found him shot full of holes. Shortly after this DeRosa was joined by officers William Whisehunt and Robert Burbridge, who, with guns drawn, searched the other cars on the drive and the garage area. As they approached the house the officers could now clearly see two bodies lying on the lawn, a man and a woman, both of whom had clearly suffered massive injuries. As the enormity of the crime dawned on them they became more cautious – the killer or killers might still be in the house. With guns ready they approached the front door, noticing the broken window screen as they were about to enter. They also saw the word "Pig" scrawled in blood on the lower half of the door and as they edged past it they caught sight of a pistol grip on the floor. With three bodies already discovered they could not have prepared themselves for the horrific scene they were about to walk into – they all stood stunned at the sheer volume of blood and were shocked to the core by the heavily pregnant female who had clearly been the victim of a frenzied knife attack. Then from the back of the house the officers heard a man's voice – warning that they were police, they instructed him to stay put and promptly arrested William Garretson, the caretaker.

As an army of police moved in to secure the crime scene and begin the mammoth task of sifting through the debris, the media lost little time in announcing the massacre to the rest of the world. As an up-and-coming movie star and the wife of Roman Polanski, the killing of Sharon Tate was big news. As was the death of Abigail Folger, society personality. The press gathered around the property and sought out anyone who knew any of the victims, eagerly planning to fill many column inches with every fact, allegation, theory and historical detail that they could get their hands on. The press were in overdrive – it had been an agent of Polanski, the Mafia, a drug-related revenge attack or someone wanting to extract revenge on Polanski himself; maybe Polanski had been the intended target but had fortunately been out of the country filming. At one time or another all of the angles were reported as fact and supported by whatever gossip and whispers were available. The truth is the police themselves were not sure of the motive, although they were able to quickly rule out burglary as a likely option. Meanwhile between the LAPD and the LA Sheriff's Office no one connected the Hinman case to the Tate murders, as both departments carried out what appeared to be entirely independent enquiries,

Back at the Spahn ranch Manson read of the events in the newspapers and revelled in the sheer shock that the murders had caused. What was apparent, however, was that "Helter Skelter" had not been triggered, a fact not lost on Manson or indeed a number of "family" members. As with LA, although America and the world were reeling from the news, there was no ensuing race war, not even a skirmish. Manson decided that the gang needed to press home the message and planned another attack, only this time he would lead the murder squad himself. On 10 August, just one night after the Tate slayings, Manson, accompanied by Watson, Atkins, Krenwinkle, Leslie Van Houten and Clem Grogan, drove to the Silver Lakes area of Los Angeles. Silver Lakes sported expensive homes and would be the choice of area for any successful middle-class family. The criteria for the attack was purely that the targets should represent white respectability. It was therefore purely bad luck for the inhabitants of 3308 Waverley Drive that Manson randomly selected their address as the next focal point of his senseless brutality. The property belonged to Leno LaBianca, a grocery store owner, and his wife Rosemary LaBianca, the owner of a smart clothing boutique.

On the night in question the "family" arrived in two cars and once again pulled into the shadows; four of the occupants climbed out, leaving Van Houten and Grogan behind. Manson, lead the gang towards the house but indicated that they should wait while he quickly broke in, armed with a sword and a gun. Once in the house he quietly headed for the couple's bedroom. When Mr LaBianca awoke he found Manson pointing the gun directly into his face; 38-year-old Mrs LaBianca was now also awake and heard Manson explain that his purpose was robbery – if they co-operated no one would get hurt. Having tied the couple up Manson then took Mr LaBianca's wallet and went back out to the car, sending Watson, Krenwinkle and Van Houten into the house. There was no doubt what the group had to do –

the occupants would be killed and the scene should be shocking, with the clues pointing to a crime committed by a black gang. For some reason best known to Manson, he told the others that they should finish the job on the LaBiancas whilst he broke in to the neighbouring house and murdered the residents there. He did no such thing, however, but simply made his way back to the Spahn ranch and waited for the others to report in. Wasting little time once they were in the house, Watson pulled Mr LaBianca into the front room and stabbed him four times with a large kitchen knife, which on the final thrust was left sticking out of his throat. Then, with a pillow over LaBianca's face, he took his own knife and stabbed him a further eight times in the abdomen. Once again, as the frenzy took hold, Krenwinkle joined in – grabbing Mrs LaBianca they stabbed her a massive 41 times, encouraging Van Houten to join in as they chanted an evil mantra. Van Houten eventually stabbed Mrs LaBianca in the buttocks 16 times but by then she would have already been dead. Watson then carved the word "War" on Mrs LaBianca's stomach, while Krenwinkle, who had picked up a carving fork from the kitchen, stabbed both bodies repeatedly, leaving the instrument sticking up out of Mr LaBianca's abdomen. As with the Tate murder, they now took a lamp flex and tied it around the victims' necks, covering their faces with pillow cases. With the place covered in blood they once more ran their fingers through it and began daubing the walls with political slogans – "Death to pigs", "Rise" and finally the phrase, "Helter Skelter", misspelled, was scrawled across the refrigerator door. Then, in the depths of all this madness and depravity the trio showered together before making themselves something to eat in the kitchen, finally leaving just before dawn. With the killing over, that left the task of ensuring that the "Helter Skelter" plan was further advanced. They drove to a service station where one of the girls took Mr LaBianca's wallet and placed it on the top of a water tank, high up on the wall, in the ladies' rest room. The plan was simple, but flawed – they assumed the wallet would be found by a black person who would then attempt to use the contents. This would make the LaBianca murders a crime of blacks on whites in their own home – and this in turn would create the social unrest needed to set off "Helter Skelter".

If being murdered is not bad enough, had events moved the time lines back a little the LaBiancas might never have been home in the first place. On the night of their murder they had been driving back from a short break. Mr LaBianca was towing his prized boat with his wife beside him and her daughter by a previous marriage, 21-year-old Susan Struthers, in the back. Dropping Susan off at her apartment they had not got back to Waverley Drive until after 2 a.m., when it is assumed they went straight to bed, only to be disturbed a short time afterwards by Manson.

At 8.30 a.m. the following day Frank Struthers, Mrs LaBianca's son, arrived with his camping equipment and was immediately struck by a couple of things that didn't look right. The speedboat was still in the drive, whereas Mr LaBianca would normally have garaged it – although they did return late – and secondly, all of the window shades were down, something he had never known them do. He got no response from knocking on the door and instead decided to call the house from a local telephone kiosk. When he got no response this time he called his sister who confirmed that as far as she knew they were heading home after they dropped her off. Susan asked Frank to hold on by the phone box while she and her boyfriend drove over. A sense of fear swept over the threesome as they entered the unlocked door into the kitchen. Asking Susan to wait while they checked the house, they walked headlong into a scene of total carnage; unable to take in the scene they ran back out of the house pulling Susan along with them. They could not bring themselves to say what they had seen, but Susan was able to put the pieces together when Frank phoned the police and asked them to rush over – his parents had been murdered.

For the second day running the police entered a house of horrors, the same chaotic bloodbath and again, cords tied round the victims' necks and bloody slogans on the walls. The similarities between the Tate murders and these were unmistakable – so far as the LAPD were concerned the crimes were committed by the same people. However the lack of collaboration with the Sheriff's Office meant that the similarities with these more recent murders and the Hinman case had not been established. Had the LAPD known that the Hinman murder had also been the scene of bloodied writing then they might have been able to get to Manson through Beausoliel, who was keeping silent while on remand. Meanwhile with the revelation of the second murders the police now had to release Garretson, the Polanski caretaker who had been held for questioning while the LaBianca murders were being committed.

The press once more had a field day – a wild bunch of killers were targeting the famous, rich and business orientated of Los Angeles; no one was safe. The sales of intruder alarms rocketed and security companies were inundated with business. Meanwhile the Hollywood elite left town in their droves, some simply moving into hotels, prepared to sit it out until the killers had been brought in.

When Sergeant Whiteley of the Sheriff's Office heard of the Tate murders he could see the similarities with the Hinman killing, and knowing that Beausoleil was in custody, it couldn't have been him. They had always believed that Beausoleil had not acted alone, but even under interrogation and with the possibility of some degree of leniency, he continued to deny that he had been helped. The one fact that Whiteley had got in his possession was that prior to his arrest, Beausoleil had lived out at the Spahn ranch with a gang of weird hippies. Whiteley phoned this information through to Jesse Buckles who was working on the Tate case for the LAPD, but he immediately dismissed the possible connection in the belief that they already had their man, a factor which seriously delayed progress with the investigation and which could have resulted in more murders. Worse still, when they were forced to release Garretson they failed to reconnect with the information provided by Whiteley.

As the police departments continued their isolationist strategies, the media ran full pelt with a range of theories and stories which held LA in siege. Among the facts which peppered the newspaper articles were the usual journalistic sensations served up to an already overactive public imagination.

Meanwhile in the aftermath of both the Tate and LaBianca murders, there was little sign of the race wars and social unrest as predicted by Manson. And with this the "family" slowly began to disband as they could feel the long arm of the law stretching out to them; many left town and others simply moved on to the next ranch to be further away from the violent epicentre of Manson's gang.

Polanski himself had returned from Europe and had walked straight into a police questioning room – they could not discount the fact that he may have arranged the murders and being abroad at the time would provide a perfect alibi. Outraged that anyone would think this, let alone print stories that he could have killed his unborn son and wife, he made a tearful statement to the press in his own defence and proposed a $25,000 reward for information leading to the arrest of the killers. Polanski wasn't alone in coming under suspicion for at various times other members of his and Tate's families were dragged into the equation, including Tate's father, Colonel Paul Tate, who subsequently started his own investigation, travelling around the hippie communes hoping to unearth information that would lead him to the killers.

Without the link to the Hinman case the LAPD continued to pursue the drugs connection – it was well known that Sebring had been involved in narcotics and it was natural therefore to assume that the murders were retribution meted out by some drug baron. However, this speculation also ran into difficulty with the LaBianca murders as they were a respected business couple and nothing in their backgrounds connected them in any way to the drugs scene. Once again a dead end. Then on 1 September a young boy found the gun which had been used in the Tate murders, discarded under a bush. The boy's father turned the gun over to the LAPD who once again failed to carry out a proper investigation.

Meanwhile the Sheriff's Office were keenly pursuing a strategy of their own. In the knowledge that Beausoleil had lived at the Spahn ranch, they dispatched officers to check for stolen cars and credit cards with a warrant to really give the place a good going-over. If nothing else came out of the search it would signal the department's interest in the "family" group and spook them a little. With a little co-operation from the Inyo County Sheriff's Department the neighbouring Barker ranch was also raided, resulting in the arrest of 24 gang members, including Manson. The Barker ranch was so extensive that the search took three days and on the last one, hidden in a ditch on the outskirts of the property, the police found the pregnant girlfriend of Beausoleil, who came out terrified and begging for police protection. The net was slowly closing in on Manson, as many of those arrested at the Barker ranch gave the Spahn ranch as their official address. The Inyo officers now called Whiteley and Guenther in as officially this was their jurisdiction. Under questioning the girl stated that she had overheard Manson telling Beausoleil and Atkins to go and rob Hinman. Meanwhile Atkins, who had fled the Spahn ranch, had been arrested on charges of prostitution and had admitted being at the Hinman house at the time of his murder. Booked on suspicion of Hinman's murder she was held awaiting trial in the Sybil Brand Institute, an LA detention centre for women, and placed in a cell with two other detainees, Ronnie Howard and her friend Virginia Graham.

The LAPD, having come to a dead end, decided to check out any other murders which had shared the same modus operandi and had gone full circle back to Hinman. They too had now established the potential link to the Manson gang and were following up lines of enquiry of their own, even though there was no proof of any connection between the Hinman murder and those of Tate/LaBianca, save for the feeling that those living at the Spahn ranch new more than they were letting on.

As part of their sweeping enquiry the LAPD called in a couple of bikers from the Straight Satan Biker gang who had also stayed at the ranch for a while. Danny DeCarlo and Al Springer were able to provide more information supporting the involvement of Manson. They confirmed that amongst the Spahn ranch group, it was common knowledge that

Manson had arranged for the "family" to carry out the hit. They also mentioned that the gang had killed one of their own members, a man named Donald "Shorty" Shea, after he threatened to tell George Spahn what was really going on at the property. That resulted in Shorty having his head chopped off and the rest of him cut into little pieces so that he could not be identified. As the interviews progressed with interesting, though circumstantial results, they finally hit upon a key piece of information when DeCarlo, asked if anything had been written on the refrigerator, stated that Manson had said, "They wrote something on the fucking refrigerator in blood . . . something about pigs or niggers or something like that."

With the noose now around Manson's neck it was Atkins who began to pull it tighter. She had started to brag to her cell mates, Virginia Graham and Ronnie Howard, about the crimes she and the "family" had committed under the leadership of their guru Manson. Graham and Howard were intrigued with Atkins, who seemed a little crazy as if she was still on drugs, dancing around the cell, often looking and acting perfectly happy. Atkins explained that she was in for the first-degree murder of Hinman, but added that the police thought she had been more of an accomplice, holding Hinman down, whereas in reality it had been she who had stabbed him to death. The two girls were taken aback by this confession – even these days it is still rare for murder of this type to be carried out by a female.

Urged on by the obvious shock effect of her story, Atkins began to reveal details of the other murders she had been involved with. Both Graham and Howard were familiar with the bloodbaths that had occurred at the Tate household and also at the LaBianca residence, and if they were not mistaken Atkins seemed to be intimating that she had been involved in at least one of these. Over the course of a number of days, Atkins spoke of Manson being Jesus, that they were all going to survive and rule after the race war, this time referring directly to the Tate murders. Addressing Howard directly she said, "You know who did it, don't you, well, you're looking at her." Howard was shocked and asked why they had committed the murders. Atkins calmly explained that the "family" wanted to commit a crime of such proportions that it would shock the world, and said that they had picked the house because of its remote location, not caring who would be there when they arrived. She then described the gang as consisting of three women and one man, describing how they cut the telephone wires to prevent a call to the police, and also that they had shot a young man four times who was leaving the property as they were arriving. With more shocking, graphic detail Atkins described how they rounded up the occupants, putting nooses around their necks to prevent them escaping, and finally after one had tried to run, how the killing had begun with shooting and stabbing. The most shocking and sickening element of the story was Atkins' description of how Tate was the last to die, that she had begged for her life and that of her unborn child, but more horrifying, how Atkins had looked her in the eye as she plunged the knife into her. The two girls were unsure of what to make of Atkins' claims – she was after all a very bizarre young lady who could have gleaned most of the details from the papers and be merely repeating them to shock or impress them. But Atkins went on to describe how the "family" had gone out the next night and had murdered the LaBiancas.

Intrigued to say the least Graham and Howard decided they would set up a way of testing Atkins to see if she was for real. Howard by chance had been to the house on Cielo Drive when it had been up for sale and had driven past, purely window-shopping, and therefore knew what it looked like. When she asked Atkins if the house was still decorated in white and gold – which it hadn't been – Atkins replied, "No." The girls were now starting to believe that the girl they shared their cell with was in fact a multiple, cold-blooded killer. Once Atkins had started talking she found it easy to continue, especially about what the "family" were planning to do with other celebrities on their list: Frank Sinatra, Elizabeth Taylor, Richard Burton, Steve McQueen and Tom Jones. She said she was going to carve the words Helter Skelter on Taylor's face and then gouge her eyes out, putting them in a bottle with Burton's penis and mailing the package to Eddie Fisher, Taylor's ex-love. Sinatra was to be skinned alive whilst listening to his own music, while Tom Jones was to have his throat slit, but not until Atkins had forced him to have sex. With Howard and Graham more scared than horrified they passed on their knowledge to the prison authorities who in turn called in the LAPD.

With the cell room confession now on record, Atkins finally admitted her part in the murders, and in December 1969, she described to a grand jury the full details of the horror that took place at 10050 Cielo Drive. Crucially, Atkins delivered a more important and undeniable piece of evidence, when she told the jury that the wallet belonging to Mr LaBianca had been left in the rest room at the service station, and for what purpose. When the police searched the rest room and found the wallet perched on the top of the water tank, they now had positive proof that Atkins had detailed inside knowledge of the killings, knowledge that would now be impossible to deny should she succumb to Manson's influences once the charges came to court. Atkins' celebrity hit list was also released to the papers and another wave of fear spread through the glitzy homes of the Hollywood elite. The media were now aware of Manson and his "family" and began to dig into the backgrounds of all of those who had been arrested in connection with the murders – the story simply ran and ran. By the time the trials began there wasn't a person left in America who had not been spoon-fed the papers' various versions of events.

As the "family" had broken up other key members were tracked down and brought in. Watson had fled back to Texas and was now fighting extradition back to California, while many of the others had been arrested after the initial raids on the Spahn and Barker ranches.

On 18 November 1969, 35-year-old Deputy District Attorney Vincent Bugliosi was assigned to the Tate–LaBianca case, his colleague, Aaron Stovitz, being appointed as co-prosecutor. Their jobs were incredibly difficult. The LAPD now knew which of the gang members were at the various murders; they had a gun which had belonged to Manson, although not registered in his name; they had numerous confessions to say that Manson was the gang leader and had instructed the killings to be carried out; Atkins had delivered the LaBianca wallet to them; they had knives and finger-prints; but none of this placed Manson at the scene of the murders and none of it showed that he had actually com-mitted murder himself. Manson was quite comfortable with his position, knowing he had not committed murder, and yet the press had already labelled him a cult figure, leading a band of murderous, drugged-up hippies. He complained at the bad publicity, that he was being judged by the papers before he had fought his case in the courts. The public were already baying for blood – the killing of the heavily pregnant Sharon Tate, beautiful and married to a successful Holly-wood film director, had driven the American public almost to the point of hysteria. Bugliosi had to consider how to provide two important elements in the prosecution case, firstly motive – why did he want these people dead? He did not know them and he had not robbed them for personal gain. And secondly, how to prove that Manson was able to exert such an amount of influence over his "family" mem-bers that they would kill in his name.

The first task was to win indictments against all of those involved; this would in effect allow charges to be brought against each of them, including Manson, and then the debate would take place in a courtroom. With the evidence available and the confession by Atkins, who was not offered immunity, the grand jury were quick to hand down their verdict: Manson, Krenwinkle, Atkins, Watson and Kasabian were all charged with seven counts of first-degree murder, while Van Houten was charged with two counts of murder and one count of conspiracy to commit murder. Although immunity was not offered to Atkins she was encouraged to give evi-dence for the prosecution in exchange for her own life. The state of California still had the death penalty as an option at this time and the prosecution, keen to pin Manson, offered not to pursue her if she continued to act on their behalf.

The complexity of the case was further compounded by the pressures exerted by the various interested parties. Manson had already managed to get the first appointed trial judge, William Keene, replaced because he believed him to be biased. The press ran story after story and the jurors had to be protected from them in order that a fair trial could be delivered – if this was indeed possible given the negative press that the defendants had already attracted before the trial had even begun. Nevertheless, the trial did begin in mid-June 1970; Judge Charles Older, the second trial judge to be assigned to the case, presided and declared that the jurors should remain under lock and key when not in court. The need to keep the media from them was paramount, as any flaw in this arrangement would have the defence screaming for a null-and-void trial – possibly their best hope, all things considered. At one point this was almost achieved when towards the end of the trial, Richard Nixon, the newly appointed President, made a comment indicating Manson's guilt, going against the concept that defendants are innocent until proven guilty. Again the press ran the scoop at full tilt until Judge Older announced that given the jurors were in a pretty much confined environment, without television, radio or newspaper, there had been no material breach of the rules, and so the trial was allowed to continue.

Bugliosi described Manson as a "vagrant wanderer" who had sought to gain power over those around him by posing as a hippie, whilst all the while being obsessed with violent death. Bugliosi was as intent on implicating Manson, the evil behind the murders, as he was with ensuring that those who committed the crimes were seen as willing accomplices – he wanted them all inside for a long time. On Manson's first visit to the courtroom he appeared sporting a newly carved "X" in the space between his eyebrows, giving him an even more menacing look.

Initially Manson had requested the opportunity to defend himself but the court had ruled against this. The chance for Manson to grandstand himself, talk round in circles and generally disregard the facts was not something the California justice system could accommodate. Given Manson's ability to manipulate people, it would be a tough job for any prosecution witness to be cross-examined by him. In the end the court imposed a lawyer upon him.

Central to Manson's defence was his need to exert maximum influence over those still left in the "family". If any of them were to give evidence against him it would certainly be the final nail in his own coffin. By now Atkins, who had initially given statements incriminating Manson, had repudiated her testimony and was telling a completely different story, one that left everyone on the hook except Manson himself. Manson needed to ensure that those who took the stand had been got at by his agents, which he achieved by sending messages via those members of the "family" who had not been arrested, and who could visit him and the others. It worked for a while – Barbara Hoyt who was to give evidence for the prosecution was initially threatened and then enticed to Honolulu by one of Manson's girls; there she was given a large dose of LSD, but managed to get medical help before the drug could cause her harm.

The "family" took on a more bizarre appearance when Manson, Krenwinkle, Atkins and Van Houten all shaved their heads in protest, the women by now having also etched crosses into their foreheads. Outside the courthouse the remaining "family" members followed suit and shaved their heads in defiant support.

Manson and the others were now having to sit through statement after statement, most of which were damning against them. Manson had adopted new tactics to minimize the effect of the evidence – whenever the evidence looked bad he or his cohorts would create a disturbance which ensured that it was their diversions and not the evidence which got all the attention. One particular incident saw Manson launch himself out of the dock towards Judge Older screaming, "Someone should cut your head off," at which point Atkins, Krenwinkle and Van Houten began chanting some Latin verse. Judge Older had the defendants removed from court and instructed the jury to disregard what they had heard and seen – but they had now seen the true character of Manson, the menacing, threatening, violent man which the prosecution had been painting all along.

After 22 days of the trial, the prosecution had had its time and it was the defence attorneys' chance to make a rebuttal.

By now the girls had decided to make a statement which had them take the entire responsibility for the murders. It was they who planned them and they who carried them out; Manson had nothing to do with them. Van Houten's lawyer, Ronald Hughes, refused to co-operate, saying, "I refuse to take part in any proceedings where I am forced to push a client out of the window." A few days later Ronald Hughes disappeared and the media speculation machine went into overdrive once more, this time proven to be right. After the trial concluded Hughes's body was found wedged between two boulders in Ventura County, and an ex-Manson follower admitted that the murder had been carried out by a member of the "family". When a replacement lawyer for Van Houten was appointed Manson accused Judge Older of killing Hughes; again the proceedings were suspended and the defendants were removed from the court.

Overall the defence teams had a difficult time. As each one got up in turn to say something positive about their client, they could do little more than claim diminished responsibility brought on by excessive drug use and mind control. They were less guilty because they were unable to resist the influence of Manson – even the defendants weren't impressed.

The world had endured the reports of the murders and then followed the twists and turns through the media – the attempted murder of one witness, the disappearance of Van Houten's lawyer, the frequent outbursts of the defendants – but now the time had come to deliver the verdicts. On 15 January 1971, some one and half years after the Tate murders, the jury were holed up in a high-security room at the Hall of Justice, ready to deliberate on their verdict. Security had been enhanced following a report that Manson "family" members had stolen hand grenades from a local marine base and were preparing a special event on what they had termed "judgement day". The seven men and five women who made up the jury took nine days to reach their verdict. As the court reconvened the Judge asked the jury to give its verdicts: they found Charles Manson, Patricia Krenwinkle, Susan Atkins and Leslie Van Houten each guilty of murder and conspiracy to commit murder. Charles Watson, who had fought extradition from Texas, had not been tried at the same time, but he too was found guilty on the same charges just one year later.

On 29 March 1971 the jury met again to agree the penalty phase of the trial, the outcome being no surprise to anyone: "We, the jury in the above-entitled action, having found the defendant Charles Manson guilty of murder in the first degree, do now fix the penalty as death." Susan Atkins responded, "Better lock your doors and watch your own kids," while Krenwinkle told them, "You have just judged yourselves." Later in the month Judge Older pronounced the court's position on the penalties, "It is my considered judgement that not only is the death penalty appropriate, but it is almost compelled by the circumstances. I must agree with the prosecutor that if this is not a proper case for the death penalty, what should be?" The Judge then shook the hands of each juror in turn saying he would have provided them all medals of service if he could have done.

Further trials were held for the murder of Hinman and Donald "Shorty" Shea, following which Manson was again found guilty, as were Watson, Beausoleil, Bruce Davis and Steve Grogan.

At the time the Manson trial had been the longest running trial in American legal history, lasting some nine and a half months and costing a million dollars, small by today's standards. It was also the most publicized case and has attracted a consistent high level of attention over the years, lasting right up to present times. The coverage made Manson more well known and infamous than any other criminal. His name and face are now known to more people than any celebrity of the time, and possibly of the present time. His notoriety and that of his accomplices precede them wherever they go and Manson still receives more letters than any other prisoner in the US penal system. They are all still alive and behind bars following the state of California's abolition of the death penalty in 1972. Their penalties were commuted to life and remain so, even though California has since reinstated the death penalty.

They are all in separate prison establishments apart from Atkins and Krenwinkle who are both housed in Corona, California. The Manson saga continued to rumble on for years after the trial – in 1975, Lynette Fromme, a former "family" member, pulled a gun on the then President of the United States, Gerald Ford, in an attempt to get Manson freed. She never pulled the trigger and managed to heap more bad press on the name of Charles Manson, as well as earning herself a prison stretch.

Unlike his associates, Manson has endured a difficult incarceration, having spent many years in solitary confinement, sometimes for his own safety and at other times as a punishment for drugs offences. He suffered further loss of privileges for an alleged escape attempt involving a hot air balloon. To date Manson has been denied parole ten times, the latest in April 2002. His next chance will be in 2007, but there is no one who believes he has any chance of release. He has spent the majority of his life behind bars and is now institutionalized; he has never accepted his role in the murders and continues to hold a grudge against society. It is almost certain that Manson will spend the rest of his days in prison; now aged 70 and apparently in reasonable health, he could have a long way to go yet.

His accomplices, however, may not have to rot in jail. They have followed a different path, each one admitting and taking full responsibility for their parts in the murders. Charles "Tex" Watson is presently serving his sentence at Mule Creek State prison in Northern California. Since his imprisonment 34 years ago he has converted to Christianity, got married, written several books and fathered four children. He has become a minister of religion and has an exemplary prison record. He was last turned down for parole in October 2001, but will have another opportunity in 2005.

Susan Atkins is presently serving her sentence at the California Institute for Women at Frontera. She has been married twice and has been a model prisoner. She was last denied parole in February 2000. Sharon Tate's sister attended the hearing and read out a letter written by her father: "Thirty-one years ago I sat in a courtroom and watched with others. I saw a young woman who giggled, snickered and shouted insults; even whilst testifying about my daughter's last breath, she laughed. My family was ripped apart. If Susan Atkins is released to rejoin her family, where is the justice?" Atkins responded with, "I don't just have to make amends to the victims and families, I have to make amends to society. I sinned against God and everything this country stands for." Atkins will not be eligible for parole until 2005.

Patricia Krenwinkle has maintained an extremely low profile during her prison term and has, like the others, led a trouble-free existence, being co-operative with the authorities. She too has admitted her part in the crimes and has expressed great regret and sorrow at what she has done. She was last denied parole in July 2004 for the eleventh time. Although aching for freedom she will have to serve a few more years before her next opportunity for release.

Leslie Van Houten failed to win freedom in July 2004 and will, like Krenwinkle, have to wait a few more years before trying again. At the last hearing Van Houten said, "My heart aches and there seems to be no way to convey the amount of pain I caused. I don't know what else to say." With these words concluded her fifteenth parole application.

The crimes were without doubt some of the worst cases to be heard in a courtroom, although not unique. It is rare for women to kill in the grotesque way in which the "family" murdered people, especially Sharon Tate, eight months pregnant. The law is a complex subject and is there to provide protection, retribution and a deterrent, but also remedial therapy. It is open to public pressure and on occasions to the public's apathy, but above all it is at the mercy of the forces of media presentation and sensationalization, and it is in this mass of conflicting interest that you must wonder if the law delivers a fair and just outcome every time. The "family" members have been in prison for 34 years now, and are themselves still the subject of much publicity – their victims were high-profile, famous individuals. To what extent is their own notoriety and the fame of their victims continuing to affect their prospects of release? As history has shown, if you murder a celebrity, you often become as famous as that person, and in the case of Charles Manson and the "family" even more so.

The Millionaire's Mysterious Murder

Harry Oakes

On 18 October 1943, at the Bahamas Supreme Court, Count Marie Alfred Fouquereaux de Marigny (known to his friends as Freddie de Marigny) stood before the court accused of the murder of his father-in-law Sir Harry Oakes. Because of the high social status of the murder victim, not to mention the circles which he moved in, this was to prove to be a massively publicized case. Outside the courtroom were hundreds of interested parties, some friends, but the majority members of the press. Despite the fact the Second World War was still raging, this new story dominated the headlines throughout the court case and beyond.

Freddie was originally from the island of Mauritius, but had moved to the island of Nassau during the 1930s. He was extremely tall, over 6 feet, and described as handsome and charming; with a French accent he was an accomplished ladies' man. He had made a profitable living on the island by running a highly successful chicken farm, also proving to be a prosperous property investor.

He lived a rather jet-set lifestyle and spent the majority of his recreation time sailing; in fact, as an accomplished sailor he regularly took part in the Nassau Yacht Club sailing competitions, which he regularly won. The now second-time divorcee spent many evenings at parties and social engagements and was never without a beautiful companion.

He was to meet Sir Harry Oakes' eldest daughter at Nassau's British Colonial Ball – Nancy was at that time only 17 years old. When she told her parents about Freddie they were immediately against her seeing him, but she was not easily dissuaded and managed to meet him privately for over a year. When she was 18 the pair decided to elope to New York and were secretly wed. When Nancy called her parents to break the news they were totally devastated – they considered that a man twice divorced, and with a reputation for being a womanizer, could not devote himself to their beloved daughter. That said, they did try their best to accept him into the family, but their true feelings towards him were never far from the surface. Oakes was seen on several occasions telling his son-in-law exactly what he thought of him, although his daughter had no complaints regarding her marriage and was so upset by her mother and father's attitude towards Freddie that she eventually gave up and stopped communicating with them, in the hope that they would one day accept him.

The accused had been assigned defence barrister Godfrey Higgs as the leader of his team, despite the fact that Marigny had previously asked the police to provide him with his own lawyer, the much revered barrister, Sir Alfred Adderley; it would appear that the police did not fulfil this request.

The jury was chosen, as always at random, and were all men, many of them working-class Bahamians. Prior to the testimonies being given, the jury were escorted to the murder scene to view the location, this being the home of Sir Harry Oakes in Westbourne, Nassau.

One of the first testimonies given to the jury was that from Sir Harold Christie, who had been born on the island of Nassau and had lived there all of his life. He was a self-made man, who had worked hard selling property on the island, and was extremely successful. He asked his employers if rather than pay his commission in cash, they would pay him in plots of land instead. They agreed, and as time passed Christie managed to amass quite a valuable portfolio of land. He used the profit from this land to buy larger, more sought-after properties and building plots.

He became extremely wealthy and as the island began to attract more rich and famous residents, Christie was usually the person who found properties and sold them. In this way he was profiting both financially and personally by his work, for he became good friends with the most successful and wealthy residents on the island.

When Oakes arrived on the island it was Christie who was his real estate agent. In fact Oakes came close to buying almost half of all the properties on the island, and, having much in common, the two men became good friends.

Christie explained to the court that as he and the victim were good friends it was common for them to spend time at one another's home. On the last evening of his life, Oakes had invited Christie and two guests to his home for dinner. These guests were Oakes's neighbours, Mr Charles Hubbard and Mrs Dulcibelle; also joining the group for drinks until around 7 p.m. were Christie's niece and her friend. After enjoying an evening meal together the four friends played chequers until around 11 p.m., when Mr Hubbard and Mrs Dulcibelle made their way home. Shortly afterwards, Christie told the court, he and Oakes chatted for a while before Oakes retired to his bedroom to finish reading the daily newspapers. At around 11.30 p.m. Christie bade him goodnight and made his way to the guest room to also catch up on some reading before switching off the light and sleeping.

During the night Christie remembered waking briefly on two occasions; the first time was because he had been bitten by a mosquito and the second time due to the noise created by a storm outdoors. Christie stated that each time he had woken, it was only briefly, probably only for a matter of a few minutes, and during this time he heard nothing unusual inside the house.

The following morning Christie recalled eating breakfast alone, and thought that Oakes must have been taking the opportunity to sleep in. He decided to go and waken his friend, and called him from outside the bedroom, but did not get a reply. He then knocked on the door and entered the room.

He first noticed that part of the bed appeared to be blackened and burnt, while a portion of the mosquito net which hung over the bed was similarly burnt. He rushed over to his friend to find that he too was burnt and had blood on the left-hand side of his face.

Unaware at this stage that Oakes was dead, he tried to get him to take a drink of water from a glass which was on his bedside table. He then went to the bathroom for a towel and used the water to try and remove some of the blood from Oakes's face. He was now certain that his friend was beyond help and called for assistance by going to the porch window in the bedroom and shouting for the servants to come, unaware at the time that it was the servants' day off. When nobody came to his aid, he went downstairs to call for help on the telephone.

Godfrey Higgs now had his opportunity to question the witness. He started out by asking why Christie had decided to park his car so far away from the Oakes property, to which Christie responded that he was wishing to conserve petrol owing to the shortage because of the war. Higgs was not satisfied and stated that he had a witness who had seen Christie as a passenger in another person's vehicle that night. Higgs then called for the Superintendent of the Bahamas Police Force, Captain Edward DeWitt Sears, to take the stand. He confirmed that he had seen Christie in a station wagon travelling from Marlborough Street in Nassau, and understood that the car had come from the harbour area at a little after midnight. Christie strenuously denied having vacated the property that evening, although this could not be corroborated by the night security guard as he had rather suspiciously drowned before the case came to court.

The jury were not informed that a speedboat had been seen in the harbour that evening and that two unknown men were observed leaving the boat and getting into a nearby parked car.

The doctor who had examined Oakes's body not long after it had been discovered was called to give evidence. Dr Hugh Quackenbush told the courtroom that when he arrived in the victims' bedroom part of the mattress was still smouldering, so the murder had been extremely recent. He pointed out that Oakes had wounds on the left-hand side of his head, and that he had been severely burnt. He described several blisters around the victim's body, from his feet to his neck, and in his considered opinion, they had been sustained before he had died. He was unable to provide an explanation as to what had caused these blisters, but did indicate that he believed that Oakes had died in the early hours of the morning of 8 July – between 2 a.m. and 5 a.m.

The post-mortem had been carried out by Dr Laurence Fitzmaurice and he came to court to testify, agreeing with the findings of Dr Quackenbush, but also offering a more detailed description of the injuries he had examined on the body. He confirmed that Oakes had suffered a fractured skull, and suggested that he had been hit about the head with a heavy, blunt instrument. He described the instrument as having a "well-defined edge" and that the wounds this inflicted were of a triangular shape around two inches in diameter. The wounds, as Dr Quackenbush had already testified, were on the left-hand side of the face, above the ear.

Several character witnesses were questioned in court, each referring to the poor relationship between Freddie and Harry Oakes. Many were of the opinion that Oakes was unhappy with his daughter's choice of husband and considered that she could have done much better for herself.

The first police officer to speak with the defendant after the murder was Police Constable Wendell Parker of the Bahamas Police Department. He explained in court that the defendant had arrived at the police station early that morning, at around 7.30 a.m., to have his car checked over, as it had recently been converted into a truck. The constable described Freddie as agitated and distressed, and considered it unusual to have somebody arrive at the police station at such an early hour.

Other members of the police force were in court to give their statements, one of the more interesting being given by Captain James Barker, who had been assigned the case along with Captain Edward Melchen; both had been brought in from Miami for this purpose. The day after the murder he had managed to locate the accused's fingerprints in Oakes's bedroom, on a Chinese screen which was close to the bed. This discovery was directly related to the arrest of the accused, which was the following day.

The manner in which Barker had obtained the fingerprints

was rather unusual – he had actually lifted the prints from the screen using a piece of rubber, thereby leaving no evidence behind on the screen. Usual police procedure for obtaining fingerprints was quite straightforward – firstly the print was dusted with a very fine black powder to make it much more obvious and easy to see. Secondly, it was photographed with a high-resolution camera whilst still in situ, to prove where the print was discovered. Lastly the print was lifted from the scene using a form of Scotch tape, which was then bagged and labelled as crime scene evidence.

When the actual screen was brought into the courtroom as evidence, Captain Barker was unable to identify where he had located the fingerprints. Strangely, his colleague Captain Melchen testified that he had not been told of the positive identification of the fingerprints until several days afterwards, by which time Freddie was already in police custody. When Higgs pushed Barker on this point he was unable to give a reasonable answer, which must have partially destroyed his testimony to the members of the jury. Higgs pointed out that in his opinion the dubious fingerprints could have been lifted from Freddie whilst in police custody, which explained the unusual manner in which they were collected.

Other anomalies came to light regarding Barker's investigation of the crime scene. Areas which should have been dusted for fingerprints were simply overlooked, including the foot of Oakes's bed. When he was asked if all the fingerprints of any visitors to the room had been taken he confirmed that this had been done, but later in his statement he admitted this had not in fact occurred.

Melchen made a further mistake when he was in the witness stand, telling the court that he had interviewed the defendant on the afternoon of 8 July, between 3 p.m. and 4 p.m. But Lieutenant Douglas of the Bahamas Police Department had made out a report at the time which disagreed and stated that the accused had left his home as early as 1.30 p.m. Higgs concluded that the case had been badly handled and recorded from start to finish.

When the defendant was called to the stand he gave a thorough testimony of the events which had occurred, and started by describing the problems he had encountered with Nancy Oakes's parents. He had not done anything to antagonize the Oakes, but they simply could not get along with him. He and Nancy had decided that they would never accept their son-in-law to be a good match for their eldest child.

Just like his father-in-law, on the evening of 7 July Freddie was entertaining friends at his home. They had enjoyed a pleasant evening together and the majority had departed at midnight: at a little after 1.00 a.m. Freddie had driven his last guest home. Also in his house that night were two others, Freddie's good friend Georges and his girlfriend, who were in a guest bedroom. By 1.45 a.m. Freddie had returned from his trip and made his way to his own bedroom at around 2 a.m. He was awoken briefly an hour later by Georges' cat; he also heard Georges leaving the house to take his girlfriend home and was aware that he had returned only a quarter of an hour later. When he came back into the house Freddie called for Georges to come and remove his cat from his bedroom, which he promptly did. Freddie only awoke once again that night, to take an indigestion remedy, and soon resumed his sleep.

He awoke early in the morning and at 10.30 a.m. his friend Mr Anderson called at his house to tell him of the death of Harry Oakes. The three shocked men made their way to Oakes's house; when they arrived they were mystified to discover that several of Oakes's neighbours were wandering around what was a crime scene. They commented on how bizarre it was, and felt sure that this was an unusual way to conduct a criminal investigation. Freddie then went home and contacted his wife by telegram before being taken by Anderson to his house for lunch, where they talked about the events of the morning.

After lunch Freddie returned to Oakes's house and was briefly questioned by the two leading police officers, Barker and Melchen. He told the court that his hands were inspected and that the officers noted that he had several singed hairs; he explained that these were the result of cooking on a gas stove. Singed hairs were also noted in his beard, which

Freddie said he had because he smoked the occasional cigar.
The two policemen and Lieutenant Douglas took Freddie
home as they wanted to examine the clothes which he had
been wearing the previous evening. He showed them the
clothing which he had in his linen basket, but could not
remember which shirt he had worn the day before; the men
looked through the clothing, but found nothing of interest.
When Barker and Melchen left the property, Douglas stayed
as Freddie had requested him to do so.

Georges was called to give his testimony to the court;
whilst being cross-examined by the prosecuting attorney,
Adderley, he repeated the account of events which had
previously been given by the accused. He even remembered
that he had been into Freddie's bedroom to retrieve his cat at
around 3 a.m. Adderley listened to the testimony before
picking up a piece of paper and reading it out loud to the
courtroom; it was a transcript of Georges' statement to the
police in which he quite clearly says that he did not see the
accused from 11 p.m. on 7 July until 10 a.m. on the 8th. This
was to prove a very critical piece of evidence, which could
well have ended Freddie's hopes of a positive verdict.

Freddie's defence counsel, Ernest Callender, immediately
took the opportunity to cross-examine Georges, and quickly
pointed out that the two men did not actually see one another
late on the night of 7 July until early the following morning,
but did talk to one another through Freddie's door. This
corroborated with Freddie's version of events, and proved
that he was at his home at that time.

The last testimony was given by the accused's wife, Nancy
de Marigny. She confirmed her husband's opinion of her
parents, namely that they did not approve of him and were
not openly friendly towards him. She went on to comment
that she had decided that she would not speak to them until
they showed her husband the respect which he deserved. She
also told the court that the two leading police officers in the
case had informed her that they had located her husband's
fingerprints on the Chinese screen in her father's bedroom.

The defence and the prosecution had their chance to sum
up the case before the court and the Judge asked the jury to

take their time in coming to their verdict. Within two hours the jury of 12 men returned to the court to give their verdict, finding the defendant not guilty of the murder of Sir Harry Oakes.

The news was well received by the hundreds of locals who had been gathered outside the courtroom awaiting the verdict. There were also dozens of newspaper reporters who were waiting with bated breath, ready to write their story for the next edition of their paper. The news travelled quickly and was soon spread, quite literally, around the world. The reason for the massive worldwide interest in the case was not only because the victim had the title of "Sir" but also because of the powerful and influential people with whom he mixed.

Sir Harry Oakes had become one of the leading figures on Nassau and was a powerful decision maker when it came to changes on the island, as he owned most of it. He was a self made man, and although his parents enjoyed a comfortable lifestyle, this was not good enough for their determined son who was adamant that he would make his own fortune.

He was born, the middle of five children, to his parents, William Pitt Oakes and Edith, on 23 December 1874. The first decade of his life was spent in Sangerville, Maine where the Oakes children attended local school. William and Edith had high hopes for their offspring and decided that as their education was paramount they would uproot the family to Foxcroft, also in Maine, because they considered that the education they would receive there would be far superior. The children were enrolled at the well-regarded Foxcroft Academy, where it has to be said, they all did remarkably well.

Harry went on to continue his education at Bowdoin College in Brunswick, Maine and later moved on to specialize in medicine at Syracuse Medical School. He stayed on his course for over two years, but a lifelong obsession with the search for gold was just too strong to ignore and he ditched his medical studies to follow his dream.

To give his parents credit, they supported their 23-year-old son in his wishes, although this must have been difficult to come to terms with as they had set so much store by giving him a good education and thorough training in an expert field. Nevertheless, they believed in their son and supported his decision; they also helped pay for his trips to far distant lands. By 1899 Oakes had arrived in the Klondike, but sadly he was out of luck as the "gold rush" was all but over. He had now been on his quest for three years, and although he had been largely unsuccessful, he was still not ready to throw the towel in. He was a determined man who had set himself a goal and was not prepared to admit defeat.

He had to fall back on his medical training to supplement his income, as by this stage he was struggling with his finances. He worked in a makeshift medical centre most of the time treating would-be gold hunters with bad cases of frostbite. Later that year he had the unfortunate experience of becoming a prisoner of the Russians after being shipwrecked near the Alaskan coastline, although he was held only briefly and subsequently released.

His gold quest continued, taking him as far afield as Australia and then on to New Zealand, before he tried California, still not ready to admit defeat. His body had been through the most extreme weather conditions, almost freezing to death in Alaska, and latterly suffering heat stroke in California, but Oakes had an iron will and would not be put off his mission.

Almost 15 years since he had set out to claim his fortune Oakes was still searching, having travelled the world following the well-publicized gold strikes. In 1911 yet another one was declared in Canada, so the resolute Oakes boarded a train and made his way there. On arriving his money was so depleted that he set about finding the cheapest lodgings available, these coming in the form of a boarding house run by Roza Brown, a formidable character who had a dislike of gold prospectors.

She was, however, quite taken with Oakes, as she recognized that he was different from the usual man hell bent on finding gold. She believed he was mentally superior to the others and admired the fact that he was hard working and respectable. As she had lived in the area all her life she was familiar with the geography of the area, and spent time with Oakes discussing where she considered would be a good area to look for the elusive gold.

These discussions were to prove very worthwhile and after studying maps of the area he convinced a group of four brothers, also prospectors, to join him in his search on the outskirts of Kirkland Lake in Ontario. The Tough brothers and Oakes made an agreement that if they were successful in locating gold they would split any money, equally, five ways.

Diligence paid off and the group enjoyed their first success. With the profits from their initial strike they went on to lay claim to other areas around Kirkland Lake. Inevitably, the happy alliance was to be destroyed as there were huge quarrels regarding the distribution of the shares, eventually Oakes was unable to work with the brothers any longer and sold them his share of the Tough Oakes mines. Not put off by mining, he decided that he would profit better under his own steam. With his money from the sale of his shares he staked a claim in an area of land further down Kirkland Lake, with financial support from his mother.

This was to be the best decision in Oakes's life as he struck gold, and this time much more than he had located with the Tough brothers. He was fast becoming a very wealthy man, and at one time Oakes's Lake Shore Mines was earning its owner over $50,000 a day. He soon became Canada's most wealthy man and he shared his success with friends and family who had supported him throughout the past 20 years.

He decided that it was time to set up house as he was now financially secure, in the most fitting place, overlooking his empire at Lake Shore Mines. For almost four years, until 1923, Oakes lived a luxurious lifestyle in his wonderful, opulent chateau. He had his own golf course built on his grounds and enjoyed entertaining his friends, comfortable in the knowledge that his gold mines were still providing a large income. But the pioneer in Oakes could not be tamed for ever, and he was soon itching to venture out and broaden his horizons, deciding that a round the world trip would satisfy his lust for excitement and new experiences. It was during this trip that he was introduced to a young Australian woman called Eunice MacIntyre who was heading for England. By now the 48-year-old millionaire was twice her age, but she was attracted to him all the same, although they made an unlikely match – Oakes was short in stature and Eunice was tall and slim.

The pair were infatuated with one another and were soon engaged; they made their way to Eunice's family home in Sydney, Australia and were soon married. On arriving back in Canada, both Oakes and his new wife applied to become Canadian citizens, which they were soon granted, and decided that they would set up home together at Oakes's home at Kirkland Lake. They initially started out married life living in his chateau, but as their family started to grow Oakes arranged to have another, larger house built to accommodate them. They were blessed with five children altogether, the eldest being a daughter whom they named Nancy, followed by a son they called Sydney (after Eunice's home town), next came William Pitt (after Harry's father), then a second daughter, Shirley, and lastly Eunice gave birth to another son, Harry P. Oakes (obviously after his father).

The family moved to the small Bahaman island of Nassau at the end of the 1930s, and Oakes changed his nationality to Bahamian, thus escaping the quickly soaring Canadian taxes. He wasted no time after arriving on the island and started to make it his own, quite literally. He was introduced to Harold Christie, a real estate agent with very good contacts, and with his assistance Oakes bought up virtually half the island to create his new empire. He installed a much-needed airport on the island and from there he ran his own airline company. He had a luxurious hotel complex built, complete with a prestigious beachside golf course, attracting many of the rich and famous to the previously discreet and somewhat overlooked holiday destination.

His arrival brought work for the relatively untapped work force, and the island fast became an upmarket resort. Oakes ploughed much of his profits back into the island's economy, providing new hospital facilities and through donations to the Governor of the island, money was spent across a broad spectrum of the island's needs. This work did not go unnoticed and his efforts were recognized by the King of England in 1939 when Harry Oakes was knighted and became Sir Harry Oakes.

The island was not without its upper echelon of society. It was also the home of the former king of England Edward VIII, who had given up the throne to marry the American divorcee, Wallis Simpson. Having given up the title of the King of England he was granted the new title of Duke of Windsor by the new king, his brother King George VI. They moved to the island during the Second World War and Edward became the first royal Governor and commander-in-chief of the Bahamas.

Wallis Simpson did not acclimatize well to the heat on the tropical island and complained that their social life was severely hampered by living on such a remote island. She was also unhappy with the accommodation which the British government had provided for them, and requested the house be renovated, but because of the war her request was declined as all available funds were needed to support the war effort.

Her lifestyle was curbed only slightly and the couple were to host many luxurious dinner parties, with high-profile, wealthy guests. They often escaped their "exile" by taking extended holidays in friends' homes throughout the United States and Mexico.

The Duke had become close friends with the wealthy inhabitants of the island, one of his shadier acquaintances being Axel Werner-Gren, who was believed to be part Swedish, but had been educated in Berlin, Germany. When he was grown up he decided to try and make his fortune in New York, where he took a job with a Swedish light bulb manufacturer and discovered that he was a natural-born salesman. He prospered and used his commission to buy shares in the company, which proved fortuitous as the company wealth rocketed when it gained the contract for the Panama Canal. He soon became the primary shareholder for the company and an extremely wealthy man, reinvesting some of his fortune to set up his own company which sold household electrical appliances.

In 1939, Werner-Gren, along with his wife and children, set sail on their new yacht (formerly owned by Howard Hughes) to the Bahamas. They loved the islands and decided to set up home on the beautiful island of Nassau. It was not long before the Werner-Grens were invited to one of the prestigious parties hosted by Edward and Mrs Simpson and were also introduced to other prominent citizens of the island, including Sir Harry Oakes and the now Sir Harold Christie. Werner-Gren proved to be a very popular guest at the many evening receptions, and soon settled down to life on this unusual island.

It came to light, over time, that Werner-Gren had other influential acquaintances. These included some rather more unsavoury characters such as Hermann Goering, the Nazi politician and close supporter of Adolf Hitler, who was head of the German air force in the Second World War. He had also some form of "friendship" with Benito Mussolini, the dictator of Italy, who had founded the Fascist party in 1919 and had taken Italy into the war in support of Adolf Hitler. And to add to his impressive, if rather dubious list of acquaintances there was General Maximo Camacho, the Mexican pro-Fascist.

None of this information was lost on the United States and British governments and the intelligence services were alerted. It was suspected that the island's newest inhabitant could well be a spy, so his movements were closely monitored. On investigation it came to light that Werner-Gren had amassed a small fortune and it was suspected that he intended to use this money to try and gain control of the Mexican economy. Whilst he was holidaying in Mexico, his bank accounts were frozen, he was blacklisted and forced to stay in Mexico pending the result of the investigation. It was also discovered during this time that other prominent inhabitants of the island of Nassau were customers at the same bank including the Duke of Windsor, Sir Harry Oakes and Sir Harold Christie.

Unlike Oakes, Werner-Gren and the Duke of Windsor, Harold Christie had made his fortune on the island and was keen to see the economy further boosted by helping create a year-round holiday resort. He had an American contact called Frank Marshall who represented a group of wealthy American businessmen who were also keen to promote the island of Nassau. Their aim was to open casinos on the island, but Christie was well aware that the laws on the island would prohibit these plans. Marshall suggested that as Christie had all the right connections he could help their plans come to fruition, but Christie was not convinced he would be able to talk Oakes and the Duke of Windsor into changing the island's laws.

His plans were further hampered when he became aware that the main investors would be the heads of the Mafia, Charles Luciano and Meyer Lansky. This information worried Christie, so he arranged a meeting with Oakes and the Duke, and alerted them of his findings; meanwhile Marshall was unaware of the meeting and was getting impatient waiting for Christie to get things moving. He therefore arranged a meeting with the island's foremost citizens and was extremely disappointed when he was told that his wishes would not be granted. Marshall was not a man who took defeat well, and was renowned for reaping his revenge.

As Freddie had been found not guilty of the murder of his father-in-law, one question remained unanswered – if Freddie was innocent then who was the guilty party? After the court case had been concluded, many theories were put forward as to who the killer was. Initially, Christie was suspected as he was the last person to have seen Oakes alive and was in the house with him on the evening of the murder. But what would be his motive? Had he reconsidered the offer put to him by Marshall and decided that it was simply too good an opportunity to miss out on? It was possible that he had tried again to convince Oakes to change his mind and allow the law to be altered to allow gambling on the island. But Oakes was notorious for sticking to his guns – could he have given Christie a point-blank no and enraged him to the point of murder? Or might Christie have enlisted a third party to murder Oakes, thus clearing his own name of the crime?

The Duke and Axel Werner-Gren also came under suspicion, as between them they could well have considered that

Oakes knew too much about their private lives, things that they would definitely want to keep quiet – although it has to be said, it is very unlikely that this was the explanation for Sir Harry Oakes's death. It is more likely that it stemmed from the rebuff of Marshall, the go-between for Charles Luciano and Meyer Lansky. Marshall had much more to lose from Oakes's unwillingness to comply with his request. Add to that his dubious contacts, he would easily have arranged a way for Oakes to be eliminated for scuppering his plans to take financial control of the island. Oakes's murder was callous – he had been beaten about the head before having petrol poured over him and had apparently been burnt alive – and would be highly unlikely to be the actions of a family member, however distant.

The mystery surrounding the death of Sir Harry Oakes still remains an enigma over 60 years after his death.

Media Circus

The Murder of Nicole Brown-Simpson and Ron Goldman

America's TV screens told a clear and compelling story. Not since the broadcast of US astronauts landing on the moon in 1969 had so many of the American public been focused on one amazing event. A police car chase in Los Angeles is hardly unique, but one involving one of America's most respected sporting heroes certainly is. Playing live for all to see was O. J. Simpson, concealed in the back seat of a Ford Bronco pick-up truck, driven by his friend and sporting colleague A. C. Cowling, being pursued down the westbound 405 Los Angeles freeway by a swarm of LA police vehicles.

The pursuit looked more like a presidential motorcade, the Bronco driving moderately fast in the centre lane, with police vehicles fanned out across the freeway behind it. Everyone was calm and no one wanted to escalate the proceedings into a full-blown high-speed chase. Come what may the police were intent on arresting Simpson for jumping bail whilst under investigation for the murder of his ex-wife, Nicole Brown-Simpson and her friend Ron Goldman.

Helicopters packed with television crews from practically all of the TV networks, crowded the skies as cameramen leaned out trying to get a shot of the fleeing American football star. As the Bronco pulled off the freeway and headed north to Simpson's Rockingham estate, the streets were clear of other vehicles, but the pavements thronged with members of the public waving and cheering, whilst the police maintained a low-key pursuit.

Eventually the Bronco pulled into the driveway of Simpson's prestigious estate in the Brentwood district, and before the engine had been switched off police officers moved in to conclude the arrest.

The ensuing trial would run for a record nine months and cost the American taxpayer a staggering 20 million dollars; it would spawn 80 books and be the subject of numerous TV documentaries. It kept the chat show circuit and the gossip columns busy with spicy titbits for a year, and in what would be the biggest televisual extravaganza the US had ever seen, beating the moon landing, the arrival of the Beatles and the assassination of President Kennedy, the court case of Simpson would on occasions capture a massive 92 per cent of the American TV viewing public.

O.J. Simpson was a true American hero, a 1968 Heismann Trophy winner as a running back for the LA Lakers, who had gone into acting as well as promoting various brands on television. Married to a beautiful young wife, Nicole Brown-Simpson, with whom he had two children, he was a classic example of the American Dream. But for Simpson the dream had turned into a nightmare when the body of his ex-wife and her friend, Ron Goldman, were found butchered at her Bundy Avenue address just a few blocks from the home she had once shared with Simpson. To many people the prime suspect was Simpson himself.

Simpson and Nicole had split up a while before and despite several reconciliations had finally decided to go their separate ways. They had endured a stormy past which had seen the police being called on a number of occasions to quell scenes of domestic disturbances, which on occasions saw Nicole on the receiving end of Simpson's fierce temper.

Simpson was known to be possessive where Nicole was concerned, and even though he could have his pick of beautiful ladies he was still concerned about the social life his wife was enjoying, and had seen off many would-be suitors.

After their initial split Nicole moved to a two-storey town house at 325 South Gretna Green, letting the spare room to her friend Brian "Kato" Kaelin. On 25 October 1993, during one of the periods when they were attempting a slow reconciliation, Simpson discovered a photograph album containing pictures of Nicole's previous boyfriends. Enraged he drove round to Nicole's house to confront her. Kaelin and Nicole were both downstairs when Simpson kicked the French doors open and stormed into the living room. He ranted for a while, becoming more and more agitated, at which point Nicole called 911 and asked for police assistance. The operator asked her a number of questions to establish the level of danger she thought she was in. During this period, when the call was being recorded, the operator could clearly hear Simpson remonstrating in the background and consequently dispatched the police. On arrival they ordered Simpson off the property, and he left quietly, agreeing to rectify the damage he had caused to the property.

In a previous incident that occurred during New Year 1989, Simpson beat Nicole quite severely, resulting in a judicial notice. He was ordered to undergo therapy by the courts but for Nicole it was the final straw – he had gone too far, repented too little and Nicole finally filed for divorce during 1992.

There had been many reports of their marital rifts and Simpson's propensity for spousal abuse. All of this damning detail would become the background to the case that followed. In addition to the evidence, he had a motive in that he was still jealous of his wife's liaisons and appeared to have a history of violence towards her. The situation looked as bad as it could get for Simpson.

However there were events which seemed to contradict this picture of Simpson as a brutal wife beater, often on the verge of anger. Nicole had become friendly with Keith Zlomwitch who she and Simpson had known previously in Colorado. When Zlomwitch opened a new restaurant in Los Angeles, called Mezzaluna, he and Nicole renewed their friendship and during another period of separation from Simpson she entertained Zlomwitch at her house. On one of these occasions her husband visited the property and could plainly see, through opened curtains, Nicole and Zlomwitch engaged in oral sex. Rather than burst in, he chose instead to call on Zlomwitch and tell him he did not think such activity was appropriate given that his children were upstairs at the time. Zlomwitch got the message and although he and Nicole continued to be friends the romantic involvement ceased.

The details of what happened next are complex, though the prosecution painted a detailed picture and provided a range of evidence to back up their claims, using Simpson's previous domestic disruptions as further evidence of a man who could be pushed over the edge and who might well have killed the mother of his children and Ron Goldman. The prosecution claimed the events that followed and the time lines to be a close representation of the situation prior to, during and after the crimes had been committed, putting Simpson firmly in the frame.

During the week prior to the murders, Simpson had spent time in Buffalo, New York, attending various functions. He was planning to return to Los Angeles that weekend to attend a dance recital by his daughter Sydney, and later that evening he was due to fly to Chicago, departing LA at 11.45 p.m. In line with these plans he had booked a limousine to collect him from his Rockingham address at 10.45 p.m. The whole family would be there to watch Sydney in her dance recital but Simpson had been told by Nicole that he would not be welcome to sit with them in the auditorium. As Nicole's family arrived, they sat directly in front of the stage, while Simpson sat off to one side. A member of the public who had videoed the proceedings caught Simpson on film chatting cordially to Nicole's mother, while smiling and being attentive to his children.

Prior to the discord in the Simpson household, Simpson had always maintained a good relationship with Nicole's mother and family. Nicole had booked a table at the Mezzaluna where she intended to take the children and family for a meal afterwards. Again, Simpson was not invited so he returned home. At this stage Brian "Kato" Kaelin was staying in the guest quarters at Simpson's house, an arrangement he had offered to Kaelin after he thought it unseemly for him to be staying with Nicole whilst he was attempting a reconciliation. At around 2.30 p.m. on that Sunday, Simpson remarked to Kaelin that his relationship with Nicole was now at an end. He was aware that he was not invited to sit with his family during the recital or indeed take tea with them afterwards, and Kaelin noted Simpson's irritation at this gesture of bad will. Nicole and her group of about nine went on to the restaurant, arriving around 6.30 p.m. and enjoyed the proceedings for the next couple of hours, leaving at around 8.30 p.m.

Leaving the restaurant Nicole took the children to a nearby ice cream parlour and bought them tubs of ice cream, some of which would later be found at the crime scene.

At about 9.45 p.m. Nicole's mother phoned to say she had left her spectacles in the restaurant and asked if Nicole would collect them. Nicole phoned the restaurant who had by then found the glasses outside on the pavement, so she asked to speak to Ron Goldman who was working there that night. Goldman said he would call round later with the glasses, after which he was intending to go on to a venue called the Marina with some friends.

At home Nicole put the children to bed and prepared a bath, whilst quickly tidying up downstairs in preparation to receive Ron Goldman. Back at Simpson's Rockingham estate, between 6.30 p.m. and 7 p.m. just after the end of the NBA play-offs between the Houston Rockets and the New York Knicks Kaelin had a brief chat with Simpson, who was still not happy at the way the day out with his children had been handled. Leaving Simpson simmering he went to his quarters for a relaxing soak in the jacuzzi; he then returned to the main house and once again bumped into Simpson who was heading out for a McDonald's hamburger. Kaelin asked if he could tag along, and they both set off in Simpson's Bentley. They arrived at the drive-through McDonald's at around 9.25 p.m., collected their food and continued the journey back to the house. Simpson ate his hamburger on the way, while Kaelin decided to eat his when he got home. Arriving back, Simpson appeared tired, retiring to his private quarters to relax, while Kaelin returned to his rooms to eat his food, calling his friend Rachel Ferrara at around 9.45

p.m. Meanwhile Ron Goldman was about to leave the Mezzaluna with Nicole's mother's glasses – the time, 9.50 p.m.

The details up to this point are accurate and were corroborated by phone records and eyewitness testimony. The next part was largely speculation on the part of the prosecution, supported by some key witness testimony and information provided by Kaelin and the limousine driver.

It was alleged by the prosecution that instead of retiring to his bedroom to rest, Simpson quickly jumped into his Ford Bronco and drove over to Nicole's Bundy address, setting off at around 9.55 p.m., just five minutes after Ron Goldman had left the Mezzaluna restaurant. It was speculated that Simpson arrived at the Bundy address and approached the house at around 10 p.m. Strangely, Simpson then waited and according to his phone records made a mobile call to a model with whom he had previously had a liaison, Paula Barbiera, at 10.04 p.m., which would be a strange thing to do for someone on the brink of committing a particularly violent and bloody murder. Simpson, however, did not get through to Paula, instead leaving a message. It was then suggested that he approached the Bundy address through the main gate, the lock of which had been suspiciously broken in the days prior to the murders. Hearing a knock at the door, Nicole answered, expecting to find Ron Goldman on the doorstep, but instead found Simpson there. It was alleged that Simpson pulled Nicole out of the door and into the outer porch area to the place where she was finally found, stabbed and with her throat slashed. With blood everywhere and no doubt panicking, Simpson was planning to exit the murder scene when Ron Goldman showed up to return the glasses. Unluckily, Goldman would have literally bumped into the murderer on the path, where he too was knifed a number of times and left for dead in a pool of blood. It was then suggested that Simpson once again jumped into the Bronco and headed home.

As the killer sped away, a neighbour of Nicole's reported that he heard the continuous barking of a dog. It was this factor and the results of the post-mortem that suggested the murders happened at around 10.10 p.m., just six minutes after Simpson made the call to Paula Barbiera. Leaving a scene of carnage behind him it was alleged that Simpson then headed home in time for his trip to Chicago.

Back at the Rockingham estate, Simpson's limousine driver, Allan Park, had arrived at 10.25 p.m. and decided to wait at the gate as he was a little early. At around 10.40 p.m. he rang the buzzer for the main house but received no reply. Inside the house, Kaelin, who was on the phone, heard three heavy thumping noises coming from outside. Terminating his call at 10.41 p.m. he headed outside to investigate the noise. Unable to immediately trace its origin, but seeing the limousine parked on the driveway, he continued to walk around the edge of the house looking for the source of the noise. At 10.50 p.m., Park called his boss to ask what he should do and was told to continue waiting. At around 10.56 p.m., Park saw the shadowy figure of a 200lb, 6-foot-tall black person cross the driveway and enter the house. At the same time he noticed Kaelin heading towards him with a flashlight. Kaelin asked Park if Simpson had overslept and also if he had heard the strange bangs, now wondering if it had been a weak earthquake. A few moments later Park once again buzzed the main house; this time the intercom was answered and the person said he would be out shortly. At around 11.01 p.m. the house lights were switched on and Simpson emerged from the house and started putting his travel bags onto the porch.

Back at Bundy, Nicole's neighbour, Louis Karpf, was now concerned about the noise from the dog and decided to go out for a quick look. At 10.55 p.m. he found Nicole's Akita dog running around the street barking. On closer inspection the dog's paws looked to be covered in blood but he could not see any wound on the animal. Whilst trying to calm the dog down, which was by now in an extremely agitated state, Karpf came across another neighbour, Steven Schwab, who was out walking his dog. They agreed that Steven should take the dog to his neighbour, Sukra Boztepe, who would be able to look after him. When the dog was at Boztepe's house it continued to act in such a distressed way that Bozetepe decided to take it out for a walk and see if it could find its own home. Now 12.10 a.m. on Monday, 13 June, Boztepe followed the dog around to Nicole's house. As they approached the gate Boztepe could see the obvious shape of a woman's body lying by the porch, a river of blood having run down the path to the pavement. Running to another neighbour Boztepe raised the alarm to the police at 12.15 a.m.

Back at Simpson's estate Kaelin and Parks helped load Simpson's luggage into the limousine, the time 11.15 p.m. They arrived at LAX at 11.35 p.m. where Simpson was fast tracked through the terminus, his plane departing the airport just ten minutes later at 11.45 p.m. He finally checked into the O'Hare Plaza Hotel at 4.15 a.m. These events and their timeline were examined carefully by the prosecution case, however, to further add weight to the supposition, another fact emerged that could be seen to further implicate Simpson. A member of the public claimed to have seen Simpson's white Ford Bronco driving without lights and a little erratically at around 10.20 p.m. on the road leading towards his home.

The police arrived on the scene and discovered the bodies of Nicole and Ron Goldman in pools of blood. Not wanting to disturb the murder scene they called for appropriate backup and then started looking around the general area. It was subsequently determined that Nicole had suffered a number of stab wounds and one fatal one across the throat, while Goldman had suffered four separate stab wounds plus one directly into the side of the neck, which was presumed to be the final cause of death. Not far from the scene where the bodies lay the policemen found a glove covered in blood and bloody footprints leading away from the scene.

By 5 a.m. the following morning LA police detectives were at Simpson's Rockingham address. They eventually climbed over the wall and woke those staying there, including Simpson's daughter Arnelle from a previous marriage. Members of the family were told of the murders and it was now that Simpson was traced to Chicago, where he was informed of the murders and instructed to return to LA, being met at the airport by the police. Simpson was immediately taken into custody, but was released on bail, pending the outcome of the police investigation. His children were temporarily housed with a family member and the police began to seal off the two addresses ready to begin an exhaustive search and analysis of both sites.

By now the media had caught wind of the events which had occurred at the Bundy address and had begun congregating at both residences. Worse, they had already started to release snippets of information regarding the stormy past of Nicole and Simpson; they also made it abundantly clear that they believed the police suspected Simpson of carrying out the murders. The media circus that began shortly after daybreak on Monday, 13 June would in due course dog the trial, enrage the judge and to some extent prejudice the proceedings.

The car chase that followed Simpson's bail violation heralded the start of a series of media-driven events which served to add further weight to the idea that Simpson was guilty. If he wasn't guilty why had he gone on the run? Why had he not turned himself over to the police for the sake of his children, who had surely endured enough? The police made it clear from the outset that he was in the frame for the murder and the media too had started down the same path, as they scrambled to portray the life of Simpson and Nicole. They ran story after story on the couple, focusing on their matrimonial troubles which had seen the police called on more than one occasion.

On arrival at the house gates Simpson could have been forgiven for thinking he had travelled back in time to the days when he was a football hero – the throng of media surrounding his property was immense, and every spare inch of ground had a television crew recording details of his arrival under police guard. The crime scene at Bundy was also crammed with reporters and film crews, ready to feed a constant stream of information to the American public. The TV crews fought for the best positions and the best angles on any story they could find. As the police fought a constant battle to protect the crime scene, this behaviour and lack of respect for the judicial process would spill over into the court case, as the presiding judge dealt with the ever-present spectre of leaked information.

After the police had sealed the respective properties a meticulous search was commenced and the details linking Simpson to the murders began to emerge. Several witnesses came forward to present further evidence, including one who remembered Simpson buying a simulated bone-handled knife, the characteristics of which matched those of the murder weapon, a 6-inch-long blade with a three-quarter-inch width.

The police, however, never found the knife during their searches, although the defence managed to find Simpson's knife in a bathroom cabinet.

Simpson had bought the manually locking knife from Ross Cutlery in downtown LA, where he had been shooting a scene for the film *Frogmen* in the days before the murder. The defence were later to present it as a keynote defence point, as analysis had shown that it had no traces of blood on it. However these points were merely circumstantial when compared to the actual evidence found.

A left-hand glove, matted with blood, was found close to the bodies and the matching right one was found behind Simpson's garage. The police also found a blue knitted cap on the grass leading away from the scene which contained hairs matching Simpson's. Bloody footprints were found round the back of the Bundy condo as were five droplets of blood that were shown to be of Simpson's type, giving a 1 in 200 chance of them belonging to anyone else.

It was noted by the police that Simpson had a cut on his middle finger, which he explained he had done on his mobile handset, a point later proven not to be true. Socks taken from Simpson's home were subjected to serological analysis and were shown to have Nicole's blood type on them; there was also much bloodstaining on Simpson's Ford Bronco and analysis again showed this to be his own and Nicole's blood type. Much later, after the advent of DNA testing, further analysis would show that the Bronco bloodstains contained the blood of Ron Goldman as well.

Whilst out on bail and overcome with the enormity of the

crimes and the evidence being presented, he and his friend A. C. Cowling took off in the Bronco, resulting in the highly televised freeway pursuit which resulted in his arrest and internment for the period of the trial.

Simpson now began assembling the legal team that would become known as the "dream team", the key players of which would become as famous as their client. America had already split into the "guilty" and "not guilty" camps with the numbers broadly equal, those against had many reasons for him not being the killer: he was an intelligent man; he would never leave such obvious items of evidence at the scene; he would not dispose of the bloody glove behind the garage as the police were bound to look there; why make the phone call at 10.04 pm? His socks were bloodstained and found in the house, but what of his shoes?

After the police had arrested Simpson he called his lawyer Howard Weitzman, who was there to meet him when he finally arrived at the house under police guard. Once the basic evidence was presented to Simpson, Weitzman was dropped from the defence team and replaced by Bob Shapiro as attorney; six weeks later Johnny Cochran joined the team, replacing Shapiro as lead counsel for the defence. The dream team was now set and spent their time preparing for the court case and probably the biggest challenge any of the team had faced in their careers thus far.

The police and media during this period were still portraying Simpson as the killer and details from Simpson's police interviews were being leaked with alarming regularity to the press, for example, how he couldn't remember how he had cut his finger, then changing this to claiming it was cut on the handset of his mobile phone. Every printed word seemed to further incriminate Simpson, and Judge Ito, who was set to preside over the court proceedings, became increasingly concerned about ensuring a fair trial, given that it was almost inconceivable that the jury would have avoided being fed the medias presentation of the facts.

Simpson throughout this period kept a low media profile, although he was filmed looking particularly stressed behind dark glasses, while attending Nicole's funeral. It was reported that shortly after the service Nicole's mother asked Simpson directly if he was responsible for the murder of Nicole, to which he replied, "I loved her too much."

The newspapers continued to report the facts as leaked by persons unknown until Judge Ito finally exploded, declaring that the media circus would now come to an end. One reporter, Tracie Savage of KNBC, reported that the blood found on Simpson's socks was a direct match to Nicole's blood type, for which she was publicly denounced by Judge Ito from the bench. He then subpoenaed the reporter and her bosses and subjected them to a severe grilling, had the attorneys make a public denial of the details of the claim and went on to warn that he would bring to bear the full authority of the court on anyone who interfered with the proceedings, including those seeking to run the justice system through the pages of the tabloid newspapers or the public's TV screens. The threats worked and finally the media settled back into a more responsible reporting style.

However, during the course of the trial the defence counsel did make use of the Savage article by claiming that it showed that a member of the LAPD knew of the results before the final results of the blood tests were known, thus indicating that the evidence was planted by a close member of the LAPD team. Accusations of this type had been thrown at the LAPD before and the public were not impervious to the facts.

Following the preliminary hearing Simpson was held for trial to answer two counts of first-degree murder. A key decision also made at this stage was to direct the District Attorney away from a possible call for the death penalty, in light of Simpson's previously good record.

The trial that followed would now run for the next nine months and hold the title of the longest-running criminal court case in American history, a title previously held by the Charles Manson trials.

On 24 January 1995, Orenthal James Simpson sat in the dock of the LA Supreme Courthouse and along with a jury of eight black people, one Hispanic, two of mixed descent and one white person, listened to the opening statements.

There followed month upon month of complex statements from so-called expert witnesses, which would then be dismantled by the defence. Throughout this period the entire proceeding were being broadcast live to a massive audience – 92 per cent of the American television viewing public were tuned into the court case. CNN's Larry King joked that if he had God booked on his show and O. J. became available he would move God. The case was heaven sent for the media and the whole world watched as Simpson played the supporting role to the extravagant and some would say flashy defence team.

During the trial Judge Ito barred media staff from both Court TV and *USA Today* for talking during the proceedings, and warned others that they too would be removed if the media's chatterings did not cease.

Amongst the myriad of evidence and counter-evidence one of the key defence positions was that one of the detectives first on the scene, Mark Fuhrman, had in fact planted the evidence that the prosecution often referred to. He was the first on the scene and had been the one to go over the wall at the Rockingham estate to see who was in. The defence claimed that it was during this period that Fuhrman had planted evidence. This was a particularly bitter dispute during which the defence asked to see Fuhrman's personnel records. It was also claimed that Fuhrman had made numerous racial remarks which could influence his attitude to Simpson. In yet another strong attack, F. Lee Bailey, a key defence lawyer, stated that he would prove that Fuhrman planted the bloody glove found behind Simpson's garage. In a private meeting with Judge Ito, Bailey said he had more evidence that Fuhrman planted the glove than the prosecution had that Simpson had committed the murders. During the whole interrogation of Detective Mark Fuhrman, Marcia Clarke, the lead prosecution lawyer, would interject with complaints that the defence team were making accusations they could not prove and were bringing the detective's reputation into question, a point the defence team said they had every intention of pursuing as it was at the heart of their case.

Another major defence position was that the LAPD had run the enquiry and especially the murder scene in a sloppy and amateurish way. The police had to admit that they had not allowed the coroner access to the bodies until ten hours after the scene had been sealed by the police, an act that meant they could not easily pinpoint the time of the crime. The police were accused of being so convinced of Simpson's guilt that they did not pursue any other lines of investigation at all. It was intimated that boot prints found at the scene were quite likely to have come from wandering police staff and that even bloodstains could have been moved around by them.

Denise Brown, Nicole's sister, made an emotional testimony, saying that Nicole was justifiably scared of Simpson, adding that she was frequently in danger of physical abuse.

Throughout the trial jurors were replaced for one reason or another, but the Judge was able to maintain a sensible balance and one that would be best placed to deliver a fair verdict, although the changing faces of the jurors meant new challenges for the lawyers involved as they sought to maintain whatever influence they thought they had achieved to date.

The courtroom also witnessed numerous arguments between the defence team and Marcia Clarke. At one point Judge Ito ordered that the two stop their "gratuitous" personal attacks on each other, claiming they were not helping the jury in their task of assessing the available evidence.

As the trial dragged on even Judge Ito became the target for criticism, with the press saying it was unfair for the jurors to have to maintain track of the trial over such an extended period of time – the wheels of justice were certainly turning very slowly, and the costs were mounting rapidly. By the end of February, just one month into the case, the court costs had reached $3.2 million.

The media, getting tired of discussing the endless evidence, some too scientifically complex to easily present in a newspaper article, took to commenting on the personalities of the legal teams and of the growing tension and arguments between them. One newspaper decided to lead on one occasion with the new hairdo that prosecutor Marcia Clarke was sporting. There were also many light-hearted moments during the trial, when even Simpson was able to raise a smile. When Brian Kaelin took the stand he was asked by a member of the defence team if he felt nervous, to which he replied, "No, I feel great," and the courtroom laughed, thankful for a break in the pressure.

The norm however was for the two teams to tackle each and every issue head on with as much effort and skill as they could muster. The defence had a stroke of luck when a female employee from the LA District Attorney's office filed a $12 million suit against Christopher Dardin of the prosecution, alleging she was being coerced to stand by details that she believed were fabricated. Whatever the strength of the evidence the prosecution's position was constantly hampered by claims of corrupt and inept policing, fabrication of evidence and so on. It would be a difficult call as to the eventual outcome.

After nine long months of deliberation the legal teams made their final summaries and the jury were retired to the Intercontinental Hotel in downtown Los Angeles to consider their verdict. After just five hours Judge Ito was informed that they had completed the task. He confirmed to a waiting world that he would reconvene the court in the morning and make known the outcome at 10 a.m. As expected the courtroom was packed the next day, as were the streets surrounding the courthouse – this was an unprecedented media offering and the whole of the Western world held its breath.

Only in Los Angeles could such a tele-visual extravaganza occur and nothing in Hollywood could rival it.

At 10 a.m. precisely Judge Ito asked the newly appointed foreman of the jury, Armanda Cooley, to stand. He then asked the question the whole world wanted an answer to. Did the jury find O. J. Simpson guilty or not guilty of the murder of Nicole Brown-Simpson and Ron Goldman? The courtroom was silent as she replied, "Not guilty." The relief was evident on Simpson's face as the news sank in that he had won and the defence teams smiled their satisfaction at winning what had clearly been a most difficult case.

The statistics for the case speak for themselves. The defence team had consisted of eleven lawyers, the prosecution had maintained a team of 25 staff and the total cost of the trial had risen to $20 million. The court had produced 50,000 pages of typescript, had called 150 witnesses and it had all been covered by some 2,000 reporters. The trial spawned 80 books including one by Detective Mark Fuhrman who had suffered much personal criticism during the proceedings.

The debating continued across the nation for months after the trial, but for O. J. Simpson the nightmare was still not over. During the trial and the period of his incarceration the court had awarded temporary guardianship of his children to their maternal grandparents, Nicole's mother and father. Simpson now prepared to go back to court to gain custody as he could not come to an agreement with the grandparents. At the same time Nicole's parents and those of Ron Goldman engaged further legal assistance, this time to pursue a civil action against Simpson.

The matter of custody was settled when the courts once again came down in favour of Simpson, but the civil trial would be a different matter. During the criminal trial the jury had to be sure beyond all reasonable doubt that Simpson was guilty of the murders, however, in civil terms they need only be convinced that he probably was the most likely person to have committed the crimes, based on the "balance of probabilities". This time the jury voted unanimously in favour of Simpson's culpability, in the case of the death of Ron Goldman, and found him liable for having committed malicious battery against Nicole Simpson. No further charge was pursued here for the death of Nicole Simpson. Following the civil action, the court awarded damages of $8.5 million to the family of Ron Goldman and a further $25 million in punitive damages, $12.5 million awarded to Nicole's estate, money that would be held in trust for her children, and the balance to go to Goldman's father.

Simpson's financial situation, however, had become a point of controversy, as those acting for him claimed he was broke. They stated that Simpson's previous estimated worth of some $10 million was now $800,000 in the red and therefore the likelihood of him making any payment was nil. Those pursuing Simpson pointed to his expensive Rockingham estate, his Bentley and other cars and the fact that he was still able to employ a large staff. The truth, however, was that the attorneys acting on behalf of Simpson had acquired security on the Rockingham house to ensure that their bill was settled.

It was estimated that even given the bad publicity of the trial, Simpson might be able to earn as much as $3 million a year from his fame, and under Californian law his creditors would be able to claim 25 per cent of his earnings at source. Simpson's final decision was that the Rockingham estate should be repossessed by the bank, which had a significant mortgage on it, and he meanwhile moved to Florida, one of two states in the US where the family home cannot be used to settle civil damages. This move also protected his estimated $4.1 million pension fund, and so nine years after the murders none of the awards have been met.

There continue to be many theories regarding the murders and the USA is still split as regards to Simpson's guilt. There are other possibilities that were not fully pursued by the police that are quite possible. One suggests that Nicole was murdered because of her interference in an illegal gambling operation that involved Simpson introducing high rollers to the mob in exchange for a fee. Simpson regularly mixed with highly paid sports stars on the golf circuit and would introduce them into a well-run, high-class gambling operation, making use of the latest technology, but which was operated by members of the East Coast mob. According to this theory, Nicole found out and threatened to spill the beans if the mob did not let Simpson leave quietly; they subsequently killed Nicole and set Simpson up, planting the evidence and even luring him to the scene that evening.

Another line of enquiry involved Simpson's son from a previous marriage, Jason. In a BBC documentary aired to shed new light on the crimes they suggested an investigation into Jason should not be ruled out. Known to have had a testy relationship with Nicole, he also had a history of violence, including an alleged attack on someone with a knife.

Nicole had also had death threats in the months before the murders and it is thought there may have been a contract out on her life. She was trailed by a friend of Simpson's, who had supplied them both with cocaine, and had been tasked with taking photographs of her and any men she might meet.

The police were aware of all of these possible lines of enquiry and yet concentrated their efforts on just one man.

In a recent interview Simpson said he was devoted to his children, but had to relearn how to be a father again. He said he was always a great father, but made a poor mom and in an interview with *New Yorker* magazine Simpson said that, "Instead of being treated like a pariah, he now gets nothing but love, and women are his biggest defenders."

Barry George, prisoner FF5227

Jill Dando

"It is just a matter of time before I am killed. I think somebody in the underworld killed Jill and now they want to silence me. I think I will die in prison. Someone will have me done away. I never shot Jill, never did it, but I don't think people in authority want to know. They would rather I die and the whole thing go away."

These are the words of Barry George, the man jailed for life in July 2001 for the murder of the popular television presenter Jill Dando in his first interview from prison. Since his imprisonment George has continued to plead his innocence and deny emphatically any involvement in the shocking crime which was carried out at Dando's Fulham home on Monday, 26 April 1999. At around 11.30 a.m. that day a man forced Dando at gun point onto her knees and fired a single gunshot into her skull, killing her instantly. Shortly after lunchtime, the news of the murder spread and sent the entire nation into shock. Dando had presented an array of popular television programmes and had become one of the BBC's main programme anchor ladies. In contrast to many of her counterparts, Dando had cultivated an image of "the girl next door", very down to earth and devoid of the attention-seeking ego which is generally symptomatic of many media personalities. A slightly harder person in real life, Dando was ambitious and would often be the one to end relationships.

By the time of her death Dando was in a fulfilling relationship with her fiancé Alan Farthing, they had announced their plans to marry and had subsequently moved in together, living at Farthing's house in Chiswick. It was increasingly rare, therefore, to see Dando visiting her Fulham address. She now only called back to collect mail and to occasionally stop there if it was easier in terms of her many television assignments. Was it purely bad luck for Dando that day that she happened to be visiting the address when her assailant was planning the attack? Or was the crime more organized, a planned strike, for reasons as yet not known? Like many personalities Dando had attracted many adoring fans, even the odd fanatic. In the months before the attack Dando had confided to friends that she believed she was being stalked. In any event the gunman timed his approach perfectly, delivered the terminal shot where it would do most damage and calmly left, giving the impression that it was more the work of a professional assassin rather than a crazed fan, who although carrying a gun had stumbled across an opportunity and had acted on impulse. It is these and many other questions which have given rise to the doubts over the conviction of Barry George. And to the confusion as to why the authorities are loath to re-examine the facts. George has on a number of occasions been denied a re-evaluation of his case at the Court of Appeal.

There are many possibilities when searching for a motive for the murder of Jill Dando – the crazed fan is certainly one of them and one which is not uncommon, as in the case of Mark Chapman's murder of John Lennon. But Dando had a more complex set of circumstances – she co-hosted with Nick Ross the *Crimewatch* programme, which presented information to and sought out information from the public, information that was passed to the police and in many cases used to bring villains to court. Dando also had a number of relationships before Farthing, some of which overlapped, causing consternation among her suitors who she would drop, claiming her work schedule was too busy to accommodate a full-time relationship. Maybe on the announcement of her engagement to Farthing, this had triggered some vengeful emotion. Dando had also been involved publicly in raising money for the Kosovans, providing help for the thousands who had been displaced following the bitter civil war between Kosovo and Serbia. It was therefore considered a possibility that Dando had been murdered by a Serbian assassin. Another perhaps less likely version has Dando knocked off by a spurned Mafia boss. All were to some extent possible, but with few convincing facts to support them; yet what are the facts which persuaded a jury of seven women and five men to convict George of this heinous crime?

Dando had been shopping on the morning of her murder; her final television appearance would be the security video footage of her leaving a department store. She had planned to make a visit to her home at 29 Gowan Avenue just to collect mail and arrived slightly before 11.30 a.m. As she prepared to unlock her front door, she was approached from behind by a man holding a pistol. She turned to face her attacker and was forced to kneel on her front doorstep; without further delay the attacker fired once, at point-blank range, into her head. Then calmly and without drawing further attention to himself, the killer walked back down the path and away from the crime scene. Dando was discovered just ten minutes later – she was dead.

These events sparked the largest and most expensive police investigation that had ever been organized in Britain. A team of 50 officers was assembled, who slowly interviewed, tracked down and eliminated literally thousands of suspects from the enquiry, which had been code-named Operation Oxborough. The police operation eventually ran to a cost of £2 million, and was headed by Detective Inspector Hamish Campbell, who was determined to bring the culprit of such a high profile murder case to book.

All the neighbours of Dando's Fulham address were interviewed and it appeared that a number of residents had seen the person likely to have been the murderer – one as he left Dando's front garden and others who had seen people in the general area. Richard Hughes, one resident, said he saw the man walking calmly away. Other witnesses came forward to describe other men who had been seen acting strangely in the vicinity of Gowan Avenue. The similarity in the descriptions led police to believe that they had all probably seen the same person and the likelihood was high that he was the person responsible. The man was described as white, thick set with collar-length black hair, combed back off his face. He was wearing a dark-coloured wax jacket and either a white or blue shirt depending on the witness giving the description. There were also conflicting reports, some suggesting that they had seen a Mediterranean-looking man, others say not. It would appear that several people had been seen in the area that morning, and to this end the police initially announced their belief that three men had been involved in the murder, although shortly afterwards they altered their stance – they now felt strongly that they were looking for a lone gunman. The reason for the change in this important assumption was driven by Hamish Campbell's firm belief that if there had been a multi-person conspiracy to murder Dando, the police would have heard something of this from their connections in the criminal underworld. The suspicious behaviour of several people seen in the area was now discarded in favour of pursuing a single person.

Over the months that followed the police interviewed many ex-cons, those who lived in London and who had previously been jailed for murder, sex crimes or stalking, and ruled out those who could provide solid alibis, which in general was most.

Barry George had not enjoyed a trouble-free existence, so when he was picked up for questioning on 11 April 2000, nearly a year after the attack, it was by virtue of his previous record. During the 1980s he had been jailed for attempted rape, following the assault of a young woman in his tower block. After his release, he had, as far as all who knew him were concerned, led a perfectly normal and crime-free life. During his questioning the police were initially satisfied that he had a strong alibi, but were concerned that George had apparently been preparing his defence in advance, as if he was expecting to be accused. In the days following the attack George had spoken to those he had been with to provide a record of his movements around the time of the attack. Although that morning George had been at the Hammersmith and Fulham Action for Disability (HAFAD) premises, as borne out by Susan Bicknell, one of the staff, the police were now highly suspicious that the man who had spent his time preparing those alibis may have had something to hide. Bicknell confirmed that George had been at HAFAD at 11.50 a.m., just 20 minutes after the attack, and even though Gowan Avenue was half a mile away and George could not drive, the police still focused their attention on him. Bicknell also confirmed that George was wearing a yellow shirt beneath his anorak, not the white or blue shirts as described by the witnesses at Gowan Avenue.

George did however fit the general description of the attacker, had a previous conviction for a serious crime and had been interviewed over the murder of Rachel Nickell, but had been released without charge. Was it the paranoia caused by previous suspicions which prompted George to set out the case for his defence before he had even been accused? Many believe so for he was always concerned when serious crimes were committed in his area and was always waiting for a knock at the door. He explained these reasonings to the police as they were clearly highly suspicious of his actions, but above all George believed that the alibi itself was what counted, although the police did not hold the same view. Just one month after his initial police interview George was arrested on suspicion of killing Dando and was charged three days after that with her murder. He was sent to Belmarsh Prison whilst awaiting trial and was frequently questioned by police, but now in the presence of his high-profile defence counsel, Michael Mansfield QC.

Convicted already by the press, George's time in Belmarsh Prison, south-east London, was a frightening experience. "It was hell," he said, "I was terrified. I really thought I was dead. I kept my head down, never spoke to anybody." Staying close to the warders for protection he could see the bigger prisoners staring across at him, trying to get his attention, but he kept his eyes averted. George was the target of much intimidation; the other prisoners would shout names and spit in his food and drink. Dando was such a popular icon of television that to some extent people thought they knew her. As an attack on a lone woman, the crime was considered as bad as a sex attack or a paedophile case as far as the other prisoners were concerned. Ironically it was the imprisonment of Lord Jeffrey Archer, an old friend of Dando's, that finally averted some of the attention from him; considered a privileged toff, he too became a target for abuse.

On closer examination of the facts the case against George was weak. Susan Bicknell, who saw George on the morning of the murder, and remembered him because he was her first case, was sure that she could place him at HAFAD at around 11.50 a.m. Yet more than a year after the event a number of her colleagues thought they remembered seeing him at around two in the afternoon, a fact which, if true does not preclude him being there in the morning. So long after the event, the police should have been wary of their recollections, yet seemed intent on using the statements of those who had not dealt with George that day, over and above Susan Bicknell, who had every reason to recall George being there. The emergence of a £250,000 reward for information leading to a conviction cannot easily be forgotten when considering the veracity of witness statements. Such an amount of money can be used to discredit statements given, just as it can potentially encourage people to embellish or slightly alter facts.

The murder weapon was never found. It never turned up in a rubbish bin nor has it been retrieved from a sewer pipe, and cannot therefore be linked to its owner or the murderer that day. Further circumstantial evidence was accumulated in respect of George and his apparent liking for guns. As a young man he had joined the TA and enjoyed telling those he knew that he was in fact in the SAS. He had always been prone to exaggerating to those who would listen, claiming once to be called Paul Gadd of Gary Glitter fame, and on another occasion taking the name Steve Majors, the first and last names of the actor Lee Majors and his character from the television series *Bionic Man*. George failed his basic training for the TA and had to leave; instead he tried to join a local gun club but again failed entry when he was unable to provide a credible reference. In a series of tenuous links, the police traced people who had known George and who were able to confirm that he had at least some interest in guns. One old acquaintance said George had been in possession of a number of gun magazines and had bought books on the subject of weapons. Another person had come forward to say that George had fired a blank round at him as a joke, using a replica firearm. All of these reported facts suggest nothing more than a passing interest, nothing that could be described as an obsession, and if taken out of the context of Dando's murder are the weakest of platforms on which to pursue a conviction. The police did recover the gun magazines, which had been in George's flat for 17-odd years and used the items as a way of confirming George's interest in guns.

Also found in the flat were some 200 other newspapers and magazines for George was a hoarder who very rarely threw anything out. On analysis of these items the police discovered that out of the 200 or so editions, only eight of them contained any reference to Dando and none of them had been highlighted or in any way marked out for special attention – not the typical find for someone who the police tried to claim was obsessed with Dando, no pictures of her on the wall, no tape recordings of her many TV appearances. He had however become interested in Freddie Mercury and the signs of this were evident in his flat, but again there was no indication that his interest had developed into an unhealthy obsession. Experts commented that whoever killed Dando was likely to have been obsessed with her and would have talked quite openly about the focus of his or her attention, yet not one person who knew George could recall him ever mentioning her name – unlike Freddie Mercury whom he talked about frequently. Like many people George was interested in celebrity and had over time managed to take a number of photographs of famous people, but not one of Dando although he lived within one mile of her home, and there is no indication that he actually knew her address.

Throughout the period in which the trial was being prepared the media ran many tributes to Jill Dando and famous personalities, including Sir Cliff Richard, one of her friends, spoke of his affection for her. The newspapers meanwhile presented the case for the prosecution – he had been in jail for attempted rape, and he was an oddball, a loner who had an unhealthy interest in guns. The conflicting facts regarding the alibi and the sightings of multiple suspects, potentially working as a team, were disregarded once George was arrested and charged, another fait accompli.

The anorak that George had been wearing was taken for analysis and was discovered to have traces of firearms discharge residue (FDR) inside the jacket pockets which matched that discovered at the murder scene inasmuch as it was made up of the same elements. Unlike a ballistics report which can confirm a particular bullet was fired from a particular gun, the FDR analysis could not be so conclusive. The fact is that residue found inside the jacket pocket could have come from one of the gun magazines that George owned, or for that matter from a common or garden firework, such is the commonplace nature of this substance. The probability of the residue arriving there from a magazine that George hadn't handled for years, or for that matter a firework, are probably slim, but there is a chance that it arrived on that article of clothing due to poor police controls at George's flat, giving rise to contamination. There are a couple of ways in which it is thought this could have occurred, the first being at the time of his arrest. The police entered his house carrying a range of guns, not unusual given that they were about to arrest a person suspected of a shooting. It was during this initial search of the house that officers turned the jacket pockets inside out whilst searching for evidence, an act which in the presence of the police weapons could have led to a cross-contamination of the jacket. At a later date the jacket, which had been stored in a protective bag to protect it from contaminants, had been sent to a photographic studio where it had been removed in order that it could be photographed. Unfortunately the bullet and cartridge were also in the studio, as well as Dando's front door and other related items, for a similar purpose at the same time, another opportunity for cross-contamination. A scientist acting for the defence, Dr Lloyd, a forensic scientist of over 30 years standing, made a study of the particles at the time and commented, "It is my view that this evidence is not reliable as evidence of the defendant's involvement in the shooting. There is no particular reason why this particle can be so related to the shooting of Miss Dando."

In a further break with procedure, the van in which the jacket had been taken away had not been prepared in line with the approved police procedures, procedures intended to protect items to be used as evidence from any form of contamination.

To contest the testimony of Susan Bicknell, who placed George at the HAFAD centre at 11.50 a.m., the police located witness, Susan Mayes, who believed she could place George in the vicinity of Gowan Avenue at around 7 a.m., hours before the murder took place. Although she claimed to have studied the man for a full six seconds, she later provided descriptions which were contradictory, initially stating that the man she saw had smart, short-cut hair, but then changing it later to saying that he had longer, untidy hair. It has been claimed since that the police tried to influence Mayes's decision. Other informants came forward, but most were only able to promote the idea of George being a bit odd – very possibly true, but not the hard-hitting evidence usually required to secure a conviction.

In addition to the mounting evidence, tenuous though it certainly was, there is George himself, a nervous, shifty sort of person, someone who finds it difficult to look you in the eye. Paranoid about police interest in him generally, he was nervous and acted like he was guilty, which for a copper with a nose for the bad guy would be a compelling enough reason to pursue him. It is strange that his "guilty" behaviour many months after the trial, had not been evident when he was seen by Susan Bicknell at the HAFAD centre less than 30 minutes after the crime and that he was unflustered, not sweating and calm, something he could not now manage whilst under police questioning.

George had been brought up on the tough White City housing estate in West London, the product of a broken home; he was a restless child who did not make friends easily.

He invented fantasy lives for himself, lives where he was important and glamorous, the motive ultimately presented by the police for his killing of Dando.

In May 2001 the respective legal teams entered court ready to debate the innocence or otherwise of Barry George. Michael Mansfield QC, George's defence counsel, commenced by saying that he believed Jill Dando was the victim of an organized underworld hit and that the case against his client was hanging by the merest of threads. The prosecution, led by Orlando Pownall, based their case on a mixture of circumstantial evidence: George had an interest in guns and some vague interest in Dando; certain eyewitnesses had placed him at the scene in the hours before the killing took place; and the forensic evidence, the speck of gunpowder found in his jacket pocket.

In a legal game of "ping-pong", one side then the other sought to dismantle the other's arguments. The defence hammered home the alibi that placed George at the HA-FAD centre at 11.50 a.m.; the prosecution claimed other witnesses placed him there after that time, giving him the opportunity to commit the crime. The prosecution argued that the forensic material found on George's jacket proved he had used a weapon; the defence claimed contamination from a bungled scene of crime investigation. Each brought forward experts on this point. Robin Keeley, acting for the prosecution, claimed that it was unlikely that the forensic material got onto the jacket after the garment was seized and that he was confident that it was the result of a firearms discharge. The police, who had denied taking guns into George's flat, now faced witnesses who claimed to have seen armed police entering the premises with their guns clearly visible, a damning piece of evidence and one that, if true, would imply a significant conspiracy of silence on the individual officers' parts. The embarrassment of a poor scene-of-crime investigation would not be as bad as a claim of conspiracy, or worse, that an innocent man should go to jail. The prosecution claimed the motive was simply that George had an unhealthy interest in Dando, a claim the defence argued could not be proven, citing the multitude of magazines and papers which contained so little reference to Dando as proof.

And finally the murder weapon had never been found, the missing link that could have provided the evidence needed to secure a safe conviction.

On balance the case did hang by a thread, however, George's own behaviour during cross-examination did not help his position. Irrespective of his "shifty" mannerisms, George at one point claimed he did not know who Dando was, clearly a lie, but given his situation perhaps understandable – he was after all fighting for his freedom. When asked by DC Tim Snowden how the gunpowder residue had got into his pocket, he replied, "I cannot explain. I have no knowledge," and then when pressed further that it had got there because he had shot Miss Dando and that it matched the residue found at the scene, he responded, "I cannot explain that."

His pathetic, confused retorts only served to make him look guilty and the defence's explanations in response to these specific points seemed to get lost along the way, even though reporters in court claimed that Mansfield was able to completely denounce the forensic arguments. After the two sides had summarized their cases, the trial judge, Mr Justice Gage, warned the seven women and five men not to allow any feelings of prejudice or sympathy to affect their judgement. The prospect of sympathy for Barry George would not have been an emotion the defence would have expected, however, the need to make a conviction, with an entire nation watching and awaiting an outcome, was a situation George and his team would have been understandably afraid of. The Judge continued, "I doubt throughout the United Kingdom there can be many adults – or even children – who have not read about her death or this case." Truer words could not have been spoken, the coverage had been immense and one sided in favour of the prosecution. Although the Judge summarized the main points of both the defence and the prosecution, it was the prosecution's main threads that seemed to carry the greatest weight as the jury retired to consider their verdict on 27 June 2001.

Just five days later the jury returned their verdict, finding

George guilty of murder on a ratio of ten to one, after one juror had been forced to leave the jury during the proceedings. The judge had agreed that he would accept a majority decision which in this instance required a minimum of ten jurors in agreement. George was then sentenced to life imprisonment. The publicity surrounding the conviction was, however, soon disrupted as a growing band of credible individuals began to voice their doubts and suspicions over the outcome. The doubts raised were soon front-page news as more and more people joined the protest group which was loosely forming – there was the pressure to get the conviction, the amount of money spent on the investigation, the trial judge's decision to allow the publication of photographs of George at the commencement of the trial. One photograph showing George in an SAS-style uniform, crouched in a shooting pose and wearing a gas mask presented him in an almost biased way. The argument over the handling of the investigation and the conflicting testimonies of the various eyewitness all seemed to fly in the face of the requirements of a criminal case, namely, that a conviction can only be brought when the evidence is "beyond reasonable doubt". Newspapers, including the *London Evening Standard*, the *Telegraph* and the *Daily Mail* all expressed grave doubts over the safety of the conviction. Callers on a Radio 4 programme seriously questioned the evidence, as did Trevor Macdonald on ITN's *Tonight* programme. Channel 4 presented the most persuasive case when they reconstructed the murder for an episode of *Cutting Edge*, titled "Did Barry George Kill Jill Dando?" Unfortunately the media's influence after the conviction could not match the pre-conviction coverage, although the public were now fully aware of the conflicts in the case.

Following the conviction, the defence team logged an immediate appeal which was accepted during December 2001, the basis for the appeal being the lack of concrete evidence. In July 2002, after considering the facts once more, Lord Woolf, the Lord Chief Justice, commented, "I have no doubt about the accuracy of George's conviction," and with this the conviction of Barry George still stands, although many lobbying groups continue to pursue another retrial.

George himself gave the following statement, "I did not murder Jill Dando and I believe that one day the truth will come out. I only hope and pray that this happens in my lifetime. I have spent over two years in prison for a crime I simply did not commit. I have struggled hard during this prosecution against me to keep my faith in the British criminal justice system. Today, that faith and belief has been destroyed."

George is now serving his sentence at Whitmoor Prison in Cambridgeshire, a top-security prison, where even his elderly mother Margaret is searched before being allowed to see her son. Prisoner FF5227 is now less troubled by the other prisoners; even they seem more inclined to believe he did not commit the crime. In a letter received by the authors in 2004, lifer Dennis Nilsen explains that this is more than just "honour amongst thieves", and that "nobody inside believes he is guilty, this was a professional hit."

George, now in his mid-forties, shows increasing signs of mental breakdown, still maintaining his innocence but convinced he will now die in prison, probably the target of some assassin. Even though he now receives fewer threats he is convinced he will die violently at the hands of one of the other inmates.

Whatever the truth behind the murder of Jill Dando, the case demonstrates a number of unique points that emerge when a celebrity is killed. The Dando murder trial commanded more public money and a larger police team than any other investigation of its type. At the time of writing a young black girl, shot and killed in a drive-by incident, has received much less police and press attention, yet the crimes are similar. No significant reward has been offered in this recent shooting and yet £250,000 was offered for information leading to the conviction of Dando's killer, an amount which, one could argue, reduced the probability of the evidence being wholly accurate. The pre-trial coverage demonstrated the innate desire for the killer to be caught – murder is murder, we hear of it every day – but thankfully it never seems too close to home, even though our extended TV family brings it into that domain.

The Girl on the Red Velvet Swing

Stanford White

Evelyn Nesbit was lucky to be born into a happy family which enjoyed a comfortable lifestyle, her father Winfield Scott Nesbit a relatively successful lawyer. She had all the privileges which are bestowed on an only child and as a youngster was very pretty. She was the apple of her parents' eyes who were delighted when they found out that they were expecting their second child. When the baby was born the couple were thrilled that they had been blessed with a son, who they named Howard; he was to be their last child.

When Evelyn was only eight years old she was to experience the first of her life's traumas – her beloved father died suddenly. Mrs Nesbit was left to raise her two children single handedly, which was to prove a terrible struggle, as the passing of her husband had left her virtually penniless. The couple had not planned on such a massive alteration to their finances and therefore had made no provision for the loss of Winfield's wages.

Mrs Nesbit tried various means of raising money for her young family, initially taking in lodgers, but as this did not provide enough money, she resorted to selling off some of her furniture. This then resulted in her no longer being able to have paying guests in the house, not one of her best decisions, but the woman was grief stricken and desperate. She made small amounts of money by working from home, taking in washing and also repairing other people's clothing, but this was not sufficient to keep them in their own home. Mrs Nesbit and her two young children moved from house to house with ever mounting bills following them.

As the children grew older they attended school less and less frequently. Howard, a sickly child tried in vain to earn money for the family, but as he was continually tired he was never able to maintain any form of employment. His fatigue and general ill health was no doubt not aided by the fact they regularly went without meals and the food that they did eat was of poor quality and poor nutritional value. This could have explained why Evelyn was much more slender than her friends – at the end of the nineteenth century the waif-like look was not fashionable, girls were much curvier. But her unfashionable slenderness was overlooked when it was added to her now obvious beauty, with flawless olive skin and a head of luxurious, wavy, auburn hair.

In her early teenage years Evelyn dreamt of a fairytale ending to her desperate existence, wishing that a knight in shining armour would come and rescue her. By the time she had reached her fifteenth birthday she was mature enough to realize that this was nothing more than a young girl's fantasy and the only way to change her predicament was to take matters into her own hands.

In her favour were her looks, so she decided that she would use them to her advantage, and the easiest and most convenient way to do this was to pose as an artist's model. After discussing her ideas with her mother, the two set about finding a reputable artist to whom they could put their proposition. Her mother was initially reluctant, but as she was virtually impoverished, she was left with no real alternative but to support her daughter.

One of the most eminent artists who worked in Philadelphia at that time was John Storm. Evelyn and her mother arranged to meet him and after some persuasion Mrs Nesbit agreed that her daughter could become the artist's model. Storm found Evelyn to be a fantastic model, she was a beautiful subject to study and soon the work he produced was highly acclaimed, and was published in magazines. Evelyn's new-found financial success was much needed and although her mother was not altogether happy with her daughter's choice of profession she reluctantly accepted the money which it provided.

Encouraged by her success, Evelyn began to consider her future – after talking with other models she was encouraged that with her stunning looks she could make much more money by working in New York. She put this proposition to her mother, who was worried that her daughter was biting off more than she could chew, but her complaints soon died away as her daughter was now bringing more money into the house than she and her son were. So the three of them made their way to New York where Evelyn soon managed to start earning good money by, once again, being a model for a number of artists working around the city, quickly discovering that there was more money to be earned by posing for fashion photographers, which was a highly popular and lucrative occupation for young girls at that time.

Her pictures were viewed by many when they were published in both the *Sunday World* and *Sunday American* fashion supplements. Evelyn was still only 15 years old, but was well aware that this publicity would not harm her career – in fact it could well open new doors for her. The beautiful new face in town was soon noticed by several theatre companies and she found herself being offered various roles in chorus lines across the city.

Evelyn accepted a role in the Broadway hit show *Florodora*, which featured six young ladies in a chorus line and was an extremely popular show, attracting large audiences. The girls chosen to take part in this extravaganza were the most beautiful and thus became the most lusted after by the male members of the audience. To have moved from Philadelphia to a hit Broadway show was an amazing feat, but now Evelyn found that she had much interest from wealthy New York businessmen.

Among the many men showing a sudden interest in her was wealthy architect Stanford White, who had designed many of the opulent houses in New York for the richest families living in the city. His designs were bold and elaborate and always very expensive, but as White always insisted, "you get what you pay for." He not only designed private dwellings but also worked on and added to decorative finishings on buildings around the city, including the Church of the Ascension, Washington Square Arch, the Lambs and the Brooks, the Players Club and Saint Bartholomew's Church. One of New York's most famous landmarks which White was responsible for is Madison Square Garden, a stunning gilded building with a fabulous rooftop garden.

White owned part of the splendid building, a prestigious apartment, where he would spend time away from his family, in seclusion, enabling himself to have time and space to concentrate on his work. He would also entertain colleagues and friends from time to time and would host lavish parties where his guests would marvel at the wonderful decorations and expensive furnishings of his private dwelling. White had a penchant for young girls, especially young ladies in the chorus line and Evelyn Nesbit did not go unnoticed by him. Initially he spent time talking to her after her show and complimenting her on her performance. She was still at this time barely 16 years old, but had already been warned sufficiently by her mother to be wary of older men making advances towards her.

A good friend of Evelyn's was also a member of the chorus line, Edna Goodrich, and White saw in her an opportunity to spend more time with Evelyn away from the crowds in the theatre. He invited both young women to have lunch with him and one of his friends in the tower of his building. Despite being over 30 years older than Evelyn, White did not consider this to be a reason to be deterred from ingratiating himself with her. He provided a banquet for the four to enjoy and after the meal he took them on a grand tour of his apartment. The young girls followed him in wonder, as he moved from room to room, each elegantly furnished with expensive decorations, from pieces of furniture to priceless tapestries which were hung from walls throughout the rooms.

When they reached a room which was filled with White's drawings and sketches of buildings, they were amazed to see in the centre of the room, taking pride of place, a sumptuous red velvet swing. What the girls didn't already know was that White had seen many a young girl enjoying taking their turn on the swing; it was quite a masterpiece. Evelyn was invited to have a go on the unusual piece of furniture, which she did and thoroughly enjoyed herself, noticing that her host appeared to be enjoying himself too.

The girls regained their composures and were about to leave when White happened to notice that Evelyn had a discoloured tooth. He pointed out to her that she would benefit from seeing a dentist and having it repaired, or better still replaced. As money was still a relative luxury to Evelyn and her family – living in New York was not cheap – she said that it was not troubling her and that for the time being she would leave the tooth as it was. White obviously saw his chance to help a damsel in distress and offered her the services of a dentist for whom he had high regard, and gave Evelyn his details on a card.

When Evelyn told her mother about the strange afternoon with Stanford White, she was immediately suspicious of him and would not allow her daughter to make a dental appointment with the famed dentist. When White next saw Evelyn he was disappointed to see that she had not taken up his offer to improve her smile. She explained that it was her mother who had refused her permission to make an appointment so White asked if he might meet Mrs Nesbit. The meeting was arranged at his offices and Mrs Nesbit arrived with the sole intention of telling White to find another plaything and leave her daughter alone.

What Mrs Nesbit was not prepared for was the effortless charm which White exuded. She was more taken in by him than her daughter and came away from the meeting giving her consent for Evelyn to visit the dentist who White had recommended.

The appointment was duly made and Evelyn benefited by gaining a perfect set of teeth to add to all her other attributes. Shortly thereafter Mrs Nesbit and her daughter relocated from their tiny cramped boarding rooms in the poorest part of the city to the sumptuous upmarket Audubon Hotel, evidently paid for by White. He also provided Howard with the opportunity to attend Chester Military Academy back in Philadelphia, which he duly accepted. Mrs Nesbit's previous unhappiness over her daughter using her looks to raise money for the family now seemed to be a dim and distant memory.

Mrs Nesbit now considered that Mr White presented no threat to her daughter's well-being and even entrusted her to him when she was to leave town on a trip to Pittsburgh with her new fiancé – Charles Holman. White now had the perfect opportunity to spend time with Evelyn and more to the point she would be alone in his care, unchaperoned.

Evelyn performed on stage in the chorus line and was quite excited at the prospect of being made a fuss of by her benefactor. She said goodnight to her friend Edna and went to meet the car which had been sent to collect her and take her to White's apartment at Madison Square. She spent the evening feeling much older than her 16 years, chatting with White, who overlooked her inexperience and her lack of social graces. If anything this endeared her to him all the more.

They were served a delicious meal, with an accompanying glass of champagne. Evelyn knew full well that her mother would not have approved of the alcohol, but decided not to let White know of her reservations in case he decided that she should not have any more. The meal over, Evelyn accepted further glasses of champagne and was later invited to try on an expensive yellow silk kimono. Owing to the effects of the champagne, Evelyn had by now lost many of her inhibitions and duly tried the garment on. The fabric was glossy and sensual, and she enjoyed the feeling of it against her skin. White asked if she would like to have a good look at herself with it on and he showed her to his bedroom where he had large floor-to-ceiling mirrors. By now feeling the effects of the alcohol she felt that she wasn't fully in control of the situation; she was still aware enough to notice that White was very attentive and was sure that he trembled when she moved close to him.

When she complained to White that she was not used to drinking alcohol and that the effects were making her feel rather sleepy, he told her not to worry as the same thing had happened to him when he had initially tried champagne. He advised her to rest on his bed until she started to feel better.

Not long after lying down Evelyn seemingly passed out. Although she was suspicious later that the drink had been drugged, she was never able to prove this. When she awoke she was immediately aware that she had been involved in some form of sexual activity as she could see evidence of it on her thighs – she had arrived in White's apartment a virgin and now her virtue had been stolen. White was unremorseful and scoffed at her anger, simply telling her that she was now his as nobody else would be interested in her.

Evelyn's outrage did not appear to last very long as she continued to see White. Perhaps she believed that nobody else would want her; or, quite possibly, she was rather attracted to him, if not for his looks, certainly his power and wealth could well have been an adequate aphrodisiac. Her relationship with White could also have been as a result of her not having a father figure in her life for such a long time, which he might have seemed.

As White was still a married man, he was not able to spend all of his time with Evelyn, so she found herself with evenings when she was free to meet with other gentlemen. She was still an extremely beautiful young woman and had no end of admirers, some of whom proposed marriage to her. One such man who found her attractive was Henry K. Thaw, preferring to be called Harry by his friends, from a very wealthy, influential American family. He was described as "smitten" with the young girl in the famous chorus line and interestingly Evelyn and Harry had one thing in common – they both came from Pittsburgh, although owing to the huge gap in their social circles they would never have met if Evelyn had stayed in her home town. Thaw's family were multi-millionaires, making a vast proportion of their wealth in the railroad and mining businesses, to which Harry was sole heir.

His upbringing was the best that money could buy; he attended the best schools, had the highest qualified servants, lived in the largest, most expensive houses and had all the luxuries that any spoilt child could wish for. With all these worldly goods bestowed upon him, Harry was rather unruly and expected to get his own way – if he did not he was renowned for having famous temper tantrums. No amount of persuasion would work and once Harry had started there was no stopping him, much to the embarrassment of his parents. Even his mother, known to all as Mother Thaw, a strict disciplinarian and a formidable character by anybody's reckonings, was unable to control her unruly son's alarming outbursts. In fact she went so far as to state that he was a problem child even before childbirth who showed no sign of mellowing with age.

At school Harry was constantly reprimanded for his behaviour and was branded a troublemaker, being passed from school to school. This fact was overlooked when his parents applied for a place for him at the prestigious and handy University of Pittsburgh to study Law, his name alone enough to grant him a place. Harry concluded his education, for what it was worth, at Harvard University. He was not an easy scholar and spent the vast majority of his time socializing, drinking and spending much of his allowance entertaining young women, and gambling. He was eventually expelled after an incident in which Harry was described as chasing a taxi driver with a firearm, albeit unloaded.

After his education was deemed over, little changed for the multi-millionaire, who continued to spend his time socialising and frequently getting into sticky situations, which were terribly embarrassing for his friends who were at a loss to explain his unusual behaviour. For some reason, Harry was either unwilling or unable to change his behaviour and was far too headstrong to accept offers of assistance.

On his many nights out, Harry would often enjoy going to the theatre, he was particularly interested in seeing Broadway shows and much admired the *Florodora* chorus line. He was soon enchanted by a young auburn-haired beauty and made it his business to find out her name – Evelyn Nesbit. He introduced himself to Evelyn, but she had already been warned about him by White so was respectful but kept her distance from him.

Another suitor to Evelyn was Mr John Barrymore, much younger than White and very good company to Evelyn, the two striking up quite a close relationship, so close that Evelyn found herself to be in a delicate condition – Barrymore again proposed marriage to her but she declined his offer. Instead she turned to her other lover, Stanford White, who assisted her out of the predicament by having her ensconced at the DeMille School for girls, taking its name from the school's headmistress, mother of the famous Cecil B. DeMille, in out-of-town New Jersey. There she concluded her schooling and enjoyed refining her singing abilities, but after around seven months of her stay there she suffered from "acute appendicitis" and was hospitalized for a short time before being moved later to a sanatorium in New York City.

On her return to New York she was immediately aware of White's change in feeling towards her. Although he continued to be interested in her, she sensed that his affections were dwindling and suspected that he might have eyes set on another younger, more innocent young lady.

Whilst in the sanatorium she was regularly visited by both White and Thaw. Although she was careful that they should never arrive together, she met them both individually. Thaw was extremely keen to make her stay at the sanatorium as pleasant as possible and made sure that she was provided with anything and everything she desired.

By the time that she was well enough to leave the hospital Thaw had convinced her to take a trip to Europe to aid her recovery. Mrs Nesbit was against the idea from the start, obviously unaware of White's waning interest in Evelyn and not wanting to risk offending him after he had been so generous to her and her family. Eventually she was talked round and was encouraged to take the trip with her daughter and Thaw. She did take it upon herself to go and see White, supposedly to seek his approval, and also came away with a generous $500 letter of credit should she find herself in financial difficulties.

She need not have bothered as Thaw was extremely lavish and spent freely on both women, buying them both several new outfits, jewellery and of course paying for the whole trip, throughout which Thaw had one thing on his mind – he was set on proposing to Evelyn and was not prepared to take no for an answer.

Evelyn managed to hold off giving him her answer for several weeks, but Thaw could not wait for ever and when pushed she eventually offered him her explanation. She told him the shocking story of being "raped" by White – having been robbed of her virginity, she wanted to clear the air before accepting his proposal. She no doubt elaborated for full effect and Thaw was so enraged that he was more protective than ever of Evelyn. Evidently he had not been informed of the real nature of her stay in the sanatorium prior to their European tour.

As they continued on their trip Thaw continued to press Evelyn for more detailed information regarding the events which had occurred on the evening of the assault by White. He was entirely committed to protecting his new love and was just as committed to gaining revenge on White when he next saw him, determined to make him pay for besmirching Evelyn.

Whilst in London Mrs Nesbit decided to use some of White's money to treat her daughter and herself – she bought them new lingerie, apparently not wanting to embarrass herself by having to ask Thaw for money for such a personal purchase. Once Thaw found out he enquired where she had got the money from. She told him that it was part of a gift from White and Thaw was furious, so much so that he could stand Mrs Nesbit's company no longer and duly sent her packing back to New York.

Evelyn now found herself alone in Europe with Thaw and was alarmed to discover that he had some secret habits – he was an intravenous drug user, probably cocaine and/or morphine, which appeared to have an unpleasant effect on his moods. The couple continued their tour and moved on to Germany, where Thaw arranged for them to stay at an isolated small castle, Schloss Katzenstein. Evelyn endured a frightful night in the castle when Thaw turned violent and attacked her whilst she was in bed, beating her with what she described as a whip. After the ordeal Thaw was apologetic and begged her forgiveness; Evelyn wasted no time in telling him that he had behaved like a monster and that he had treated her terribly. As she was at his mercy she continued the trip, but encouraged him to return to New York earlier than they had originally planned.

When she was finally back in New York she didn't have to wait for long before she was visited by White. She told him of her trip but eventually broke down into sobs and described Thaw's strange behaviour, and of how he had beaten her in the castle in Germany. White, no longer romantically involved with Evelyn, offered support in the form of a good lawyer, as he believed that she could protect herself from Thaw if she had everything recorded officially.

White's interest in Evelyn diminished, and it was now common knowledge that he had turned his affection to another younger member of the chorus line, but continued to show a fatherly consideration toward Evelyn. Thaw on the other hand was still besotted and continued to woo her to gain her trust once again. As she was now "spoilt" goods Evelyn decided to take what she could get – to marry a multi-millionaire, if somewhat strange, was in her eyes still a good deal.

Strangely Evelyn was stricken with appendicitis again – seemingly Thaw did not grasp that this was impossible – was hospitalized and spent a long time recovering. It was during this time that Mrs Thaw decided that she should have her say and called on her "would be" daughter-in-law to encourage her to marry her love-struck son. She was of the opinion that her son would settle down if he married, and that she could share the burden of his tantrums with another woman.

The wedding was confirmed and the ceremony took place in their home town of Pittsburgh. After a honeymoon, Mr and Mrs Harry K. Thaw moved into the palatial Thaw family mansion, joining Mother Thaw. Mrs Thaw senior made her best efforts to introduce her new daughter-in-law to the local upper cut of society, but her reputation had preceded her and she was politely given the cold shoulder. She found herself to have no close friends, her husband would go missing for days on end and she soon started to yearn to return to New York.

After some persuasion Thaw relented and in the summer

of 1906 the couple returned to the city which Evelyn felt was her home. This was to prove a terrible decision, as Thaw was still harbouring a terrible grudge against White and was merely biding his time before he confronted him.

On the evening of 25 June 1906, White was in the garden at the top of the building which he had designed – Madison Square Garden – where he was enjoying the premiere of a musical review and clearly had a keen interest in one of the young lady performers. He had a table in front of the stage and did not want to miss any of the routine, unaware that a young man was making his way towards him. The young man in question was Harry Thaw; unusually for the time of year he had turned up in a long black overcoat, although his clothing went unnoticed by other people as they were either too busy watching the show or were engrossed in their own conversations.

Thaw stood and watched the 50-year-old man whilst he applauded the young dancers. Then, quite deliberately, he took a pistol from his coat and fired three shots into White's face. White slumped over the table, which collapsed and he fell to the floor. People nearby were not sure whether this was in some way a bizarre part of the act, as it was the opening night and it could have been an unusual "extra" to the show. The mood suddenly changed when Thaw then held his weapon above his head and made his way to the door. The shocked onlookers quickly rallied to aid the victim, but it was soon evident that he was past their help.

Outside the room Thaw walked towards his wife, still holding the gun above his head. "Good God, Harry, what have you done?" she asked. "All right, dearie," replied Harry. "I have probably saved your life." He made no attempt to leave the scene and was soon arrested by the police as they arrived at the theatre.

Due to the fact that Stanford White was a well-regarded architect and that his murderer was from one of the most wealthy families in America, the trial was dubbed the "trial of the century", no mean feat, considering that the year was still only 1906.

The trial was recorded and covered by all the news

agencies. Reporters were at court every day throughout the trial, making sure that they got photographs of all the witnesses before they entered the building. Many character witnesses came forward to tell the press that in their opinion Stanford White was a pillar of the community and in their eyes had done no wrong. Surprisingly Mrs Nesbit (now married and known as Mrs Charles Holman) also gave a statement to the press and confirmed that she knew Mr White to be an honourable, decent man. She went on to describe her daughter as "head-strong, self-willed and beautiful and that led to all her trouble".

The main witness in the court proceedings was surely Evelyn. She was rarely seen during the course of the trial, preferring to keep out of the public eye. Reported to have struck a deal with Mother Thaw, whereby she agreed to support her husband, in return for financial security after the trial, she was granted the opportunity to quietly divorce him after the interest in them had died down.

Thaw had the best defence team that money could buy, headed by eminent defence attorney, Delphin Delmas, who decided that the best way to get a good result in this case was to plead not guilty by way of insanity.

The head of the team for the prosecution was District Attorney William Travers Jerome, who did not share the opinion of Delmas; he considered the case to be a clear example of premeditated murder.

Numerous witnesses were brought before the court who had been in the room at the time of the murder, all of them able to identify Thaw as the killer. The doctor who had performed the autopsy confirmed that White had died as a result of gunshot wounds to the head.

Other doctors were brought to give their opinion of Thaw's mental health which, taking into account his previous tantrums and uncontrollable rages, provided the jury with a fair indication of his mental instability.

Evelyn was eventually called to give her testimony; as requested by her mother-in-law she dressed very demurely, not wanting to spoil her chances of getting the money at the end of the trial.

She fulfilled Mother Thaw's wishes to the tee. She told of her initial friendship with White and that she found him to be a kind man. She then broke down in tears when she described to the court the terrible night when she was attacked by him when only 16. The reporters took down every word and hurriedly relayed their stories to news hungry readers. This trial was turning out to be the biggest story for years and the news presses were quite literally working overtime to meet their demands.

Delmas took his opportunity to emphasize to the court that his client had been told the same harrowing story by Evelyn, still loved her and wanted to marry her.

The prosecution team took their chance to try and sully Evelyn's name by bringing up her former employment as an artist's model and more recently as a girl on a chorus line. He also implied that Evelyn was well aware of White's reason for asking her back to his apartment and stated that she was a willing guest into his bedroom.

He then asked her why she had continued a relationship with him after he had apparently attacked her. She confessed that her family had come to rely on the financial security which White offered and that it was for this reason alone that she carried on seeing him. He asked her why she had visited the lawyer Abe Hummel with a deposition against Thaw; she told him that she had made the deposition whilst under great emotional strain. The prosecution had attempted to dishonour Evelyn, but this had proved a mistake, public opinion warmed towards her and she was much pitied in the press.

The first time the jury provided a verdict, it was inconclusive – seven believed that Thaw was guilty of first-degree murder and the remaining five found him not guilty as charged.

It was nine months before the second jury managed to conclude that Thaw was not guilty by reason of insanity and he was duly incarcerated at an asylum in Matteawan. Several attempts were made to have him released, or at least transferred to a private hospital, but these requests were denied. Eventually Thaw had taken enough, escaped from the asylum and made his way to Canada; he was duly apprehended and returned to continue his incarceration. However, as a result of the well-publicized court case, Thaw was seen as a Robin Hood character and had won the admiration of the public. Massive public debates managed to sway the ruling and Thaw found himself a free man. This was indeed a very unusual case and there were still many who considered Thaw to be guilty of first-degree murder, but it has to be said that he definitely suffered from some form of mental illness. In this day and age he would surely have been diagnosed and offered the correct type of drug therapy to enable him to control his violent outbursts.

Once he had been declared a free man he went on to divorce his wife and his life continued in much the same vein until his death at the age of 76 in 1947.

Evelyn had carried a child through the court case and when the baby was born she named him Russell Thaw, although her husband never recognized the baby as his own. She was never paid a penny by Mother Thaw, despite carrying out her part of the bargain to the letter, and lived out her days trying to make ends meet. She found it difficult to return to her old profession after the trial as she was now a single parent and her infamous past didn't help her situation – the chorus line was usually a place in those days where you found innocent young women, not divorced single mothers, no matter how pretty they were.

A Nation in Mourning

JFK

John Fitzgerald Kennedy was arguably one of the world's most influential state leaders. For Americans in particular he stood for a new dynamic phase of American history. Leading them to post-war wealth and prosperity he also presided over a period epitomized by the cold war, the communist eastern bloc contrasting heavily with the democratic freedoms enjoyed by those living in the West. Kennedy initiated the space race when he declared America's intention to put man on the moon before the end of the 1960s. In 1962 he held firm as the world watched a superpower stand-off, with Kennedy threatening to blow Russian ships out of the water if they attempted to deliver nuclear weapons to Cuba, the small communist country lying just 90 miles off the American coast. History records Russian vessels turning around and heading back across the Atlantic, and with that the threat of an all-out nuclear exchange receded and the world breathed a mighty sigh of relief. Kennedy was a hero and was now more popular than ever – even his countless extra-marital indiscretions could not mar his public image, although when rumours began of an affair with another icon of the times, Marilyn Monroe, his gloss finish did lose some of its otherwise brilliant shine. His wife and the USA's first lady, Jackie Bouvier Kennedy, became somewhat of a style icon herself, as together they cut a charismatic swathe through the world of international politics.

But not all Americans were impressed with the Kennedy administration. The Mafia were being heavily targeted by JFK's brother Robert, who had assumed the office of At-

torney General, while JFK himself tackled the "tax concessions" enjoyed by Texas oil tycoons. Dallas in particular was
a hotbed of right-wing extremism, the town least likely to
offer a warm welcome to a liberal democratic president. Here
in particular, Kennedy's approach to the Cuban missile crisis
was considered a missed opportunity to demonstrate America's might against the communists. The nuclear test ban
treaty signed with the eastern bloc and the decision to sell
American grain to them looked like a climbdown to those
living in the South; and to top it all the withdrawal of
American troops from Vietnam would for many right-wingers be the ultimate humiliation. The President's visit to
Dallas was therefore brave – even if one excludes the possibility of an assassination, he could at the very least expect a
frosty welcome.

This unique period of American history ended just under
one hour after Air Force One, the President's personal
aircraft, touched down at Love Field airport, Dallas, at
11.38 a.m. central time, on Friday, 22 November 1963. As
the door to Air Force One swung open, the Kennedys were
struck by the crowds who had gathered from all over Texas
to give them a warm welcome. It was to be a brief visit – an
open-topped motorcade would deliver the President to the
Trade Mart where he was due to give a speech and then he
would be whisked back to the airport from where he was due
to visit Lyndon Johnson, the Vice President, at home on his
ranch.

Security was heavy on this particular visit – Texas, and
Dallas in particular, was hardly a hot-bed of Kennedy
support. The local police chief, Jesse E. Curry, had deployed
over 300 police officers at the airport and a further 60 were
stationed at the Trade Mart, considered an area most likely
to be a potential trouble spot. Along the route the motorcade
would travel, Curry had scattered a number of other officers,
a precaution against overzealous, anti-Kennedy demonstra-
tors. Earlier that morning officers had already removed a
number of individuals whose placards were too graphic for
public display, but apart from this the visit was expected to
pass without further incident.

The crowds along the way surged onto the road, slowing the progress of the motorcade, bringing the speed down from its expected 15 to 20 miles per hour to just seven. Finally the President's car swung into Dealy Plaza, a trio of parallel roads made up of Elm Street, the street which would take the President right past the crowds, Main Street and Commerce Street, which would eventually bring him to the Trade Mart. As the President's car slowed to make the sharp left turn into Elm Street, Jackie noticed an underpass which crossed Elm Street just ahead, whose shadows looked inviting with the temperature soaring that day – especially as she was wearing a bright pink woollen suit and feeling distinctly uncomfortable. As the President's car straightened up to head down Elm Street a sharp crack rang out. Jackie thought that a motorcycle had backfired; Chief Curry thought it was the sound of a small explosion on the railway line; but when the President lurched forward, grabbing at his neck, the unthinkable reality set in – the President had been shot; the time 12.30 p.m.

Riding in the vice-presidential car ahead of the president's, Rufus Youngblood thought he could smell gunpowder and with the sight of the President grasping at his neck, he knew for sure that he had been shot. Thinking faster than the President's own secret service agents Youngblood threw himself onto Lyndon B. Johnson, forcing him lower into the footwell of the car, using his own body as a shield. The slow rate at which the President's driver reacted allowed a further two shots to be fired, one missing whilst the second exploded into the president's skull, jerking his head sharply. Amateur footage shot at the time shows the shocking images of the bullet's impact, with pieces of the President's skull spraying over Jackie and the back of the car. It was now clear to most who were in, or close to the President's car that he had been fatally hit. The motorcade now sped away, heading directly to Parkland Hospital which had been warned of the President's impending arrival. At the same time, the police and officers who had been amongst the crowds began searching for the would-be assassin. The feeling was that the gunshots had been fired from a sixth-floor window overlooking Dealy Plaza.

Just six minutes later, at 12.36 p.m., the President's car arrived at Parkland Hospital and he was rushed through to the emergency suite. No one really imagined that any amount of medical intervention could save the President – anyone else would have been classed as dead on arrival (DOA). But this was Jack Kennedy and so the medical team went through the motions, performing a tracheotomy to aide breathing and then providing a blood transfusion, even though his pulse was already non-existent. Finally the doctors opened his chest and massaged his heart, but it was already too late and it probably had been since the second shot hit him. Jackie entered the emergency room with two Roman Catholic priests who had been called, determined to be in the room at the time of the President's officially recorded time of death, even though she too knew the actual time of death had been much earlier. Seeing the frenzied action surrounding her husband she briefly wondered in fact if there might be a chance after all, but the hope soon faded as the doctors and nurses moved away from the operating table and began pushing the wheeled medical equipment aside.

Unlike previous presidential assassinations, the news of Jack Kennedy's death revolved around the news screens of the world within minutes. It is said that anyone of a certain age can remember where they were at the time they heard the news of the assassination. In terms of a world-changing event there could have been nothing quite like it as America went into deep shock and sought answers to how it could ever have happened. The assassination has spurned hundreds of books, movies, documentaries and above anything else, numerous conspiracy theories. For if the death of the President shocked the world, it would be the murder of his assassin that would provoke a mixture of delight, then disbelief and finally confusion as to the question of who really lay behind the murder of JFK.

In the immediate aftermath of the shooting police officers fanned out and headed to the areas most thought to have been the gunman's vantage point. Motorcycle police officer Marrion Baker had heard over the police radio that the shots had appeared to come from a sixth-floor room of the Texas

School Book Repository building, which overlooked the assassination zone. Baker pulled up at the repository building and sprinted up the back staircase hoping to find the gunman. On the second floor he passed two men, Lee Harvey Oswald and his boss, Roy Trudy; both said they were employees and Baker allowed them to pass, whilst he headed up to the sixth floor. On reaching the sixth floor, Baker found the area empty, but he did find a rifle hidden behind some old boxes. Over the police radio he then heard a description of the gunman as provided by a member of the public who had seen the man in the window from his position opposite the repository building. The description given matched that of Lee Oswald, the man he had passed on the second floor.

Oswald had by now left the building, heading into Elm Street via the front door. Banging on the door of a passing bus he managed to gain entry and travel a short distance before the bus became ensnared in traffic, largely caused by the chaos following the shooting. Jumping off the bus he then flagged down a taxi and made his way back to the rooming house he had been using, getting out of the taxi a few blocks short of his destination, with the intention of collecting a pistol and a jacket and then disappearing. Leaving the house he walked along the road, waiting for a while at a bus stop before walking on again. The streets were now crawling with officers, all of whom knew the description of the man who had allegedly killed the President; it was quite by chance therefore that patrolman J.D. Tippit spotted Oswald at the intersection of Patten Avenue and Tenth Street and pulled in to talk to him. Once he was sure the man matched the description given, Tippit climbed out of the patrol car and joined Oswald on the sidewalk. Not having pulled his own gun first, he was allegedly met by Oswald with his .38 already drawn and was shot dead there in the street. Thirteen people witnessed the shooting of Officer Tippit and identified Oswald as the culprit – the question of whether Oswald was indeed the shooter appeared to have been answered. He emptied his revolver at the scene and reloaded. Knowing he was now his own identikit picture, he struggled to stay out of view. Leaving his jacket in the parking lot of a nearby petrol station he headed away, bobbing in and out of shop doorways to avoid the constantly passing patrol cars, eventually finding refuge in the Texas Theatre. Unfortunately he drew attention to himself by avoiding payment and the manager called the police. To his surprise the police arrived in larger numbers than he had expected, pouring into the cinema and scouring the seats with their flashlights. It was officer M. N. McDonald who spotted the hiding Oswald, sat low in his seat at the rear of the theatre. Approaching him he asked Oswald to stand, but instead he punched McDonald and drew his gun. In the struggle that followed McDonald was able to wrestle Oswald to the ground, at which point other officers moved in to help conclude the arrest.

News of the president's death had spread fast and the crowds who now gathered outside the Texas Theatre were of the opinion that the police had arrested the assassin inside. On his removal to the waiting patrol car the crowds began chanting for Oswald's death, even though at this point the police were unaware of the link to Kennedy's murder – as far as they were concerned they were making the arrest in connection with officer Tippit's death. Oswald had succeeded in eluding the police for a mere hour and 20 minutes.

Once in custody Oswald was quickly linked to the assassination of Kennedy and although he was never officially charged because the arraignment hearing was interrupted, it was generally accepted that he had pulled the trigger whilst knelt at the sixth-floor window of the school repository building. Oswald however denied both of the murders and intriguingly referred to himself as a "patsy", a comment that fired the imaginations of those who believed the assassination was a conspiracy. Since that point there have been many suggestions as to who the conspirators were: communists, Republican right-wingers, the Mafia and even Lyndon B. Johnson himself, as the individual who won the presidency through the tragedy.

A famous person can be murdered for a variety of reasons, including the simple act of making the perpetrator more famous themselves. When a president is murdered there is the added dimension of politics, reprisals from groups of individuals with something to lose from a particular policy decision, such as large-scale criminal activity that is likely to be curtailed due to an administration's focus on their particular brand of crime. So which could have spurred Lee Harvey Oswald to commit what history recalls as the most terrible individual murder of the last 40 years?

It is not the purpose of this chapter to examine in detail the concept of the President's assassination as being the act of conspirators. However, it is important to note some of the peculiar facts that have emerged since that fateful day, facts that question the notion that Oswald acted alone or that he was involved at all. For justice to be dispensed fairly, those who have to consider the facts must do so without any preconceived ideas, without any prejudice and without the pressure to provide a result which will suit the public's needs. There is no doubt at all that the public's and the media's opinion was heavily in favour of Oswald being a lone gunman, a crazy communist sympathizer who had planned to escape to Cuba after the event.

But we should briefly consider the following observations in relation to the events that day. When the initial shot rang out it has been asserted that the first bullet entered the President's back somewhere between his shoulder blades, exiting through his neck. The official investigation after the assassination concluded in the Warren Commission that this same bullet then hit Governor Connally in his shoulder, exiting at the front and then struck him in the wrist before finally lodging itself in his thigh. This became known as the "single bullet theory" or the "magic bullet", as it had to enter and exit a human body five times, changing direction on each occasion in order to achieve this end result. To change direction the bullet would have had to strike bone and in doing so it would have lost most of its velocity. One must also consider the angle at which Oswald was meant to have shot the President: he was on the sixth floor, shooting down at about a 60-degree angle, it is therefore surprising that the bullet should head down into the President's back and yet emerge from his throat, a significant change of angle once inside the body.

At the time of the shooting many spectators believed that the shot rang out from the rear of the area now famously referred to as the "grassy knoll", directly adjacent to the President's car. In archive film footage shot at the time, spectators can be seen looking over their shoulders at the fence at the top of the "grassy knoll", where a shadowy figure can be seen prior to the shooting and then disappearing directly afterwards. There were many who headed for that fence in order to assist in the capture of the gunman, but who were stopped by individuals displaying secret service credentials, yet the secret service denied having agents in that area.

Other witnesses claim to have heard a shot coming from the front of the motorcade, possibly from the vicinity of the underpass. Were all these people right? Were they simply picking up the gunshot sound nearest to them? Certainly shots were heard coming from high up on the repository building. It has emerged since that police walkie-talkies did pick up multiple gunshot reports, supporting the claim that there was more than one gunman operating from around the assassination zone.

Further confusion surrounds Oswald's disposition when the police arrived. He was passed by Officer Baker and was seen drinking a coke with his boss on the second floor of the building. Officer Baker arrived at the rear door of the building within one minute of the shooting, and had to take the stairs to the sixth floor as the lift was not in operation. How could Oswald have dashed to the lower floor, got a cola from the drinks machine and been stood with his boss, without any sign of exertion?

When other officers arrived at the repository building they examined the gun and all three confirmed that it was a German Mauser, but later two of them changed their minds and claimed that it was in fact a Mannlicher Carcano rifle, a completely different weapon. The third officer however stood firm, refusing to concede the gun was anything other than a Mauser; he was subsequently run off the road by an unknown person and shot.

When Kennedy arrived at the Parkland Hospital the medical staff wrote in their report that the wound in the President's neck was in fact an entry wound, suggesting a shot from the front of the motorcade, not from the repository building which lay to the rear of the vehicles. The wound in the President's back being the exit wound, normally the larger of the two, now makes more sense. The hospital had every reason to recall these facts as the doctors took the decision to use the bullet hole as part of the tracheotomy procedure. The Warren Commission later concluded that the larger hole on the President's neck was of the size it was because it was the exit wound, not because of the work the doctors had carried out.

The footage of the President being shot shows his head being thrown backwards and the matter that is thrown off is also spraying towards Jackie and the rear of the car. Again this would be consistent with a shot hitting from the front, however, the Warren Commission concluded that the President's head movement was caused by a spasm, at the moment of being shot. It becomes easier to see why the public's trust in the Warren Commission was significantly less than total and why the conspiracy theory continues to be supported.

And last but not least in this complex story is the simple fact that Oswald himself was shot dead by local bar owner, Jack Ruby, as the police were transferring him to another jail. The public waiting outside the jailhouse cheered as news broke that Oswald had been shot. For a moment Ruby was a hero, the man who shot the assassin – many people even believed that Ruby should be given some sort of a medal, certainly not any form of a reprimand. But soon questions began to emerge – supposing Ruby had not shot Oswald in a revenge attack for the President's murder; what if he had shot him to prevent him from talking? There was Oswald's own description of himself as being a "patsy"; now he was dead anything further he might have said was lost for ever.

Oswald's background was more complex than his seasonal job at the Texas School Book Repository building. He was in fact allied to the CIA and had been on missions to Russia, acting as a Soviet sympathizer. Documents relating to his service record have emerged to confirm this and there is evidence to suggest that he was expecting to be sent on another mission, this time to Cuba, at the time of the shooting. Could it be that Oswald's history was in some way his undoing? To many people, including the Warren Commission, Oswald's Russian forays were proof positive of his communist sympathies.

Other facts that have emerged since the conclusion of the Warren Commission indicate that Oswald, along with two other unidentified individuals, had made enquiries at a Dallas airfield to hire a small aircraft a couple of days before the President's murder. The aircraft's owner was suspicious that the trip they intended to take was to Cuba and declined to do business with the trio. A few days later the front pages of America's newspapers carried the photograph of Oswald, the man he identified as being at the airfield that day. Was this just another part of an elaborate plan to further implicate Oswald, to conclude in the public's mind that he was indeed a communist? Or worse, was this one element of the plot meant to implicate Fidel Castro, the Cuban dictator, in the assassination of the President. It would be an easy plot to believe – there had after all been bad history between the two men over the Bay of Pigs invasion and the Cuban missile crisis. There were many senior government officials who would have preferred to blast Cuba into submission when they had the opportunity but instead had to back down when the crisis was over.

There is no doubt that had Oswald ever gone to court he would have lost his case and been sentenced to death. The country wanted revenge and they had their eyes firmly on the man in custody. Although there were many doubts expressed over the findings of the Warren Commission, most Americans believed that they could implicitly trust their own government. Many of the facts that have emerged since that time, and which paint an entirely different picture of the events unfolding on that November day, did so decades after the actual event and would have come too late to have been of any use to Oswald.

Oswald was saved the prospect of a trial in which he would have had the steepest of hills to climb, vilified from the moment the news broke. He was instead found guilty of being the lone gunman, by virtue of the findings of the Warren Commission, the official government investigation team set up by the newly inaugurated President, Lyndon B. Johnson. The Commission, which was set up on 29 November 1963, carried out its investigations in total privacy – even at the time of writing the majority of the files associated with the investigation are yet to be released; some will be kept out of the public domain until 2030, fuelling further speculation as to what is hidden in those top secret government files.

Jack Ruby therefore is the only character in this whole event who ever went to court. Born to Polish immigrants and of the orthodox Jewish faith, Ruby entered the world in June 1911, to a large family, with four older siblings and three younger. The Ruby household did not enjoy great wealth and it is generally thought that Ruby was somewhat deprived. He struggled at school and was considered to be a delinquent, at times being moved out of the family home to spend brief periods with foster parents. His early move to paid employment fell short of being impressive as well, initially selling horse-racing tip sheets before moving on to work for a scrap collectors' union.

However it was bars, night-clubs and strip joints where Ruby eventually found permanent employment. Ruby arrived in Dallas in 1947 and jointly managed the Singapore Supper Club with his partner Eva Grant. When Grant moved to the West Coast she left Ruby in full control of the club, whose main concern was to sell beer to its patrons and provide basic dance hall facilities. The club was positioned in a rough area of Dallas and the name just didn't seem to sit well with the local clientele so he changed it to the Silver Spur Club. In 1952, borrowing $3,700 from a friend, Ruby then purchased the Bob Wills Ranch House with a partner and ran it as a Western-style night-club. What should have been a burgeoning business, however, soon ran into financial difficulties as Ruby found it difficult to maintain the interests of both outlets and eventually lost both. Depressed at his misfortune he sank into depression and basically locked himself away in his hotel room for the next four months.

In early 1953 Ruby once again managed to take an interest in a club, this time the Vegas Club, which he managed with another friend, but again history repeated itself when the club failed to meet its obligations and was taken away from him. He eventually bought his interest in the Vegas Club back again and this time managed to hang on to it right up until his arrest.

Throughout the years Ruby bought himself in and out of club interests, most failed and he never managed to reach the heights of club ownership that would have made him a "name" in Dallas, or provide him with the money and power he craved. Clubs were not his only foray into the world of private enterprise – amongst other things, Ruby tried to sell American jeeps to Cuba and created a vitamin mix which he attempted to sell through shops – but none of his attempts at business seemed to bear fruit.

At the time of his arrest Ruby was not unknown to the authorities – between 1949 and 1963 he had been arrested eight times by the Dallas police department. The charges against him were varied: in 1949 he was fined for disturbing the peace; in 1953 he narrowly avoided arrest over a charge of carrying a concealed weapon; but fell victim to the same charge in 1954 and in addition was charged with violation of a peace bond. He frequently fell foul of the state liquor laws by selling alcohol after hours and was also charged with allowing dancing after hours. The year in which he murdered Oswald had already been a busy one in terms of trouble with the authorities – in February 1963 he was charged with common assault, a charge he managed to walk away from; and later that year he was arrested again for ignoring traffic summonses. Throughout this entire period Ruby acquired many motoring tickets and was frequently suspended by the alcohol licensing authorities for breaching their many regulations.

Those who knew Ruby had a wide-ranging set of views on him, his employees in particular being divided over how he behaved as an employer. His normal operating style seemed to be frequent outbursts of temper and threats of discharge, followed by the occasional apology. Most however portray Ruby in a more sympathetic light – he was generally interested in the welfare of his staff and could be quite pleasant, although there is much evidence to suggest that he dominated his employees and often resorted to violence, tried to cheat them out of pay or make late salary payments. Certainly he used foul language to vent his frustration and his staff were often the focus of this. His physical outbursts are well recorded, at one time beating one of his musicians, Willis Dickerson, who in turn bit a chunk off the end of Ruby's index finger. In a more serious incident Ruby beat another musician with brass knuckle dusters, causing serious damage, the unfortunate man needing stitches to his mouth.

And then there is the matter of Ruby's links to organized crime, although to anyone who knew him there was no doubt that if he was anything, he was small time. There is evidence to suggest that he had been involved in smuggling, drug-running and certainly pimping and prostitution. In 1956 Ruby met James Breen to discuss the management of three prostitutes and the possibility of selling pornographic photographs, which, together with the club scene would lead one to expect him to have links with organized crime, but if he had any associations in that direction he was at the bottom of the tree. His personal wealth, or lack of it, would suggest he was not one of the recipients of the proceeds of crime, while his reputation as someone who could not keep his mouth shut suggests that others would not trust him with delicate information. Therefore the idea of him shooting Oswald to silence him would seem misplaced, as someone else would then need to silence Ruby.

On the day in question Ruby had been hanging around the police headquarters where Oswald was being held. He had managed to gain entrance to the area concerned by posing as a member of the press and was armed with a pistol. When Oswald emerged, flanked on all sides by police officers, Ruby stepped forward and shot him at close quarters. As Oswald sunk to the floor, other officers moved in to arrest

Ruby, who did not resist or try to make a run for it. Some would say he was expecting thanks rather than a prison term. Outside, members of the public who had been waiting to jeer Oswald clapped, as news of the shooting spread amongst the crowd.

Initially Ruby appeared to take the position that he had shot Oswald on the spur of the moment in a bid to save Jackie Kennedy the trauma of a Dallas trial. However his behaviour around the police headquarters suggest a more calculated attack. Conspiracy rears its head again when one considers how Ruby managed to get down to the basement of the Dallas jailhouse; some believe Ruby must have had cooperation from someone in the police department.

The American population now faced a more complex question. Initially they were pleased to have their assassin in custody and were even more pleased when a patriotic Dallas man killed him in a reprise attack. Soon though questions of conspiracy emerged and Ruby himself became the focus of public hatred.

After his arrest the prominent attorney Melvin Belli agreed to represent Ruby for free, many believing that with the right preparation the charge of murder could have been handled as a "murder without malice" charge, broadly equivalent to manslaughter. The resulting sentence would therefore have been probably not more than five years and with good behaviour possibly in the region of three. If the public believed that Ruby had carried out a public duty and saved the taxpayer the cost of an expensive trial and execution, then his stay in jail need not be such a difficult stretch.

Strangely though Belli decided to defend the case by claiming that Ruby was legally insane, citing some vague family history of mental illness as proof. Following his trial Ruby was convicted of "murder with malice" and was handed a death sentence.

The complexities of the situation surrounding the President's murder were such that it would be almost impossible for anyone involved to have obtained a fair trial. Oswald would surely have been convicted – even the might of the Warren Commission concluded that he was the lone gunman, although the basic facts suggested otherwise. During a review of the assassination in 1970 another committee concluded that the President's death was "as a result of a conspiracy". The conspirators, however, could not be found and the two who had been in custody were now dead.

The case against Ruby could have gone either way – if he could have proved that he simply wanted to avenge the murder of the President, a lighter sentence might well have been achieved, but those in authority did not seem interested in this as the claim of insanity would have meant that anything he claimed after being jailed would have been disbelieved. And if he was found guilty of murder and competent, then he would suffer the death penalty.

Either way the press and the public were avenged – they had Oswald dead and if Ruby was involved then he was behind bars; if he wasn't a conspirator then he was at least a murderer and a cold-blooded one at that.

Whilst in custody Ruby alluded to a conspiracy and asked the Warren Commission on a number of occasions to be taken to Washington as he did not feel safe in Dallas. He never got his wish to be moved and sank into a delusional state whilst awaiting an appeal, dying of an embolism on 3 January 1967.

Although it is generally now accepted that Kennedy was assassinated as the result of a conspiracy, the exact details will probably never be known. The subject still attracts much attention as it was after all a major world event. As recently as 1981 Oswald's body was the subject of an exhumation which sought to prove or disprove a thesis developed in a 1975 book by British writer Michael Eddowes, that following a trip to Russia, Oswald was replaced with a clone. Dental records showed conclusively that the body in Oswald's grave was indeed him.

No doubt in 2030, when more of the Warren Commission papers are released to the public, the controversy will rage once again, and perhaps the truth over the involvement of these two famous bit players will finally be known.

No Time for Another Comeback

Sal Mineo

James Dean, Natalie Wood and Sal Mineo all shot to fame when they starred in the massive silver screen hit *Rebel Without a Cause*. They were the pin-ups in teenagers' bedrooms throughout the United States and beyond. Who would have guessed that tragedy would befall all of them? They were all to die suddenly, a total waste of three promising lives and a sheer waste of talent.

On 30 September 1955, James Dean was tragically killed while out enjoying one of his great pleasures, driving his beloved Porsche sports car. The 24-year-old star worked hard and played hard, and was on the way to compete in a motor race when he failed to negotiate a bend at high speed. On 29 November 1981, at the age of 43, Natalie Wood was sailing near Catalina Island, California, on the yacht she shared with her husband, Robert Wagner, and their friend Christopher Walken. Natalie drowned while trying to board the dinghy tied up alongside the yacht. Sal Mineo was shot down and killed outside his apartment building by a would-be robber.

Salvatore Mineo Jr was born on 10 January 1939. He grew up in the tough Bronx area of East Harlem, New York City. He was the third of four children for his parents Sal Sr and Josephine, having two older brothers – Victor (born in 1936) and Michael (born in 1937) – and later in 1943 the family was completed with the arrival of his only sister, Sarina.

His parents had emigrated to the US from Mineo in Sicily; his father had his own company making caskets. Young Sal would be teased at school because of his father's profession, but Sal was extremely proud of his father's work and would defend him, saying, "So he makes caskets – what are you going to do about it?" Invariably, nobody ever did do anything about it. In fact, the whole family was involved; it was truly a family business. His father would design and make the caskets, his mother would do the paperwork and the children would do general chores to assist their parents. When they had time to play, they even used the caskets as a good place to hide when playing hide and seek. On one occasion, the young Sal had been hiding in a casket for so long that he actually fell asleep in it; when he awoke he was understandably rather shaken up, but maintained his cool, casually climbed out and went to find his brothers and sister.

By the time he was nine, his family was able to move, to a larger three-storey, family-sized house. Initially he found it difficult to fit in; it's never easy being the new kid on the block. But he managed to impress a local gang of youths when he was challenged to smoke a cigar – he actually smoked the whole pack and thus became their front man.

It was also at this time that Sal made his first stage debut. He was attending his local parochial school, where he was asked by the nuns to play the role of Jesus. He learned his lines well and, when it came to the stage performance, he was surprised how much he enjoyed the experience. He was also aware that his performance had gone down well; he showed a great deal of talent and thoroughly enjoyed the whole event. He was considered a natural.

Problems persisted at school and Sal was often involved in fights – to such an extent that he was excluded and was even considered to have minor behavioural difficulties. In a bid to keep her son on the straight and narrow, his mother enrolled him in dancing school at the age of ten. The lessons were a total success, as Sal had found something that he excelled at and enjoyed. His enthusiasm didn't go unnoticed, and it wasn't long before he had been spotted and requested to take a part in a TV programme called *the Ted Steele Show*.

From there his life took off. At the age of 11 he was asked by Broadway producer Cheryl Crawford to audition for a small part in *The Rose Tattoo*, a Tennessee Williams play, to appear on Broadway. He was thrilled when he was offered the part and even more so with the $65 a week pay cheque, for the single line: "The goat is in the yard." This is what he and his mother had dreamed of. Even if it was just the one line, he would be working twice a week at the theatre alongside Eli Wallach and Maureen Stapleton. He could hardly believe his luck.

Before his debut on Broadway, the show was to have a trial run in Chicago. This was to prove a daunting trip for Sal; it would be the first time away from his family, and he was in tears on the train while saying goodbye to his mother. He was so upset that Tennesse Williams, who was also travelling on the train, sat and comforted him.

The show returned to Broadway and Sal would take the subway from the Bronx to Broadway, but found that he received a lot of unwanted attention from small groups of gangs using the subway and was also propositioned by men. He would have to run through the stations or switch trains to get away from them, although he wouldn't always manage to outrun the gangs and would arrive at the theatre in some disarray on several occasions. He even went to the extreme measure of carrying a toy gun. He often found the travelling scary, but would be completely professional when he arrived at work. He stayed with the company until the show closed a year later in 1952.

This was to prove timely, as he had just been successful in landing the role of understudy for the Crown Prince of Siam in the Broadway play *The King and I* at the St James Theatre. The star of the show was Yul Brynner, who played the role of the King of Siam, and Gertrude Lawrence, who played the King's English teacher. For this role, Sal had far more lines to learn and also had to sing; he was needed at the theatre for every performance, although he was only able to assume his role when the boy who played the part of the prince was either taken ill or on holiday, such as during the summer of 1953, when he went on his annual summer holidays, leaving the eager Sal to take his place.

It must be said that Sal was nervous of appearing on stage and also of the show's star, Yul Brynner. Sal was in awe of the talented actor, but got to know him and found that he was very supportive and easy to talk to. Yul even offered Sal advice on his acting skills, and it wasn't long before Sal was offered promotion to the part of the Crown Prince of Siam on a permanent basis. He obviously accepted and was very successful, earning himself great reviews, which his mother and father were truly proud of. He stayed with the show until its close in 1954. By then Sal was 15 and ready for his next challenge.

This challenge was to be a part in a weekend series called *Omnibus*, in which he acted alongside Leslie Nielsen and Anne Bancroft. His new "mentor" was the director, Yul Brynner, and with Yul's coaching Sal was to do well. From this success he was offered many other television roles. He was receiving good recognition and it was obvious that he was about to hit the big time.

Sal was offered the role of young Chandler in the film *Six Bridges to Cross* – the role of adult Chandler was given to Tony Curtis – and this was the beginning of his movie career. While filming, he auditioned for another role in the movie called *The Private War of Major Benson*; the part was the character of a cadet colonel and the star of the film was Charlton Heston. Sal was successful and at the tender age of only 16 his career was in no doubt: he was able to act, dance and sing and had a huge female following thanks to his stunning good looks.

While still in Hollywood, he visited the Warner Brothers Studios to audition for a role in a movie called *Rebel Without a Cause*. The lead character, Jim Stark, was to be played by a new actor, James Dean, and the female lead character, Judy, was to be played by a 16-year-old actress, Natalie Wood. After winning over the casting director, Nick Ray, Sal secured the role of Plato, Jim Stark's friend. He and Dean became friends both in character and off the set and would often spend time together after filming.

The movie's strong teenage rebellion theme and the blatant homosexual desire between the two male characters proved a massive success around the world, shooting Dean and Mineo to stardom. Dean, who had previously admitted that he was bisexual, encouraged Mineo to express his feelings towards him during the shooting of the film, in order to portray more genuine characters, something that was not lost on the viewing audience. Many believed that the two men had a romantic relationship off screen, but this was never more than a rumour. It was years later that Sal admitted that he was bisexual, but didn't realize this until long after the filming of *Rebel Without a Cause* was completed, and by then it was too late as Dean was no longer around.

Sal's next movie role was the part of Angel Obregon II in the movie *Giant*, which again starred his good friend James Dean, along with Rock Hudson and Elizabeth Taylor. He and James were particularly close and, after the movie was completed, Dean helped him to get his next role. Shortly before the release of *Rebel Without a Cause*, Sal signed a contract to play the part of Plato. The filming took place in Texas in a town called Marfa. Sal was only to act in a few scenes; to his disappointment, many were cut from the finished movie. He swiftly signed a contract with MGM for his next movie, *Somebody Up There Likes Me*, in which he would star again alongside James Dean.

Tragically on 30 September 1955, just a few weeks after the completion of *Giant*, James Dean was killed in a car accident. This was a terrible shock for Sal, who had admired the talents and acting skill of Dean, describing him as young, brilliant, shy and hating hypocrites. Sal even took up some of the hobbies Dean had introduced him to, including working out with weights, boxing and playing the drums. Another love of his was waterskiing, which he was taught by Yul Brynner. The role of Rocky Graziano, which Dean was due to take in the new film was then given to the acting newcomer Paul Newman.

It was while filming *Somebody Up There Likes Me* that Sal discovered he had been nominated for an Oscar for his role of Plato in *Rebel Without a Cause*. Despite being the youngest person to be nominated for an Oscar for best supporting actor, he was not successful, losing out to Jack Lemmon for *Mr Roberts*. However, Sal managed to achieve critical acclaim, being described as "brilliant" and "sensational", and his popularity was soaring.

He continued his success by taking roles in movies and television dramas, notably one called *Dino*, which earned him an Emmy nomination. In the movie *Crime in the Streets*, Sal played a resentful criminal and it was after its release that he earned the nickname "The Switchblade Kid". During 1957, Sal recorded several records, which his already strong fan base were ready to welcome with open arms. It didn't take long for him to achieve a Top 10 hit, with his song "Start Moving"; in fact, this record was in the charts for over 13 weeks. His album sales did well also, selling over a million copies and earning him a gold record.

During all this success, he didn't forget his family. His mother, Josephine, managed and guided him, and his brothers and sisters also worked for him. After studying law at New York University, Victor became Sal's lawyer. Mike was always with him to offer a helping big-brother hand, while Sarina assisted him with the masses of fan letters which were constantly arriving. By now Sal's earnings were in excess of $200,000 a year and he was able to enjoy the luxuries that this provided. He bought his family a large home in Mamaronek, New York and for himself a New York apartment, also renting a large house in Beverly Hills.

In 1960, he signed a contract to star as Dov Landau in the film *Exodus*, in what would be one of his most acclaimed roles. The other members of the cast included Paul Newman, Eva Marie Saint, Ralph Richardson, Peter Lawford and Jill Haworth. The latter played Karen Hansen, Dov Landau's love interest. Directed by Otto Preminger, this was a screen adaptation of the novel by Leon Uris, telling the story of the Jewish people's struggle for the liberation of Palestine following the Second World War. Sal's character, Dov, was a Polish Jew making his way to Palestine to create a Jewish homeland after having survived the atrocities of the Auschwitz concentration camp, only to be diverted and imprisoned by the British. The majority of the filming was on location in Israel. It was during the filming of *Exodus* that Sal and Jill Haworth became romantically involved;

they were together for a while after filming, but the romance faded. However, the pair remained friends for years to come.

The film was released and was again well received. At 21 years of age, Sal gave a brilliant performance and was the only one who was nominated for an Oscar in the movie. It was his second nomination for supporting actor. Sadly, again he was not to receive his prize, despite his confidence prior to the ceremony.

In the early 1960s, Sal was still acting, but not continuously as he had done previously. He found that he had time to spend enjoying himself and relaxing. He took pleasure in his hobbies, spent time at home and, more intriguingly, started to discover his sexuality. He found himself to be more interested in men and had several short-lived homosexual relationships. During this time, homosexuality was still frowned upon, and actors who displayed this side of their character soon became aware that they were limiting their acting range. Who wanted to see an openly homosexual man cast as the lead in a romantic film? This also answers the question why many homosexual actors kept their private life strictly private – to name Rock Hudson for starters. With this in mind, Sal started to be more discreet with his relationships, especially those with men.

The work gradually started to dry up and, for the first time, Sal found himself short of money. In a bid to keep himself from being financially embarrassed, he decided to sell many of his possessions. The most difficult decision was having to sell the house which he had bought for his family, but these were dire times and he had to raise money by whatever means he could. Thankfully, he was offered two movie roles including *The Greatest Story Ever Told* and *Who Killed Teddy Bear?* His earlier loss of money had not taught him any lessons; his healthy bank balance would soon be diminished as he lavished gifts on his friends and treated himself to many luxuries, including a new motorcycle.

For the next few years, he spent his time earning money to enable himself to start spending again. He really needed to get his life back on track and decided to buy the rights to a play entitled *Fortune and Men's Eyes*. This was the story of a man named Smitty, who suffered homosexual rape and degradation at the hands of other inmates while he was in prison for a minor offence. Sal directed the play himself and started the process of auditioning the cast. He was very clear in his own mind regarding the type and look of the cast, and sought perfection in those who auditioned for the play. For the leading role of Smitty, he cast a young 18-year-old actor named Don Johnson (who later went on to *Miami Vice* fame). Sal himself took the role of the character Rocky.

The play opened at the Coronet Theatre in Los Angeles and received good reviews, commending Sal for his efforts in the production. A very strong scene in the play, which portrayed a brutal homosexual rape, caused a great stir. As expected, it became of huge interest to the gay community. The play was deemed a successful hit and ran for over a year.

One of the worst situations a young man can find himself in must be at the bedside of a dying parent. Sal spent five days at his dying father's side. Sal Sr., still only in his 50s, died in 1973; he was laid to rest at the Gates of Heaven Cemetery in Hawthorne, New York. Sal gave a moving eulogy at his father's funeral, and in his grief he decided that from that day he would take life with both hands, because one never knows what might be waiting around the corner.

Over the next few years, Sal was having relationships almost exclusively with men, and was, when interviewed, openly admitting to being bisexual. He continued to take roles in television and plays, but did not manage to achieve his former success. Rather than living the high life, as he had enjoyed in the past, the money was used primarily to maintain his standard of living and keep him out of debt.

By 1976, Sal's career was starting to pick up again and he was experiencing a "comeback". He had won financial backing to direct his first movie, entitled *McCaffrey*. He had also managed to get the role of Vito in a play called *P.S. Your Cat is Dead*; his character was, appropriately, a bisexual burglar. After the show opened in the Montgomery Playhouse in San

Francisco, Sal was to receive the reviews he was so desperate to hear – his acting skills were commended and his performance was described as brilliant. As the play was doing so well, it was decided to move to the Westwood Playhouse in Los Angeles – which, fortunately for Sal, was only a few miles from his Hollywood apartment.

His life was truly coming together and Sal was now satisfied that he was no longer struggling to find the right job for the right price. His happiness was to end abruptly as on 12 February 1976 Sal was making his way home after rehearsals for *P.S. Your Cat is Dead* and was brutally attacked. He was viciously stabbed which pierced his heart and was left for dead.

A young child, Monica Merrem, who was in her bedroom at the time of the attack, recalled hearing voices from outside. "Oh, no!" a man shouted. "Oh, my God! No! Help me, please!" She went to her window and was able to see a man running away; she described him as a pale white man.

Monica wasn't the only person to be alerted; in another apartment, Ron Evans also heard a man screaming. He quickly ran to find out if he could be of assistance. When he reached the man, who was now on the ground and bleeding, he immediately recognized his acquaintance Sal Mineo. He found Sal covered in blood, lying face down. He turned Sal over and, as he was obviously having trouble breathing, offered mouth-to-mouth resuscitation. It wasn't long before Ron was joined by others who had heard the commotion and the emergency services were summoned.

Unfortunately, by the time the ambulance arrived, it was too late – Sal had already passed away.

Several witnesses saw a man fleeing the scene of the murder, but their descriptions varied immensely. A security guard, Stephen Gustafson, recalls a white man with either dark blond or brown hair. Another, Scott Hughes, thought the man was Italian or Mexican with dark curly hair, and believed that he made his getaway in a yellow Toyota.

When the police searched the body, they concluded that the death was not caused by a robbery, as Sal still had his money in his pocket, was wearing jewellery and his car keys were lying beside his body.

Sal's autopsy concluded that a stab wound to his heart caused his death. It was also noted that parts of his body, especially around the buttocks, contained small puncture wounds. Some of these were explained by a former lover of Sal's, a man named Michael Mason, who told police that Sal was having hormone injections to enable him to overcome his low libido. But it was suggested that the other wounds may have been caused by intravenous drug use.

Five days after his death, Sal's family arranged his funeral for 17 February at the Holy Trinity Roman Catholic Church in Mamaronek. Hundreds of mourners came to pay their respects. Among them were family, friends, fans and members of the entertainment industry, including Warren Beatty, Yul Brynner, David Cassidy, Dennis Hopper, Peter Lawford, Paul Newman and Natalie Wood. Sal was buried beside his beloved father, whose own funeral he had attended only a three years previously.

After a search of Sal's apartment, police found a large amount of homosexual pornographic magazines and were coming to the conclusion that the murder was sexually related. They then started their investigation by interviewing as many people as they could who had any connection with Sal, including his many colleagues in the entertainment industry.

Press speculation was immense and daily reports of the murder investigation were there for everybody to read. Public opinion varied wildly, but everybody wanted the murderer of the movie heart-throb to be found and found quickly. However, this was not to prove the case.

Unfortunately, the investigation didn't manage to produce any firm leads and for many months the police were unable to come up with a firm suspect. Then, out of the blue, several months later, a fresh line of enquiry was opened as a new witness came forward with information which was to prove very interesting.

Theresa Williams told the police that her husband had arrived home on the night of Sal's murder with his shirt covered in blood, and confessed to her later that evening while they were watching a news report about Mineo's murder on television. She claimed that her husband told her, "That's the dude I killed." He said that he had murdered Sal with a hunting knife, which he had recently purchased for just $5.28. She also said that he had used the same knife in other robberies he had committed. She claimed that his motive was to rob the star. Sadly, the police would never get this witness to testify in court, as shortly after giving her statement she took her own life.

The police then focused on Lionel Williams. They found that he had a criminal record involving robbery and was already being held in prison because of bad cheque charges. The only problem they faced was that their new suspect did not fit any of the previous witness descriptions, as Lionel was a black man, although it has to be said he was reasonably fair-skinned.

While in jail, prison guards heard Williams telling other prisoners that he did in fact kill Sal Mineo. They duly contacted the police and Lionel Ray Williams was charged with murder and was extradited to Los Angeles in January 1978 to face the charge of murder as well as lesser charges of attempted robbery. At a pre-trial hearing, he pleaded not guilty to first-degree murder and bail was set for $500,000. He returned to jail to await his trial, which would not take place for a year. The judge presiding over the hearing was Judge Ronnie Lee Martin. The prosecution was led by Deputy District Attorney Michael Genelin, and the defence lawyer was Mort Herbert; the jury was an even mix of men and women.

The prosecution claimed that the murder was premeditated. If this were proven it would mean that Williams could face the death penalty. Their case was based on the evidence provided in Theresa's statement to the police prior to her death, and on testimonies from the medical examiner and that of a colleague of Williams. They stated that in their opinion Lionel was sitting in wait for Sal on the night of the murder with the intention of robbing him. They produced a knife similar to the one which Theresa Williams had described her husband using in the robberies. When the knife was examined by the medical examiner, Dr Noguchi, and placed inside the wound in Sal's heart, it was found that the blade was an exact match.

Herbert told jurors that it was difficult to guess which knife Williams had used and it would be wrong to assume that the replica was an exact copy, pointing out that Theresa was not there to testify that it was identical to the one she had earlier described.

A witness for the prosecution was Allwyn Price Williams (no relation to the accused), who was brought from prison whilst serving a sentence for kidnapping to testify that Lionel Williams had boasted about stabbing Sal Mineo while he was being robbed. He claimed that Williams had described driving around the area looking for somebody to rob. He said that Williams was alarmed by Mineo's cries for help and in his panic stabbed him and fled without taking any of his belongings.

But his statement was challenged by the defence, who claimed that he was not telling the whole truth and was hoping to have his sentence shortened by assisting in the Sal Mineo murder case. Under cross-examination, Allwyn confessed to embellishing his story, claiming he had made things up because "I was hoping to get out of jail" and thought a "strong" story would do the trick.

"Would you lie again?" Herbert asked, "if it was absolutely necessary to get off the hook?"

"I guess so, sir," Allwyn admitted.

The defence then produced the three witnesses who saw a suspicious man fleeing from the scene of the murder. None of them stated that the man was black; their descriptions ranged from a white man with light hair to a Mexican-looking man with curly hair. One witness described the getaway vehicle as a Toyota. Herbert therefore concluded that Lionel Williams was not the person who was seen at the crime scene.

The prosecution were quick to show the jury a photograph of Williams at the time of the murder; he appeared to have light skin and had long bleached hair. They also pointed out that they had records to prove that Williams was using a light-coloured Dodge Colt on the night of the murder, and that this vehicle resembled a Toyota.

In his summing, up the Judge described Williams as "a predator, a man who wants the world to know how tough he is". He then went on to instruct the jurors to connect the dots of evidence and that the portrait drawn "is the face of the defendant".

It was now over three years since Sal had died and over two months since the trial began, but on 16 March 1979 Lionel Williams was found guilty of second-degree murder and sentenced to 51 years to life. He would be eligible to apply for parole in 14 years. The judge allowed Williams a chance to speak in court, following his sentence. William was critical of his attorney and the Judge, claiming, "He wasn't in my corner. I didn't want him but you put him on me. I asked you to get rid of the man twice but you didn't do it. I fault you for my going to the penitentiary."

The case failed to conclude satisfactorily why Sal was murdered and indeed whether Williams actually committed the crime. With no real motive and the fact that the murder weapon was never found, there were many people who believed that he might have been framed. Could public opinion have forced the police to take Williams to trial, knowing that this would quash tabloid jibes regarding their inability to bring forward a suspect in over 12 months? Speculation continued to grow and there were various theories put forward. Some believed that the murder was drugs related, but surely Sal's drug use was not anywhere near severe enough for him to be a large-scale user, and therefore he would not have run up large drug debts. Others believed that the crime might have been related to Sal's sexual leanings and could have been the result of a homosexual dispute. The truth is that nobody will ever know for sure; the mystery died with Sal Mineo on the roadside outside his apartment block.

Lionel Ray Williams did receive his parole in the early 1990s. He subsequently returned to his old ways of crime and it wasn't long before he found himself back in prison, a habit that was to recur on several other occasions.

Another Conspiracy

Robert Kennedy

At best the Kennedy family, America's one-time royals, are either unlucky, jinxed or the target of an organized group, whose ultimate purpose has never been fathomed. The family has certainly had its fair share of bad luck. The eldest son of Joe and Rose Kennedy, Joe Jr, was killed whilst on a secret bombing raid during the Second World War. It was this event that placed John F. Kennedy as the son who would run for President. During the course of JFK's presidency, his wife and first lady, Jackie, lost their first son Patrick during pregnancy. Only weeks after this tragic event Kennedy himself was killed in Dallas, Texas, the victim of two gunshots, leaving the way clear for Robert Kennedy to run for President just four years after the murder of his brother. In a rerun of his elder brother's assassination Robert Kennedy too was laid low by an assassin's bullet, whilst campaigning for what was looking like a successful bid for the Presidency. Later, and not the subject of this chapter, the youngest Kennedy brother, Senator Edward Kennedy, was involved in a near fatal situation when he ran his car off a bridge at Chappaquiddick, killing his female passenger, Mary Jo Kopechne. The mystery surrounding this event was sufficient to put an end to any thoughts that he might have had for the top job in American government.

The debate has raged for years over the mystery surrounding the various events which have affected the Kennedy family. It persists with good reason, for in each event there has been significant reason to suspect that there was more to the events than the law could uncover, yet researchers and investigators have provided evidence to support conclusions other than those reached in either official government investigations or in the courts themselves.

The "celebrity factor" would seem to play its hand in different ways for different people, sometimes positively and sometimes negatively. If you do not believe the Kennedys have been the subject of a conspiratorial vendetta then you would need to explain in other ways why evidence has been ignored. Perhaps the "celebrity factor", when a president or would-be president is assassinated, displays itself as the authorities and the public looking to hang the first person who fits the bill. On the positive side of the "celebrity factor" is the fact that researchers, writers and investigators continue to sift through the details, perusing every strand of evidence and often taking decades to get at the truth. Just like President Kennedy's assassination, which was originally thought to have been the work of a lone gunman, Robert Kennedy's shooting, which at first looked to be the result of one man's murderous thoughts, turned out to be more complex and the Kennedy name ensures that three and a half decades after the event we continue to look for the truth.

In the wake of President Kennedy's assassination, Vice President Lyndon B. Johnson was sworn into office vowing to continue the foreign and domestic policies of his predecessor. The Vietnam War dominated the nation's front pages, with the loss of countless American lives. The Johnson administration pursued a strategy which increased the number of American servicemen in Vietnam from 20,000 to half a million. At home, Martin Luther King lead the way in establishing black civil rights, a movement which sat awkwardly with a certain faction of the white population.

Having served out the balance of JFK's initial term in office Johnson successfully regained the position by winning the 1964 presidential election. Robert Kennedy, who had completed his role as Attorney General during what would have been his brother's first term in office, now successfully transferred his political ambition to the senate.

During the next four years Kennedy watched the American people divide themselves on both domestic and foreign policy. He strongly believed that the Vietnam War could only be brought to a satisfactory conclusion by diplomatic means, and at home he wanted all Americans, black and white, to live together, sharing the same freedoms and aspirations. He pointed to the heavy price paid by black Americans in Vietnam, and asked if they were fighting the same war for the same reasons.

As Johnson's first elected term was drawing to a close Kennedy decided he had no choice but to take on the President for the Democratic nomination – their views on the main areas of policy were too disparate to be compromised.

As the time approached for those who would be president to declare themselves, it was Senator Eugene McCarthy of Minnesota who first announced his candidature, and he was soon building a healthy following on the campaign trail. Kennedy, who did not see McCarthy as presidential material, was the next to join the race, spurred by Johnson's decision to send a further 200,000 men to war.

Kennedy was a seasoned campaigner with great energy, not to mention the plentiful charisma he oozed when reaching out to the public. Those involved in the campaign would later say it was an experience never to be forgotten. Once the bandwagon was rolling, it gathered pace and volume, and Kennedy was able to win over most of his audiences through his warm and compelling messages, finally stepping out of the shadow of his brother. He spoke compassionately of the plight of the poor, the need for civil rights for all, of brave young men dying in the swamps of South-East Asia and of the roles these young men could play if they were not sacrificed for the vanity of their country.

His speeches touched the hearts of Americans of all creeds and colours; Martin Luther King was sure to support Kennedy's nomination had it not been for his own premature demise at the hands of another assassin. It was Kennedy who stood and faced the crowds in an Indiana ghetto, against the advice of local police, to announce the death of King and his own fight for social justice.

Somewhere along the way, with a backdrop of ever-increasing support and with this the chance to take up residency in the White House, someone or some group decided that Kennedy had gone too far. The risk of him taking the Presidency was too great for the shadowy powers that be, and his demise was planned.

After his speech in Indiana his victory there was decisive, although he lost Oregon, Orange County and Nebraska to McCarthy. By now Johnson had withdrawn from the contest leaving it a two-horse race. Kennedy headed for California, with speeches planned for Los Angeles, San Francisco, Sacramento, Oakland and San Diego; there was a real buzz around the campaign as Kennedy entered the largest of the primaries. The newspapers had their new target and gave unprecedented coverage of the Democratic nomination contest. When asked if Kennedy had all it would take to go all the way, one reporter, John J. Lindsay of *Newsweek*, responded, "Of course he has the stuff to go all the way, but he's not going to go all the way . . . somebody is going to shoot him . . . he's out there waiting for him now."

On 5 June 1968 Kennedy stood on the podium looking out at the screaming audience who had come to listen to his campaign speech at the Ambassador Hotel in Los Angeles. He had delivered what some described as his best speech of his campaign so far. Smiling his broad Kennedy smile he gave the victory sign to the 1,800 strong audience, before concluding, "My thanks to all of you and now it's on to Chicago and let's win there." To all present there would be few who would doubt they were looking at the next President of the United States.

It had been a tiring few days, but before he would get a chance of sleep there was one more appointment he had promised to keep – with the ladies and gentlemen of the press who were gathered in a separate room, elsewhere in the hotel. Exiting the podium, Kennedy was shepherded away by his small group of close-knit helpers and taken the shortest route through the hotel to get to his next venue.

Kennedy had made the decision himself that he did not want an army of security people shrouding his every move, partly because he didn't like the restriction of close-quarter body guarding, but mostly because he was trying to appeal to normal individuals who associated that type of self-important gang-handedness with people with whom they had nothing in common. On this particular night Kennedy was accompanied by his inner circle and a number of security personnel supplied under contract to the Ambassador Hotel. Behind the core group led by the hotel maitre d', Karl Uecker, a large number of the audience had followed the senator who was heading into the hotel's pantry area, which was deemed the quickest way to get to the appointed press room. One of the agency bodyguards, Thane Cesar, had moved in behind Uecker and now lightly held the senator's arm in a bid to steer him along the pantry corridor which was set with all types of stainless steel tables and utensils. Hotel staff had gathered in the pantry area and were pleased when Kennedy stopped to shake their hands, turning to the left and then the right. After one handshake Kennedy turned to the front to continue his progress when the first shot rang out. It was 12.15 a.m.

A young man of eastern appearance had jumped out of the crowd in front of Kennedy and shouted, "Kennedy, you son of a bitch," and started to fire over and over again. Reminiscent of his brother's shooting the scene broke into pandemonium, with the crowd dispersing, not knowing which way to run. In an act of pure bravery, Karl Uecker lunged for the gunman and managed to contain him in a headlock with one arm whilst trying to control the man's gun hand with his other. Bashing it against one of the stainless-steel steam tables he hoped to make him drop the weapon, but the gun continued to fire until the last bullet was spent.

When the noise stopped and the chaotic scene had calmed down, Robert Kennedy lay on his back on the pantry floor, his blood pooling around his body. Juan Romero, a member of the hotel staff, cradled the senator's head in his lap. "Come on Mr Kennedy, you can make it," he encouraged. Surprisingly, Kennedy was still conscious, and enquired if everyone was alright, seemingly unaware of his own plight. A member of the crowd handed through some rosary beads and a doctor who had been found gave what little assistance he could. Kennedy's wife, Ethel, was ushered through to the front of the crowd, where she immediately knelt beside him in the expanding pool of blood and offered shocked words of comfort. Kennedy, barely audible, asked Ethel if he was alright, but by now he was losing his fight as his life blood slowly seeped away.

The police were on the scene within three minutes of the attack, quickly taking charge and arresting the gunman. The ambulance was painfully late, taking 17 precious minutes to reach the hotel, taking Kennedy first to the Central Receiving Hospital before being sent on to the Good Samaritan Hospital, where they arrived at 1 a.m., some 45 minutes after the shooting.

Once there he was rushed into the operating theatre where he endured a three-hour operation to save him, but the damage was too great and Kennedy died of his wounds, the second Kennedy to be killed by an assassin's bullet.

The man arrested for the crime was Sirhan Bishra Sirhan; born in Jerusalem, his family had moved to the United States after they had become refugees in Israeli-occupied territory. During the course of the police investigation that followed, they found a diary kept hidden by Sirhan at his home, in which he appeared to make threats against Kennedy. It was suggested that Sirhan's motive was his disapproval of Kennedy's support for the sale of 50 Phantom jets to the Israelis. On top of the eyewitness testimonies, Sirhan had been seen earlier in the day practising rapid-fire shooting at the San Gabriel Valley Gun Club and was known to have communist sympathies. The gun Sirhan had used at the gun club was the same calibre as that taken from him after the shooting had occurred. If ever there was a case which could be classed as "open and shut", this must surely be the one.

The media machine rolled into action once more as the name Kennedy hit the front pages, reminiscent of his brother's tragic demise just four years earlier. Again there was outrage, another Kennedy assassinated, and another opportunity for dynamic leadership of the American people had been lost through one man's actions. And like the last time the public were fed the facts as they emerged, the obvious ones – Sirhan was seen to have shot Kennedy, had been wrestled to the floor, had his gun taken and had left evidence to demonstrate his disdain for his victim through his diaries.

The public once more wanted to see justice done and were in no mood for a complicated enquiry. But Kennedy's celebrity, his worldly importance, would not allow the simple facts as presented to just sail through unquestioned.

Examination of Kennedy by coroner Thomas Noguchi revealed that he had been struck by three bullets, a fourth one having travelled through his suit, exiting through the shoulder pad of his jacket. The first bullet hit Kennedy just around his right shoulder blade, coming to halt after getting lodged in his spine. The second bullet entered just a couple of inches below the first, exiting his chest, the entry and exit wounds showing that the bullet had been travelling steeply upwards and forwards at the same time. The third bullet struck just to the rear of and slightly below the right ear, causing heavy damage to the neck tissue.

When the pantry area had been cleared the police began to take witness statements from those who were present, including many members of the public and those who worked at the hotel. The Los Angeles Police Department's forensic expert, De Wayne Wolfer, was also in attendance and began to draw up his own picture of events that evening by creating a "ballistics map", through which he intended to show where each bullet had ended up, from which direction they were fired and their trajectory once launched.

The ballistics map and the coroner's report form the starting point of another assassination mystery which carries through into the LAPD investigation and the reports which were ultimately released for public consumption in 1988.

An evaluation of the evidence from the forensic and medical perspective reveals that Kennedy was shot from behind, not from in front, the position adopted by Sirhan. All the bullets that struck Kennedy show entry wounds to the back of his body and the more obvious exit wounds to his front. Closer examination of the injuries show that the trajectory of each bullet is steeply upwards and forwards. The coroner's report also suggests that the nature of the injuries would indicate that the gun involved would need to have been practically touching Kennedy to create the effect uncovered in the examination. The ballistics report confirms similar findings – the bullets that were retrieved were found in the ceiling space, consistent with a steep angle of trajectory and in a wooden door jamb, again in front of Kennedy.

If Sirhan had been a lone gunman then his bullets would have been found behind Kennedy and the entry wounds would have been obvious on Kennedy's front. Eyewitness accounts are clear that Sirhan made his attack from the front and that at most Kennedy only ever presented the side of his body as he shook hands with the kitchen staff. More specifically, the most common account is that Kennedy was facing Sirhan full on when he fired his first shot. Sirhan had after all shouted, "Kennedy, you son of a bitch," thus drawing the senator's attention fully to the front. In conflict also is Sirhan's distance from Kennedy when he opened fire. It is estimated that he was at least one and a half feet away, possibly up to six feet away depending on your perspective, whereas coroner Noguchi's evaluation suggests that the shot that hit Kennedy behind the ear was fired from not more than a couple of inches away, and the others which hit him in the back were fired with the gun's barrel pressed up against Kennedy's body.

Again reminiscent of JFK's murder, there was a type of "magic bullet" conundrum. If one ignores the directions the bullets were fired from for a moment there is the angle of entry. Given the positions of Kennedy and Sirhan in relation to one another, it would appear to be geometrically impossible for Sirhan to have fired bullets which could achieve such entry angles. Supporting this further are the eyewitness accounts which state that Sirhan's gun arm was parallel to the ground for the initial shots, which would indicate he was firing at a 90 degree angle to Kennedy's perpendicular body. Only after Uecker grabbed him did the angle of shot change. The circumstances the eyewitnesses found themselves in would have made it difficult to recall everything perfectly, but the forensic and medical proof is difficult to ignore – though it ultimately was.

And then there was the matter of the number of bullets fired and the number of bullets accounted for at the scene. Kennedy was not the only person to have suffered gunshot wounds that night – five other people were injured, including Kennedy's friend Paul Schrade, newsman Ira Goldstein and others unlucky enough to have been in the vicinity. Sirhan's gun contained a maximum of eight bullets and he was able to keep firing until it was empty. He was prevented from reloading his weapon, therefore if more than eight bullets were found there must have been another gunman in the kitchen at the same time. All of the bullets were accounted for except for one which had been lost in the ceiling space. Comments passed by officers of the LAPD at the time suggest that there were many other bullets which had been found in the door frame, which when added to the ones removed from those who were hit add up to more than the eight Sirhan had fired. These additional bullets were never mentioned in De Wayne Wolfer's ballistics report. Other witnesses at the time also identified men in suits who had their weapons drawn; Don Schulman claimed he saw one of the security guards firing his gun, but in the pandemonium could not be sure who at.

As Kennedy was a presidential candidate rather than the President, the crime committed that night was not a Federal offence, therefore it was appropriate for the LAPD to handle the enquiry themselves. Their police chief, Ed Davis, was heard to say, "this will not be another Dallas," making reference to the government-based investigation carried under the leadership of Earl Warren. What was specifically meant by this comment is not known but what is clear is that the investigation was much less vigorous than it should have been. Early on the LAPD began to come to conclusions which the evidence did not support, and where evidence emerged which did not fit the pre-formed conclusion it was discarded.

One would think that the medical and forensic evidence would have been sufficient for questions to be asked, but there were other pieces of the jigsaw which were officially ignored. Shortly after the shooting one witness heard a man and a woman, who were running away from the Ambassador Hotel, say, "we shot him, we shot him." Sergeant Paul Schraga was the officer who took that particular statement and he subsequently put out an All Points Bulletin (APB) on the two suspects. At LAPD headquarters they were so sure they had got their man that Schraga was told to cancel the APB – when he didn't do so his superiors stepped in and cancelled it for him. One can draw one's own conclusions as to why this action was taken – conspiracy involving the LAPD, incompetence or the sheer wanton desire to be able to close the case without complication. When someone of Kennedy's public stature is killed the net result can be difficult to deal with – the press will invade, the government may intervene, the LAPD's effectiveness will be scrutinized – however, if an arrest can be quickly concluded it is possible to look good and avoid all of the chaos which would surely follow. The power of celebrity should not be underestimated; it can have a dizzying effect on all concerned. Eventually the witness statement was explained away as a simple case of mishearing, the couple actually saying, "They shot him, they shot him," which is of course possible, but those who heard it would be more likely to recall accurately what was said than those who were not present.

Others in the room that night claim to have seen all manner of suspicious men acting strangely; two people say they saw armed men other than Sirhan and the contract security man, Thane Eugene Cesar, with guns drawn. Lisa Urso stated she saw a blond-haired man in a grey suit putting his gun back into his holster. Another witness saw a tall, dark-haired man, dressed in a black suit, fire two shots and then run out of the pantry, heading back in the direction Kennedy had originally come from.

With all of the above information seemingly contradicting the official version of events, the press were happy to report that the lone gunman, Sirhan Sirhan, had committed the crime because of his political beliefs, the whole event was unfortunate and demonstrated the need for more security. Certainly had Kennedy had the benefit of official security he might have been a more difficult target, as his bodyguards would have shielded him from any would-be attackers. However suspicions are aroused by the contract security provided by Ace Guard Service that evening. Given the ballistic and forensic evidence, Thane Cesar, who had only been with the security company for one week prior to his assignment, was the man closest to Kennedy when he was shot; he was guiding him by the elbow and was therefore in a position slightly to Kennedy's rear, a position best placed to deliver the wounds that were sustained. During the LAPD investigation that followed, the gun Cesar had been carrying that evening went missing – it has never been found.

Sirhan himself presented a rather odd persona on his arrest. Clearly he had drawn a gun and fired several shots which were presumably intended for Kennedy, and to this extent he was heavily embroiled in the events that evening. The police, the press and the public were to that extent quite right to conclude that Sirhan was guilty; the issue comes as to whether he acted alone or acted as part of a group. Those who saw Sirhan on the night of his arrest were surprised at his demeanour. Given that he had been arrested for a very serious crime he was unnervingly calm; he smiled and his glazed expression gave the impression his mind was elsewhere, giving rise to the notion that he had been hypnotized. During interview he mumbled incoherently and claimed he could not recall anything of the shooting. Many people had seen Sirhan in the company of others earlier in the evening, seemingly in deep discussion, but he couldn't recall what he had been doing or with whom. His forgetfulness seemed to fit nicely with the LAPD – talk of others who might have been involved that evening simply complicated the situation – who for some reason were much happier to conclude that Sirhan had acted entirely independently. The detailed descriptions provided by those who had seen Sirhan in the company of others were simply dismissed, even when one witness claimed to have spoken briefly with one of Sirhan's party that night.

In due course Sirhan was charged with first-degree murder and his defence team constructed a "diminished responsibility" plea as their main defensive argument. In doing so they entirely overlooked the opportunity for a defence based on the evidence supporting a conspiracy, one which would have claimed that although Sirhan was involved, it was not his weapon that ended Senator Kennedy's life.

There is something quite unique about a crime involving a high-profile celebrity. If the criminal investigation itself had been wanting then the trial of Sirhan would prove equally perplexing. Following his arraignment Sirhan requested to see a lawyer from the American Civil Liberties Union (ACLU); renowned for their championing of minority causes, they also came with the added benefit of providing their services free. After consultation with Sirhan 65-year-old Grant Cooper was appointed as his defence counsel; he was a former president of the Los Angeles Bar Association.

Heading the team for the prosecution was Lynn "Buck" Compton, Chief Deputy District Attorney. Supported by two assistant DAs, Compton made it clear he was looking to restore the trust in American law enforcement.

To get the proceedings underway Sirhan pleaded not guilty at a hearing on 2 August held on the second floor of the Hall of Justice. With many political and judicial cogs now turning the clocked ticked on to October before Herbert V. Walker was appointed as magistrate. Coming to the end of a long and impressive career Walker was known amongst his colleagues as a hard but fair man: hard because of his track record in handing down 19 death sentences; fair because of his reputation for sticking to the letter of the law.

As pre-trial proceedings began Sirhan was already looking at a predetermined outcome. In mid-October the defence and the prosecution agreed, based on the findings of the LAPD's investigation into Kennedy's assassination, that Sirhan had acted alone in the shooting. With this prior agreement in place the respective teams entered the court.

After a small delay whilst the court decided if the diary obtained from Sirhan's house could be submitted as evidence, due to a question of whether the LAPD had been granted appropriate authority to enter the house, the trial eventually opened on 7 January 1969. It was held on the eighth floor of the Hall of Justice in a packed 75-seater court. Security was placed on maximum alert.

When the court proceedings finally commenced there was doubt as to whether there would be any need for a trial as the defence and the prosecution had agreed a plea bargain. Sirhan would plead guilty in exchange for immunity from the death penalty, which on the face of it would seem a fair outcome, given the defence had done little to establish an alternative story to the one commonly presented in the papers or suggested by the LAPD.

Judge Walker however would not agree to the plea bargain, in this instance – saving the taxpayer the cost of an expensive trial was significantly less important than demonstrating to an extremely eager public that justice would be fairly dispensed. It was a sensible decision given that Lee Harvey Oswald had never been brought to book for his alleged role in the assassination of John Kennedy. The prosecution, however, did not necessarily have the public purse in mind when they agreed the position with the defence. The prosecution's own psychiatric assessment of Sirhan had concluded that he was psychotic and therefore not medically liable for his crime, which would mean that they were much less likely to win the ultimate outcome.

In February of the same year the prosecution produced the first of its witnesses, including those members of the senator's group who sustained injury on the night. Forensic experts, gun experts, the arresting police officers and William Jordan, who first interviewed Sirhan after his arrest, were all called to give testimony to the events that evening. Neighbours who thought they had heard Sirhan say negative things about Kennedy were called and a damning entry from Sirhan's diary was read aloud to the court before being interpreted by the prosecution.

The media continued to present the case for the prosecution, feeding it to an eager public who had no reason to question any aspect of the LAPD's findings – after all, why would they wish to ignore evidence of there being anyone else involved?

By late February 1969, the defence commenced its counter-attack by trying to establish Sirhan's unbalanced state of mind. They started by defining Sirhan's rough childhood in war-torn Palestine, and described the abuse he suffered at the hands of his uncaring father. Psychiatrists proclaimed that he was of unsound mind and therefore not capable of committing a premeditated murder. They pointed to a horse-riding accident which had resulted in a severe head injury, ending Sirhan's hopes of becoming a professional jockey and contributing to his present muddled state of mind.

Sat in the dock, Sirhan could only watch and listen whilst his defence team declared him almost insane. Looking distinctly uncomfortable with the assertion that he was completely mad, he at one point jumped up out of his chair and shouted towards the Judge, "I withdraw my original plea of not guilty and submit a plea of guilty as charged . . . just execute me."

After the defence team managed to calm him down, the part of the trial that everyone had been waiting for had finally arrived – Sirhan was now to take the stand and act in his own defence. Those who waited with baited breath were to be disappointed. When Sirhan was questioned about his role in the assassination of Kennedy he claimed, as he had done to the LAPD, that he could not remember any details at all about the night in question. When pushed to at least offer some explanation as to his alleged role in the shooting, he simply suggested that he must have either been intoxicated or had suffered a temporary bout of insanity, brought on by his severe anger at Kennedy's apparent support for the Israelis.

The case which had been classed as "open and shut" by the LAPD had lost none of its appeal in the courthouse. When the trial was brought to a close on 14 April, after 15 weeks of battle and having had the benefit of 89 testimonies, there seemed little doubt as to the outcome. The three-day recess as the jury considered its verdict seemed excessive to most people but when they eventually emerged to give their decision there was little surprise when they announced that they found Sirhan guilty of first-degree murder. Everyone seemed pleased, the court, the LAPD, the media and the public – they would all have their revenge and no one seemed too concerned with the evidence which had not been aired in court.

When Judge Walker passed sentence on 21 May, there was little surprise again when Sirhan was condemned to death in the gas chamber. The only voice to spring to the defence of Sirhan was that of his mother, Mary Sirhan, who claimed that her son had not received a fair trial. If the death penalty seemed harsh given the actual evidence, then at least some degree of justice was dispensed when California declared the death penalty no longer legal, and with this Sirhan's sentence was commuted to life.

He was sent to serve his sentence in California's Corcoran State Prison, where it is assumed he will remain for the balance of his life. Now in his sixties time is running out if Sirhan harbours any hope of winning a retrial.

Those whose voices were absent during the trial in respect of the real facts surrounding Kennedy's death soon emerged after Sirhan had been sentenced. The conspiracy theorists began to examine the facts and wrote volumes in support of an official investigation. When someone of Kennedy's celebrity status is murdered there are many agendas at work. The need to satisfy the public's desire for retribution may be the reason why the LAPD overlooked the obvious contradictions in the evidence and if this is so then we must assume that their ultimate destruction of much of the evidence was motivated by the same thoughts. Photos, files and the door frame, along with many other items of evidence have been destroyed, apparently taking up room that is needed for more current investigations. Much of the information though does still exist and there is now a swell of public desire to explore the case further and maybe even review Sirhan's prison term. Vincent Bugliosi, famed for his prosecution of the Manson gang, was retained by Sirhan in 1975 to peruse the LAPD over additional bullet holes that were found on the door frame, as shown on X-rays taken of the wood. The LAPD had by then disposed of the door frame and the X-rays could no longer be found – another dead end and once again the

District Attorney's office could see no reason to reopen the case.

This case, like many other high-profile events, lives on through the continued attention it is given by the media, who have u-turned to some extent. They were happy for Sirhan to be given the death sentence at his trial but now present the shortcomings of the case. During a June 1998 press conference held outside the Pasadena home of Sirhan's sister Adel, the press turned out in force to hear her defending her brother, stating the inconsistencies in the evidence that had been aired some 30 years earlier, but without effect.

Sirhan has always claimed he could not remember any of the events that occurred on the evening of the assassination, a fact which has driven the conspiracy theorists to suggest that he was under hypnosis at the time. In June 1997 Sirhan attended his tenth parole board hearing and declared that he thought he was innocent of the crime. He pointed out the conflicting evidence that has been mentioned and then suggested that he thought he had been used by others who had directed him whilst he was in some sort of trance. The prosecutor assigned to the hearing, Thomas L. Trapp, called Sirhan's claim "preposterous". He was denied parole.

In March 2003 Sirhan was again turned down for parole on what was his twelfth hearing, still declaring his innocence and with a model prisoner record. A senior commentator from the Loyola University Law School commented, "Parole hearings for such high-profile prisoners are not intended to consider their eligibility for release, but to let justice be seen to be done, for the public's sake."

The press, who were so keen to declare him guilty at the time, are now probably the only people who have a powerful enough voice to demand a review of the second Kennedy murder to shock the nation.

With remarkable insight, or some deeper knowledge, Jackie Kennedy had predicted the demise of Robert Kennedy during a conversation with a friend: "Do you know what I think will happen to Bobby? The same thing that happened to Jack." Sadly she was proved to be correct.

The Farcical Trial of the Funny Fatman

Roscoe Arbuckle

Justice for all, except if you are a celebrity. These words could have been Roscoe Arbuckle's epitaph. He was cruelly hounded by the press, who, when they get the sniff of a celebrity scandal, let alone a suspicious death, are determined to prove that it's the media who make a killing.

Roscoe was initially charged with first-degree murder of a young girl who died at one of his parties, although by the time the case went to trial the charge had been reduced to manslaughter. In what can only be described as a farce of a trial, the first jury failed to reach a firm agreement on his guilt, or indeed innocence, although the majority sought his acquittal. The second time round the jury were still unable to come to an agreement, although strangely this time they favoured finding him guilty. By the third and final time they found him not guilty and even prepared a statement to apologize to the now totally humiliated and depressed accused. But by now the damage was done, the press had had their pound of flesh and had managed to stir up so much public animosity towards Roscoe prior to the trial, that everybody had already formed their own opinion as regards his guilt. The jury obviously struggled to reach their verdict, but truth will out and Roscoe was deemed a free man.

Sadly though it would be many years before he would be able to take up his acting career. His name had been well and truly dragged through the mud and was considered to be the proverbial hot potato; nobody therefore wanted to be associated with his name, worried that the public would boycott any production that he was involved with. Amazingly, after he had been acquitted, people were still very suspicious of his guilt. It's probably true to say that if you read a scandal in the press about a celebrity, you tend to remember it (whether it's true or not) rather than a favourable review of a movie.

From the moment of his birth on 24 March 1887 Roscoe "Fatty" Arbuckle was no lightweight – reportedly weighing in excess of 13lb on delivery this was to prove something of a shock to his slim mother and father. Indeed the large birth weight of her child did in fact cause his mother health problems which troubled her until her death some 12 years later. His father, William Goodrich Arbuckle, was suspicious of the size of "his offspring"; considering his wife's and his build, there was always a niggling doubt that he may have not fathered the child. He was unable to prove such, but did make life hard for Roscoe, who was aware that his father was unduly harsh on him, although unable to guess the reasons for his behaviour. He was born in Smith Centre, Kansas, but while he was an infant, his parents, by now with nine children, moved to California.

Unfortunately for Roscoe he became the butt of many childhood jokes and was often taunted and bullied by the other children. It was at a young age that he was given the nickname of "Fatty", which stayed with him until his death. Like many large children who find themselves in this situation, he sought comfort in food which only compounded his problems and his weight continued to soar in this cruel vicious circle. As a result of being bullied, Roscoe became a self-conscious, shy and quiet child who tried his best to blend into the background, and not bring unwanted attention to himself.

Extraordinarily, Roscoe found his confidence would soar when he took to the stage to perform in front of an audience. He was found to have a wonderful singing voice and was extremely agile in spite of his large size. He performed on stage from the age of eight, thoroughly enjoying the applause and adulation from the audience. His mother was immensely proud of her son's hidden talents and often came to the theatre to enjoy his performances.

Sadly his mother died in 1899 when he was only 12. His father soon stopped supporting him so the youngster began making ends meet by doing odd jobs in a local hotel. He consoled himself by singing at work, and it was here that a professional singer overheard him, suggesting he attend a local amateur night at a nearby theatre.

Roscoe watched several acts perform on stage – if their work was not considered good enough the crowd would jeer and then, to his horror, a long hook would come out and pull the poor performer off the stage. At that point Roscoe decided that he would not put up with such humiliation and determined that he would do well. He sang a few songs and danced, concluding with clowning around and doing somersaults – when he saw the dreaded hook appearing he somersaulted into the orchestra pit in panic. The audience loved him, he was applauded heartily and won the competition.

No longer a failure, he was spotted by important people in show business and in 1904 was invited to sing for Sid Grauman at the Unique Theatre in San Jose. From then he began to tour with the Pantages Theatre Group and travelled the West Coast of the States. By 1906, he took a job in Portland, Oregon working for Leon Errol at the Orpheum Theatre, from where the company, including Arbuckle, began touring other theatres with their show. Often Arbuckle would take centre stage and being extremely versatile was hugely popular with the audience; he was able to turn his hand to any form of entertainment and was a credit to the company.

Arbuckle's acting career was to start in 1909; while in California, he took a part in his first movie called *Ben's Kid*. He thoroughly enjoyed the work and with the money it provided he was able to dress well, becoming a rather striking figure who took great care of his appearance. He refused to let his size be the cause of "mickey taking" and would not allow his friends and colleagues to refer to him as "Fatty" – he would always interrupt and simply remind them that his name was Roscoe.

Roscoe met a beautiful, slim, young singer called Minta

Durfee, whom he affectionately called "Minty". They were soon married and were indeed a happy couple, although they were a strange match as Roscoe towered over his petite wife.

Arbuckle resumed his stage career by joining the Morosco Burbank Stock Company. The work took him and Minta through China and Japan, Minta enjoyed the sightseeing but was not happy at the sight of her new husband drunk with the male members of the company. When he took to drinking his personality changed for the worse, and rather than being considerate and jovial, he would become argumentative and spiteful.

To Minta's relief the couple returned to America later that year and Roscoe started work at Mack Sennett's studio, Keystone, where he became one of the famous Keystone Cops. They were hugely popular, silent slapstick films in which Roscoe was involved in much pie throwing and clowning around. He was in many brilliant films and worked with great actors of the time, including the undisputed greatest – Charlie Chaplin.

Roscoe still refused to use his size to get a cheap laugh – for example, he would not allow himself to get stuck in a doorway or chair, although it must be said he was well aware that his weight did add a comedy value to an already comical routine.

By 1914, Arbuckle had started to direct some of the films in which he acted and was able to prove that he could produce almost feature-length films moving from one-reelers to two-reelers.

Being such a heavyweight tends to result in medical problems and in 1916 the comic had a severe health problem – an infection on his leg turned into a carbuncle, which proved to be so bad that he almost had to have his leg amputated. Fortunately this was not the case but the illness took its toll and Roscoe was briefly addicted to morphine as he lost around 80lb.

After recovering from this bout of illness he went into partnership with Joseph Schenck, and they formed their own film company called Comique. This partnership was to provide Arbuckle with more creative control over his work and it wasn't long before they started to enlist young up-and-coming stars to come and work for them, one very successful name they added to their team being Buster Keaton. This was to prove highly successful and the pair starred together in their 1917 film *The Butcher Boy*.

Although Arbuckle was enjoying a highly successful professional life, unfortunately the same cannot be said for his marriage. The couple were now struggling, partly because of Arbuckle's drinking, but also the amount of time spent away from each other whilst he was filming. Unable or unwilling to give up his drinking, they were unable to resolve their differences and the couple separated in 1917.

Comique films went from strength to strength and they managed to produce some of the best movies of the silent era. After two years Arbuckle was once again ready for a change and decided to relinquish control of Comique to Keaton and signed with Paramount, reportedly for $1 million a year.

It was whilst with Paramount that he worked on his first real feature movies. The pace was much faster and he was expected to make around half a dozen a year. He was working flat out and suffering as a result. Eventually, in need of a break, he decided to take a short vacation in San Francisco with Fred Fischbach, his long-time friend, and actor Lowell Sherman.

Just before leaving for his holiday, Arbuckle managed to sustain second-degree burns during filming to both of his buttocks. Reluctant to cancel his long-awaited trip he decided to go ahead with the planned vacation. By way of anaesthetic he packed cases of booze into the boot of the car and the trio set off with Arbuckle at the wheel.

On arriving they booked into the St Francis hotel and took three rooms – one for Fischbach and Arbuckle to share (1219), one for Sherman (1221) and 1220 to be used as a party room. They were all set to enjoy the Labour Day weekend of 1921.

Among the guests at the party was a young actress called Virginia Rappe. Rappe had been born to a single-parent mother, who died when the child was only 11; Virginia was then raised by her grandmother in Chicago. She had grown up seeking the affection of men and had had several abortions by her mid teens before giving birth at 17 to a child which she had put into foster care.

She had begun a modelling career and moved to San Francisco where she worked as an artist's model. She finally seemed to have found happiness when she became engaged to a dress designer named Robert Moscovitz, but this was to be short lived as Moscovitz was tragically killed in a trolley-car accident.

She began getting small parts in motion pictures and started dating director Henry Lehrman. Her acting ability was only mediocre and the best award she managed was in 1918 when she was awarded the title "Best Dressed Girl in Pictures".

Virginia had showed up at the party with her manager, Al Semnacher, and another woman called Bambina Maude Delmont. Delmont had a dubious background, had been in trouble with the police on charges relating to extortion, bigamy, fraud and racketeering, and was reported to have been hired in divorce cases to provide compromising photographs. Other guests came and went including actresses Zey Prevon and Alice Blake.

The party was much as one would expect, with plenty of food, drink and music. Apparently at some point Arbuckle left to take his friend Mae Taub (daughter-in-law of Billy Sunday) into town. He went to his own room to get a change of clothes for the drive into town, not realizing that his life was about to change forever.

According to Arbuckle, he entered his bathroom to find Rappe lying in a dead faint on the floor. Assuming she had had too much to drink, he carried her to the bed in order that she could sleep it off. When he lay her down she asked for a drink of water so he went and got her a drink before leaving the room in order to change his clothes for the journey.

When he re-entered the room he found what Virginia had fallen off the bed and was now on the floor, moaning and writhing. He managed to get her back on the bed and left the room to get a bucket of ice. The reason for this was two-fold: Arbuckle believed that the ice would calm the woman down;

also, he would use a trick he had been taught to distinguish a person who has faked fainting. His friend Buster Keaton had said that if you held ice to the skin you should only get a reaction from someone faking it.

After waiting for Arbuckle, Delmont decided to come to his room to find out why he was taking so long. When she entered she found him holding an ice cube on the woman's thigh. Arbuckle explained the situation and she too thought that Virginia was drunk, but she then began screaming and tearing at her clothes, which alerted Zey Prevon and Alice Blake who came in to see what was happening. By this time Arbuckle was losing his patience and, still considering the girl to be drunk or faking it, he asked the guests to remove her from his room. Fischbach now came in to see what was happening to find the girl shouting at Arbuckle, "Stay away from me! I don't want you near me!" Then she turned to Delmont and said words that would damn the entertainer, "What did he do to me, Maudie? Roscoe did this to me."

They decided to quieten her down by putting her into a bathtub of cool water, which did in fact have a calming effect on her. Arbuckle and Fischbach helped her to room 1227, where Arbuckle called the hotel manager and doctor. On the doctor's examination he concluded that she was drunk, so she was left on the bed and the party continued. Arbuckle took Taub into town and returned to the hotel where he was told that the hotel doctor had given Virginia morphine and she was now asleep.

The following day Dr Beardslee gave Virginia another dose of morphine and fitted her with a catheter as her friend had pointed out that she had not been to the bathroom in hours.

Later, Delmont called Dr Melville Rumwell and apparently repeated to him the same thing she had told Beardslee, that Virginia became ill after she had been raped by Arbuckle. Although the doctor found no sign of rape he did give her painkillers as she was still experiencing trouble and pain when trying to pass urine.

By Friday, 9 September she was dead from peritonitis, an acute infection caused in this instance by a ruptured bladder.

It would be alleged later that her bladder tore as a result of being raped by the grossly overweight comedian.

The newspapers were filled with headlines about the possible rape of a young actress by comedy fat man "Fatty" Arbuckle, a scandal that was to live with him for many years. Several newspapers boosted their sales with the "Arbuckle rap" headline and took it upon themselves to increase their readership by exaggerating tales regarding Arbuckle's lifestyle. His weight was now used against him and rather than being portrayed as a loveable, good-natured, chubby man, he was cast as a gross, overweight monster – which Virginia had seemingly no defence against.

The stories in the press had a dramatic effect on the public's opinion of their once-loved comic. Arbuckle read as many of the articles as he could manage, but was devastated by the animosity thrust at him and struggled to come to terms with the virtual hatred that he was subjected to.

Arbuckle was formally arrested for first-degree murder; at a later date the charge was reduced to manslaughter that carried a possible ten-year prison sentence.

The first trial began on 14 November 1921, the Judge being Judge Sylvain Lazarus. Prosecuting was San Francisco District Attorney Matthew Brady, who argued that the sexual attack on Virginia had ruptured her bladder, thus causing her ultimate death.

Roscoe Arbuckle's defence was the lawyer Gavin McNab, also from San Francisco, who was often hired by celebrities.

Arbuckle's estranged wife, Minta Durfee, had visited her husband in prison and believed his version of events, often attending the court hearing to show support for him.

The prosecution's first witness was a nurse named Grace Halston who said that Rappe's organs had been torn in a way that suggested force and that she had sustained several bruises to her body. She eventually agreed that if somebody had bladder cancer it could cause the bladder to rupture.

Dr Arthur Beardslee testified that the bladder seemed to be injured from force inflicted from outside her body and under cross-examination admitted that at no time did Rappe mention she had been assaulted by Arbuckle.

One party-goer, a model, Betty Campbell, testified that she had seen Arbuckle looking relaxed and enjoying himself just after the alleged attack, showing no signs of remorse and obviously unconcerned about Rappe's condition. Under cross-examination she admitted that she had been threatened by Brady if she didn't testify.

The Judge was then presented with affidavits from Alice Blake and Zey Prevon backing up the claim of intimidation by the prosecution. Prevon was called to the stand and testified that she had signed the statement saying Rappe had claimed "He killed me" under duress. Alice Blake made similar claims from the witness stand.

By 28 November the defence was ready to call Roscoe Arbuckle to the witness stand. He was more than willing to testify; after listening to the proceedings he was glad to have his say. The press noted that he was well dressed and that he appeared to look very tired, with large dark circles under his eyes.

When asked his whereabouts on the night of the alleged attack, he confirmed that he was in the St Francis Hotel and that he did indeed see Virginia Rappe. He described that he was planning to take Mae Taub into town and went into the bathroom to get dressed. It was here that he discovered Virginia on the floor in front of the toilet; she appeared to have been vomiting. He described how he picked her up and placed her on the bed to lie down. On returning to the room some two minutes later he discovered that she was on the floor holding her stomach. He then asked Mrs Delmont and Miss Prevon to come in to assist him with the sick woman.

He told of how a frantic Virginia had torn at her clothes and he had helped her off with her dress as Fischbach came into the room. He said that Fischbach had taken Rappe to the bathroom and put her in a tub of cold water. This was done, Arbuckle claimed, in the hopes of calming her down. When Virginia was carried back to the bed, Maude Delmont rubbed her with ice.

Under cross-examination by the prosecution Arbuckle gave little away and many thought that his testimony had helped his defence.

On examination of Virginia Rappe's bladder the experts agreed that it was ruptured, there was evidence of chronic inflammation and signs of acute peritonitis, and that the examination failed to reveal any pathological change in the vicinity of the tear preceding the rupture. In short – the rupture was not caused by external force. This was deemed another success by the defence.

The first trial came to an end on 4 December 1921 when, after over 40 hours of deliberation and at least 20 ballots, the jury were unable to reach a verdict, deadlocked, 10 to 2, in favour of acquittal.

At the second trial the victim's past was dragged through the mud, claiming that she was a heavy drinker and had enjoyed many sexual partners. Zey Prevon testified that she had not heard Rappe accuse Arbuckle of hurting her. But a deadlocked jury again voted 10–2, this time for a conviction, the entire opposite to the first jury.

The third and final trial ended with an apology from the jury: "Acquittal is not enough for Roscoe Arbuckle. We feel that a great injustice has been done him. We feel also that it was only our plain duty to give him this exoneration, under the evidence, for there was not the slightest proof adduced to connect him in any way with the commission of a crime.

"He was manly throughout the case, and told a straight-forward story on the witness stand, which we all believed.

"The happening at the hotel was an unfortunate affair for which Arbuckle, so the evidence shows, was in no way responsible.

"We wish him success, and hope that the American people will take the judgement of fourteen men and women who have sat listening for thirty-one days to evidence, that Roscoe Arbuckle is entirely innocent and free from all blame."

This leaves the question of what did happen to Virginia Rappe? The reason for her death is undisputed – peritonitis caused by a ruptured bladder. But why did the bladder rupture? Public opinion, encouraged by the press, the theory that she may well have undergone a botched abortion. Unfortunately, several organs were destroyed after the autopsy, including her uterus, so it was impossible to guess whether or not she had been pregnant at the time of her death.

The 35-year-old actor was a free man again, but his life was in ruins. The defence team had cost him a small fortune and to add to that he was given a $500 fine for bringing liquor to the party. He had lost his place in Hollywood as a comedian and found himself blacklisted from films. Even the films he had already recorded were withdrawn from circulation because of his tarnished reputation.

On 18 April 1922 Will Hays issued a statement saying, "After consulting at length with Mr Nicholas Schenck, representing Mr Joseph Schenck, the producers, and Mr Adolph Zukor and Mr Jessy Lasky of the Famous Players-Lasky Corporation, the distributors, I will state that at my request they have cancelled all showings and all bookings of the Arbuckle films. They do this that the whole matter may have the consideration that its importance warrants, and the action is taken notwithstanding the fact that they had nearly ten thousand contracts in force for the Arbuckle pictures." The ban was lifted later that year, but the damage had been done and Arbuckle would not act in front of a camera for over ten years.

He did find work as a director using the alias of "William B. Goodrich", directing several films including *Special Delivery* and *Windy Riley Goes to Hollywood*. Acutely depressed he and Minta divorced in 1925. He did manage to pull his life back into shape and married his second wife, Doris Deane, but the marriage only lasted three years because of Arbuckle's depression and drinking.

By 1930 he managed to get a part in the movie *Buzzin' Around*, which thankfully for Arbuckle was well received and he was able to prove that he was still capable of exhibiting his special gift for slapstick humour – to his delight audiences enjoyed the film. Indeed his devout fans came out in force and flocked to see his comeback, thoroughly pleased with the delightfully funny movie.

In 1932 his personal life turned a corner and he met very pretty dark-eyed actress Addie McPhail. Roscoe invited her out and took her to a special restaurant, where after he had managed to calm his nerves the couple enjoyed a lovely meal and Addie soon warmed to his charms. He was very attentive and she found that she was swept off her feet by his romantic gestures – he regularly sent her flowers and small gifts. After a courtship of a few months, Roscoe plucked up the courage to ask Addie to be his bride. To his delight and surprise she accepted and he was elated, believing that his life was now on the up; the couple were married in June 1932. His movie career continued to be a success and he was now enjoying the happiest time of his life.

Everybody knows that nothing lasts for ever, but in a cruel twist of fate his life was to come to a sudden end. At the tender age of 46 Roscoe died peacefully in his sleep, too young to die, but the years of heavy drinking, hard work and of course his weight would have been contributory factors. A quiet end to a very eventful life.

The Life and Death of a Rascal

Carl Switzer

Carl Switzer found fame as a child in the hit series, *The Little Rascals*. His portrayal of the character Alfalfa was his only major acting success, and he was always known as Alfalfa or Alfie to his friends. His death was premature and was brought about as a result of an argument over money – Alfalfa was shot at close range and died shortly afterwards. But was justice served? His murderer walked away a free man.

Carl Switzer's death coincided with that of the highly acclaimed Hollywood director, Cecil B. DeMille. The press favoured the story of DeMille's death, pushing the murder of Carl Switzer to the more obscure inner pages, so that his passing did not command many newspaper columns.

This was the second time that Switzer had been cheated in his life, for having worked throughout his childhood, financially supporting his family, he found himself low on funds. Owing to poor contractual decisions, he never earned the income his movie roles should have provided, a situation Switzer would sorely regret as his youthful fame gave way to adult obscurity. By the time he reached his twenties his acting career was all but over.

Carl Dean Switzer was one of three children born to devoted parents, Fred and Gladys, in Paris, Illinois. Janice Genevieve, the eldest, was born on 18 March 1923, followed two years later by Harold Frederick, who arrived on 16 January 1925. Carl, the youngest, was born on 7 August 1927 and was fortunate to have all four grandparents alive at the time of his birth. It was Gladys' parents, John and Hattie

Matthews, who lived to see their precocious grandson's rise to fame.

During the Great Depression the Switzers, like many others at that time, struggled to bring up their children. Paris was a small, residential, semi-rural farming district in eastern Illinois. Money was scarce and it became increasingly difficult to make ends meet, their financial problems compounded by the fact that Fred was an invalid, having accidentally shot himself in the foot which had resulted in amputation. This severely impeded his chances of gaining employment, especially in this district as the majority of unskilled work on offer was hard, manual, farm work. Unaware of their parents' financial problems Carl and his siblings were happy children who, along with their friends and neighbours, attended Redmon Elementary School. In their leisure time the local residents enjoyed picnicking and swimming at the Twin Lakes Park.

The Switzers were imaginative in the ideas they came up with to earn money. They had two very outgoing young boys who displayed a raw, but charming talent for singing. The children performed from time to time at local shows and fairs; they proved to be very popular and their parents were extremely proud of them. The additional revenue which their performances generated was unexpected but gratefully received by Fred and Gladys.

The family, encouraged by friends, believed that the children were stars in the making and were keen to seek fame and fortune in Hollywood. Fred and Gladys decided that they had nothing to lose, so when Carl was six years old they decided to take their children and visit members of their family living in California.

On their arrival they spent time reacquainting themselves with relatives, and were soon encouraged to take the children on one of the Hollywood studio tours. One such trip was a visit to the film studios of Hal Roach, where the Switzers joined the public tour of the studios. At the end of the tour, visitors were given the opportunity to use the studio cafeteria which was especially exciting for them as all employees of the studio went there too, so there was always the chance of spotting a star. Rumour had it that whilst visitors were enjoying their refreshments, movie executives used this opportunity to "talent scout" unsuspecting diners, and was probably the reason why the Switzer youngsters were encouraged to run through one of the routines which they had performed back in Paris. This may indeed have been the plan all along, and soon the boys were brought to the attention of Hal Roach himself who was sufficiently impressed to ask the boys to return for auditions.

Hal was in the early stages of putting together the cast for a new show to be called *Our Gang*. The plan was to record a series of comedy sketches using a cast of youngsters, primarily focusing on their adventures.

Hal was renowned for having an eye for talent, and as he was the creator and exclusive producer of the show, he was the decision maker. He was immediately impressed with the quite extraordinary ability that the young Carl had of learning, reciting and performing his lines. Carl had the gift of timing, even at the tender age of seven – a quality that was not lost on the famous Hal Roach. Initially, the boys were offered roles in an episode aptly entitled "Beginners' Luck", and were given the names Tom and Jerry, being dubbed the "Arizona Nightingales".

Carl's performance was quite remarkable and he was offered a lead role in the next episode of the show, in which he would be known as Alfalfa. Carl's elder brother Harold was also offered a part, though not quite as prestigious. Harold was given small roles throughout the course of the shows in which he would act as different characters, usually for just a few scenes. The two characters which he played most often were Deadpan and Slim, but his limited acting ability meant that he was never as successful as his younger brother. This was never a bone of contention between the siblings as Harold was aware that Carl had an ability which he did not possess and was never bitter about the attention his brother received.

The news of the children's success in Hollywood soon travelled back to Paris, Illinois and they were front-page news in the local newspaper, the *Paris Beacon News*. The report reads:

Harold and Carl Switzer, sons of Mr. and Mrs. Fred Switzer, formerly of Paris, have passed the motion picture tests in Hollywood, California, and according to word received here will appear in Hal Roach comedies. The two boys are between the ages of six and eight and are talented in music and comedy.

The Switzer family left Paris during the latter part of October and motored to California by way of Texas, New Mexico, and Arizona. It was while playing in one of the large hotels in Phoenix that the boys came in contact with many picture folk who were holding a convention there.

The Switzers were eager to have their sons' employment formally recognized and swiftly applied for them to receive Social Security cards. Having obtained these documents Fred was quick to clinch the deal and signed the studio contract on behalf of his sons. Fred now assumed the role of manager to Harold and Carl and was often on set; with their best interests at heart, he ensured that his boys were given a fair deal. He would complain bitterly if he was not happy with the amount of screen time they received, and would demand that Carl's name be prominent on the billing and all associated advertising literature.

In 1938, due to a change of parent company ownership, the name "Our Gang" was dropped in favour of "The Little Rascals". Hal Roach had all the references to Our Gang removed from the original titles and credits and they were replaced by the new name prior to being shown on television.

The show was a long-running success and Switzer starred in over 60 episodes, but by the age of 13 he was growing tired of performing as Alfalfa and decided to quit the show. He still wanted to continue with his acting career and went on to have some success in movies. In his first film he starred alongside Elizabeth Taylor in *There's One Born Every Minute*, Taylor's screen debut at the age of 10; Switzer was 14. He was also in the big hit *It's a Wonderful Life* and enjoyed acting with many of the Hollywood greats, including William Powell, Bob Hope, Jimmy Stewart, Henry Fonda, Spencer Tracy and Katharine Hepburn.

As Switzer matured, his acting career started to dry up, the offers coming more sporadically. Not in the slightest bit bitter, he felt that he had already been very fortunate with his acting success; he accepted that he had already had his share of fame, and as long as he could live comfortably, he was satisfied and did not complain. It has to be said that with more skilful payment negotiations, he could have earned more from all his acting work – if he had received a share of the royalties from the shows, he might well have been a rich man.

During his adult life Switzer continued to act whenever the opportunity arose, and spent the rest of his time following various occupations. He worked as bartender in a local bar, at times he was employed as a bear-hunting guide in the high Sierras, and he also worked as a dog trainer.

In the early 1950s Switzer had become a good friend of popular actor Roy Rogers and with Rogers' encouragement Switzer got a role in a television series, though this was only short lived and he soon found himself back behind the bar. Switzer married his long-time girlfriend, Diane Collingwood and when they were blessed with a son, Switzer asked Rogers to be the boy's godfather. The marriage unfortunately did not last and the couple were divorced in 1956.

In the mid 1950s Switzer began to show an interest in becoming a Freemason, a member of an international fraternity for mutual help and fellowship, with elaborate secret rituals. His interest in this society was possibly encouraged by Rogers who was already an active Freemason. Until his death, Switzer was intrigued by the society; his headstone bares two freemasonry symbols, one on either side of a picture of a dog and the words "Beloved father, son and brother – Carl 'Alfalfa' Switzer".

His life continued rather uneventfully until January 1958, when in circumstances never satisfactorily explained, let alone investigated, Switzer was shot by an unknown assailant whilst getting into his car. Fortunately the wound was not life threatening, as he was hit in the arm. After limited police investigation, the crime went unsolved. One year later, when he was hit by a bullet for the second time, the injuries proved fatal, although the outcome was much the same as the first time he was shot for the man pulling the trigger. Later in 1958, Switzer had a brush with the law when he was arrested for felling pine trees in Sequoia National Forest, for which he was ordered to pay a $200 fine and given one year's probation.

That same year Switzer continued his acting career with a supporting role in the movie *The Defiant Ones*, with the lead roles going to Tony Curtis and Sidney Poitier. The film was released the following year and was very well received by both movie critics and audiences alike.

By January 1959 Switzer was still awaiting the final payment for his role in *The Defiant Ones*, continuing to work in the bar and make money dog training. That month he borrowed some hunting dogs from an acquaintance called Moses "Bud" Stiltz in order to take some tourists on a bear-hunting trip near Lake Shasta. During the time that Switzer had the dogs, one of them managed escape whilst chasing a bear, and Switzer was unable to find it. As Switzer did not wish to let Stiltz down, he decided to advertise for the dog's safe return, and offered a reward of $35 if the dog was found.

Whilst Switzer was bartending a few nights later a local rancher approached him with the missing dog, asking for the reward money. Switzer was so relieved that he handed over the reward and by way of extra thanks he gave the man several drinks. Later when he added up the money he had spent on drinks he estimated it had added another $15 to the reward bill, totalling $50.

Switzer brooded over his lost $50 for several days, until the evening of 21 January 1959, when he was short of cash. He and his friend, Jack Piott, a photographer and small-time actor, decided it was time to get the money back from Stiltz, Switzer having come to the conclusion that Stiltz should pay for the reward as it was his dog that had run away. Stiltz, however, was adamant that the dog was left with Switzer for safekeeping and that it was down to him to look after it.

The pair arrived at the home of Stiltz's employer, Ray "Crash" Corrigan and his wife Rita, in San Fernando Valley.

Corrigan was a star of western movies, and had a mutual friend with Switzer in Roy Rogers. He employed the 38-year-old Stiltz in various capacities, including mechanic, welder and also as a bodyguard, which meant that Stiltz was not a man to be trifled with. This was to be Switzer's downfall as the pair were not well matched, but Switzer was reluctant to back down and wanted his money. What he was not aware of was that Stiltz was past talking about the money, was fed up with Switzer complaining about the $50, and was ready to put a stop to his moaning once and for all.

Between the men's arrival and their eventual departure the events have become difficult to pinpoint, but the outcome is clear – Carl Switzer was shot by Stiltz and would die as a result, at the age of just 31.

Stiltz offered his version of the evening's events to the police when he was brought in for questioning. He claimed that Switzer had banged on the door shouting, "Let me in, or I'll kick in the door." Stiltz had opened the door and let Switzer and Piott inside, whereupon Switzer apparently said, "I want that fifty dollars you owe me now, and I mean now." Stiltz still felt that as the dogs were in Switzer's care, he was responsible for their safe return – if he had to offer a reward to achieve this, then that was his problem. He told Switzer as much and a violent argument erupted, during which Piott grabbed a glass-domed clock and hit Stiltz in the face with it. With a bleeding and swollen eye Stiltz then took a loaded .38 calibre revolver from a drawer, but Switzer panicked and made a grab for the weapon. The pair ended up wrestling on the floor, during which the gun went off, luckily not hitting anyone, the bullet lodging itself in the ceiling.

Stiltz later told the police that by this time Switzer had the gun and that he also pulled a knife on him and shouted, "I'm going to kill you." He then added, "I took the gun away from Alfalfa and he threw the knife at me. That's when I shot him." On investigation of the crime scene, the police did recover a knife, which would add weight to Stiltz's story, although the blade was found to be closed.

The second version of the evening's events offered to the police was given by Switzer's companion, Jack Piott. He claimed that he and Switzer had gone to Corrigan's house to collect a debt due to Switzer. During the visit an argument erupted, escalating into much more than they had bargained for. He then claimed that after a brief struggle, Stiltz pulled out a gun and shot Switzer in the stomach. Piott, worried for his own safety, begged Stiltz to spare him, fully expecting the gun to be turned on him.

The alarm was raised from a neighbouring house from where the emergency services were called. With sirens blazing, the ambulance arrived ready to deal with a major gunshot injury but had not expected the damage to be as extensive as it turned out to be. Their plans to rush Switzer to hospital were stalled owing to his massive internal injuries. After struggling to resuscitate Switzer the ambulance team were forced to accept that their patient had suffered too much trauma and blood loss. Switzer's one-time girlfriend and now sister-in-law, Beverly Osso, was at the hospital when Alfalfa was pronounced dead; the time was 7.27 p.m.

The following morning, 22 January 1959, when Moses Stiltz was arrested on suspicion of the murder of Carl Switzer, he maintained that he had acted in self-defence. Before the coroner's jury, whilst giving his testimony, Stiltz was very emotional and at times was reported to have broken down in tears. He told the jury how his friend of over 18 months had come to him, demanding money for the recovery of a lost dog. He described Switzer as intoxicated and that his demands were unreasonable. He said that Switzer wanted reimbursing the $50 which he had paid in reward money for the dog but Stiltz felt that Switzer was responsible for its welfare and safety. He explained that he refused to pay the money and that as Switzer and Piott had been drinking they were uncharacteristically aggressive. Stiltz described having a scuffle with them during which Switzer had pulled a knife and charged at him with it. Stiltz then explained, "Alfie charged me with a jack-knife, I was forced to shoot."

After giving his testimony the coroner's jury ruled that Carl Switzer's death was deemed a justifiable homicide. Stiltz's self-defence plea had worked and he was able to leave court a free man.

This ruling was deemed a washout by the press, who only briefly reported on the coroner's jury hearing as Hollywood was reeling from the announcement of the death of Cecil B. DeMille. Switzer's death slipped through the net as far as the press were concerned, so there was little public interest.

During the police investigation, Los Angeles police detective Pat Poe had interviewed Tom Corrigan, the son of Roy, as the 14 year old was at home on the night of the shooting. When questioned by the detective Tom recalled that after Switzer and Piott had entered the house there was a struggle in which Piott broke the glass-dome clock over Stiltz's head, causing the swelling around his eye. He then added that in the struggle the .38 revolver had gone off and that the bullet had lodged in the ceiling, although a small amount of shrapnel had hit Tom on the leg. This alarmed his two younger sisters, who ran to a neighbouring house to call for help. Tom then made to leave, but as he went out of the door another shot rang out, this time hitting Switzer. Although Tom did not witness Switzer being shot, he immediately looked back into the house and saw him collapsing to the floor. It was at this moment that he saw the closed penknife beside Switzer. He turned and saw Stiltz threatening Piott with the gun, but fortunately the police sirens managed to bring him to his senses and possibly stopped another pointless shooting. After Tom had concluded his statement, Poe asked the boy if he would be able to give his account to the Judge. Although Tom was afraid of Stiltz he agreed to be a witness. Poe never did ask for his witness to come forward, so his side of the story was never related to the jury.

Frank, Switzer's father, took his death very hard and mourned his son until his own death the following year in California in May 1960. Some describe Frank as in deep mourning and after a fishing trip with his surviving son Harold, he complained of feeling unwell and rather hot. As he sat in a chair, being comforted by Harold, he suffered a massive heart attack. He was buried next to his son at Hollywood Memorial Park.

Carl's brother Harold was the next family member to die when he took his own life in Los Angeles on 14 April 1967.

Janice Switzer, Carl's sister, sadly died of cancer in 1988.

The longest-living member of the original Switzer family was Carl's mother Gladys. In her later years she preferred to be known as Pamela as she had decided it sounded more elegant and dignified than her original name. She and Frank had been divorced before the death of their youngest son, but the pair were always good friends – in fact Frank was a frequent visitor at the home of Pamela and her new husband, Jess Doerr. Pamela's marriage to Jess lasted until his death in 1992. She lived a long and eventful life and had the unfortunate task of attending the funerals of each of her children and both of her husbands, until on 8 March 1997, at the age of 92, she too passed away.

The Would-be Hero

Bob Crane

As you might expect from a man recognizable to millions as a television star, he showed entertainment promise even as a youngster. He was a natural and spent much of his recreation time as a youth entertaining his family and friends with his various talents.

He was born on 13 July 1928, in Waterbury, Connecticut, to loving parents who christened him Robert Edward Crane. He was an outgoing, happy, healthy child and displayed many talents for showmanship, regularly amusing his peers with his comic ability. He loved being the centre of attention and was a very popular boy, never short of companions, who loved his ability to invent games. His favourite pastimes were undeniably all things musical, from singing to playing instruments; he was particularly keen on jazz and the big bands which were prevalent at this time.

Despite being very popular at school he was not a child who enjoyed schoolwork, so he didn't shine in the classroom, nor did he excel on the sports field. His education lasted through to high school, at which point he dropped out, confident that there was more to life than sitting at a desk learning things parrot fashion. He was able to secure a job with the Connecticut Symphony Orchestra as a drummer, where he managed to earn a living for 12 months, but owing to his high spirits, it was considered that he was not serious about his job and he was duly dismissed.

At the age of 21 Crane was married to his long-term girlfriend, Anne Terzian, and they had a wonderful white wedding surrounded by their families, friends and loved ones. By this time money was short with Crane holding down a shop job and supplementing his earnings by playing the drums in various local clubs. The couple commenced their married life living with Anne's parents in Stamford, Connecticut, an arrangement which turned out to be short lived. Soon after moving in Anne announced her pregnancy and with it the need to move to a home of their own. Their family grew quite quickly and they eventually had three children, Bob Jr, Debbie and Karen.

Crane now needed a good wage, and was looking for stability, something which playing the drums just couldn't guarantee. He managed to get a salaried position as a radio announcer for a small station called WLEA, based in Hornell, New York, a job he loved, but sadly one which took him away from his wife and family. Money was so tight that he was living in the YMCA whilst Anne was bringing up the kids back home in Stamford. Eventually Crane secured a job at a radio station nearer to home, this time working for the WBIS station based in Bristol, Connecticut. The job was convenient for home and the salary was reasonable – after a lot of stress the Cranes were finally happy, so much so that he kept his position at WBIS for over five years. Crane, though, was ambitious and had enjoyed his stint as a local celebrity, but yearned for more.

Crane was 28 years old when he was offered his first big break from KNX, a much larger radio station based in California, this time as a programme host. With the opportunity of more money, Anne and the children joined him this time. It wasn't long before Crane's programme began to command quite a large following; his natural wit and cheerful personality came across well and he proved a very popular host.

The secret of Crane's success lay in the fast-paced style of his radio programmes, which proved very popular with his fast-growing audiences. The fact that he had such a devout following didn't go unnoticed, or unrewarded – as "the King of the LA airwaves", his new nickname, he became the highest paid disc jockey in America, commanding an annual salary in excess of $100,000, a sum previously unheard of in the realms of radio.

His show was so well regarded that even big Hollywood stars graced his programme, during which he was able to interview some of the all-time greats, among them the likes of Frank Sinatra, Marilyn Monroe, Bob Hope, Mary Tyler Moore, Jayne Mansfield and the soul king, Marvin Gaye.

Crane had reached the top of his chosen tree – there was no one better in the world of radio; he had fame and was enjoying the money it brought. Most men would have been satisfied with this new-found fame and fortune, but Crane was still hankering for more. Having met the stars of Hollywood – and their star qualities were infectious – Crane's new ambition was to become an actor, and when he set his mind on something, he threw his entire energy into it, determined to succeed.

His introduction into acting was gradual, initially guest appearances on a number of popular television shows, including the very popular *Dick Van Dyke Show*. Crane's quick wit and repartee, coupled with his easy conversational style, went down well with the audiences and he settled in easily to the world of television – he was after all well practised at talking to hundreds of thousands of listeners; the only difference now was that they could see him, and he was more than comfortable with this.

His first acting role on the big screen came in 1961 when he played a relatively minor part in the film sequel, *Return to Peyton Place*, following this up in the same year with another small role in the movie *Man-Trap*. These really set him on his way in his new-found acting career and his family were overjoyed at the way things were progressing.

In 1963, Crane auditioned for a regular part on the *Donna Reed Show* and was ecstatic when he heard the news that he had been chosen, determined to make his mark and improve his already blossoming profile. He managed to maintain his character for two years, until 1965, when his contract was not renewed as the producers were concerned that Crane's character had developed away from their original brief. The problem was Crane's interpretation of the character. Knowingly or not, he had managed to bring out the flirtatious and suggestive side of his character, a style which sat awkwardly with the wholesome, "family values" type of show which the *Donna Reed Show* represented.

The loss of his part in the *Donna Reed Show* came as a huge blow to Crane, who genuinely believed he was adding something unique and wonderful to the show. For many actors this rejection would have spelled trouble – although rejection is part of the game, not getting the part is acceptable, whereas losing a part which had been secured and expertly executed for two years would have caused a severe dent in the most thick-skinned thespian. Crane's confidence however remained strong and his sacking only a short-lived blight on his ambition to become a famous actor. Later that same year he won the part that would make him a star in his own right when he was given the lead in a new and controversial television comedy called *Hogan's Heroes*.

The new sitcom was pioneering from the very start, based as it was in a Nazi prison camp. Many would be excused for wondering how on earth this setting would be deemed amusing as the Second World War was still a terrible memory for millions of ex-soldiers. The show was truly ambitious, possibly ahead of its time, but then again so was Crane. When he first read the scripts he was in no doubt at all that he would accept the starring role, impressed as he was at the brilliance of the scriptwriters.

With some degree of nervousness the show was aired in 1965, and to everyone's delight was extremely well received, the viewing figures were good and the show quickly grew in popularity. The way that the characters were presented and acted managed to take the edge off the controversial setting and the audiences came to love the way the Germans were portrayed as bumbling buffoons, easily fooled by the more astute American prisoners.

Crane had finally arrived and although the show wasn't without its critics, it was without doubt a resounding success. Those elements who were offended were either Jewish, unhappy at the trivialization of a terrible chapter in world events, or neo-Nazis, upset that their German heroes were portrayed as fools. Both groups undoubtedly sent hate mail, some even threatening Crane and other members of the cast, but most people simply enjoyed the entertainment. Ironically, the two main Nazi characters were played by Jewish actors, namely John Banner and Werner Klemperer who played Colonel Klink. Banner had lost his family in the concentration camps when he was just 28 years old and enjoyed the fact that he was able to poke fun at those who held such views.

The show was a long-running success and in 1966, and again in 1967, Crane was nominated for an Emmy, his fame beyond doubt and his wealth increasing beyond all expectations. Along with the fame came the adulation, and Crane, a womanizer at heart, found that his new Hollywood credentials gave him the sort of appeal he had always dreamt of. He pursued his interest in women the way he had pursued his acting goals – with energy and enthusiasm. All of his conquests were willing, some were married and many were scorned.

By now Crane's career had matured and he found himself in perpetual demand, his schedule was such that he was hardly ever at home and the pressure was taking its toll on his marriage to Anne. During his long absences she was left to look after the house and bring up their three children, a difficult task at the best of times, but worse when rumours of Crane's extramarital encounters began to circulate. For Crane absence did not make the heart grow fonder – when Anne suggested they separate, he was more than happy to oblige.

Patti Olsen, a new member of the *Hogan's Heroes* cast, had become quite close to Crane. Pretty and blonde, she had not escaped his attention. As Crane's marriage was over – he was in the process of getting divorced from Anne – the relationship with Patti soon blossomed. After a whirlwind romance Crane proposed to her and the pair quickly began preparing for their marriage. Having been married in the conventional confines of a church once, the pair now sought the permission of the studios to hold their ceremony on the set of *Hogan's Heroes*. On 16 October 1970, Bob Crane and Patti Olsen were married before their friends, work colleagues and family on the film set.

Shortly after his second marriage, just when Crane was enjoying himself most, the president of the CBS network, Robert Wood, announced a review of all programming schedules. Wood was concerned that his audience was ageing and wanted a slice of the advertising budgets aimed at the younger market. Among the first shows axed were the very popular *The Beverly Hillbillies* and *The Ed Sullivan Show*, a decisive move by CBS; however the decision which would have Crane reeling was the culling of his prime-time show, *Hogan's Heroes*.

Crane was devastated; he felt that the show could easily carry on running, and that the viewing figures could still be maintained. His words however were lost on the CBS executives whose commitment to a new, younger audience was unfaltering; they had made their decision and were not going to change it, not even for the Emmy nominated Crane.

Crane still received offers, but he could never find a role which measured up to his character in *Hogan's Heroes*. He searched in vein for his next sure-fire winner but could find nothing which would fill the void left by his high-profile television show. He took roles in several movies and managed a number of guest appearances, but none of the work was fulfilling for him, it merely kept him ticking over financially.

In 1973 Crane tried his hand at stage acting and joined the cast of a play called, *Beginner's Luck*. He was not one for doing things half-heartedly and accepted both a starring role and responsibility for the directing, a new and challenging experience for him. The play did exceptionally well and went on to tour for almost five years.

In 1975 Crane was back on television, this time presenting his own show, appropriately named *The Bob Crane Show*. He was hoping that he would be able to achieve the same success with his new venture as he had enjoyed with his radio show and *Hogan's Heroes*. Initially all the signs were good, but after a very well-received launch, the show started to weaken, after only three months NBC pulled the plug, and once more Crane found himself out of a job.

Over the years, indeed for much of Crane's adult life, he

had pandered to the whim of his considerable sexual appetite. He was an expert flirt and enjoyed chatting with his many female fans, his favourite type being busty blondes. He was partial to both reading and watching all forms of pornography and was quite happy to chat about his sexual conquests, much to the embarrassment of those around him. His sexual activity increased further after the culling of *Hogan's Heroes*, and depressed at the way his career was heading, Crane decided to prove himself in other ways. He was fast becoming a sex addict and his indiscretions were once again the cause of great trouble with his wife, who managed to keep tabs on her husband through the Hollywood grapevine.

Not only did Crane enjoy the chase, he enjoyed every aspect of his interactions with women – the chatting up, the seduction and also his natural ability to attract young women; his star quality certainly gave him the edge in the dating game. Crane's conquests were many, and he could prove it too, for he liked to keep tangible evidence of his encounters, often taking Polaroids of the naked girls with whom he had slept, and occasionally, if the girls would comply, he would take videos of their love-making. The photographs were all stored in a series of albums, beautifully laid out and always on hand. Crane enjoyed showing them to his friends as he was proud of them and enjoyed watching the reactions on their faces; strangely, his delight was even greater if they seemed offended by the contents of his little book of reminders. The videos were watched over and over again; Crane was never bored of viewing them and would often let his close friends watch his perverse activities.

One such friend was John Carpenter, part American and part Spanish, with thick dark hair, a long nose and thin lips. Carpenter had endured a period in Korea as a tank commander before taking up the job which would bring him into contact with Bob Crane. During Carpenter's time in the Army he had shown an interest in electronics and had used his time wisely, expanding his knowledge in this area, hoping it would help him get work once he was back in civvy street. Sure enough, on leaving the Army, he managed to secure a job with Hoffman Easy Vision, a television manufacturing company. After a couple of job changes Carpenter was offered a role with Sony, the Japanese giant of the consumer electronics market. It was through his job at Sony that he began coming across people from the world of acting, Bob Crane being one of them. Carpenter was keen to demonstrate the new technology, especially the VCR and video camera, which blended nicely with Crane's aspirations to film his own sex shows.

It was whilst discussing the new recording equipment that Crane and Carpenter became good friends, with Crane keen to learn all about the equipment, warming to the idea of what he might achieve with it.

One such private viewing was to take place on the morning of 26 June 1978, when the phone suddenly rang, putting a brief halt to the planned screening. On the other end of the phone, a young actress who had obtained Crane's number asked if he would be prepared to listen to an audio tape she had produced. Crane, thinking fast, and almost certainly hopeful of a potential sexual encounter, invited her over to his house. Unfortunately for him, however, his reputation as a womanizer had gone ahead of him and the would-be actress declined his offer, wary of visiting him at his home. She asked instead if he would meet her in a public bar, to which Crane agreed, before returning to watch his latest screening. He had tried his hand and failed with the young actress, a type normally so motivated to succeed that they would often agree to anything. Whether he actually turned up or not has never been established.

Later that same day Crane was reminded by his co-star, Victoria Berry, that his presence would be required at a barbecue party thrown for the cast and crew of his new show, *Beginner's Luck*. Crane surprised the other guests when he arrived with Carpenter – he would normally have had a girl on his arm. The two men laughed and enjoyed the proceedings, Crane having his photograph taken by a number of people and Carpenter happily watching his famous friend turning on the charm. When it was time to leave, however, Crane had managed to arrange some company and left with yet another beautiful young woman, leaving Carpenter to make his own way home.

The following day Crane and Carpenter met up again and decided to check out some new video equipment. Whilst out shopping Crane was enjoying the usual attention while Carpenter checked out the specifications and prices on Crane's proposed purchases. Having bought some equipment the two men did a little clothes shopping in preparation for the night ahead. They were planning a night of entertainment, some steamy passion and with any luck, a bit of amateur photography. After they returned home Crane made a number of phonecalls, the first to his son Bobby wishing him a happy birthday, the second was to a waitress he knew, looking to set up a date for that evening. He also asked if she could bring a girlfriend along to make a foursome with his friend John Carpenter. There is no doubt that the two men got on well as friends, but they were out of different stables. Crane was good looking, famous and a natural with the ladies. Carpenter on the other hand was not. He certainly benefited from his association with Crane and was always first in line for the woman Crane overlooked. The only thing Crane appeared to get out of the friendship was admiring glances and minimal competition. Others have suggested there was more to the relationship, something more complex.

With the date agreed the four went out to dinner, but immediately it was clear that Carpenter was unimpressed with his "date" and privately told Crane as much. With the mood distinctly frosty, Crane and Carpenter decided not to pursue their two guests, instead choosing to head out on the town to see if they could round up some other willing fillies. Later that evening the two men arrived at the famous Bobby McGee's bar in Scottsdale where they were served by a waitress called Linda Robertson, who could not help but notice that they appeared to be in deep conversation, possibly arguing, later referring to them as tense. Most of the people in the bar that evening appeared to be having a good laugh, out to enjoy themselves, but her two punters were certainly not in high spirits, and looked as if they were trying to sort out some disagreement.

For a short while Carpenter was left by himself as Crane disappeared from the bar, returning a short while later with the waitress they had lunched with earlier. The three were soon chatting and appeared to be enjoying a few drinks before leaving together. It is thought that Crane dropped Carpenter off at a rental car pick-up point before taking his lady friend home. She later recalled Crane's annoyance at Carpenter's pickiness earlier in the evening – he thought Carpenter could have shown a little more gratitude, as he had after all set up the date, something he didn't think Carpenter could have achieved by himself.

The following day the pair met up again and went out for a meal at a restaurant called Little Gregory's, where they bumped into Ralph Tirrell and Frank Grabiec, the owners of a local electrical store. Crane asked if they would let him try out a new video camera, a Sony one he had been recommended. Grabiec arranged to let him borrow it on the understanding that it was returned in a few days' time. Grabiec noticed the tension which seemed to exist between the two men and also how it eased when they left with the camera, clearly eager to set it up.

With some free time Crane's mind turned to sex, so after a quick telephone call to one of his girlfriends he set out satisfy himself. The girl said later that Bob was not quite himself and seemed distant, the only comment he had made that stuck in her mind was that he told her that John was not as popular as he was.

Crane was on stage again that night in *Beginner's Luck*, and although the audience thoroughly enjoyed the performance cast members noted that Bob didn't seem to be his usual enthusiastic, energetic self; there was something just not quite right. He stayed behind after the show and signed autographs as usual, then at a little after 10.30 he went with Carpenter and three of the cast members to the Monte Carlo Bar.

By 11 p.m., Crane and Carpenter had returned to Crane's house. Carpenter remembered Crane calling his estranged wife Patti, during which the conversation became heated and an argument erupted, resulting in Crane slamming the telephone down. The bitter row caused Crane's neighbours to wonder what was going on at the actor's house. He then made a second telephone call, to another one of his girl-friends, during which he made it quite clear that under no circumstances would there be reconciliation between him and Patti; he was clearly angry.

After a brief discussion the men decided it was time to find some action and went to one of their favourite pick-up joints, a late-night bar called Bogies. But the bar was dead, it was late and it started to look like there would be little action that evening. Crane though had other ideas, made a quick tele-phone call to one of his lady friends and arranged to meet her at the Safari Bar, another favourite haunt and one not too far away.

At around 1 a.m., the two men arrived at the Safari Bar where Crane's short-order girlfriend was waiting. After a few greetings Crane spotted an old colleague, Andrew Gel-lart, with whom he had worked on *Hogan's Heroes*. The two reminisced for a while and enjoyed a couple of drinks before Crane turned his attention back to his date. Leaving Car-penter to his own devices he then left the Safari with her and returned home. For once Carpenter managed to bag his own date, a woman who was alone in the bar who he managed to cajole back to his motel room, but sadly for Carpenter that is as far has he got. Having arrived in his room she appeared to have had a change of heart and declined his advances, asking instead to be driven home. Somewhat aggrieved, Carpenter drove the woman home, arriving there at 2.30 a.m. Carpenter then claims to have driven home.

Crane too had been unsuccessful with his date that night and she too decided not to accompany him back to his home. The details of Crane's movements, and those of Carpenter, are unclear from this time onwards; what is clear is that Crane was viciously attacked and murdered in his own home. He died in the early hours of 29 June 1978.

The actor was apparently asleep in his bed when he was attacked by someone who battered him around the head with a blunt instrument. The killer then strangled Crane with a VCR flex which had been cut, apparently to shorten it, which he left tied around his victim's neck. When the autopsy was carried out it was shown that Crane was already dead from his head wounds long before the flex was tightened around his throat.

It was not until shortly after lunchtime the following day that Crane's body was discovered when his co-star Victoria Berry called at his house after he had failed to turn up for a meeting, during which the pair were to be interviewed to promote their show. It was quite out of character for him to miss such an appointment; his acting career meant everything to him, and not just in professional terms – it was also the vehicle by which he attracted his many women friends.

On arriving at his home she knocked at the door a few times and waited in vain for a response. After hanging around for a while she decided to try the door and was surprised to find it unlocked – Crane was fastidious about keeping his house secure, for he was after all a target for star spotters, thieves and ex-loves.

On entering the property Berry was met by the usual disarray one might expect after a night of partying; the place was littered with magazines, address books and various newspapers. She also noticed the video camera which had been set up close to Crane's fireplace. As she stood there surveying the mess, she called out to Bob, half expecting him to come tumbling out of the bedroom with some floozy on his arm. When he didn't respond she assumed that he was down in the pool and as she walked across to the window to take a look, again surprised that he wasn't there, a small knot of fear began to tighten in her stomach.

As she walked around the apartment she continued to call his name, hoping that he might eventually hear her and call out. Eventually she entered his bedroom, more just to check than because she thought he was there – she had already been shouting his name. When she entered the room she immediately saw his body curled up on the bed. There was nothing initially to suggest he was anything other than sound asleep, but as she moved cautiously towards him she became aware of the dark patches which stood out on the light-coloured walls behind his bed. When Victoria looked more closely she realized that the marks were actually blood, and that Bob was not asleep, he was dead and she was the first one at the murder scene. Stumbling back out of the bedroom, her heart pounding and her brain racing, she phoned the police and quickly reported his death. Panicking, she asked them to hurry up, now afraid that the murderer might still be somewhere on the property.

When the police arrived they sealed off the house and allowed scene of crime investigators to get to work. The entire place was swept for fingerprints, then inch by inch every surface was examined for evidence which would help identify the murderer. Soon the slow process of investigation would begin, piecing together Crane's last movements, interviewing all who knew him and trying to establish the all-important motive.

Who would have killed this popular television personality was the question that the police needed answer to. When the press became aware of Crane's murder they pounced on the story; he was popular and successful, yet lived the epitome of the Hollywood lifestyle – fast talking, fast cars and even faster women. Crane's womanizing ways were at the heart of the media coverage; by their reckoning any number of men might have had reason to kill Crane, who would never allow a wedding ring to come between him and a conquest.

Investigating officers were of the opinion that Crane must have known his murderer as there was no sign of a forced entry and it was therefore assumed that he had let the individual into the house. After the scene had been thoroughly investigated, medical examiner Dr Heinz Karnitschnig was inclined to believe that the murderer was a man. The force of the impact on Crane's head had been huge, causing immediate and severe damage. By studying the blood spots which were spattered all across the ceiling, Heinz was able to show that a second blow had been delivered almost immediatly, again with deadly force. The rapid bludgeoning action was therefore attributed to a man, one who was intent on killing Crane, someone particularly spiteful. The blood traces were the key in establishing the sex of the attacker – the small amount of blood on the ceiling was indicative of a fast second blow travelling in a short arc. The blunt object which inflicted the damage would have been covered in blood from the first blow; it was from the raising of the killer's arm for the second strike which sprayed Crane's blood across the ceiling. If the killer had raised his arm fully for the second attack, more blood would have been spread across the ceiling. But as the killer had sufficient strength to deliver another solid blow with what would have been a very heavy object, from such a short strike, the conclusion was that the killer was almost certainly male.

The bedroom revealed three clues which were deemed to be of some importance to the investigation. The first was a black bag which was found on the bed close to Crane's body. The bag had two zippers on it, one on the side and one on top; both were open. All that was inside the bag were some papers and a few tickets; police officers therefore wondered if some other contents had been what the murderer was after.

The second was a bottle of Scotch, half drunk and with the top off, although it was common knowledge among Crane's friends that he never touched Scotch. Had he had a guest with him that evening or had the killer helped himself?

The third clue was the VCR flex which had been tied around Crane's neck and pulled tight, as if strangulation was the purpose. Yet the police were sure that the killer would have been aware that his victim was already dead from the first assault, unless the flex was symbolic. Why use a VCR cable? There were numerous electrical cords in the house, but the use of that particular one seemed to be of significance. The possibilities seemed endless – perhaps one of Crane's women had found out she had been secretly filmed, an unwilling participant in one of his "adult" movies. Or perhaps the boyfriend of one such woman, someone with an axe to grind. All possibilities would need to be considered during the course of the investigation.

Some who were closer to Crane thought that the VCR flex would lead directly to John Carpenter and even surmised that the severed flex symbolized the end of their friendship – a fanciful idea perhaps, but one which many believed; they had not enjoyed the easiest of relations in the days prior to Crane's murder.

Crane had many contacts and work colleagues who had to be interviewed by the police. His promiscuous lifestyle was well known and those who had been involved with him would have to be ruled in or out as a suspect. Every aspect of Crane's life had to be examined to see if it would yield a clue, even as far back as his days in *Hogan's Heroes*. The police would have been well advised to read the papers which had a wealth of information on Crane and a number of hypotheses, most of which they were happy to share with their readership on a day-by-day basis. But for the police, the answers were slow in coming.

Even Crane's estranged wife Patti was considered to be a suspect, the ex-wife who had suffered the embarrassment of Crane's extramarital indiscretions. The suspicions were short lived as she had a cast-iron alibi for the night of the murder – she was in Washington, miles from the murder scene. Examination of her bank accounts did not reveal any suspicious money movements which might have suggested a hired hand. The phone records showed she had spoken to Crane that night and others confirmed that the conversation had turned into a row.

Then rumours emerged that Carpenter was bisexual and that he had wanted more than friendship from Crane. This wild speculation was given more credence when video footage of the two men was found, although they were sharing the romp with a woman who appeared to be the centre of their attention. This, and the strained relationship they had endured just before the attack, left Carpenter well and truly in the frame for murder.

With a dead celebrity and a pack of media hacks chasing down every story, the police would need to be sure that they had checked out each and every motive. The obvious starting place was to retrace Crane's movements on the evening of his death – where he had been and who he had been with. Carpenter had played a significant part in Crane's life in the days prior to his death and for this reason his movements would need to be checked thoroughly too. The first person they spoke to was the manager of the Sunburst Motel where Carpenter was staying on 29 June. Cathy Nugent, the manager in charge on the day of Crane's discovery, recalled a conversation she had had with Carpenter, describing his voice as urgent and a little shaky as he asked her to alter the time his limousine was due to collect him for his airport run. Seemingly Carpenter had become confused about his departure time and no longer wanted to be collected at 11 a.m. as previously arranged, but needed to bring the time forward an hour to 10 a.m. As she was unable to reschedule his car she offered to call him a taxi which arrived early, getting him to the airport at just before 9.20 a.m. When police checked the flight times they discovered that Carpenter's flight had left on time and as planned at 11 a.m. His flight brought him into LA airport at 11.35 a.m., from where he went home. A simple case of confusion or a subterfuge? His tickets or booking confirmation would have shown the flight details and if he did not have these then the hotel reception would have been pleased to make a call to the airport for him. The police were looking at everything as being suspicious and this change of plan on the morning of Crane's body being discovered was certainly no exception – it looked as if he wanted to get out of town in a hurry.

Carpenter's behaviour became more suspicious later the same day. After spending a short time at home, he dropped his car off for repairs before going to work. At around 2.30 p.m. he telephoned the Windmill Theatre and was told that there had been an incident at Crane's home and that the police were there. Carpenter's telephone records show that he waited for a period before telephoning the theatre again, this time asking for Bob, but again was told he was not there. He asked if he could leave a message for him to say that he had arrived home safely. Carpenter then called Crane's son, Bob Jr, chatting for a few minutes before terminating the call. His telephone activity proved of great interest to the police. Why had he called the theatre twice after being told on the first call that Crane wasn't there? Why did he feel the need to leave an innocent message confirming his safe arrival in LA? Was he planting evidence to put the police off his trail? If he was it had backfired, the police enquiries un-covered the call and focused their attention on him even more. When he spoke to Crane's son why did he not enquire about the police activity at his father's house?

It was not until after 3 p.m. that Carpenter eventually decided to call his best friend's apartment to see what was going on. Surely a concerned friend would have immediately telephoned to see if he needed any assistance and to check that he was alright. When he rang Crane's house it was answered by Victoria Berry, who was still there with the police officers. She handed the telephone to Ron Dean, a police lieutenant, and he explained to Carpenter that the police were investigating an incident at the property. Again Carpenter's demeanour was odd – instead of enquiring about what was going on, he simply offered some brief information about the previous night. He explained that he had called Crane at 1.00 a.m. to inform him that he would be returning to Los Angeles the following day and that Crane had re-quested that he shouldn't be disturbed in the morning as he was tired and wanted to sleep in.

Thirty minutes later Carpenter decided to call back once more; he spoke to Ron Dean and this time answered a few questions, leaving his contact details in case they wanted to talk to him again. Raising yet more suspicion, for the second time Carpenter saw no reason to ask the officer what it was that had actually happened. Perhaps more surprisingly, given that in theory he was not aware of Crane's death, he did not ask to talk to his friend or even enquire if he was OK – very strange behaviour indeed.

The police investigation gradually homed in on Carpenter who had been one of the last people to see Crane alive, had fallen out with him over the issue of girlfriends and had made a strange combination of telephone calls. With the focus on Carpenter the police began to examine the details of his life during his time with Crane. The first task they carried out was to locate the rental car which Carpenter had been using whilst with Crane, bringing it in for forensic examination. This revealed a few tiny spots of blood which were discov-ered on the inside of the passenger door. Forensic analysis showed the blood type to be the same as Crane's, which although it raised alarm bells with the police, was not quite sufficient to bring charges as roughly one in ten Americans would have the same blood type.

The police called Carpenter in for questioning, during which he resolutely denied having fallen out with Crane and was adamant that he had not killed him. The police could only hope that he would crack through guilt, remorse or stress, but he didn't and the evidence they had was too weak to sustain a court case. They speculated that Carpenter's motive was either jealousy or anger over Crane's success with women, but could not prove it. Even the reputed argument with Crane proved difficult to establish as all they had was one waitress's interpretation of their body language. It wasn't the full-blown public argument which would have been undeniable, and so, without the evidence to hold him, Carpenter was allowed to leave.

The media had followed the case closely, speculating that Carpenter would be named as the alleged killer. Through the publicity the case had attracted the public expected the same result and were seemingly disappointed when Carpenter was not indicted. Worse still, the police had no other leads, all other lines of enquiry having produced a blank. The officers themselves felt hollow inside – they had their suspect within their sights and were convinced that he was guilty, but could not follow it through; it left a bad taste in their mouths and a lasting stain on Carpenter's character.

John Carpenter, whether guilty or not, had to live with the stigma of being suspected of killing a very popular comic. He sought comfort from his estranged wife Diane, and the two managed to patch things up and get back together. They lived together for a further 14 years, and throughout this time Carpenter was never allowed to forget that he was the main suspect in the horrific murder of Bob Crane.

In June 1992, exactly 14 years since Crane's death, the police arrested John Carpenter for his friend's murder. After more than a decade of waiting, the "knock at the door" finally came, and Carpenter was hauled off to face trial, an unpleasant position to be in, yet he was described as being relieved that the time had finally come for his guilt to be tested.

Carpenter appointed Gary Fleischman to run his defence, and he also described Carpenter as having had Crane's murder hanging over him for 14 years. Carpenter and Fleischman prepared their defence well and were to some extent surprised at the new turn of events which had prompted the police to make the charge. Years after the event the police had revisited the crime, appointing one of their officers to re-examine the evidence. During analysis of one of the many photographs which had been taken, the officer noticed a small speck on the door panel of Carpenter's rented Cordoba car. The speck was shown to a forensic pathologist who believed it to be a piece of brain tissue. The speck was tiny, around one sixteenth of an inch across, but if it was what the pathologist suspected it to be then it would be sufficient to secure a conviction.

When the trial came to court it was of course the wider picture which the prosecution aimed to exploit – Carpenter's quick flight out of town, his two calls to the theatre, then one to Crane's son and much later one to Crane's house; and throughout them all, no enquiry as to Crane's well-being, no questions as to what was happening.

During the trial it was Bob Shutts, the Maricopa County Deputy Attorney who pointed out to the jury that John Carpenter had nothing to gain by killing his friend. Indeed it was because of his association with Bob Crane that he enjoyed the ability to mix in glamorous circles. It was also thanks to Crane that he was able to enjoy the company of many attractive women. So the real question was why on earth would he want to put an end to Crane's life? A life that gave him access to the type of social whirl he could never have achieved on his own. The reality for the defence was simple, Carpenter had absolutely nothing to gain by Crane's death, but plenty to lose.

The prosecution team countered by saying that Bob Crane was already growing tired of his "hanger-on" and was making attempts to spend less time with him. It was this, they claimed, that provoked such a violent attack on

Crane – Carpenter was humiliated and dejected by Crane's imminent withdrawal of his friendship, and in a fit of anger had murdered him. Carpenter knew full well that Bob Crane did not need his company as much as he had come to rely on Crane's. The fact that he had been with Crane in the days prior to the murder was brushed under the carpet – apart from the suspected argument, the two men had enjoyed a busy few days socializing.

The prosecution struggled with their flimsy evidence and resorted to more outrageous means to win the jury's votes. The photographic evidence of the suspected brain tissue was hotly disputed and after much debate seemed at best weak, at worst ridiculous. With one piece of photographic evidence dead in the water, the prosecution now sought to win the jury over by playing them one of Crane's home-made adult movies. As well as a woman the other guest star was none other than Carpenter himself. The defence put up a spirited fight to have the film show denied, saying it was nothing more than gratuitous sensationalism. Strangely, the Judge allowed it to be shown and the jury were subjected to ten minutes of animated pornography. When the film ended it proved nothing other than the two men were friends and that they enjoyed a wide range of sexual activities.

The prosecution's shock tactics had not worked and after the other photographic evidence failed to deliver conclusive proof, the jury returned a verdict of not guilty. The foreman of the jury, Marine Sergeant Michel Lake, added that the evidence which inspired the case, namely the photograph of a substance on the door of the rental car, could not be positively identified and consequently the jury had found Carpenter not guilty.

Carpenter and his wife Diane were jubilant – after 14 years of waiting and being talked about they were now free to leave. On leaving court John Carpenter announced, "My life is back together again after 16 years," and with this he returned to his family.

By now the media and the public had cause to wonder why public money had been spent in the pursuit of Carpenter when the case was so weak and flimsy. Why had the police suddenly reopened the case and started looking through the old evidence? And where was this evidence previously? These and other questions made the case look like a witch-hunt, the pointless showing of Crane's home movie a clear attempt to show that, if nothing else, the man in the dock was somehow perverted.

Police files are never fully closed on unsolved murders, yet once again we see the power of celebrity reaching through time and stealing the headlines just one more time. Meanwhile this case remains unsolved, inactive, but not closed.

When Life Comes Crashing Down

Charles Lindbergh

In 1902, a flying legend was born; his name, Charles Augustus Lindbergh. As a child Lindbergh longed to become a pilot, spending his free time in overalls, taking machinery apart, whilst his friends simply hung out and played ball. The mechanically minded Charles had an enquiring mind and yearned to understand how technology worked – his inquisitive nature would see him flying high in every sense of the word.

His flying days started in April 1922 whilst employed at the Nebraska Aircraft Company. It was here that he took his first flight in a Lincoln Standard, an experience which cemented his lifelong love of flying. He was soon referred to as "Daredevil Lindbergh" owing to his stunts, including wing-walking and parachute jumping. His daredevil antics earned him enough money to buy his first aeroplane, a Curtis Jenny, after which it was "the sky's the limit" for the young Lindbergh. The joys of owning his very own aircraft were, however, short lived – before he had clocked up many flying hours he crashed the plane after suffering a technical problem, and although he was unhurt, the plane was not, being damaged beyond repair. He now found himself without a plane or the money to replace it, his flying days seemingly over. Lindbergh though had a flash of inspiration and decided to join the National Guard as an army pilot. He was of course successful and achieved the rank of Lieutenant, after which he joined the US mail service, flying a De Havilland DH-4 betwen Chicago and St Louis. It was while working for the US mail service that Lindbergh decided to compete in the New York to Paris non-stop flying competition, a demanding task in those early days and one which would almost certainly end in death if the pilot was unlucky enough to ditch in the mid-Atlantic.

Lindbergh began to make plans to build a new aeroplane for his epic Atlantic crossing. After making calculations regarding the specification of the aircraft he estimated that he would need around $13,000, a massive amount in those days and an amount he just did not have. He therefore decided to seek sponsorship from his friends and a number of businessmen from St Louis, as a result of which the plane was named the "Spirit of St Louis". Incredibly the plane was built in just 90 days, largely by Lindbergh himself, in the Ryan factory in San Diego. To produce an aeroplane in such a short time frame was difficult enough, but to produce one to such a high specification, one where every nut and bolt had to be specially made, was a rare feat in itself. Cost and weight issues were crucial considerations – there were no luxuries on board, the pilot's seat was made of wicker and there were many pieces of equipment missing which most people would consider vital – he did not for instance have a radio, a parachute or even a life jacket, three items which would be of paramount importance in the event of a crash at sea. Perhaps even more surprisingly the aeroplane's design did not cater for a forward-looking view – most of the time Lindbergh would either fly blind, or use a periscope technique that he had perfected; or worse, he would risk life and limb leaning out of the cockpit to see ahead.

Many people before Lindbergh had tried and failed, usually at the cost of their lives, but he had an iron will and was determined that he would take the all-important prize money. On 27 May 1927, at 7.52 a.m. Lindbergh took off from New York and after $33\frac{1}{2}$ hours non-stop flying, he arrived in Paris. He had achieved his goal and in doing so had secured his place in the history books, changing his life forever. Almost immediately he found himself famous the world over, a new celebrity, and with his new-found fame and wealth came a new title, "eligible bachelor". At 6ft 3in and extremely handsome, he was the apple of many girls' eye.

The USS *Memphis* brought the jubilant Charles Lindbergh and the equally famous Spirit of St Louis back to the US. It appeared that everyone in America wanted to see him and congratulate him; life couldn't have been any better for Charles Lindbergh. On his return he was paid $200,000 to make a grand tour of all of the 48 US states, keeping him busy until the end of October.

Lindbergh's career as a pilot continued with many high-profile positions; he pioneered new flight routes and even took the risky job of flight-testing new aeroplanes, typical of the adventurous aviator. He initially took the position of Technical Advisor to the President of Pan American Airlines before joining Trans Continental Air Transport as a technical consultant, flying the coast-to-coast route from New York to Los Angeles, a route which became affectionately known as "The Lindbergh Line".

Lindbergh's new status meant he was now mixing with the rich and famous, one high-profile gentleman he met being Dwight Morrow, the American Ambassador to Mexico. It was through this meeting that he was eventually introduced to his future wife, Morrow's daughter, Anne, to whom he was quickly attracted. The couple started spending more and more time together until they eventually married.

The press couldn't stay away, they were the new "golden couple" and always seemed to be in the news. The press attention came as a great shock to Anne, who had left a rather dull life living with her parents to be thrust into the limelight; it seemed to her as though she had married the most famous man in the world. She found the attention quite suffocating, convinced that normal life had been removed from her – she no longer felt safe shopping or meeting friends for meals in restaurants. The only time that she felt totally free was when she and Charles were flying together, something he taught her to do, and she soon shared his love of flying, eventually the two finding space and freedom on numerous flying expeditions.

On 22 June 1930, Anne gave birth to a son, Charles Lindbergh III, after his famous father. The public were desperate to see the new addition to the Lindbergh family, creating another media circus for the new parents. He was one of the most photographed children in America; the public, it seemed, would buy any amount of newspapers to find out as much as possible about America's "golden couple" and their baby.

In contrast to most Americans at this time the Lindberghs were living the high life. Although the 1929 stock market crash had ruined many businesses and unemployment was stressfully high, they continued to enjoy the spoils of their celebrity status. The Lindbergh household was run in military style with a small army of employees, including a butler, several cleaning staff, a cook, a chauffeur and even a nanny for young Charlie. The Lindberghs spent their weeks split between Anne's family home in New Jersey and their own home near Hopewell in the Sourland Mountains.

On Tuesday, 1 March 1932, they had chosen to stay on in Hopewell as Charlie was unwell. Even though he was poorly he was still put in his crib in the nursery at 7.30 p.m., following the normal routine which meant that he would not to be disturbed until 10 p.m., at which time he would be instructed to use the toilet. His father was fastidious and strict, and the house staff followed his word to the letter. His nurse placed the youngster in his cot at the prescribed time and then closed the three sets of window shutters which hung on the nursery's windows, leaving one window open a fraction to let the child have some fresh air. At 7.50 p.m. the nanny briefly checked on the young infant and reported that he was sound asleep, and that she had switched off the lights and closed the door behind her.

At approximately 8.25 p.m. Lindbergh arrived at the house. Although he hadn't seen his son since the previous day he would not break his own rule and disturb the boy after bedtime. Instead he retired to the dining room to have supper with Anne, after which they moved into the living room to relax for the evening.

The baby's nurse, Miss Betty Gow, returned to see to him at 10 p.m., as instructed. On entering the room she was struck by how cold it was and immediately closed the open window. Worried that the temperature was now too low she decided to switch on the electric heater to take the chill off the room. While she stood over the heater warming her hands she realised that she couldn't hear the child breathing and immediately sensed that something was wrong. She looked towards where the sleeping infant should have been, only to find that the crib was empty. Panicking, she raced downstairs to raise the alarm and breathlessly explained that the young child was gone. Lindbergh and his wife ran upstairs and found the crib empty; they raced from room to room shouting out for young Charles Lindbergh before realizing that the boy wasn't there – he had vanished. Lindbergh then instructed his butler, Ollie Whately, to telephone the local police station in Hopewell. Whilst waiting for the police to arrive Lindbergh took control and insisted that his wife and household staff should leave everything untouched, especially in the nursery. He then loaded his shotgun and went outside to see if he could find any sign of the kidnappers, for this is what they had now concluded, that the infant Lindbergh had become a victim of their fame and fortune. Whilst he was busy outside his staff started another search of the house, looking through all of the rooms and cupboards, but their search was fruitless. Lindbergh re-entered the house and returned to the nursery, desperate for some sign of his child's whereabouts, at which point he found a previously unnoticed envelope sitting on the window sill, by the closed but unlocked window. Rather than opening the envelope he thought it would be wiser to wait for the police, not wanting to risk losing any evidence which might be on it.

The police arrived in the form of police chief, Harry Wolfe, and his assistant Mr Williamson. Lindbergh was still in charge, just as he liked to be, in control of his own destiny but sadly no longer that of his childs. He showed the officers the note but insisted that it be untouched until a fingerprint expert arrived. After he and the nanny had briefly explained the situation to the officers, they decided that they should first make a thorough search of the grounds, in case the child, or whoever had taken him, were still in the vicinity. There were signs that a ladder had been propped up beneath the nursery window – there were deep indents in the soil – and around the ladder marks were the footprints of a single person. Further searching revealed the makeshift ladder only a short distance from the house, at the edge of a wood. On examination it was noted that its rungs were covered with mud. It appeared to come in three sections, with each section fitting one inside the other, getting progressively narrower towards the top. Strangely, the ladder also displayed another unique design characteristic, the rungs were very far apart, almost six inches deeper than a conventional ladder. The footprints were traced across the soft earth until they reached the perimeter of Lindbergh's property, where they ended abruptly. At the point where the footsteps stopped, tyre marks could be seen – the kidnappers had clearly made their escape in a vehicle.

The police and Lindbergh continued to search the grounds with torches until late into the night, meanwhile a small army of police were scouring the estate and checking all vehicle movements in the area surrounding Hopewell. The envelope was dusted by fingerprint expert Frank Kelly, who examined it but could find no prints; he then opened it and dusted the note inside, but disappointingly this also showed no fingerprints. With the note now opened they were at least able to say with some certainty what had happened to the young boy. The note contained a demand for $50,000, in exchange for the safe return of the child.

The note read:

Dear Sir!
Have 50000$ redy with 25000$ in 20$ bills 15000$ in 10$ bills and 10000$ in 5$ bills. After 2–4 days we will inform you were to deliver the Mony. We warn you for making anyding public or for notify the polise the child is in gut care.

At the bottom right-hand corner of the sheet of paper was a drawing of two interlocking circles, each about an inch in diameter. The area where the circles intersected had been coloured red and the remainder of the circles were coloured blue. Three small holes had been punched into the design.

Whilst Lindbergh and the police considered the ransom demand, other officers began dusting the nursery for finger-prints, but none were found, not even from the child's nanny or parents. Had the room been cleaned since the abduction? The police made no note of this unusual fact.

The press once more had a field day at the expense of the Lindberghs, and the day after the kidnapping their home was swamped by over 300 journalists and photographers. The staff of the International News Photo Service had managed to set up two ambulances with developing equipment, ob-viously hoping the priority given to ambulances would enable them to get to New York with their photos before their competitors. The public were keen to keep up with the case and it was reported that circulation rose by over 15 per cent throughout Lindbergh's dreadful ordeal. Bizarrely, no precautions were taken to preserve the site containing the footprints, consequently Lindbergh's grounds were turned to mud, resulting in more loss of vital evidence. Although the press were to become Lindbergh's sole route of communica-tion to the kidnappers, the police did not appear to worry that the enormous publicity surrounding the kidnapping had great potential to cause panic among those involved, inad-vertently putting the child in even greater danger.

Anne was in a dreadful state; she could do nothing more than stay at home and wait for news on the whereabouts of her poorly baby. When the search of the grounds yielded little in the way of clues, Lindbergh's only remaining option was to pay the ransom. But in an oversight by the kidnap-pers, the note gave no instructions regarding the method of communication, leaving the newspapers as the only way of trying to get a message through to them.

The police now began to suspect that the kidnapping had been achieved with the help of one of Lindbergh's many staff – an inside job. The whole situation seemed to have been achieved too easily – the kidnappers had gained entrance to the grounds and were able to use a ladder to reach the first-floor window; one window had been left open whereas all the others had been closed and locked. These facts proved of interest to the police but provided nothing in the way of substantial evidence. If they had not missed the significance of the complete lack of fingerprints in the nursery then they might have been able to advance the case faster. Whoever cleaned the room after the kidnapping did so knowing they were likely to be removing evidence. Each staff member was interviewed in turn and background checks were carried out, but the investigation made little progress.

A second ransom note was received on 4 March, in which Lindbergh was reprimanded for involving the police and as a result the kidnappers were increasing the ransom demand to $70,000. On examination the note revealed the same symbols which had been on the the original ransom letter, a sure sign that the demand was from the same person or group.

When the time came to meet the kidnappers' demands, Lindbergh's friend, John Condon, offered to act as go-between saving his friend the ordeal of having to deal directly with his son's captors, a plan which the kidnappers agreed to. By now the kidnappers had obtained Condon's telephone number in order to organize the exchange. Condon was asked to bring the money to Woodlawn Cemetery in the Bronx district of New York City; he described the kidnapper as having a German accent. When Condon arrived at the cemetery he explained to the kidnappers that he would only hand over the money once he had seen the baby, a demand which they were unable to meet. They had arrived without proof that they were able to carry the deal through. After a brief discussion a deal was struck whereby the kidnappers would bring the child's sleep suit to prove that they had him, but they would not bring the child. With this the kidnappers said they would be in touch with a new set of instructions and the two sides went their separate ways. To ensure the child's safety Lindbergh had insisted that the police should not attempt an arrest or even a covert tracking operation; he simply wanted his child back – justice would have to wait.

At the next meeting Condon arrived with ransom money, $70,000 in two parcels, one of $50,000 and the other of $20,000; the notes were not marked but the serial numbers had been recorded. The rendezvous was another cemetery, St Raymond's; this time Lindbergh drove the car, desperate to see his child at the earliest opportunity. When they arrived at the cemetery one of the kidnappers called out, "Hey, Doctor. Over here! Over here." Lindbergh waited in the car while Condon went ahead to conclude the deal. Having seen the child's sleep suit Condon handed over the money in exchange for a note, in which, the kidnappers assured him, would be the location at which the child could be found. With the money and note exchanged the kidnappers fled, leaving Condon with nothing more than the piece of paper, on which were the instructions that the baby was on board a boat, tethered between Horseneck Beach and Gay Head, near Elizabeth Island. The two men raced to the location, desperate to reach the boy, who they anticipated would now be on his own. After searching up and down the stretch of river, they were unable to find any boat, so it appeared they had been tricked. Feeling desperate and empty the two men returned home, hoping that the kidnappers, having collected the ransom, would now release the child into a public place unharmed; sadly no further communication was received and the boy's remained unknown. On 12 May the child's body was discovered just 4 miles from the Lindbergh estate. It was obvious that he had been dead for some time. During the autopsy the skull was examined and four fracture lines were found, under which the doctor discovered a decomposed blood clot, concluding that the cause of death was a blow to the head. It appeared that the infant could even have been murdered in his room, or possibly have been dropped while the kidnapper was carrying him down the ladder. Lindbergh identified his son's body and immediately ordered a cremation, which was carried out within the hour. He might have wanted to spare his wife the agony of seeing her dead baby, but the swift disposal of his son's body meant that there would be no more opportunities to carry out further tests, tests which might have provided clues to the murderer's identity. The rather quick cremation, denying many family members the opportunity to say goodbye, would, decades later, become a point of interest in one particular conspiracy theory.

The police investigation provided little in the way of

comfort for the Lindberghs, as nothing emerged which gave them any hope of finding the kidnappers. As month after month passed with no news, the Lindberghs began to believe that the murderous kidnappers had succeeded in their plan and had now fled, taking his money with them.

It wasn't until 15 September 1934, some two years later, that the ransom money was used and became traceable, when the $10 gold certificate was used to buy petrol. The manager of the petrol station was so surprised to receive the gold certificate, so rarely did he see one, that he made a note of the driver's car number on the back of the bill. When questioned by police he also recalled that the driver had spoken with a German accent. From the details that the garage manager was able to supply, the police were able to confirm that the owner of the vehicle was a 35-year-old German-born carpenter, Richard Hauptmann.

Hauptmann was an illegal immigrant who had been in the US since he was 23 years old, and was married to a German waitress, Anna Schoeffler. When the police searched his house they found more of the Lindbergh ransom money hidden in the garage, but Hauptmann insisted that the money belonged to Isador Fisch, his business partner, who had returned to Germany the year before. Fisch had left a shoebox with Hauptmann before departing, asking him to look after it. He also left owing him $7,000, money that Hauptmann had loaned to Fisch. After checks were made on the men's backgrounds a number of facts emerged – the police established that Fisch had been a buyer of "hot" money, but that he had died in March of that year. Hauptmann meanwhile had decided that he was within his rights to spend some of the money Fisch had left with him. The police, however, were so convinced that Hauptmann was the kidnapper that they decided to carry out a more detailed investigation of his house and activities. When officers climbed into Hauptmann's attic they discovered that there were pieces of wood missing from the rafters, the same wood that had been used to make the kidnap ladder; his voice was to be identified as the voice heard in the cemetery and his handwriting matched the writing on the ransom note. With such a broad range of supporting evidence the police arrested Hauptmann, charging him with the kidnap and murder of Charles Lindbergh III.

Throughout the ordeal Lindbergh and his family had been a constant source of media speculation, and if anything the arrest of Hauptmann sent the media into a frenzy. The imminent trial of the "Lindbergh kidnapper" had the media and the public baying for blood – a child had been killed and the family of an American hero ruined. Public opinion was fierce and people just couldn't get enough of the riveting drama which was unfolding day by day in the newspapers. Lindbergh's trauma though became a pawn in the editors' bid to win what had become a hard-fought battle in a circulation war – they assumed the right to embellish their stories and worse still, invent news. The police had already been critical of the newspapers throughout the ransom negotiations, and plans to meet the kidnappers were hampered when papers got wind of the arrangements and made them their front-page story. The behaviour of the press reached an all-time low after the child's body was discovered three months after the kidnapping. In an appalling and callous act, photographers broke in to the morgue and took pictures of the badly decomposed body. By the time Hauptmann was arrested for the kidnapping he was declared guilty by the press, who hadn't wasted any time in delivering their version of events to the waiting public. Reporters resorted to dubious journalistic practices to enable them to get ahead of the pack, in some cases paying the police for inside information. Indeed one daily newspaper actually paid defence lawyer, Edward J. Reilly, of Brooklyn, $10,000 to defend Hauptmann – in return they were to receive inside information on the progress of the case and in particular, Hauptmann's defence. Reilly though was aware that he was up against it and concluded that he would be unable to handle such a high-profile case alone, turning to three New Jersey lawyers, Lloyd Fischer, Egbert Rosecrans and Frederick Pope, for assistance.

The streets around the courthouse, including those at the back of the building, were packed with people, the whole area being described as having a carnival atmosphere. In scenes more reminiscent of the current time, posters were on sale outside the courthouse and replica "Hauptmann" ladders apparently sold very well. Bets were taken at the local betting office, ranging from the outcome of the case to how long it would take before a verdict was announced. Every spare room within a 10-mile radius of the courthouse had been taken to house the hordes of press, newscasters, magazine writers and those bloodthirsty, morbid members of the public who wanted the chance to see the Lindbergh kidnapper in the flesh. The public's fury was such that if Hauptmann had been released onto the streets he would have been beaten to death within an instant – if he did not already know, he was safer inside his prison cell.

The trial started on 2 January 1935; Lindbergh was present throughout the trial. The specially selected jury consisted of six men and six women, representing a fair cross-section of people from a range of backgrounds and age groups. In command of the proceedings sat the experienced Justice Trenchard.

By the time the case had been brought to court, Hauptmann had been in solitary confinement for over three months and had obviously lost weight; his appearance must have been a shock for his wife, who was also in the courtroom. She too had run the gauntlet of the public's outrage, and would do so on each visit to the courthouse.

At the end of each day the jurors were escorted to a local hotel and were sworn not to discuss the case; they were also banned from reading newspapers, watching television and were not allowed to listen to the radio. Even so it was virtually impossible for them not to notice the several thousand-strong crowd gathered outside the courthouse each day, chanting, "Kill Hauptmann."

The foreman of the jury was Charles Walton Sr, who had been interviewed by the press prior to the trial. When asked if he had made up his mind regarding Hauptmann's innocence or guilt, he replied, "Not exactly." When asked to elaborate he added, "Not more than anyone else." It was common knowledge that Walton had made these comments prior to the trial, so it was assumed that Judge Trenchard also knew of them. It appeared therefore that the need for a fair trial, based on the jurors' impartiality, was not a requirement of what had been dubbed the trial of the century.

The prosecution's case was built around the facts provided by the police, namely the discovery of the $14,600 worth of ransom bills which had been found hidden in Hauptmann's garage; Hauptmann's cupboard had Dr John Condon's address and telephone number written discreetly on the wall, hidden by a shelf; Hauptmann was identified by Dr Condon as the man he had met in Woodlawn Cemetery in March 1932, and was the same man who he had given the ransom money to in St Raymond's Cemetery on 2 April 1932. The next damning piece of evidence was the wood found in Hauptmann's attic which matched the wood used to make the kidnap ladder. A "wood expert" was called, Mr Arthur Koehler, who testified that a quantity of the wood which was used to make the rungs of the ladder had been sold to a lumber yard near to Hauptmann's home. He also suggested that the rails of the ladder were made from floorboarding similar to that found in Hauptmann's attic. The handwriting on the ransom notes was examined by handwriting experts, who, after comparing them with samples of handwriting provided by Hauptmann, testified that the ransom notes were written by the accused.

When Lindbergh took the stand he was asked to recall the events in the cemetery, when the ransom money was handed over. He confirmed that he had very clearly heard a man's voice coming from the cemetery. When asked if he had heard the voice since that day he replied, "Yes, I have. That was Hauptmann's voice." By the time Lindbergh's comments were reported in the press, the public appeared to have made its collective mind up – Hauptmann was guilty and they wanted revenge. The daily visits to the court became an ordeal for Hauptmann and his defence team, all of whom came under verbal attack. If the police had turned their back on Hauptmann for a single moment he would surely have been the subject of a public lynching.

As the trial continued, Hauptmann's plight became worse

as three separate witnesses gave evidence that they had seen Hauptmann in the area of the Lindbergh estate at the time of the kidnapping. The first eyewitness called, Mr Amandus Hochmuth, who was 87 years old by the time the case came to trial, lived in a house which had a view of the lane leading to Lindbergh's home. He described how he was sitting on his front porch when he noticed a passing car with a three-section ladder inside. When asked if he had seen the driver, he replied that he had and pointed at Hauptmann, who sat dejectedly in the dock. A second sighting of Hauptmann was made the week before the baby's disappearance, near to Princeton Airport. Mr Charles Rossiter described how a car had stalled on a road near the airport. When he approached the car to offer some assistance, the driver declined; he too confirmed that the driver was Hauptmann. The third person to provide an eyewitness testimony had even more damning evidence to offer. Mr Millard Whited, who lived within a mile of the Lindberghs' home, had noticed Hauptmann apparently crawling out of the undergrowth on the roadside as he drove past just days before the kidnapping. He added that he had seen the accused again a day later, this time standing at a crossroads, looking as if he was checking the area out.

As the main defence witness, Hauptmann was unable to explain why his handwriting was so similar to that on the ransom notes or to produce alibis for the dates in question. Indeed his defence attorney, Mr Fisher, struggling to provide any meaningful retort, suggested that the defence were unable to provide any expert witnesses because of a lack of funds, claiming that all of the defendant's money had been confiscated. The prosecution lawyer, David Wilentz, objected to the defence using that information as part of the case, to which Judge Trenchard agreed, declaring that it was irrelevant to the trial. It appeared once again, that in this particular case, justice did not require a level playing field; unfortunately for the defence, it was them being forced to play uphill all the time.

The Judge appeared to agree with the prosecution team so regularly that some observers felt he was heavily on their side. Some of the information provided in the trial could well have been lost on the accused as his native tongue was German and his English skills were at best mediocre. The court however did not feel that the accused had to understand what was being said or what was going on and therefore denied him the benefit of an interpreter. He therefore found it difficult to keep up with the trial and struggled when cross-examined. He was hardly given time to work out what the question was before prosecutor Wilentz fired another one at the puzzled Hauptmann. The Judge never stepped in to slow the proceedings down and when the defence objected, or asked for extra clarification, they were promptly overruled.

The trial finally closed on 13 February, after the summarizing statements had been heard. The jury were retired and asked to consider their verdict, but quickly returned with their response. Under direction from Judge Trenchard, the clerk of the court stood to address the jury. "Members of the jury," he asked, "have you agreed upon your verdict?"

"We have," replied each of the 12 jurors in turn.

"Mr Foreman, what say you? Do you find the defendant guilty or not guilty?"

"Guilty. We find the defendant, Richard Hauptmann guilty of murder in the first degree."

A ripple of agreement spread throughout the courtroom before the Judge turned his attention upon Hauptmann. "The defendant may stand," he said, and Hauptmann stood up between the two guards.

"Richard Hauptmann, you have been convicted of murder in the first degree. The sentence of the court is that you, the said Richard Hauptmann, suffer death at a time and place, and in the manner provided by law. And the court will hand to the Sheriff a warrant appointing the week beginning Monday, the eighteenth of March, 1935, as the week within which such sentence must be executed in the manner provided by law. You are now remanded to the custody of the Sheriff."

The handcuffed Hauptmann did not show any emotion when the verdict was read, not even looking at his terrified wife. He simply stared ahead, as if in a trance, before being lead away to the cell by police guards. At that moment the courtroom bell began to toll, announcing to everyone outside that a guilty verdict had been reached – but it was soon drowned out by the crowd as they roared their support for the outcome.

Hauptmann did launch an appeal, always proclaiming his innocence, but it failed. The date for his execution was finally set for 3 April 1936. The execution went ahead as planned at 8.47 p.m., within the confines of the state prison in Trenton, New Jersey. It was carried out by Robert G. Elliott, the executioner who had operated the electric chair during the executions of Sacco and Vanzetti nine years before. Reporters were again on stand-by, hoping for a last-minute confession from Hauptmann, but he proclaimed his innocence to the last.

Whilst the appeals process was going ahead the Lindberghs and their new son, Jon, arrived in England for an extended holiday. They could not escape the press though, and found themselves besieged by paparazzi everywhere they went. It seemed that they were still hot news, especially their new son Jon, who everyone wanted to get a glimpse of. One daily paper ran a front-page headline claiming that the Lindberghs were sailing to England in search of a safer home, falsely stating that Jon had been the subject of threats. The story of the forced exile received mix reviews in the press, some editorials sympathizing with their plight, others not. The truth is that Lindbergh had endured the undiluted attention of an out-of-control press, throughout which his own countrymen had become obsessed with his family's every move. He wanted to enjoy his post-trial time out of the spotlight, and England, with its more reserved culture, was able to provide the environment in which he could enjoy a much lower profile.

Meanwhile, not everybody was convinced that Hauptmann was responsible for the kidnapping and murder of the Lindberghs' child, indeed public opinion began to shift as it became clear that the media had provided a very one-sided account of the proceedings, promoting the notion that Hauptmann was guilty from practically the moment he was arrested. Hauptmann's wife continued to declare his innocence, standing by her long-dead husband until her death in 1994. In her nineties when she died, she had strongly maintained that he was an innocent man.

The celebrity status of the Lindbergh family, which had created the furore during Hauptmann's trial, suddenly began to turn against them. The public's fickle opinion turned against them when they were fed a new line of information on America's one-time hero. Tiring of reports describing the Lindberghs' high living, the final twist came when it was reported that Lindbergh had become an admirer of the German Luftwaffe, even being awarded a medal by Hermann Goering. He was reported to have suggested that the rest of Europe had no defence against the mighty and admirable Germans, though he had little to say regarding the fascist dictatorship that was intent on war.

As the tide of opinion was turning against Lindbergh, the public began to see Hauptmann as a quiet, unassuming, happily married man, with a devoted wife. Lindbergh by contrast appeared arrogant, affluent and worst of all, unpatriotic. Many pages have been written regarding the possibility of Hauptmann's innocence, although none produced the quality of evidence used to convict him. The fact is that Hauptmann was put to death on the strength of the evidence, but the concern is that the outcome would have been the same had the evidence not supported the conviction. There wasn't a bigger case in America – everyone wanted to have someone pay for what had happened. The glowing embers of anger were fanned by the press, whose sole goal was to sell more papers, but what they really sold out was justice – Hauptmann was not given a fair trial; the jury had already decided upon the verdict before the first piece of evidence was shown; the Judge was biased and supported the prosecution; and the defence were left with a bankrupt client, deprived of the funds needed to pay for a fair trial.

As with all high-profile cases a range of alternative theories emerged, some gaining support over the years since the events unfolded.

The most widely spread conspiracy theory suggests that

Lindbergh himself might have accidentally killed his own child, and panicking, staged the kidnapping in order to avoid a criminal prosecution of his own. This could explain why nobody heard any suspicious noises at the time of the kidnapping, why the guard dogs did not bark and why the baby did not cry. It might also explain why the ransom letter was apparently overlooked on first inspection of the nursery – Lindbergh hadn't written it then, doing so as an after-thought to support the kidnapping story. The Lindberghs had a strict routine and would normally have been at their other house on the night of the alleged kidnapping. Either the kidnapper had some inside knowledge, or as the con-spiracy would have it, it was Lindbergh himself. The con-spiracy theorists are also encouraged by the burial of the child so close to the Lindbergh house, firstly for convenience – Lindbergh wouldn't have had time to travel further afield – but perhaps more importantly, because he wanted the com-fort of having the child close by. There was no suggestion at the time of Lindbergh's involvement in his child's death – indeed, would he have paid a ransom knowing full well the boy was dead?

Hauptmann's guilt was based on the evidence which was presented, however alternative theories have been put for-ward which suggest that although he was guilty of using the ransom money, maybe he was not guilty of the murder.

Other theories suggest that the Judge and the police were complicit in providing the evidence to implicate Haupt-mann. It has been suggested that the police planted the evidence in a bid to clear up a case which was demanding much of America's attention. One point of controversy surrounds the name and address of Dr Condon, written in pencil on the inside of the cupboard. As the kidnappers had been careful to remove all fingerprints from the child's bedroom, would it not seem a significant lapse in judgment therefore to leave this rather important piece of evidence in such an obvious place. Since Hauptmann did not have a great grasp of English, it has been speculated that Condon's details were actually written there by the police. In fact, to read the words at all would have involved taking out the shelving and, with the use of a torch as there was no other illumination, squeezing into the space and craning one's neck at an acute angle. If this information was important to Hauptmann, why choose the inside of a cupboard to record it? If he was wishing to secrete the address and telephone number, surely it would have been much easier to have written it on a piece of paper and then hidden the paper? In any case, as he didn't have a telephone, he would have needed to take the number with him so that he could dial it from a public telephone box. And then there was the question of why bother to record the name anyway? Condon was listed in the telephone directory, of which there was a copy in each and every public telephone kiosk. Which leaves the police themselves – how were they able to spot such a well-hidden message on the wall? They didn't remove the shelving, yet they still found the details.

The trial came to court some two years after the murder had taken place yet no one questioned why Lindbergh and Condon were so sure that it was Haupmann's voice they had heard in the cemetery. Could it be that Lindbergh, just like the rest of America, wanted revenge. Indeed, had he been involved in the child's disappearance himself then having someone else in the dock would be the ideal distraction.

The eyewitnesses also came under scrutiny, some proving to be less than reliable. After the execution of Hauptmann, Governor Hoffman called for one of the eyewitnesses, Amandus Hochmuth, to visit him in order to clarify if he was entitled to any of the reward money. Hoffman had heard a rumour that Hochmuth was having trouble with his eyesight and began to question his ability to identify Hauptmann. When Hochmuth arrived at his office he asked him to identify an object in his room, namely a silver cup filled with flowers, to which Hochmuth, staring intently, observed that it was a lady's hat. Hoffman was said to have been shocked – if his experiment was correct, then that eyewitness testimony should have been wiped from the records. Hoffman wondered if the financially embarrassed Hochmuth had simply come forward in order to collect the reward. He was given a total payment of $250. Perhaps Hochmuth had, like everyone else who read the papers, assumed he was doing a public service that justly deserved a small payment.

Another witness, Millard Whited, was also called before Hoffman; he too admitted that the lure of the reward money was hard to resist. His statements had changed from the time he first came forward, often contradicting one another. Nevertheless he was paid $150 initially and $35 a day for his expenses during the trial, money which was provided by the prosecution.

The final witness, Charles J. Rossiter did not come forward with his information until Hauptmann was in police custody, claiming that until he had seen his face in the newspapers, he hadn't realized the significance of the encounter. Rossiter though had unresolved issues with his statement. Despite the fact that he was able to convince the jury, two years after the event, that it was Hauptmann he had seen by the stalled car, he had in fact failed to pick Hauptmann out of a photographic line-up just weeks after his arrest. That didn't deter the police as they arranged for Rossiter to see Hauptmann in the flesh, after which his memory was jolted and he was able to confirm that Hauptmann was the driver of the car. Whether or not he had seen Hauptmann, or even anyone vaguely resembling him, is not known for sure; what is known is that Rossiter was another man who could really use the reward money – just before coming forward to the police he had lost his job.

With Hoffman now carrying a significant doubt as to the validity of the verdict, he continued to ponder the evidence which had been presented. The only physical evidence which tied Hauptmann to the crime was the wooden ladder, and the suggestion that it had been made from floorboards out of Hauptmann's loft. Just as he had with the other witnesses, Hoffman now arranged to meet the "wood expert", Keohler, only this time at Hauptmann's home. Taking the wooden rail upstairs they compared it to the floorboards which were in the loft, immediately seeing some obvious discrepancies. The floorboards in Hauptmann's loft were nailed down with seven nails per segment, whereas the one they were holding contained 23 nail holes. The biggest and most obvious discrepancy though was the width of the rail – it measured some 16th of an inch thicker than the rest of the attic boards, a difference the expert found hard to explain.

The case will remain shrouded in mystery, but the Lindberghs soon managed to get their lives back and indeed had five more children after Charlie. Lindbergh lived until he was in his mid seventies, passing away in 1974, just before completing his autobiography, entitled *Autobiography of Values*, in which he allocated a dozen or so paragraphs to the kidnapping and death of his son, the $2\frac{1}{2}$-year manhunt, the ensuing trial, and how these events affected his family.

If Hauptmann didn't murder Lindbergh's son, then the ease with which he was convicted must surely be down to the press, whose headlines practically insisted that he was guilty. And then, just as they have on many occassions, though this time far too late, the press altered their stance – having been hard on Hauptmann after the child's murder, they became hard on Lindbergh and the witnesses after Hauptmann's execution, thus extracting a second story out of Lindbergh's loss.

The Lindbergh story did not end with the execution of Hauptmann, indeed it continues to this present day, still managing to fill precious column inches. There is one conspiracy theory which did not die with Hauptmann, one which suggests that young Charles Lindbergh was not killed by his kidnappers. The conspiracy still raging today suggests that Lindbergh may have had his son adopted, embarrassed by a physical affliction the poor boy had been born with. When a man claiming to be Charles Lindbergh III requested that DNA tests be taken both from himself and other members of the Lindbergh family, all members of the Lindbergh family refused.